WILDLIFE PHOTOGRAPHY

PROVEN TECHNIQUES FOR CAPTURING STUNNING DIGITAL IMAGES

JACK BALLARD

FALCON®

Essex, Connecticut

FALCON®

An imprint of The Globe Pequot Publishing Group, Inc.
64 South Main Street
Essex, CT 06426
www.globepequot.com

Falcon and FalconGuides are registered trademarks and Make Adventure Your Story is a trademark of Rowman & Littlefield.

Distributed by NATIONAL BOOK NETWORK

Photos by Jack Ballard unless otherwise noted

British Library Cataloguing in Publication Information available

Library of Congress Cataloging-in-Publication Data

Names: Ballard, Jack (Jack Clayton), author.
Title: Wildlife photography : proven techniques for capturing stunning digital images / Jack Ballard.
Description: Guilford, Connecticut : Falcon, [2017]
Identifiers: LCCN 2017041766 (print) | LCCN 2017042663 (ebook) | ISBN 9781493029563 (e-book) | ISBN 9781493029556 (pbk. : alk. paper)
Subjects: LCSH: Wildlife photography.
Classification: LCC TR729.W54 (ebook) | LCC TR729.W54 B354 2017 (print) | DDC 778.9/32—dc23
LC record available at https://lccn.loc.gov/2017041766

Printed in India

To Lisa, the love of my life, and all the magical moments we've spent together photographing wildlife

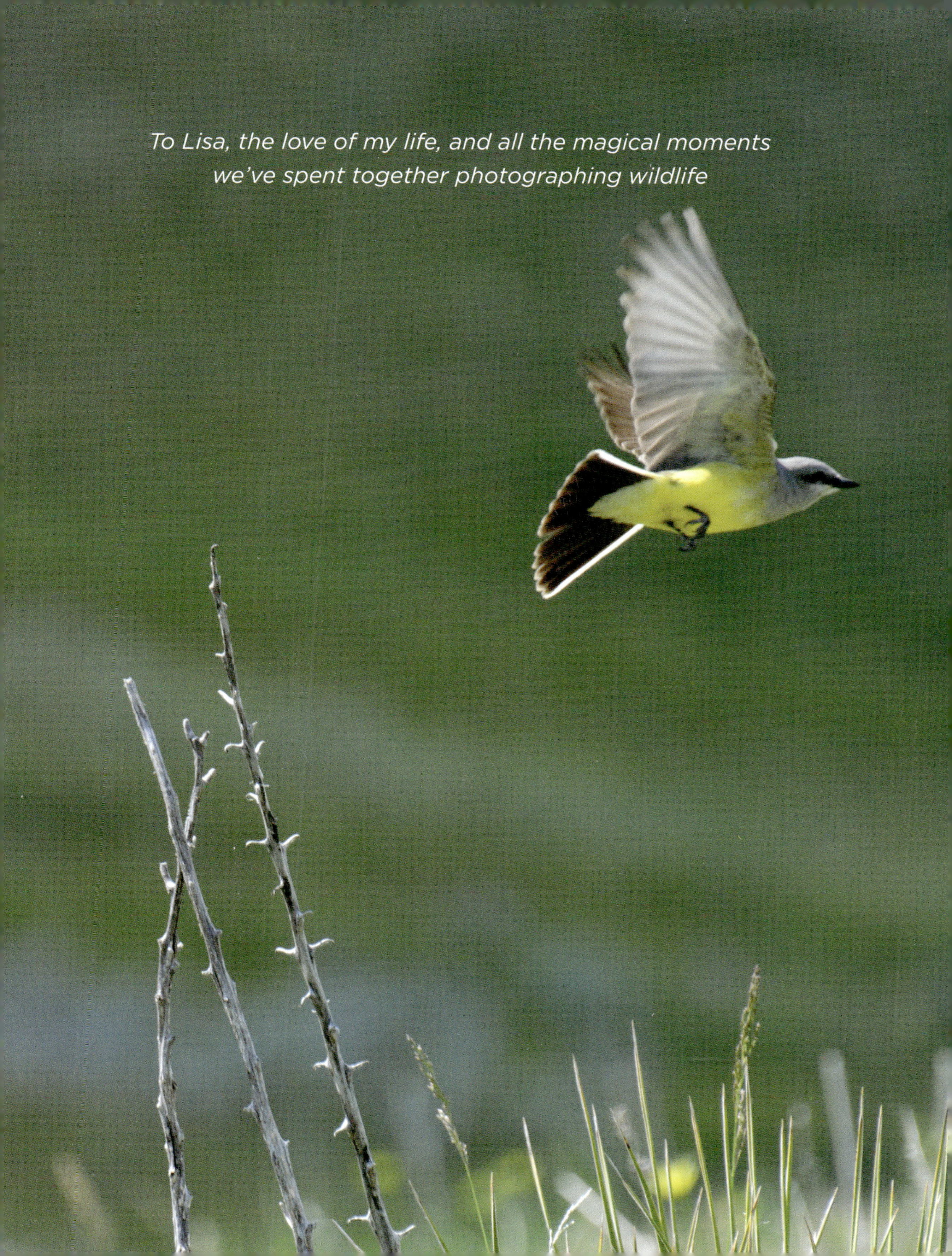

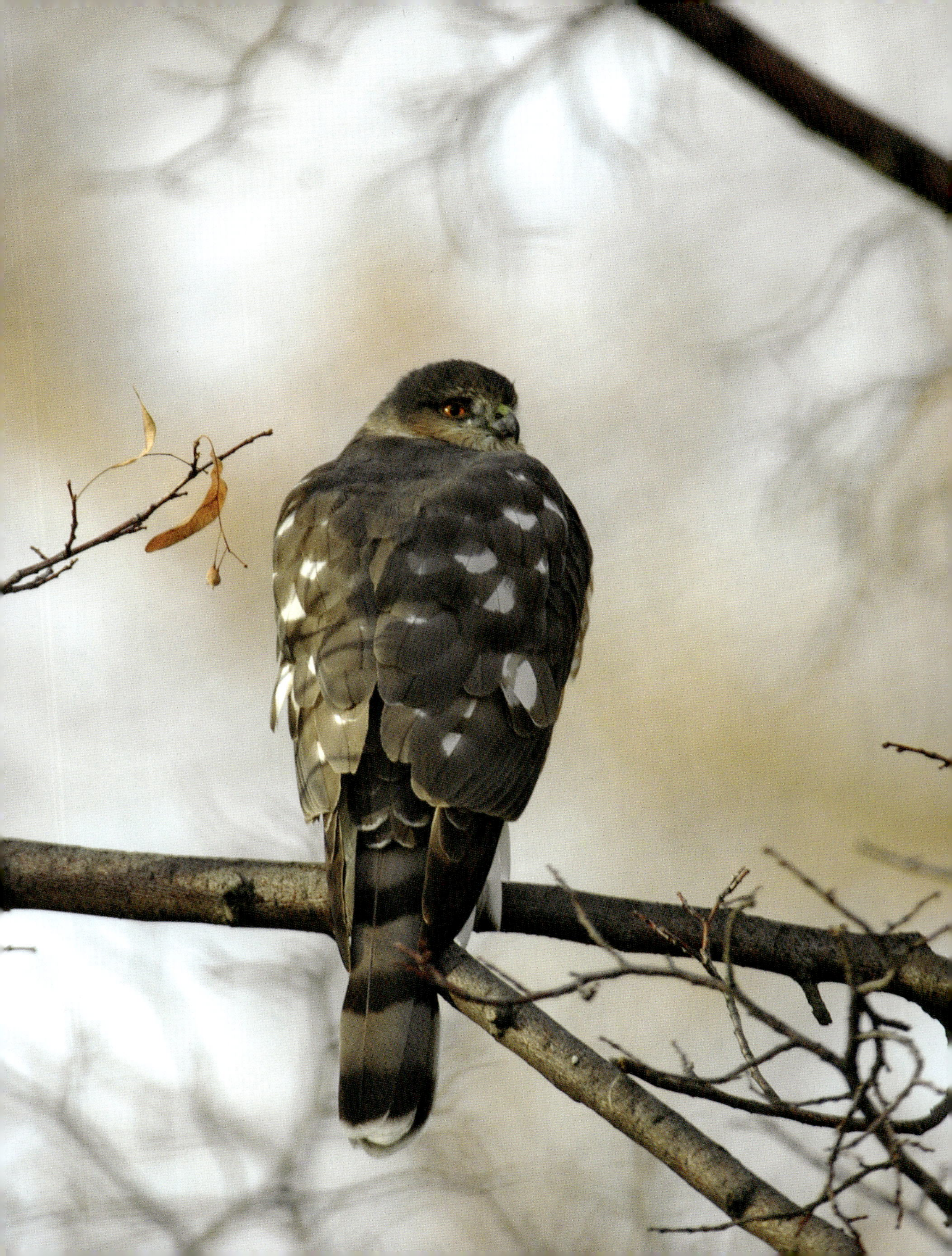

CONTENTS

ACKNOWLEDGMENTS viii

INTRODUCTION ix

CHAPTER 1 – Gearing Up: Cameras, Lenses, and Accessories 1

Cameras for Wildlife Photography 3
- DSLR Cameras 3
- Mirrorless Cameras 11
- Compact Cameras 12

Lenses for Wildlife Photography 14
- Magnification 14
- Aperture Characteristics 16
- Sharpness 17

Teleconverters 19

Accessorizing Your Camera Setup 21
- Tripod 21
- Flash 23
- Packs and Bags and Other Accessories 25

Photographing Wildlife with Tablets and Smartphones 26

Caring for Your Camera and Lenses 28

CHAPTER 2 – Exploring Exposure 31

Exposure Defined and Explained 31

Elements of Exposure 35
- Shutter Speed 35
- Aperture (Depth of Field) 36
- ISO 37

Relationship of Exposure Elements 39

Exposure and Camera Settings 43

Exposure Compensation for Difficult Subjects 44

CHAPTER 3 – Working with Light 49

Basic Light Patterns in Wildlife Photography 50
- Front Light 51
- Sidelight 53
- Backlight 55
- Overcast (Flat Light) 58
- Silhouettes 61

Daily Changes in Natural Light 64

CHAPTER 4 – Composition 69

Composition Defined and Explained 69

Basic Compositional Rules 71

Rule of Thirds 71

Level Horizons 74

Subject Framing 76

Focus 78

Depth of Field 82

Perspective 83

Composition Killers 88

CHAPTER 5 – Finding Wildlife 91

Urban and Backyard Wildlife 92

Zoos and Other Facilities 95

State and National Parks 99

Wildlife Refuges and Wilderness Areas 103

Local Hot Spots 106

Photo Tours and Safaris 107

Other Travel 111

CHAPTER 6 – Photographing Birds 113

Bird Behavior Basics 114

Movement Patterns 115

Seasonal Activities 117

Migrations 119

Backyard Bird Photography 121

Photographing from a Blind 124

Photographing Nesting Birds 129

Flight Photography 134

CHAPTER 7 – Photographing Mammals 143

Mammal Behavior and Habitat Basics 145

Movement Patterns 148

Seasonal Activities 158

Pelage Transitions 161

Urban Mammal Photography 163

Photographing Dangerous Mammals 164

Photographing from a Blind 168

CHAPTER 8 – Photographing Reptiles and Amphibians 171

Reptile and Amphibian Behavior Basics 172

Movement Patterns 174

Seasonal Activities 178

Appearance Transitions 182

Photographing Dangerous Species 184

CHAPTER 9 – Photographing Small Subjects and Macro Photography 187

Specialty Equipment for Small Subjects 188

High-Magnification Lenses 188

Macro Lenses 190

Adaptable Cameras 193

Basics of Macro Photography 194

Photographing Insects 201

CHAPTER 10 – Special Techniques and Situations 207

Flash Photography and Wildlife 208
Enhancing Motion 211
  Panning Techniques 213
  Shutter Speed 214
Photography in and on Water 216
Underwater Wildlife Photography 219
Dealing with Extreme Environments 222

CHAPTER 11 – Image Processing, Storage, and Sharing 227

Storage and Backup 228
Filing Systems 230
Photo Processing Software 232
Basic Photo Processing Techniques 235
  Cropping 235
  Exposure Adjustment 235
  Leveling 236
  Color Correction 236
Photo Sharing 238
To Sell or Not to Sell? 240

INDEX 244

ABOUT THE AUTHOR 252

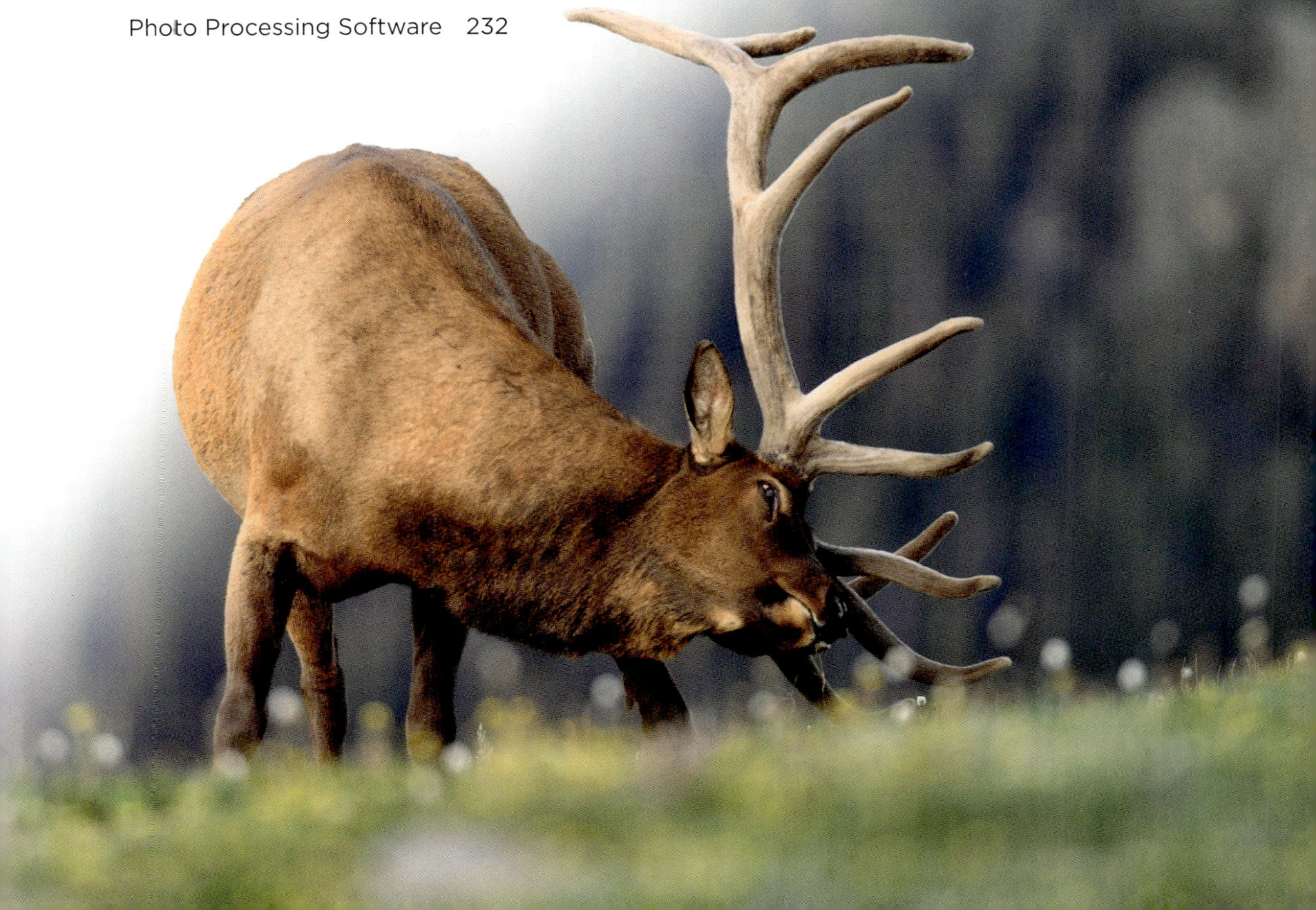

ACKNOWLEDGMENTS

I am deeply indebted to more individuals than can be mentioned when it comes to the acquisition of the information contained in this book. Numerous photographers affiliated with the Outdoor Writers Association of America (OWAA) gave me encouragement and invaluable advice after I joined this organization early in my career, including Lee Kline, Tom Ulrich (deceased), Michael Furtman, Bill Mullins, and Tim Christie, among others. Dr. Russell Lord, my former department head at Montana State University–Billings, was very helpful in adapting my schedule as I was transitioning from university lecturer to photographer/writer.

Lisa, my wife, is responsible for many of the photos in this book. We have shared countless hours together in the field photographing wildlife, some of our most treasured time together as a couple. My son, Dominic, is also a skilled photographer and has generously offered images from his files for this book. I am also indebted to John Burbidge and Katie Benoit of Rowman & Littlefield for developing the original concept of this book and making valuable suggestions on its basic outline.

Swarovski Optics generously provides outstanding optics for my viewing and observation of wildlife. Thank you.

INTRODUCTION

I remember the exact moment I became addicted to wildlife photography. While visiting Yellowstone National Park one autumn, I followed a herd of elk at a distance up a mountainside. A regal bull shepherded the cows. Halfway up the slope, his herd collided with two other bands. In the melee that followed, two more dominant stags ousted the bull. He stood in a clearing as the other animals departed, bugling his frustrations to the world, his breath coming in great clouds in the frosty air.

Camera in hand, I had 36 frames on a roll of film to capture the stunning image. Or so I thought. The camera required manual advance of the film via a thumb-operated lever. When the frame counter moved to 37, I was happy to get a bonus photo, which sometimes occurred with film. When it went to 38 and then 39, my heart sank.

Those of you reading this who remember the film days are chuckling. I had no film in the camera (later film cameras that used LCD displays and DX coding eliminated this problem). But the images I have of that singular experience are recorded in the electrochemical memories of my brain, impossible to share with others except as verbal descriptions. For me it was the beginning of my quest to photograph wildlife.

Along with earning a living as a wildlife photographer, I have written hundreds of articles regarding various aspects of the biology of many creatures. I have also authored a series of books about large mammals of the Rocky Mountains

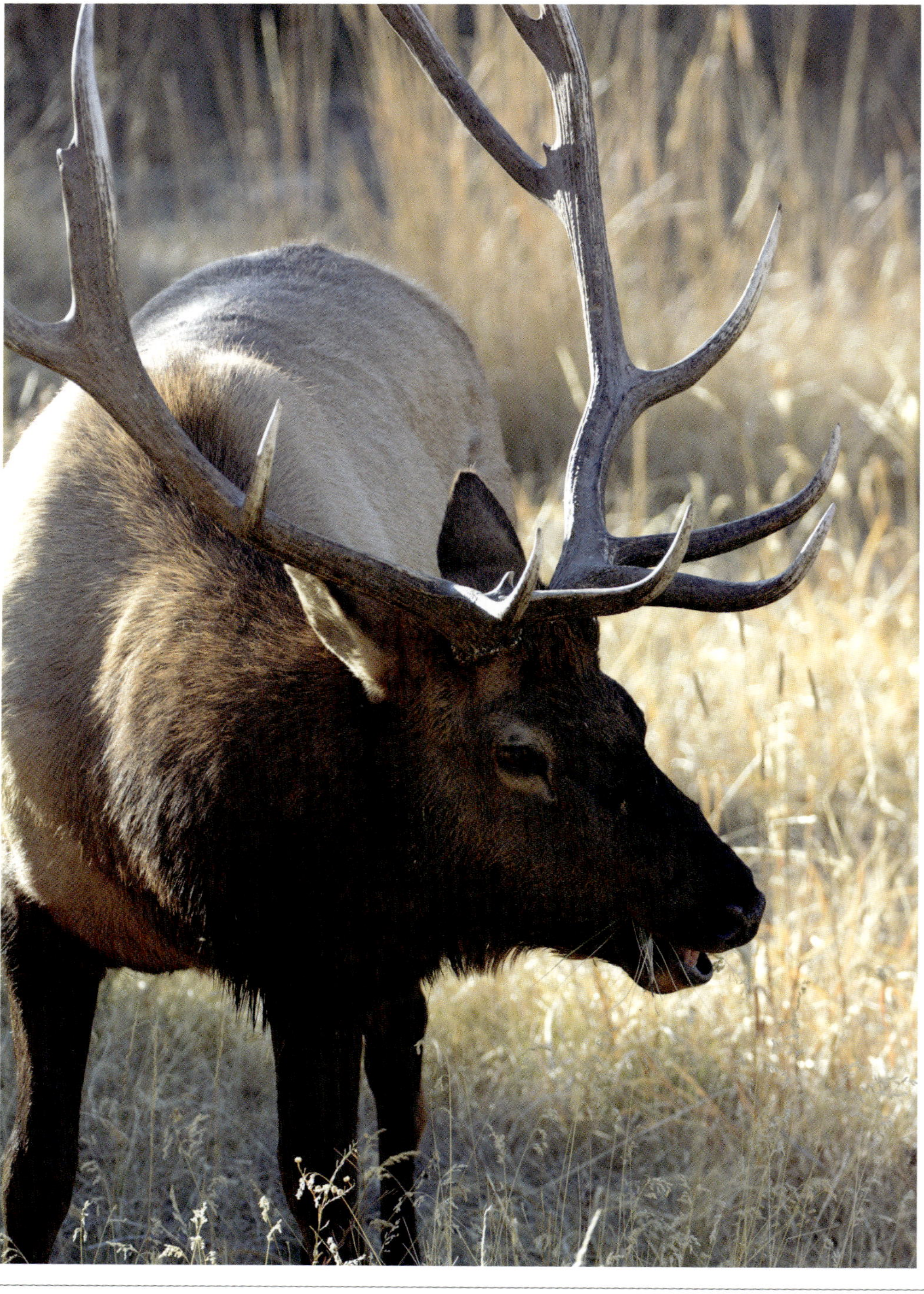

(published by Falcon). The intersection of my photography and prose in relation to wildlife has led me to conclude that the best wildlife photographers may not be the best technical photographers, but they are the best biologists. Consistently locating and photographing wildlife species demands an intimate understanding of their preferred habitat and behavior. As such, much of this book is focused on behavioral aspects of various creatures and how those behaviors influence wildlife photography. There is also enough information contained in chapters pertaining to basic technical photography to educate individuals whose skills are lacking. The material in this book is intended as a basic primer in technical photography as it pertains to wildlife subjects.

Along with the technical information, I hope readers find this work inspirational. Wildlife photography has greatly expanded my interest in, and understanding of, many creatures I did not know existed prior to taking their photo. The very survival of many wildlife species worldwide is currently in jeopardy. The more aware a person is of a wildlife species, the more likely he or she will value it enough to advocate for its conservation. As such, wildlife photography may be a powerful, driving force in a global human society that frequently sacrifices wildlife habitat for some type of material "progress."

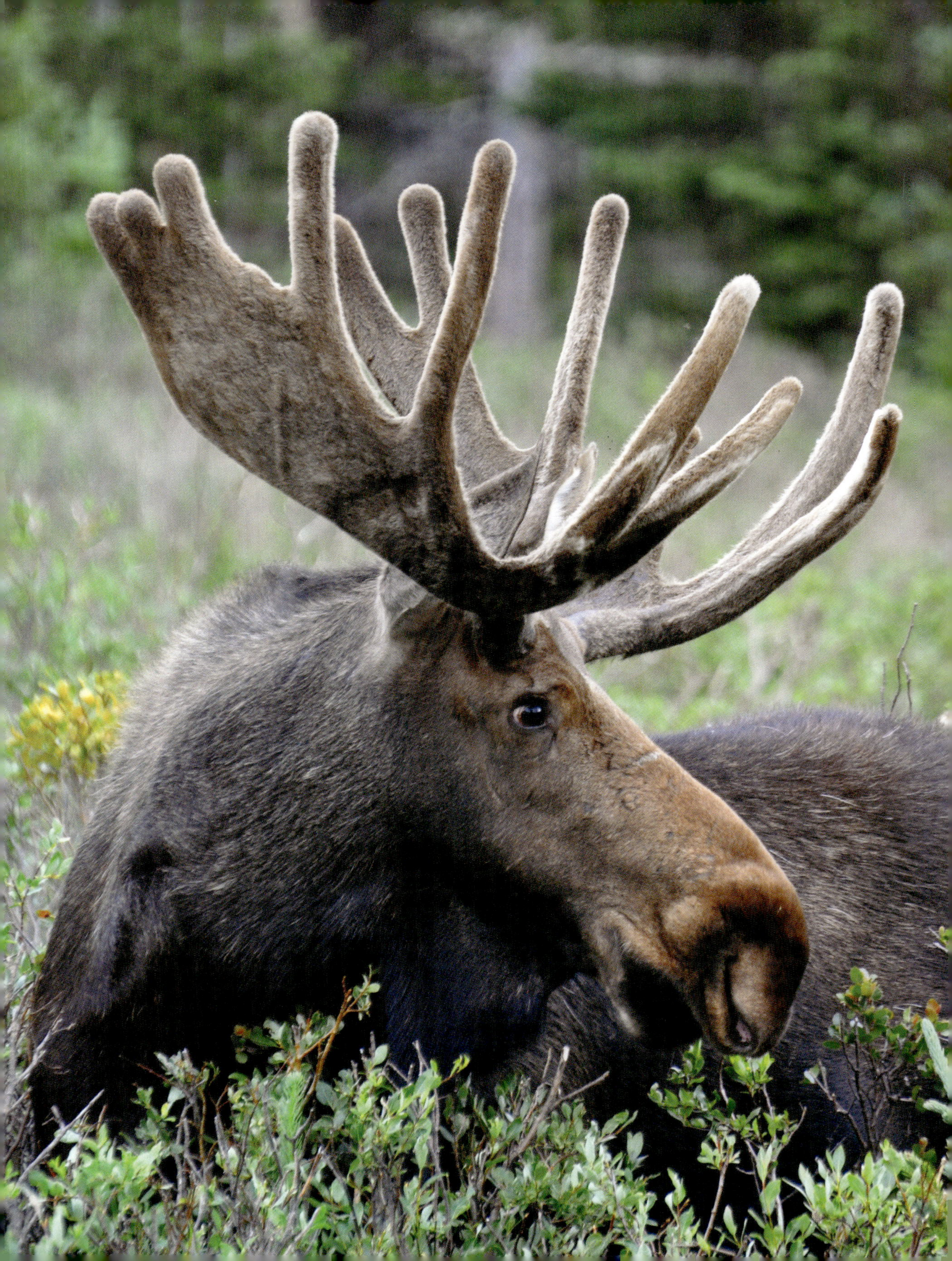

CHAPTER 1

Gearing Up: Cameras, Lenses, and Accessories

In my childhood days, a time that seems not so far away on the stopwatch of human history, cameras were a singular apparatus. A camera was, well, a camera, an instrument used to capture photographic images on film, pictures that were then most often printed on shiny paper and "shared" by transferring them from one human hand to another for viewing. Today cameras seem a ubiquitous device. As I write this, a tiny aperture peers at me from the top of my computer screen, a camera, ready to capture images of my furrowed brow and surroundings (on an airplane) with its activation via software. Cameras reside in our cellphones and automobiles. They record our images in banks, box stores, and motel lobbies. From satellites high in the heavens, they ceaselessly record

Bull moose. *Jack Ballard*

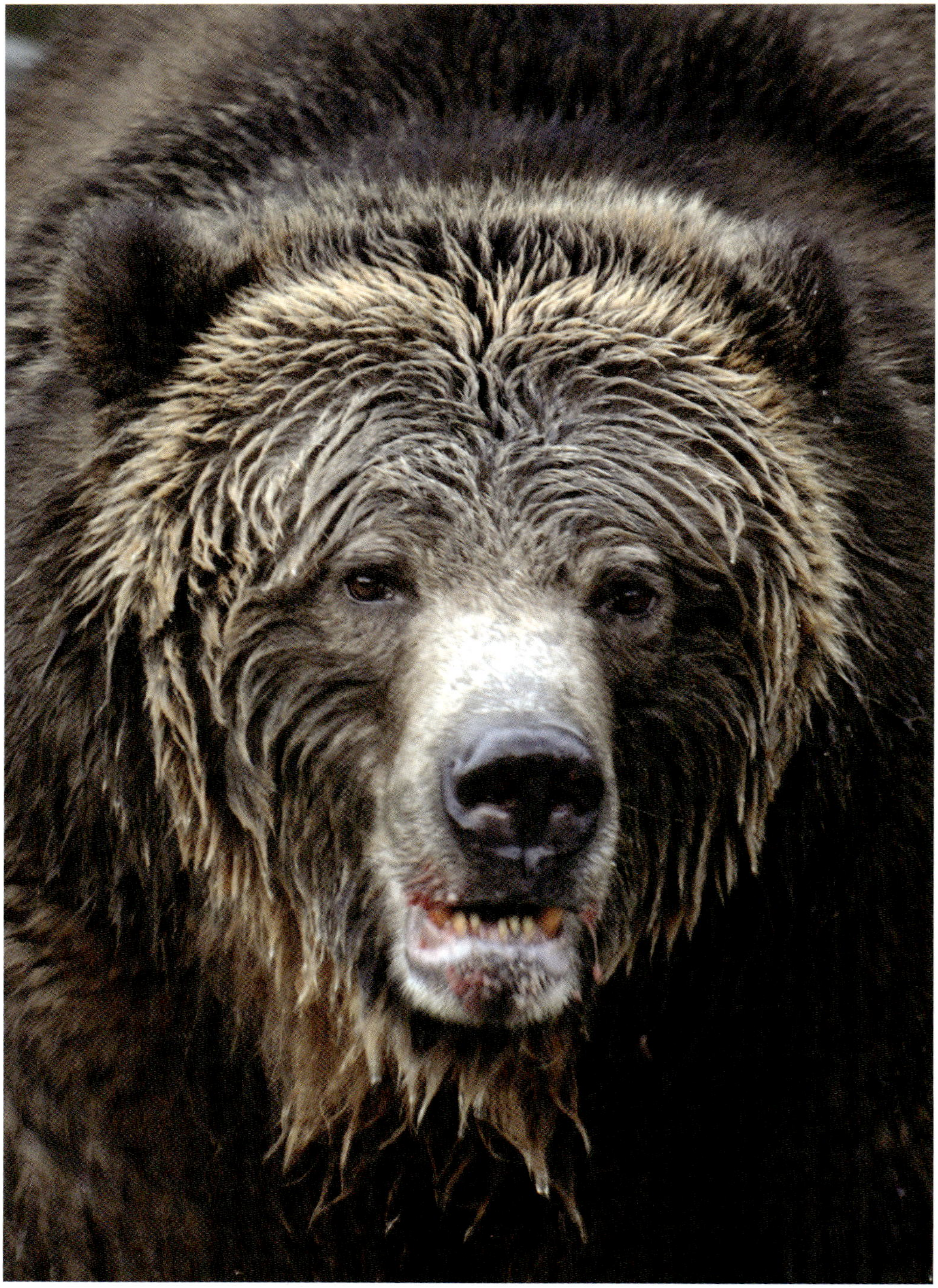

events on earth. Misbehave in public and the odds are quite high your actions will be recorded on a camera.

CAMERAS FOR WILDLIFE PHOTOGRAPHY

Despite the proliferation of photographic devices in contemporary society, none are capable of fulfilling all the purposes for which still or motion pictures are recorded. When it comes to wildlife photography, certain types of cameras are vastly superior to others in many, many respects. As is the case with any other hobby or occupation, having the proper tools makes the task much easier and leads to superior results. Individuals desiring pleasing images are advised to acquire the proper gear up front as opposed to adapting cameras designed for other purposes to capture images of the world's wildlife.

DSLR Cameras

The acronym DSLR stands for "digital single-lens reflex." Without going into too much detail, think of these as the cameras "serious photographers" carry slung over their shoulder. They consist of a camera body and interchangeable lenses. The "single-lens reflex" (SLR) part of the descriptor refers to the camera's use of a mirror to reflect the image created by the lens into the viewfinder of the camera. SLRs have been around for a century and dominated the world of serious amateur and professional photography (film) for the latter half of the twentieth

Left: Cameras devoted to the purpose of photography (versus those integrated into other devices) are vastly superior when it comes to wildlife photography. This photo of a grizzly bear at Knight Inlet, British Columbia, was taken with a long telephoto lens, a shot impossible to get with inferior equipment. *Lisa Ballard*

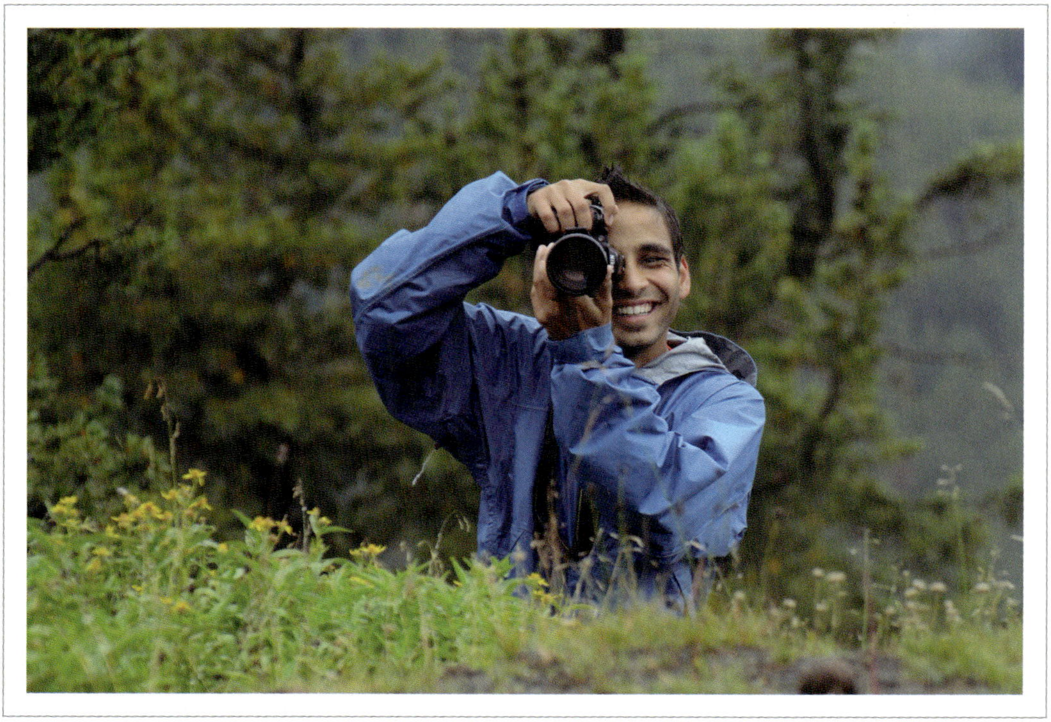

DSLR cameras are currently the most popular for wildlife photography, offering the widest array of camera models and interchangeable lenses from numerous manufacturers. *Lisa Ballard*

century. They maintain their dominance at this writing with the modification of a digital sensor capturing the photographic image instead of film. The vast majority of professional and committed hobbyist wildlife photographers rely on DSLRs as their tools of choice.

The advantages of DSLRs for wildlife photography are many. Due to their popularity, they offer an exceptionally wide array of lenses from not only the major camera manufacturers but also "aftermarket" companies that craft quality lenses. DSLRs have virtually no lag time between tripping the shutter and image capture, a disadvantage in some other camera formats. From a consumer standpoint, DSLRs are available in a broad range of prices. Like other implements, there is a strong correlation between useful features and price. The old adage "you get what you pay for" is certainly true when purchasing such a camera.

Some debate exists among technically proficient wildlife photographers regarding necessary features in DSLRs. In fact, except for the most inexpensive entry-level models (and some of those are quite good), any DSLR will capture pleasing wildlife photos under the right conditions. However, a higher price tag generally yields two advantages: higher image quality and features designed to allow the competent user to achieve superior results in difficult conditions related to tricky exposure, fast action, and tough physical environments.

Dozens of articles in photographic and other magazines are devoted to camera features each month and may prove to be a source of bewilderment to the novice wildlife photographer. However, certain features are invariably the most valuable to wildlife shooters, no matter the make, model, or format of the camera. Here are the most important to evaluate when purchasing a DSLR (or any other type of camera):

IMAGE QUALITY

Highly related to image size, the "in-camera" quality of a photo is evaluated in terms of color accuracy, clarity, and the ability to greatly enlarge it without loss of sharpness. Image size is typically rated in terms of "megapixels" (MP), which refers to a unit of area containing one million pixels (the smallest singular element in a digital photo). For most purposes, current mid- to high-priced DSLRs capture an image with more megapixels than needed. For example, lots of cameras create images with more than 20 MP. However, a quality 8x10 print can be made from 7 MP. Higher megapixels allow for greater enlargement and cropping of images, but they do not always correlate accurately with image quality. Image sensor design, optics, firmware, and other aspects of image capture profoundly affect quality. Think of it like this: A minimum of megapixels is required for a certain level of image quality, but simply meeting the minimum doesn't necessarily produce the desired results. There is one downside to more megapixels: As image size increases, so does the need for computer power when editing the photos.

EXPOSURE CONTROL

The ability to designate how a camera controls exposure (how light or dark the image appears) is important to professional photographers. Entry-level DSLRs often have limited options in relation to exposure control and compensation. The ability to designate exposure priority to shutter speed or aperture and the option of controlling exposure manually are important to advanced photographers. Additionally, the possibility of exposure compensation (having the camera read overall exposure as lighter or darker) is nearly invaluable in some situations. Finally, different metering modes are also important. Standard metering in most digital cameras of all types involves the camera evaluating the light in numerous zones of the frame and then averaging them for an overall exposure. A "spot meter" function, where the camera reads the final exposure from a very tiny portion of the frame, is extremely useful in tricky exposure situations.

Right: Very dark or very light subjects like this whooping crane can create difficult exposure situations. Cameras with sophisticated exposure systems allow a competent user to adjust for such challenges. *Jack Ballard*

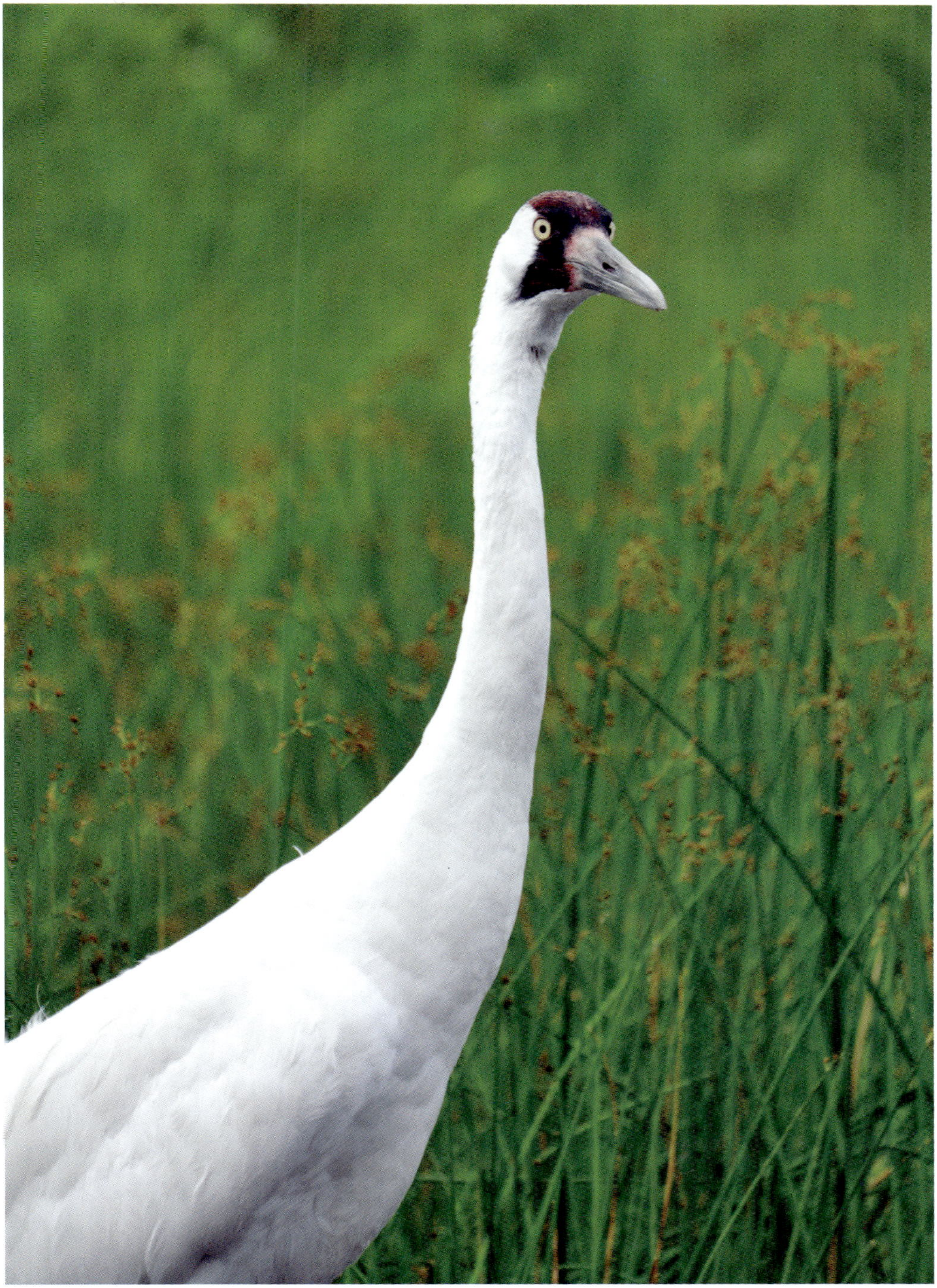

FOCUS CAPABILITIES

Most DSLRs have quite sophisticated automatic focusing capabilities. Focus can be set to lock on a subject after the shutter button is depressed partway or to continuously adjust the focus in relation to whatever object is in the designated focus point. Focus "tracking" is a mode in which the camera rapidly adjusts the focus to keep a moving subject in focus. This is a very valuable feature for wildlife photographers, especially those aspiring to photograph flying birds or other action subjects. However, not all focus-tracking systems are equal. Reviews by expert users or the ability to "demo" a particular camera are the best ways to evaluate focus tracking, but it's important to remember that the focus capabilities

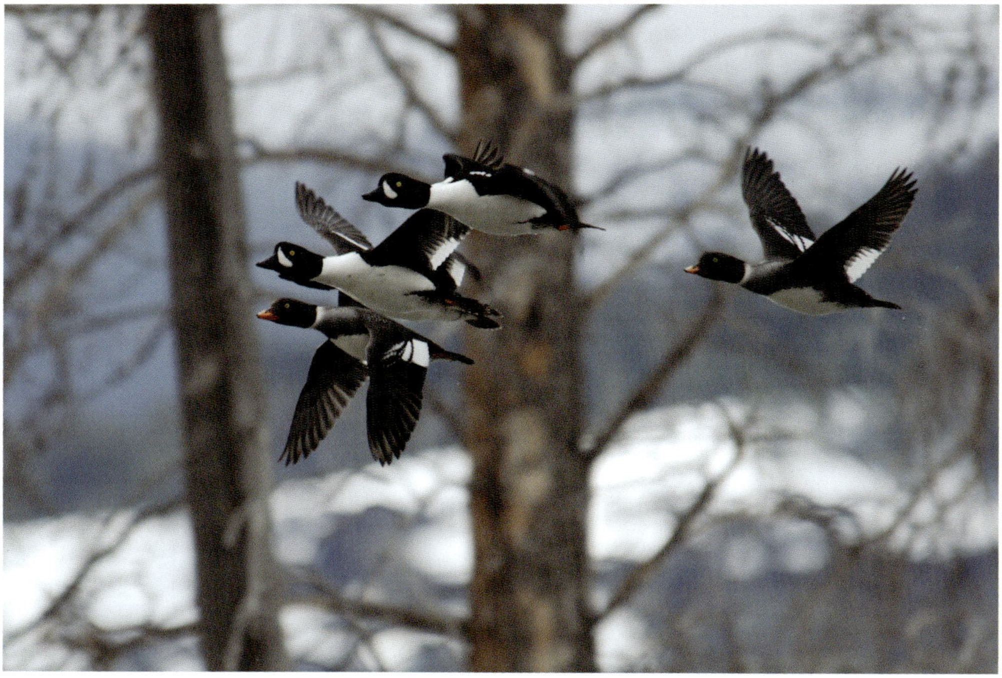

Advanced focusing systems dramatically enhance a photographer's ability to capture images of moving wildlife subjects like these flying common goldeneyes. *Lisa Ballard*

of some lenses are better than others. A lens with inferior focus characteristics may not accurately reflect the focus-tracking abilities of the camera body.

IMAGE CAPTURE SPEED

Since the days of film cameras that could automatically advance the film in the camera body, manufacturers have sought to increase the number of frames a camera can capture in a given amount of time. With film cameras, this involved a tiny electric motor that moved the film in the camera body. Photographers were thus concerned with the capabilities of the "motor-drive," terminology that's still used (inaccurately) to conceptualize how fast a camera can capture a sequence of images. A more accurate way is to think of it is in terms of frames per second (fps), which applies to both digital and film cameras. A camera that can shoot 5 fps captures a maximum of 5 frames per second, never more. Under some shooting conditions and settings, it may capture less. The maximum number of frames per second on a digital camera is limited by several things—some mechanical, others electronic. It is also affected by the memory card used in the camera. Some memory cards allow for much faster image capture than others. Cameras with high fps rates should always be paired with quality memory cards.

In addition to fps, the number of images that can be captured in a short period of time (sometimes longer than a second) is limited by the camera's ability to internally process (buffer) the pictures. If the shutter button is held down and the camera is set in continuous shooting mode, the camera will eventually slow down or stop shooting. Its "burst rate" is the number of images that can be captured in a continuous sequence. It should not be confused with frames per second. For example, suppose a camera shoots at 6 fps and has a burst rate of 24 frames; this means the camera will continuously shoot for 4 seconds (24 frames ÷ 6 frames per second = 4 seconds). Burst rate sometimes varies from the manufacturer's advertised rate in relation to image quality (the advertised versus actual rates may differ slightly as well). Shooting in the RAW mode for maximum image quality increases file size and decreases the advertised burst rate. Some cameras (both DSLR and other types) offer a "burst mode" or "sport mode" which greatly increases the burst rate, but does so by decreasing the size (and quality) of the captured images.

In general, fps and burst rate increase with the cost of the camera. Cameras capable of 6 fps and a burst rate of a few seconds are adequate for most wildlife action situations in the hands of a reasonably skilled photographer.

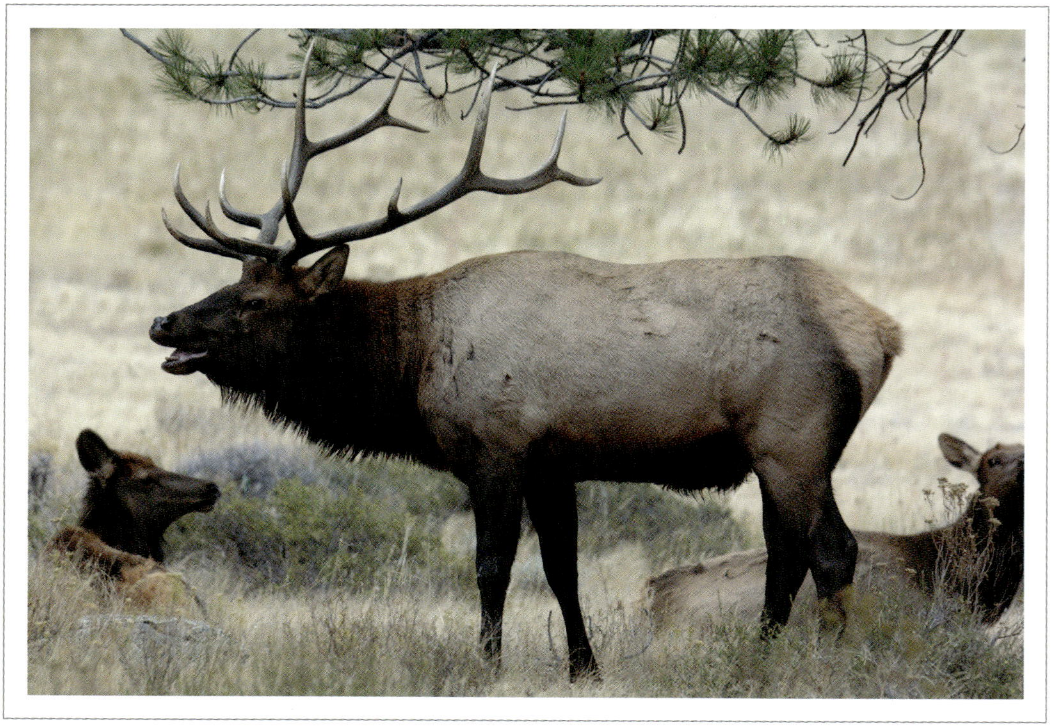

Camera bodies capable of shooting numerous frames per second are valuable in catching just the right moment in an action sequence, like this bugling bull elk in Rocky Mountain National Park, Colorado. *Jack Ballard*

Mirrorless Cameras

Mirrorless cameras operate without the mirror that a DSLR uses to reflect the image created by the lens into the camera's viewfinder. These cameras instead rely on an electronic viewfinder to preview the photographic image the camera is set to capture. While DSLRs are still the standard for the vast majority of professional photographers, mirrorless cameras are increasing their market share in the consumer camera world and steadily increasing in capabilities. At this writing, mirrorless cameras are considered advantageous over DSLRs due to their smaller size and weight (made possible by eliminating the internal mirror). Their electronic viewfinder also allows a more accurate look at how the previewed image will represent the final image in terms of depth of field and other aspects.

On the downside, lens selection for mirrorless cameras with interchangeable lens is limited compared to DSLRs (though that is likely to change if popularity continues to increase). Most models use smaller sensors than full-frame DSLRs, which limits image quality, although mirrorless cameras are very capable of producing professional-quality photos. Their focusing mechanism operates more slowly than DSLRs', a distinct disadvantage for wildlife photography, particularly in action situations. Their battery capacity in terms of how many frames the camera can shoot on a single battery charge is much less than DSLRs', due to the small size of the battery (which coincides with a smaller, lighter camera) and the electronic viewfinder, which requires constant battery output to operate. At this point, mirrorless cameras are certainly capable of capturing excellent wildlife images for hobbyist photographers but are not the camera of choice for serious shooters or professionals.

Compact Cameras

Compact cameras, or "point-and-shoot" models, are small enough to slip into a pocket. Their lens is integrated into the camera and is not interchangeable. Some have zoom lenses; others are fixed magnification. The zoom feature often relies on two types of magnification to obtain maximum reach. For the initial zoom, the camera relies on optical enlargement, which magnifies the image via the increasing focal length of the lens and does not necessarily degrade image quality. As the magnification increases, it switches to digital enlargement, which magnifies the image electronically and necessarily causes quality loss. A compact camera with a 24–130mm reach might thus use optical magnification from 24 to 90 and switch to digital magnification from 91 to 130, which is essentially the same as shooting the photo at 90 and then cropping it with editing software. Compacts are limited in their potential for general wildlife photography primarily due to the magnification of their lenses, most of which have limited reach in the optical zoom range.

However, compacts are a very useful tool in macro and underwater photography, as described in chapters 9 and 10. Some have surprisingly good capabilities in these areas. Both my wife and I use compact cameras for exactly these purposes and have seen numerous photos taken with them in publication. The key to satisfaction with a compact as a macro or underwater camera is to thoroughly understand its limitations and shoot only when conditions make it possible to achieve the desired results with a particular model. Magazine and online reviews are invaluable in evaluating a compact's capabilities.

Right: Compact cameras can be extremely useful in wildlife photography for close-up and underwater photos.
Jack Ballard

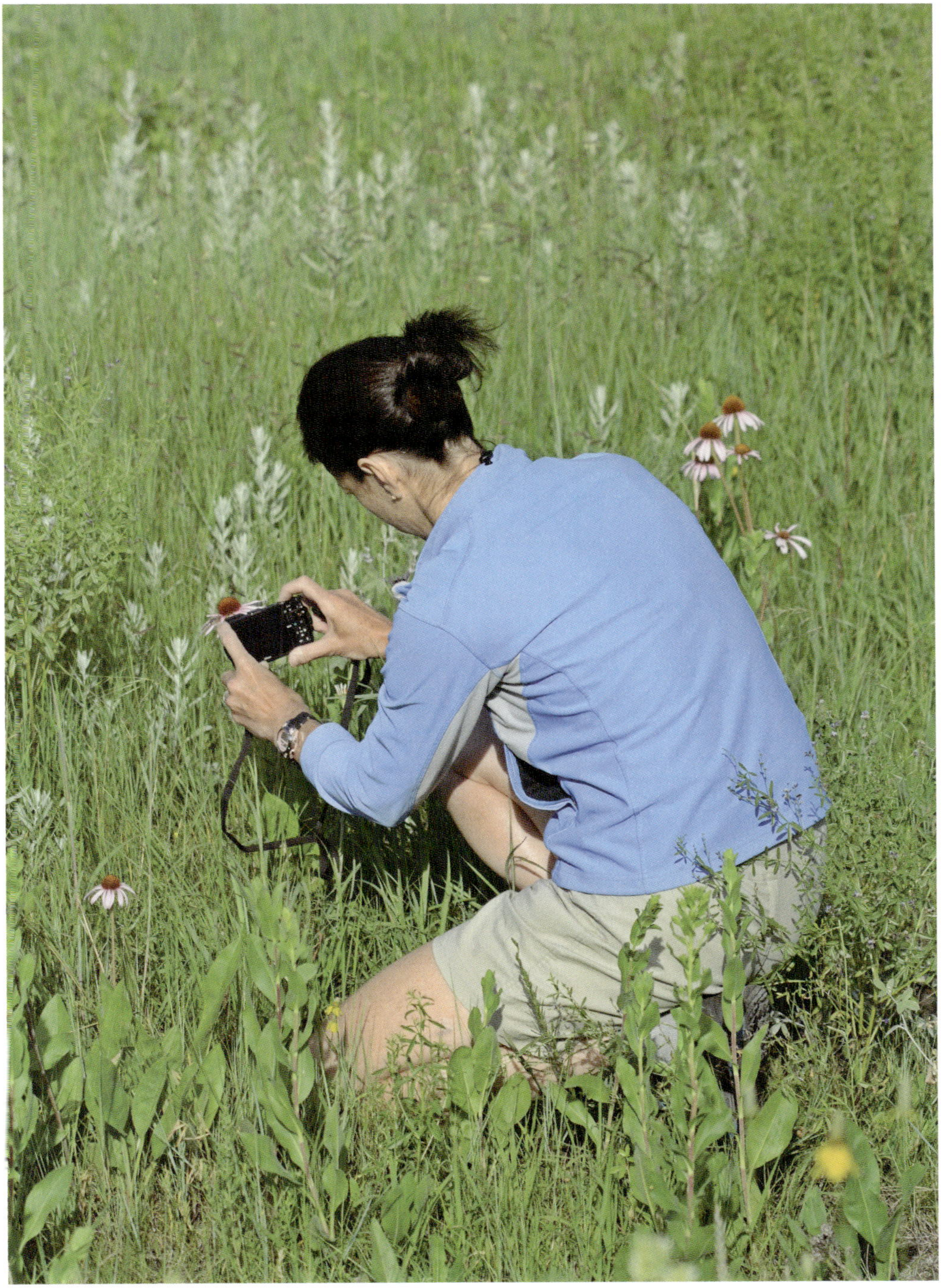

LENSES FOR WILDLIFE PHOTOGRAPHY

Cameras with interchangeable lenses are the best bet for wildlife photographers. The flexibility of changing from a wide-angle lens for habitat shots to a super-telephoto for frame-filling images of a skittish subject is invaluable for obtaining precisely the desired photographic representation of the subject. However, few photographers have a limitless budget for camera equipment. Useful wildlife lenses (purchased separately from a camera body) might range from $150 to $15,000. Selecting lenses invariably involves trade-offs between features and price. Here are the most important to consider when purchasing lenses for wildlife photography:

Magnification

Lenses nearly replicate or profoundly alter the perspective of the human eye as it pertains to the portion of a person's visual field captured in a photograph. Digital cameras with "full-frame sensors" and film cameras are commonly said to most closely replicate the perspective of an unaided human eye at a 50mm focal length. DSLRs with "crop sensors," most mirrorless and compact cameras, and cellphone cameras record their images to smaller sensors, which effectively increases the focal length (magnification) of the lens. A 50 percent magnification gain is often estimated for DSLRs with crop sensors. Thus such a camera outfitted with a 34mm lens would approximate the magnification of the human eye (34mm × 1.5 = 51mm). Lenses shorter or longer than these benchmarks either reduce or increase the magnification of the subject in the photo. For wildlife photographers, the desire most often falls on the side of increasing magnification. Thus telephoto lenses that provide extra magnification are the prized possessions of wildlife photographers.

Interchangeable lenses come in fixed or zoom configurations. Zoom lenses allow the photographer to choose a range of magnifications while shooting, as in the case of an 80–400mm zoom lens. The magnification of fixed lenses cannot be changed. Astute beginners thus raise an obvious question: Why not always buy zoom lenses, which amounts to having a bunch of fixed lenses in one package? The dominant reason involves image quality. Because the glass elements in a fixed lens do not move, they have inherent advantages in providing

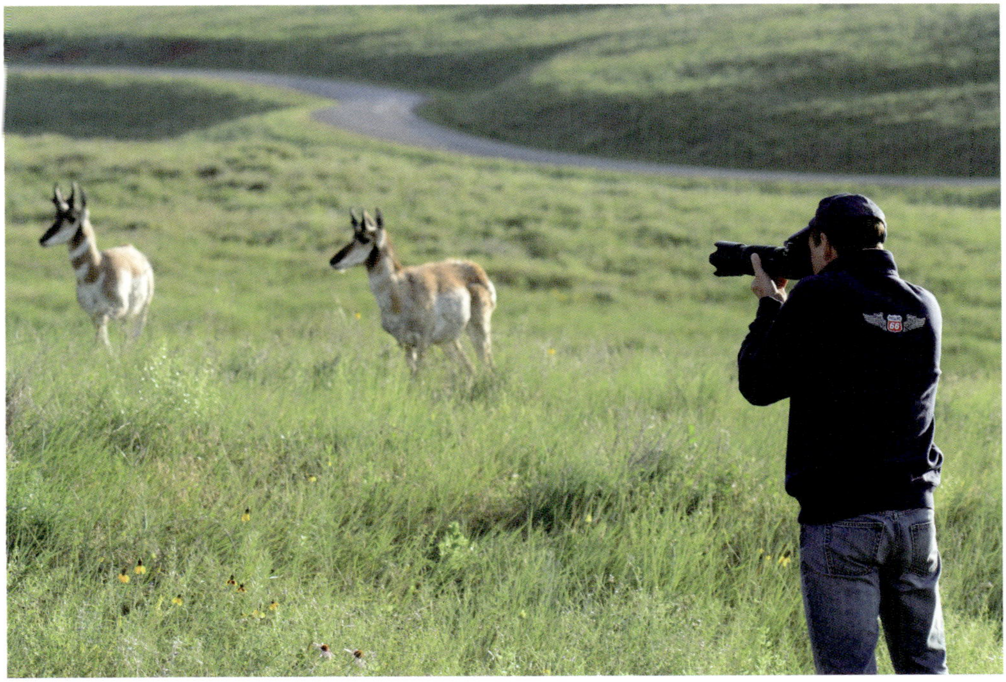

Zoom lenses are considered "bread and butter" equipment by most professional wildlife photographers. Here the author uses a 70–300mm zoom to photograph pronghorn in Custer State Park, South Dakota. *Lisa Ballard*

greater image quality. That is not to say zoom lenses aren't good. I would wager that next year far more published images of wildlife subjects will be shot with zoom lenses than fixed. However, those demanding the very best image quality at all aperture settings on the lens turn to fixed lenses over zooms.

How much magnification is needed for wildlife subjects? That depends on the subject's size (think an elephant versus a bumblebee) and the distance at which it can be approached. Many camera kits (camera body plus one or more lenses) come with a telephoto lens in the 60–300mm range. This is an excellent choice for general wildlife photography. Longer telephotos reside in the camera bags of professional and serious amateur wildlife photographers, but they are physically larger, heavier, and more expensive. Most require the support of a tripod to use them to their fullest advantage, though some incorporate a gyroscopic device for "image stabilization" or "vibration reduction" that allows sharp images when handheld at rather low shutter speeds.

Aperture Characteristics

An aperture is an opening. In the case of a camera lens, there are two openings, one at the front and another at the rear. A long lens with a large front aperture looks impressive, but more important than the actual size of the aperture is its diameter in relation to the length of the lens. This ratio is expressed as the f-ratio. This important number will be described more fully in chapter 2, so for now let's limit the discussion to noting that larger apertures on lenses of the same focal length yield a smaller f-ratio, which signifies a greater capacity to transmit light. Thus a 300mm lens with an f/2.8 can shoot effectively in lower light and at faster shutter speeds than a 300 f/5.6. However, the difference in size and weight of the two lenses is considerable. Technological advances have steadily increased the low-light capabilities of cameras in recent years, yielding cameras that can record sharp images in low light at much higher shutter speeds than a decade ago. These have negated, to some extent, the need for lenses with very small f-ratios in low-light conditions.

Another aspect of aperture involves "fixed" versus "variable" aperture zoom lenses. With a fixed aperture zoom, the maximum aperture (lowest f-number) does not change as the lens is extended or zoomed. The maximum aperture on variable aperture lenses decreases as the focal length is increased when the lens is zoomed. In fact, the aperture changes any time the lens is zoomed no matter the aperture setting. This configuration yields cheaper lenses and isn't usually a problem when shooting in an automatic camera mode. However, there are situations in which a wildlife photographer might choose to use a manual camera mode or one that prioritizes shutter speed. In both of these modes, adjustments must be made to maintain the desired settings as the lens is extended or retracted.

Sharpness

Ever-improving sensor capabilities continuously increase digital cameras' ability to record more detailed images. But just as in the film days, a photo's sharpness is limited by the lens. No matter how good the recording medium (digital or film), it cannot compensate for an inferior image projected by a mediocre lens. Perhaps the strongest argument for spending several thousand dollars on a fixed magnification telephoto lens is the razor-sharp image it projects to a digital camera's sensor.

Photographers working with more budget-friendly lenses can maximize the sharpness of their photos in a couple of ways. The first is to make sure the lens

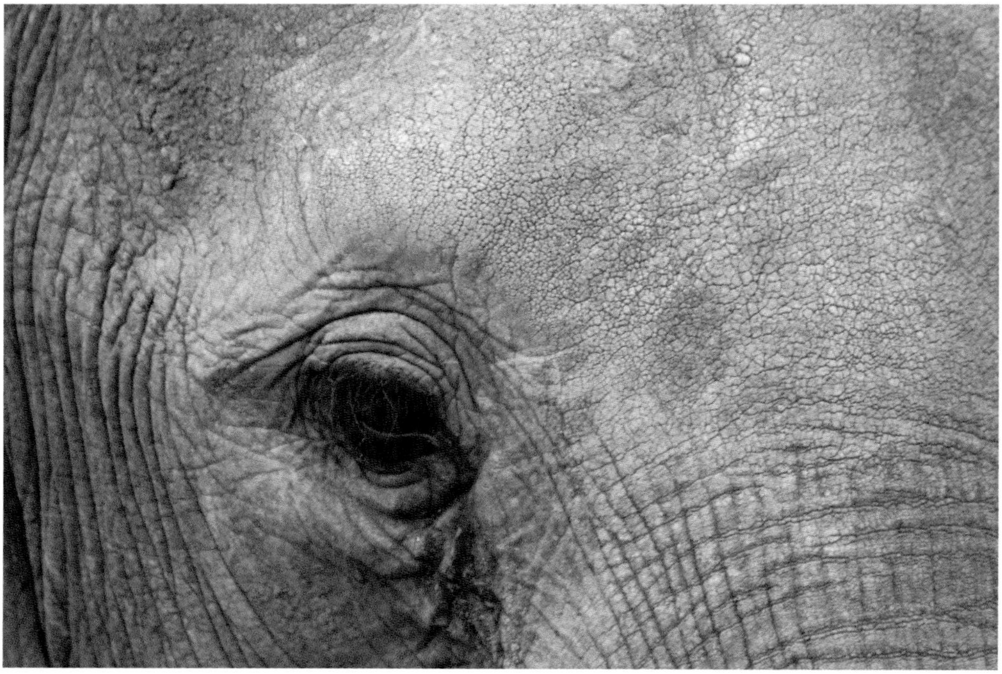

Lenses with superior sharpness are more expensive but allow perception of detail like the patterns and texture in the skin and eye of this elephant in Tanzania. *Jack Ballard*

is appropriately supported to minimize movement, using a tripod if necessary. The second is to shoot in the lens's "sweet spot," which is the range of aperture settings yielding the sharpest images. For most lenses, settings in the middle of the aperture range are the sharpest. For example, a lens with apertures from f/4 to f/32 will probably be the sharpest from around f/6.7 to f/18. Lenses from major manufacturers are usually reviewed at some point by photography magazines or online. When these reviews include technical evaluations of sharpness (as opposed to the reviewer's subjective perception), they can be very helpful in both informing a purchase and identifying the sharpest aperture settings of the lens.

TELECONVERTERS

Most wildlife photographers are on a never-ending quest for more magnification. It seems a situation always arises in which it would be helpful to have just a little more magnification on a faraway or very small subject. One "sneaky" way to find it is through the use of teleconverters. Also referred to as "tele extenders," these devices amount to an additional lens that's mounted between the primary lens and the camera body. The most popular extenders are 1.4X and 2.0X, referring

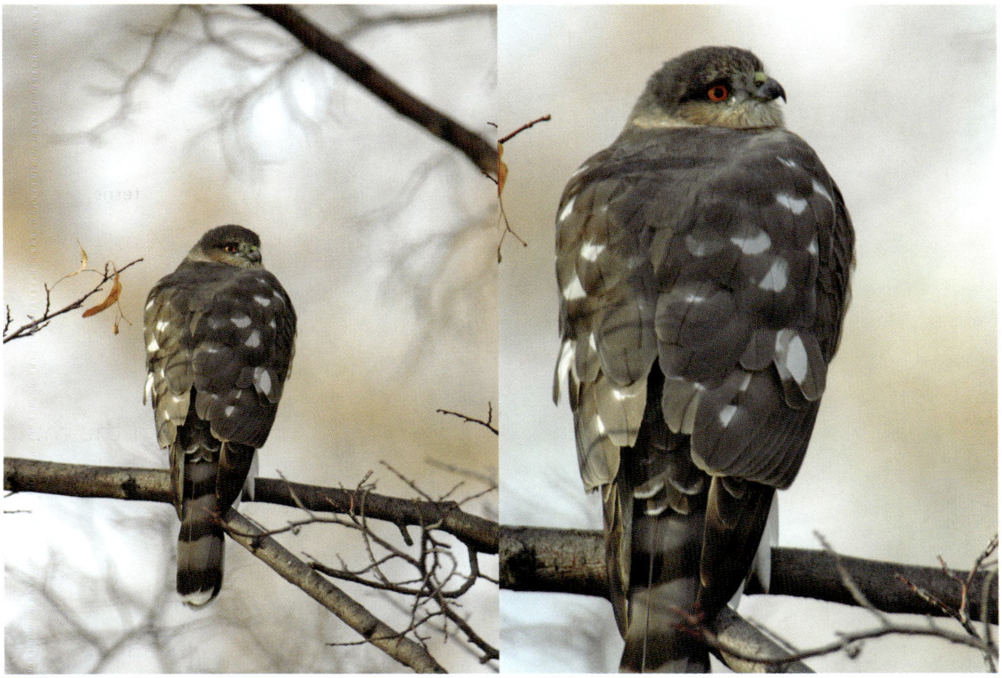

This Cooper's hawk was photographed from the window of the author's home in Billings, Montana, perched near a bird feeder. The first image was taken with a 500mm lens and yields a pleasing photo of the raptor in its habitat. A 2.0X teleconverter was added to capture the second photo that emphasizes the bird's plumage and striking red eye. *Jack Ballard*

to the amount by which they effectively increase the focal length of the lens and the magnification of the subject. Mounted behind a 500mm lens, a 1.4X converter increases it to a 700mm equivalent. A 2.0X extender ramps it to a 1000mm equivalent.

Despite their attraction, teleconverters come with some downsides. First, they decrease the lens's aperture. One f-stop is lost with a 1.4X converter; two stops are dropped with a 2.0X converter. A 200 f/2.8 lens becomes a 280 f/4 with the 1.4X and a 400 f/5.6 with a 2.0X. Converters thus decrease the ability to shoot in low light and decrease the maximum shutter speed available for proper exposure. (Look for a more detailed discussion of aperture, shutter speed, and exposure in chapter 2 if you're unfamiliar with these concepts.) They also decrease a lens's sharpness by magnifying any of its aberrations. Finally, teleconverters can disrupt the automatic focusing function of some cameras and may need to be manually focused.

Despite these drawbacks, the small size and relatively low cost of teleconverters make them a valuable addition to the wildlife photographer's equipment locker.

ETHICS AND ETIQUETTE

DRONES

At this writing, drones are one of the latest crazes in outdoor photography. They're fun, trendy, and can yield very good still and video images when controlled by a skilled user. They allow an aerial perspective at a fraction of the price of former times, when aerial images pretty much required the use of some type of aircraft.

However, drone use for wildlife photography is controversial. It holds high potential for significant disturbance to sensitive subjects such as nesting birds and reclusive predators. The welfare of birds and animals that may attack a drone as a defense response is also a concern. Drone use is illegal in many state and national parks. Some states have laws regulating the use of drones in relation to wildlife viewing and photography. There may be some situations in which drones offer an ethical option in wildlife photography, but their use is discouraged in most situations.

Additionally, the best teleconverters from major lens manufacturers yield very good image quality when paired with a sharp lens. I use both 1.4X and 2.0X on occasion, but only when lighting conditions are good and I'm shooting with a very sharp lens securely supported on a tripod or a solid surface.

ACCESSORIZING YOUR CAMERA SETUP

Cameras are a lot like laptop computers. They function fine on their own, but are greatly enhanced by accessories. Just as a computer user might opt for a larger monitor, a memory stick, and a mouse, most dedicated wildlife photographers have a host of accessories that enhance their camera's capabilities and facilitate the organization and transportation of gear. Here are some of the most essential.

Tripod

A tripod earns its keep as a stabilizing platform for the camera and lens. It reduces or eliminates the shake and vibration that's an inevitable part of hand-holding the camera. Many useful zoom lenses for wildlife photography incorporate a gyroscopic device that stabilizes it when handheld. These work very well, making sharp images possible at lower shutter speeds than when hand-holding a lens without such a device. However, not all lenses have these, and there are times when a tripod-mounted, completely supported lens is more desirable. Thus a good tripod is generally the first accessory to make its way into a wildlife photographer's kit.

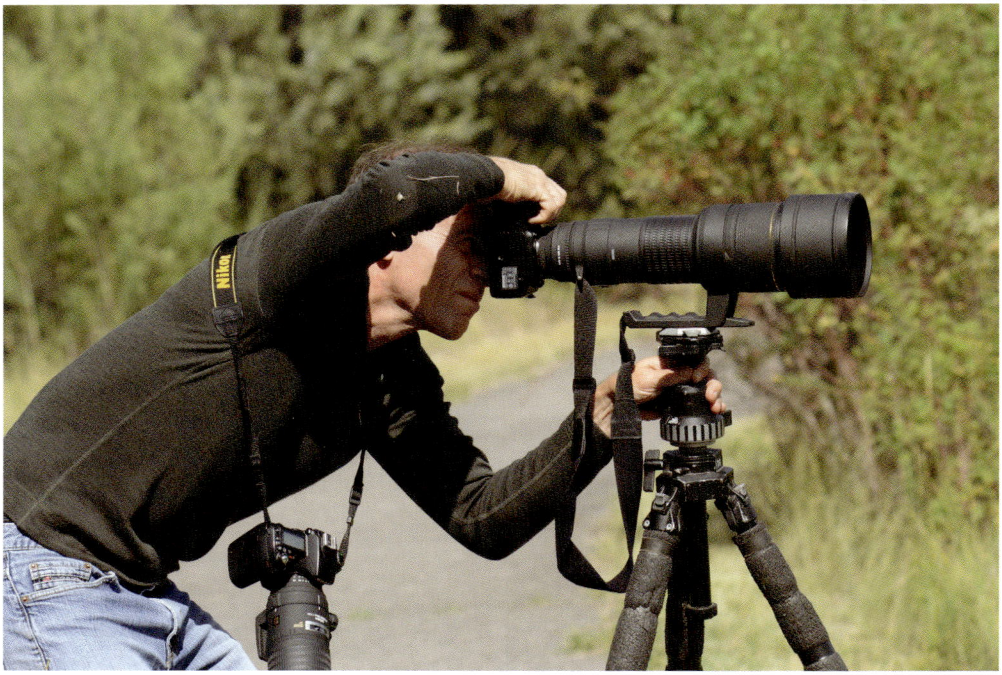

A tripod is essential equipment when using long, heavy telephoto lenses. A quality tripod will outlast many camera bodies. Here the author uses a tripod he's had in service for over two decades. *Lisa Ballard*

Choosing a tripod is best accomplished by matching it to your heaviest lens. Quality tripods from major manufacturers are rated according to the weight of the camera and lens they can support. Most higher-end tripods can be used with interchangeable heads, the part of the tripod to which the camera is attached. Heads come in various configurations. Specialty heads for supporting very heavy lenses have a correspondingly weighty price tag. Many wildlife pros opt for a stout ball head, which easily adapts to a range of shooting situations. If you plan to add a longer, heavier lens to your arsenal at some point, purchase a tripod that will handle it initially to avoid another major purchase later on. Tripods are one accessory where it's much preferred to be over-gunned than underpowered.

Tripods are usually advertised in relation to maximum and minimum heights as well as other features. The minimum side of the equation is as important as (if not more important than) the maximum. I often shoot from a low-angle position, and a tripod with a 28-inch minimum height isn't so useful in such situations. Some tripods have independently movable legs that will allow the head to nearly rest on the ground. These are very useful when photographing small subjects at earth level. A good tripod will probably outlive several camera bodies (I've used my main tripod for nearly thirty years) and should therefore be viewed as a very important, major purchase. A great addition to a tripod is a head with a quick-release plate that allows the camera and lens to be rapidly detached from the tripod for handheld shooting.

Flash

Many DSLR cameras come with a "pop-up" flash integrated into the camera body. These can be very useful for wildlife photography, especially to add "fill flash" to lighten shadows on the subject (more about that in chapter 10). However, they have two primary limitations. First, their range and output levels are quite limited. Second, they are permanently mounted into the camera and can't be moved. Sophisticated use of flash sometimes demands that the flash be tilted, swiveled, or moved off-camera (via a cord or remote control) to change the angle at which its light strikes the subject.

Early on in my wildlife photography career, I purchased a powerful external flash for my camera and have regularly used flash to enhance wildlife photos. Flash power is normally rated by the unit's "guide number" (GN). The guide number can give an informed customer a very good estimate of the distance at which the flash can illuminate a subject. Traditionally, the

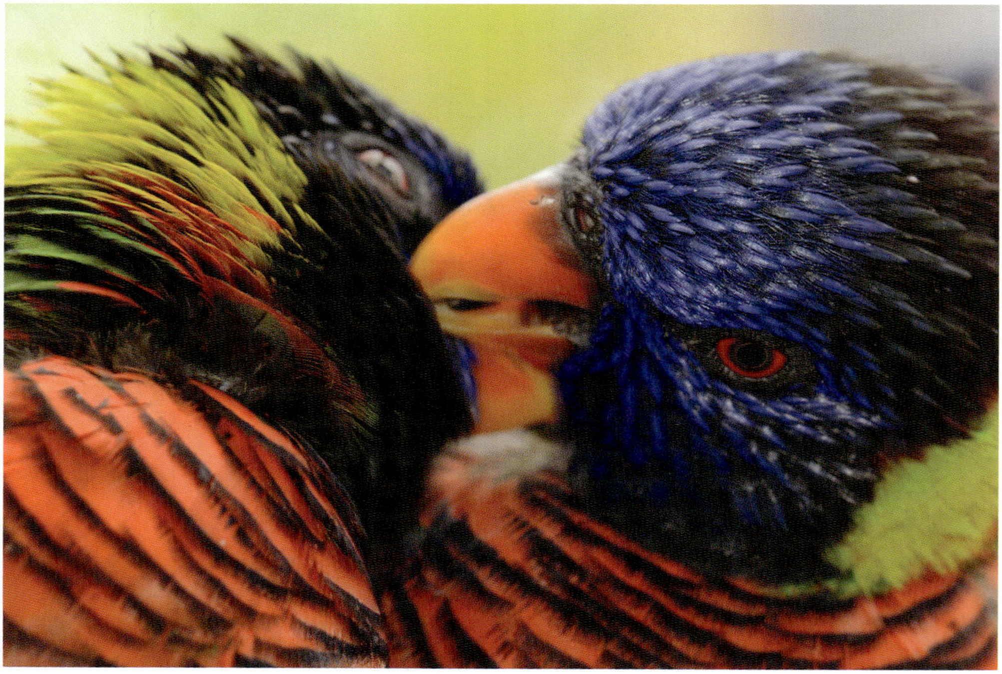

A flash is very useful for reducing shadows and adding light to wildlife subjects. The author used flash to lighten shadows and increase the detail seen on the feathers of these preening lorikeets at a captive bird facility. *Jack Ballard*

GN was given in reference to ISO 100 film. Nowadays, the information may vary from manufacturer to manufacturer. However, users who understand the mathematical relations between ISO and f-ratios (see chapter 2 for more information) should be able to calculate the flash's effective range for the preferred settings on their equipment.

Powerful flashes with heads that tilt, swivel, and zoom give the most flexibility for artistic lighting. As with tripods, you may regret being underpowered but are not likely to rue the purchase of a unit that meets your needs and then some.

Packs and Bags and Other Accessories

Transportation of gear can be a serious issue for professional wildlife photographers working in faraway locations or near home. It's often not possible to photograph near a vehicle, so camera bodies, lenses, a tripod, and other accessories may need to be transported for miles on foot. Most quality camera kits come with some sort of carrying bag, but these will not accommodate much extra gear. A sturdy camera bag or pack is necessary gear for serious wildlife photography.

A variety of specialty cases, backpacks, and bags are available. Pick one that fits the environments in which you plan to shoot and will house any planned expansion to your kit. For example, a waterproof case is desirable for shooters specializing in marine and aquatic life. Photographers who hike into the backcountry will be more satisfied with a backpack with an integrated rain cover versus a bag. Traveling photographers should check a case's dimensions against airline requirements for luggage. My wife and I often shoot in the backcountry and travel frequently.

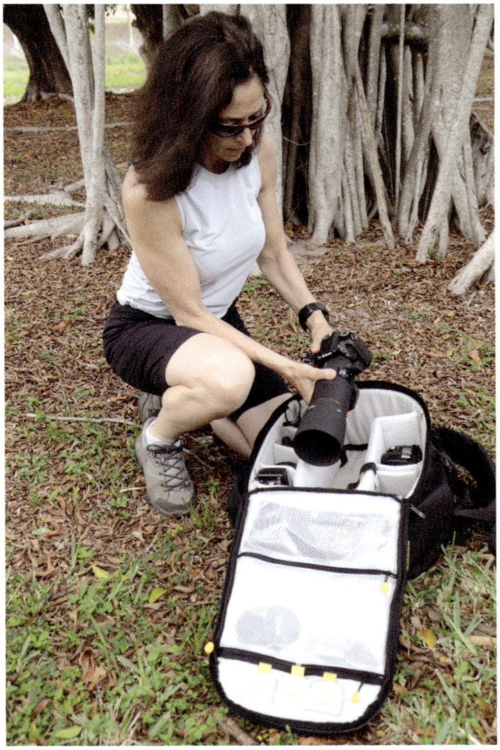

Camera cases and bags play an important role in protecting and organizing gear in the field. They should be chosen to match the photographer's modes of travel and favored shooting environments. *Jack Ballard*

We primarily opt for backpacks that fit the requirements for carry-on luggage, allowing us to keep tabs on our equipment at all times when flying.

Other accessories are also extremely helpful to wildlife photographers. I almost always carry binoculars for spotting wildlife from a distance. They are much easier to use than a telephoto lens when scanning expanses of habitat. A reflector is usually found in my bag as well, especially when working with a partner who can hold it to bounce light onto a subject, typically a reptile, amphibian, or insect. As your skill and preferences as a photographer grow, a natural winnowing process will occur that determines what accessories you find necessary and what can be left behind.

PHOTOGRAPHING WILDLIFE WITH TABLETS AND SMARTPHONES

It is a mistake to believe photos of any kind can be shot with a tablet or smartphone that rival the quality of a good camera. These devices record images to very small sensors and have other optical limitations that make them inferior to a dedicated camera. However, some have quite good capabilities. For wildlife photography, they are severely limited in terms of magnification. A handful of smartphones now have two lenses, a normal lens and either a supplemental "wide" or "telephoto." Otherwise the zoom feature on a smartphone is a digital zoom that provides more digital magnification but quickly degrades image quality.

The desire for more magnification with a smartphone has led to a variety of adapters that increase its camera's range. Some of these are external lenses that

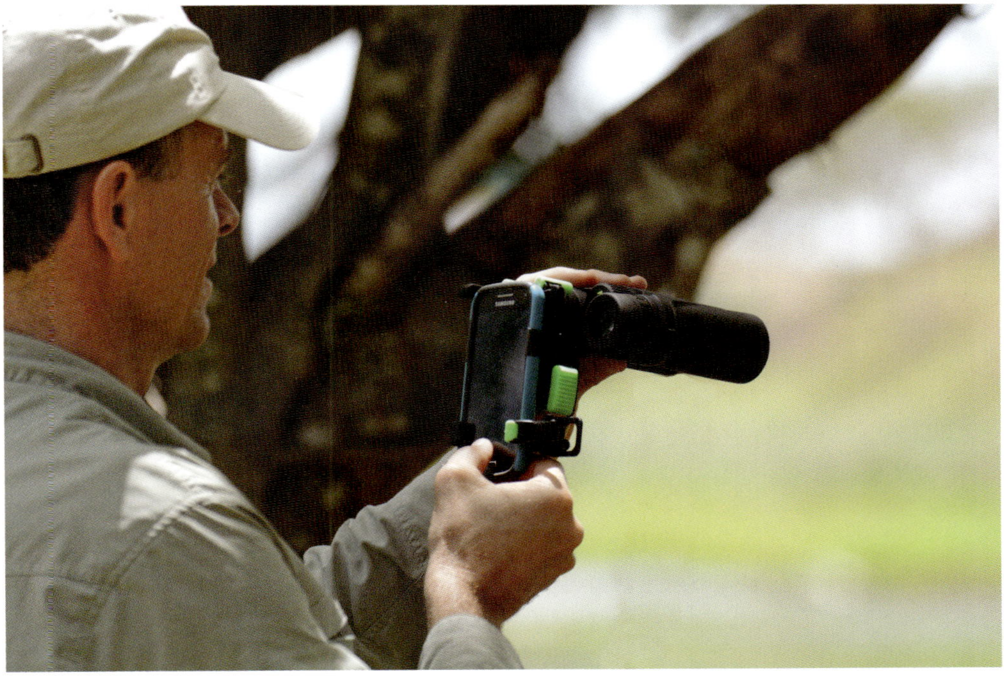

The cameras in smartphones are very limited for wildlife photography, especially where magnification is needed. Adapters that pair them with quality binoculars allow for much better images when shooting at a distance. *Lisa Ballard*

attach to the phone; most are budget priced and offer correspondingly modest image quality. Others allow the smartphone camera to be mated with another optical device such as a binocular or spotting scope. Paired with high-quality

ETHICS AND ETIQUETTE

PROXIMITY

Smartphone and tablet users confronted with intriguing wildlife subjects are often tempted to compensate for their camera's limitations by getting closer to the subject. This is fine with a butterfly, foolish with a bison. Large mammals and reptiles, no matter how docile they appear, are potentially dangerous. I've also been in countless situations where smartphone users cut in front of other photographers in an attempt to get a closer photo. No matter what camera is in your hands, respect its limitations, your subjects, and other photographers.

optics of this type, they allow reasonably good results when photographing distant subjects with a smartphone.

CARING FOR YOUR CAMERA AND LENSES

A good-quality basic kit of camera, lenses, and tripod for wildlife photography normally represents an investment of $1,500 to $5,000. Working with the best available equipment easily multiplies those numbers fivefold. Care and maintenance of sturdy equipment will greatly increase its life. A number of my wildlife pro friends shoot with lenses and tripods that they've used for two decades or more.

Care starts with protection from impact. The only serious damage my equipment has ever sustained was the broken barrel on an 80–400mm telephoto I dropped after slipping on a stone while photographing ducks on the Yellowstone River. When not in use, my gear stays in a padded backpack or case. Like many other photographers, I add a quality UV (ultraviolet) filter to the front of most of my lenses. This filter cuts the haze created by ultraviolet light, but more importantly serves as a relatively inexpensive way to protect the glass and coatings on the front of the lens from damage.

Dust and moisture are the two primary enemies of camera equipment. In severe cases, both can totally ruin lenses and camera bodies. Salt spray is also tough on equipment, as are some insect repellants and other substances. Be sure to study your owner's manual regarding care for your specific equipment. My camera bag always houses a microfiber towel and numerous cleaning cloths

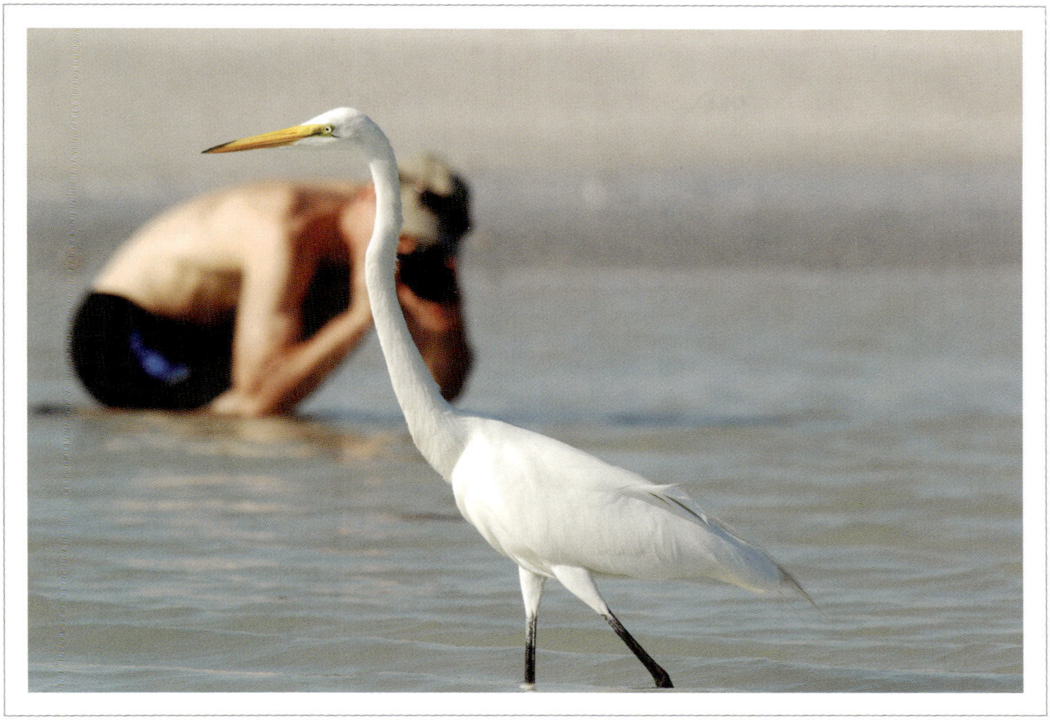

A number of wildlife environments can be very hard on photographic equipment. Saltwater mist and spray can be highly corrosive. Good care can greatly extend the life of equipment. *Lisa Ballard*

that are used to wipe dust, moisture, and grime from equipment in the field. When shooting around saltwater and dust, be sure to clean your equipment at the end of each day. Do not use paper towels, facial tissues, or a shirt sleeve to clean the glass on your lenses. Lens coatings that aid in light transmission and image enhancement are easily scratched. Opt for cleaning cloths specifically intended for optics.

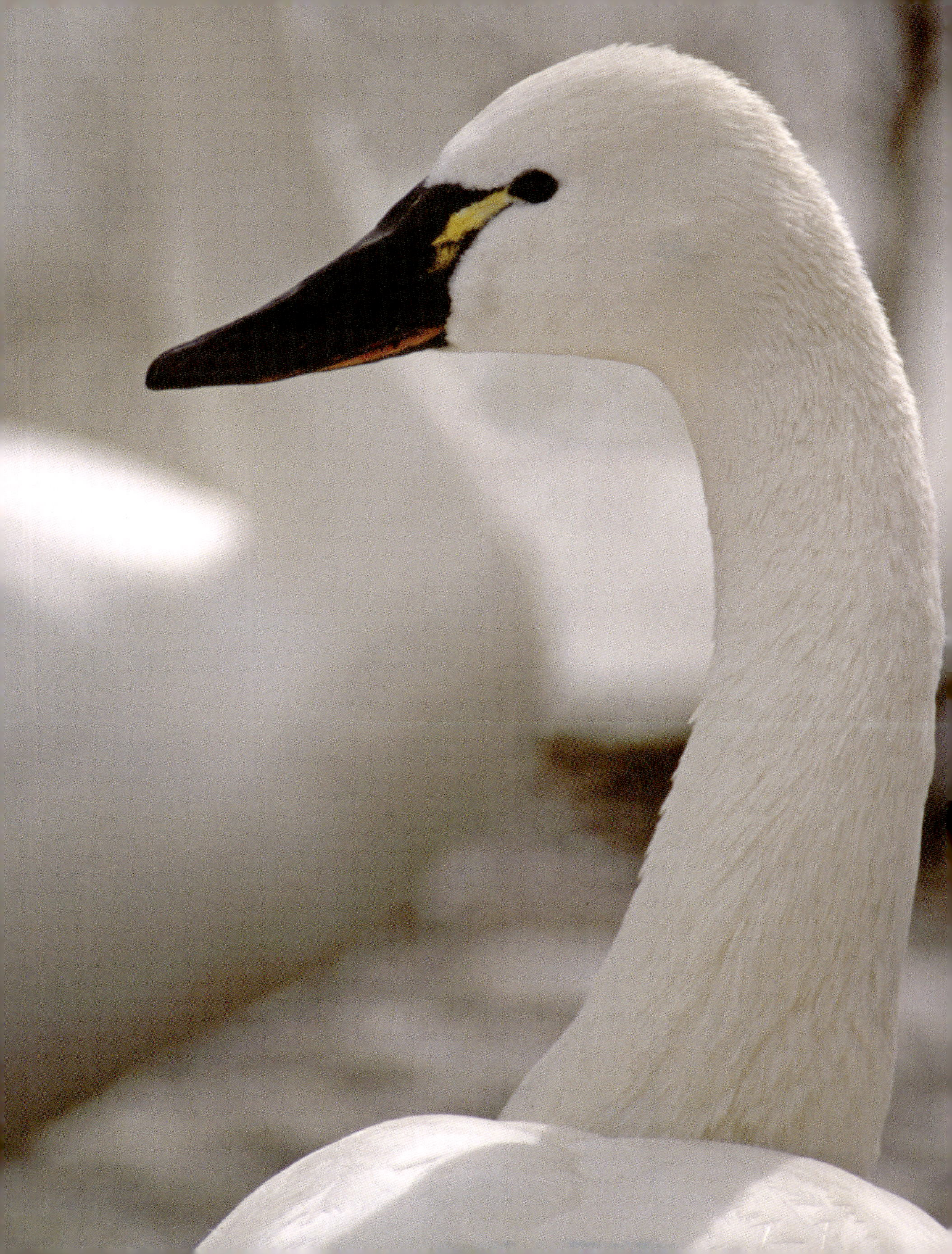

CHAPTER

2

Exploring Exposure

EXPOSURE DEFINED AND EXPLAINED

In photographic terms, "exposure" refers to the amount of light reaching some defined area of a photographic medium. When I started as a photographer more than three decades ago, the standard photographic medium was film. Today it is the electronic sensor of a digital camera. In either case, the amount of light stimulating the medium determines the exposure of the final photograph, which in very simple terms refers to how light or dark the image appears. The error that results in a photo being overly dark is often described as "underexposure." In this instance, an insufficient amount of light reached the medium. The opposite

Tundra swan. *Jack Ballard*

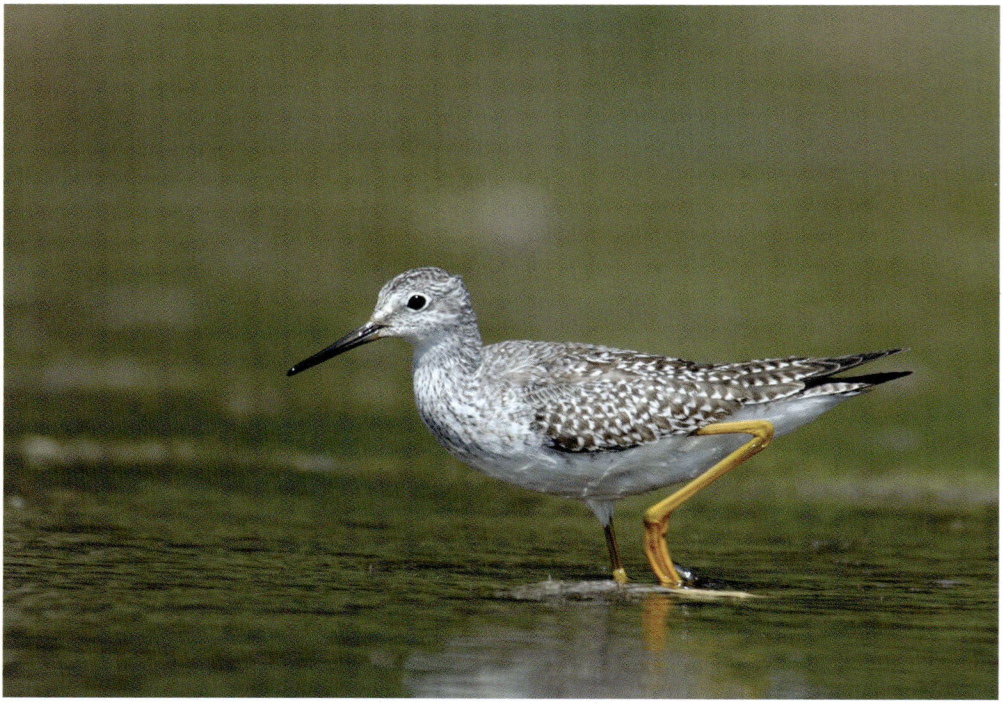

Proper exposure occurs when both the light and dark elements of the photo show some detail, as in the black bill and white feathers on this lesser yellowlegs photographed in Wyoming. *Jack Ballard*

mistake results in "overexposure," which occurs when too much light reaches the medium and portions of the image that should show detail are "blown out" by white tones lacking depth or definition.

In the film days, understanding and control of exposure was one of the noticeably differentiating characteristics between professional and amateur photographers. Film was exposed in the field, then processed at home or in a laboratory. The exposure latitude (the range in the amount of light that would still render an acceptable image) on many of the slide films used by professional wildlife photographers was very limited. Miscalculated by a single stop (we'll get into that terminology later), the resulting photo may have lost its commercial value. Wildlife of the northern Rocky Mountains was the focus of my photography in those days, and I knew the exposure values of many creatures down to the various differences on their body parts. Exposing for the blonde shoulder of a bull elk in December? Open up 2/3 of a stop from the metered value. Foiled by the dark face of a bison? Meter from the dirty base of its horn instead. My wildlife camera body was seldom set to any metering scheme but "spot metering," which allowed the precise evaluation of exposure in a tiny portion of the frame.

Today, wildlife photographers benefit from improved light metering systems in quality cameras and the ability to immediately view and assess the exposure of a photo on the viewing screen of the imaging apparatus. However, wildlife photography often puts the artist in situations where the ability to instantly react to changes in light is critical to obtaining an acceptable image. For example, on a recent winter outing I pulled our car into a pullout along a rural highway to allow my wife the opportunity to photograph a rough-legged hawk we saw perched on a fencepost. Shortly after she shot a few frames of the hawk on its perch, it dove into the snow-covered grass on the ground, its talons probing for prey. The incident allowed perhaps thirty seconds of shooting, but the resulting frames were all incorrectly exposed. The excitement of the moment caused us both to forget that the change in lighting required a different exposure. Despite vast improvement in camera technology, understanding and controlling exposure in extreme or complex lighting situations is critical to consistently obtaining superb wildlife images.

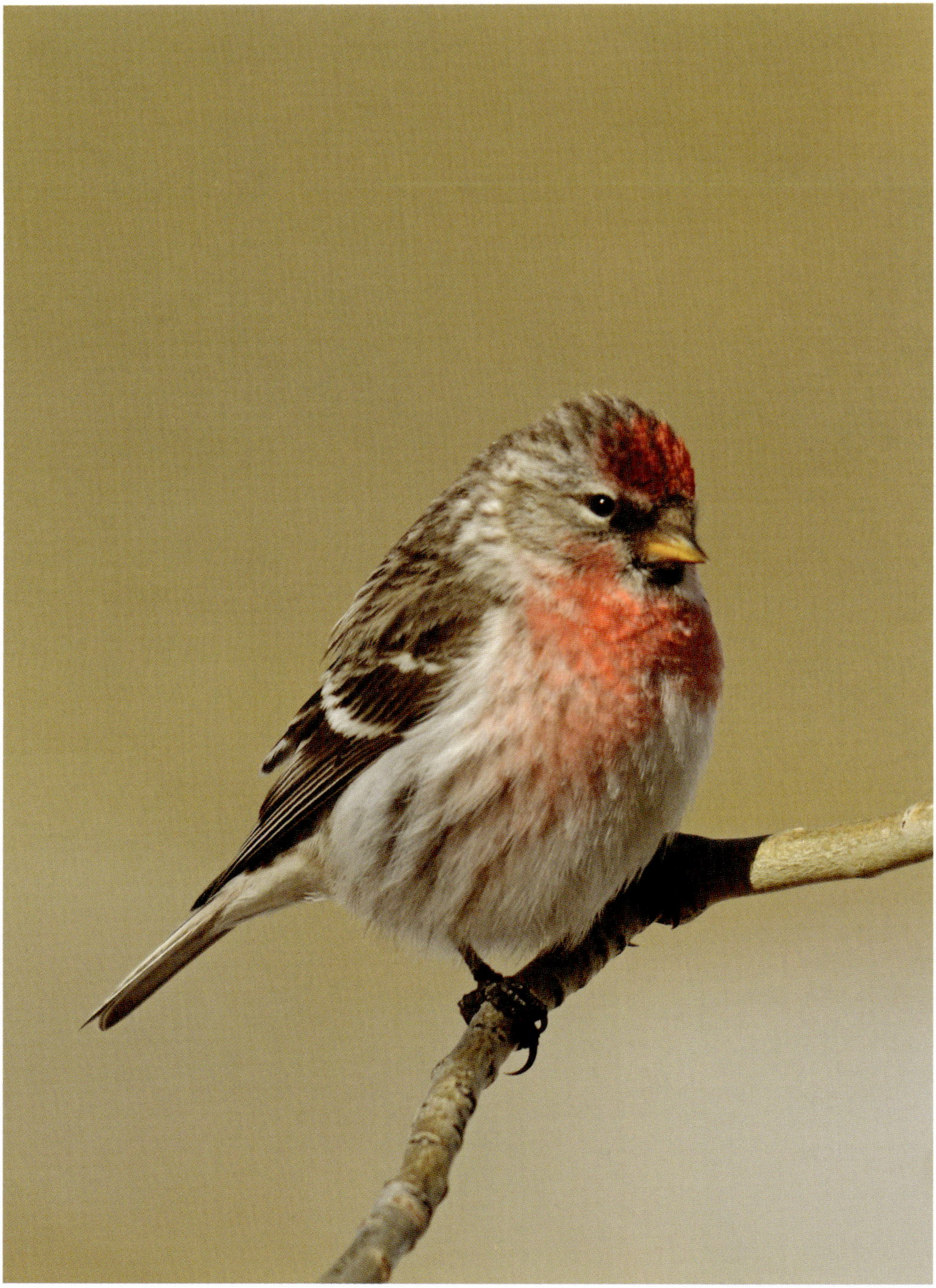

ELEMENTS OF EXPOSURE

The modern digital camera, just like very early film cameras, determines exposure in relation to three factors: shutter speed, aperture, and the sensitivity of the photographic medium to light (ISO). These three elements are sometimes characterized as the "exposure triangle," as a change to any of the three affects exposure. Countless other analogies are also used to explain how these three elements blend to determine exposure. The key to understanding exposure is to remember that each of these elements influences the amount of light that reaches the photographic medium (film or sensor) or its sensitivity, thus determining the gradation of the final image on a scale of light (white) to dark (black). Exposure depends completely upon light irrespective of color.

Shutter Speed

For illustration purposes, let's think of exposure in terms of adding food coloring to the batter of a kid's birthday cake. In my hand is a beaker filled with a cup of red food coloring for this immense cake. The amount of coloring will be determined in part by how long I tip the beaker to allow the dye to run from it into the batter. Thus the amount of time the dye is poured is part of the color equation for the cake batter.

Similarly, the shutter on a camera body opens for a specified amount of time to allow light to strike the photographic medium. A shutter open for 1/10th of a second allows twice as much light to reach the sensor as one opened for 1/20th

Left: Exposure has to do with dark and light tones and is not influenced by color. The red breast and head on this common redpoll affect the image's color but not exposure. *Jack Ballard* of a second, yielding more exposure. If the correct exposure needed for a scene is 1/20th of a second, the 1/10th exposure will allow too much light to stimulate the sensor and yield an overexposed (too light) image.

Aperture (Depth of Field)

Inside a camera's lens is an opening that allows light to pass through. The size of this opening, or aperture, determines how much light can pass through the lens in a given amount of time. Some lenses have fixed apertures that cannot be adjusted, eliminating this factor in exposure. Other lenses have adjustable apertures that can be manually or electronically widened or narrowed by the camera operator.

In relation to our food coloring analogy, think of the aperture as the diameter in the neck of the beaker containing the food dye. A larger neck means more dye will be dispensed in a shorter amount of time than with a smaller neck. Thus the volume of food coloring reaching the cake batter is determined not only by how long it is poured, but the amount allowed to pass through the neck as it is narrowed or enlarged.

The size of a lens's aperture determines the depth of field of a photograph as well as exposure. "Depth of field" refers to how much of the image, measured in distance from the lens, will be in focus in the final photo. The "f-number," also known as the "f-ratio" or "f-stop," refers to the ratio of a lens's focal length to the diameter of its front aperture. A 200mm lens with a diameter of 72mm will be advertised as an f/2.8 lens (200 ÷ 72 = 2.78). A large aperture such as f/2.8 creates a shallow depth of field, while a small aperture such as f/22 creates an extended depth of field. Shot head-on at fairly close range, an f/2.8 depth of field might see only the eyes and a small portion of the face of an American alligator in focus. The f/22 aperture shot from the same position will see more of the gator's form in focus, from its snout to the end of its tail. Thus a smaller aperture (larger f-number) yields greater depth of field but reduces the amount of light striking the sensor or film in the camera, requiring more exposure time than a large aperture (smaller f-number). This is why telephoto lenses with a maximum aperture of f/2.8 are often called "fast" lenses (they allow faster shutter speeds), while those with a maximum aperture of f/5.6 are considered "slow."

ISO

The third element of exposure is ISO, which essentially references a photographic medium's sensitivity to light. To which the astute student replies, "Wouldn't STL be a better acronym for 'sensitivity to light' than ISO?"

In fact, the acronym ISO has no logical connection to light or photography. It refers to the International Organization for Standardization headquartered in Geneva, Switzerland. As one of the things the organization has standardized is film and image sensor sensitivity to light, ISO has rather oddly become the photographic jargon for sensitivity. Some decades ago photographers threw ASA around as an equivalent term for film sensitivity, this time referencing the American Standards Association.

Returning to our food coloring analogy for exposure, think of ISO in terms of the concentration of dye in the food coloring. A highly concentrated food coloring will require perhaps half as much liquid to give the cake the same color as a less concentrated tinting agent. Similarly, because of its higher sensitivity to light, an ISO setting on a digital camera (or film speed) of 400 requires less (half as much) exposure to light as a setting of 200.

In the heyday of the film era, wildlife photographers were ever on the hunt for higher ISO films that would allow them faster shutter speeds, making it

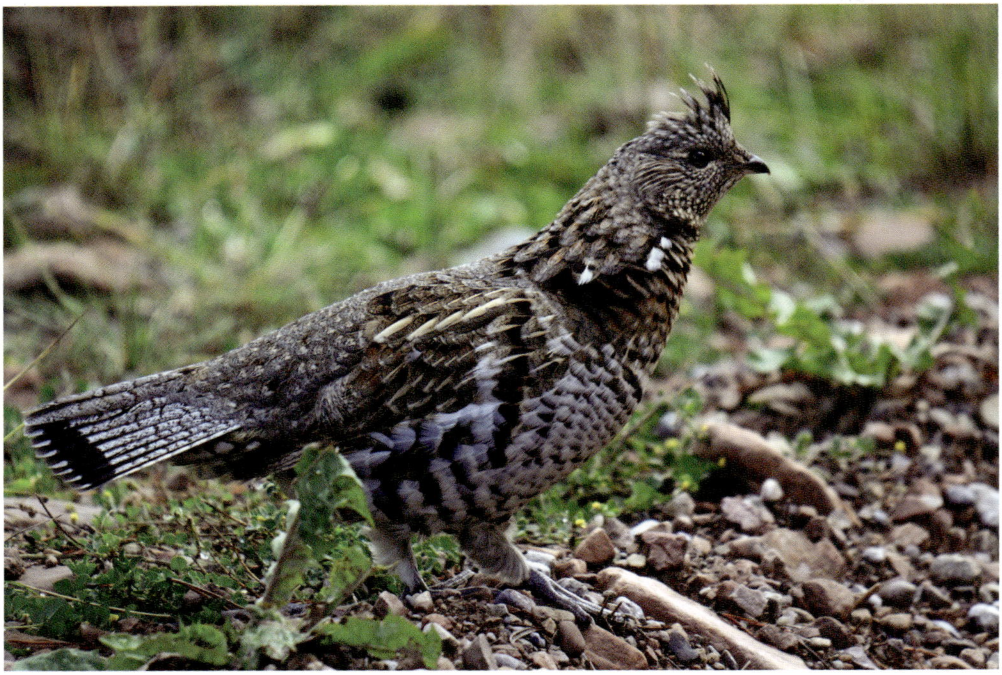

Today's digital cameras produce sharp images at much higher ISO than the color films previously used by wildlife photographers. This ruffed grouse was photographed just outside Grand Teton National Park in Wyoming at ISO 1000. *Jack Ballard*

easier to handhold cameras or stop action without blurring images. The nasty trade-off concerned image quality. In general, slide films with ISOs greater than 400 were considered of marginal use to obtain publication-quality photos. ISO 100 slide films were viewed as professional standards, with the vibrant, high-definition characteristics of ISO 50 films favored by some.

Today, digital shooters enjoy sharp images at ISOs of 2000 or higher. However, there is still an important correlation between image quality and ISO. High ISO settings are reserved by professionals for working in very low-light conditions to achieve more shutter speed, while low ISOs are used for most of the daylight hours to maximize image quality. An ISO of 400 is a good starting point for most wildlife images, yielding excellent sharpness and allowing sufficient shutter speed to handhold a lens and stop most action in daylight setting.

To summarize, exposure is a product of shutter speed, aperture, and ISO. Changing one of these alters the amount of light striking the sensor or film in the camera, varying the exposure. It is similar to an individual pouring food coloring into cake batter from a beaker. The amount of time of the pour, the diameter of the beaker, and the concentration of the dye will determine the color of the cake. Modify any of these three factors and dessert will be served in a different hue.

RELATIONSHIP OF EXPOSURE ELEMENTS

Shutter speed, aperture, and ISO combine to determine exposure. They work together in a mathematical way that allows a photographer to make rapid decisions about exposure independently of a light meter or camera.

One of the best ways to understand this relationship is via the "sunny f/16 rule." Even before cameras had built-in light meters, photographers utilized this rule to manually calculate exposure. I did so with a fully manual Nikon F camera body loaded with slide film for several years at the beginning of my career with excellent results. The sunny f/16 rule simply states that on a sunny day with the sun at the photographer's back, the correct exposure at f/16 will be the shutter speed closest to the ISO. Thus when shooting 100-speed film, the correct shutter speed at f/16 is 1/125th of a second.

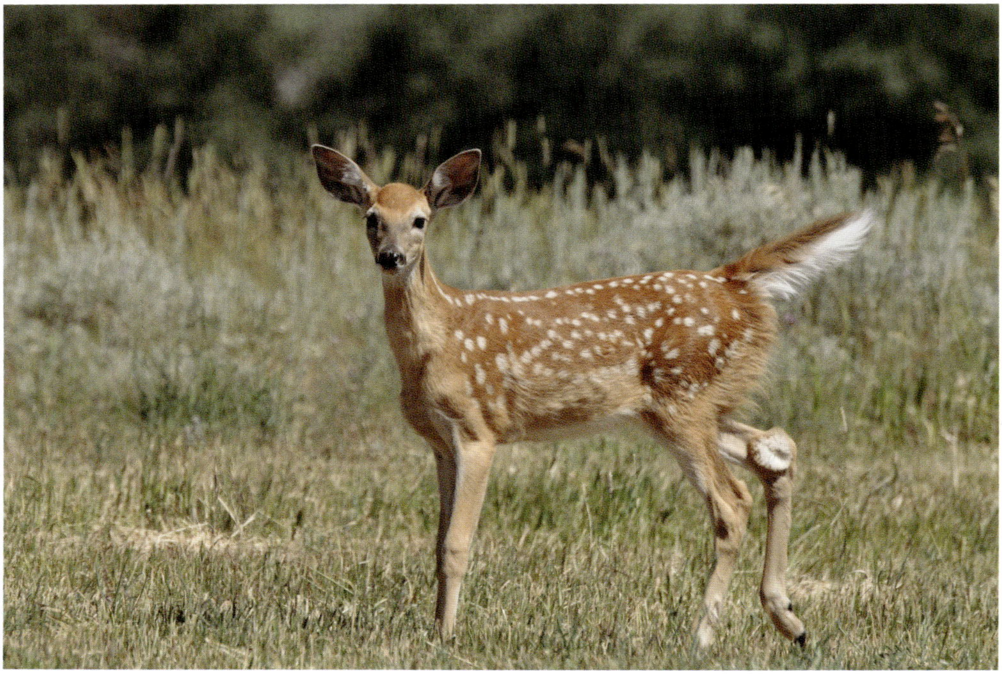

Photographed on a sunny day with the sun behind the photographer, the correct exposure for this curious whitetail deer fawn can be easily determined with the "sunny f/16 rule." *Lisa Ballard*

Prior to electronically controlled cameras, shutter speed, aperture, and ISO were set on the camera by the photographer via manual controls. ISO settings on camera bodies were developed with the invention of light meters built into the camera body. A ring on the lens was rotated to set the aperture, and settings were marked at an indicator line and could be felt by a click or a stop. Thus to move from f/2.8 to f/11, the ring was rotated through clicks at f/4, f/5.6, and f/8 before reaching f/11. Each of these clicks represented a "stop" both mechanically and in terms of light.

Most camera bodies also had a rotating dial to control shutter speed. Like aperture, shutter speeds were organized along a series of stops. Shutter speeds essentially doubled or halved depending on which way the dial was turned. For example, from 1/125th of a second, the dial was turned one click or stop to reach 1/250th in one direction or 1/60th in the other. With the invention of built-in light meters, camera bodies also had mechanical dials to set the ISO.

The numbers represented by aperture, shutter speed, and ISO are mathematically related in a simple way. Doubling the ISO represents one full "stop" of light. Doubling the shutter speed represents one full stop as well. Doubling the aperture number (slight rounding is sometimes required; e.g., as going from f/5.6 to f/11) represents two full stops. Maintaining the same exposure for a scene involves keeping the mathematical relationship intact by adjusting the three elements of exposure.

For example, if the photographer desires less depth of field on a sunny scene and wishes to shoot at f/11 instead of f/16 (one stop difference), the larger aperture (allowing more light to enter the camera body) must be compensated for by halving the shutter speed (one stop difference to allow less light to enter the camera body). The light sensitivity measured by ISO also affects the equation. Doubling the ISO from 100 to 200 yields a photographic medium that is one stop more sensitive to light. Thus a shutter speed of 1/250th of a second at 100 ISO yields the same exposure as 1/500th of a second at 200 ISO. An aperture of f/4 at 100 ISO is the same exposure as f/5.6 at 200 ISO and so on. The chart below shows the mathematical relationships between the various elements of exposure.

Shutter Speed	1/15th	1/30th	1/60th	1/125th	1/250th	1/500th	1/1000th	1/2000th
ISO	50	100	200	400	800	1600	3200	6400

Shutter Speed	1/15th	1/30th	1/60th	1/125th	1/250th	1/500th	1/1000th	1/2000th
f-stop	32	22	16	11	8	5.6	4	2.8

f-stop	2.8	4	5.6	8	11	16	22	32
ISO	50	100	200	400	800	1600	3200	6400

In an age of digital cameras with increasingly sophisticated exposure metering systems, why bother learning the mathematical relationships between aperture, shutter speed, and ISO? Why not simply set the camera to an automatic exposure profile and let it do its thing?

Knowing the mathematical values of exposure allows the photographer to make fast, accurate decisions regarding camera settings in the field. Suppose you're shooting a flock of seagulls resting in very shallow surf along a beach at sunset. To blur and soften the gently surging surf around the birds and obtain maximal depth of field, you've chosen a slow shutter speed (1/15th of a second) and a small (f/22) aperture. Suddenly you spy a flock of incoming brown pelicans some distance away. To get the flight shot, you know you'll need a faster shutter speed, ideally around 1/250th of a second or faster. Simply changing the aperture from f/22 to f/5.6 will yield a shutter speed of 1/250th, but more depth of field, say f/11, will give better seascape composition and margin for error on the focus. Your camera is currently set at ISO 100. A thorough understanding of the exposure triad allows you to make the split-second decision to change the ISO from 100 to 400 and the aperture from f/22 to f/11. The higher ISO will still produce exceptionally detailed images but allows you to shoot at 1/500th of a second at f/11, yielding sufficient shutter speed for a flight shot with a nice fudge-factor on focus.

Despite advances in camera technology, learning the relationships between exposure elements is foundational in photography programs at colleges and universities. Professional and amateur wildlife photographers desiring the greatest technical control over their images are likewise instructed to master the mathematics of exposure.

EXPOSURE AND CAMERA SETTINGS

The extent to which the photographer can independently control the three elements of exposure varies widely in relation to tablets, cellphones, and stand-alone cameras. Entry-level cameras may offer limited control in relation to exposure. Some allow the photographer to adjust the overall exposure of the scene, but don't indicate whether it results from altering aperture, shutter speed, or ISO. In the case of cameras with fixed apertures (such as those found on most tablets and cellphones), exposure compensation is necessarily a result of altering ISO and/or shutter speed.

Fully featured DSLR cameras, the type most commonly used in wildlife photography, allow complete control over the three elements of exposure to the full limits of the camera and lens. The "manual" mode of such cameras allows completely independent manipulation of the three elements by the photographer. Set to "shutter priority," the user sets the shutter speed while the camera adjusts the aperture. In "aperture priority," the user sets the aperture while the camera chooses the corresponding shutter speed.

It should be noted that overall exposure compensation can be chosen on many cameras, even entry-level models and those found on cellphones. On a DSLR, the exposure compensation will honor the shooting mode. For example, if set in aperture priority, an exposure compensation of +1 will result in a slower shutter speed, leaving the aperture the same. In shutter priority, manipulating exposure compensation will alter the aperture, not the shutter speed. In program mode, exposure compensation might alter both the shutter speed and aperture depending on the camera.

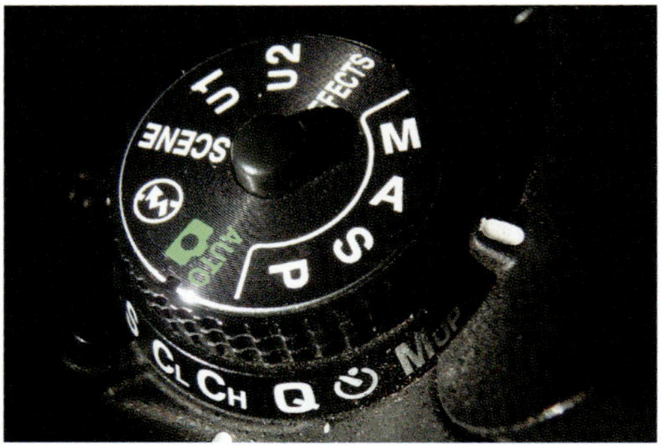

Fully featured cameras allow the photographer to prioritize various aspect of exposure. This camera is set to "aperture priority," where the user selects the aperture and the camera calculates the shutter speed. *Jack Ballard*

Understanding how your camera deals with exposure compensation is very important to the wildlife photographer. The ability to quickly activate this feature can mean the difference between acquiring a well-lit shot or regretting an image that is hopelessly over- or underexposed.

EXPOSURE COMPENSATION FOR DIFFICULT SUBJECTS

Evenly lit, middle-toned subjects such as a yawning hippo in a mud hole are easily exposed by the camera. Others such as a white short-tailed weasel bounding about in the snow will routinely fool the camera's metering system. Subjects that are overall very dark or very light usually need some compensation to achieve the proper exposure. A small, dark subject against a light background or a light subject against a dark background is also difficult for the camera's metering system to evaluate properly.

The root of the problem stems from the fact that cameras meter primarily on the assumption of a middle-toned subject, such as green grass or the blue

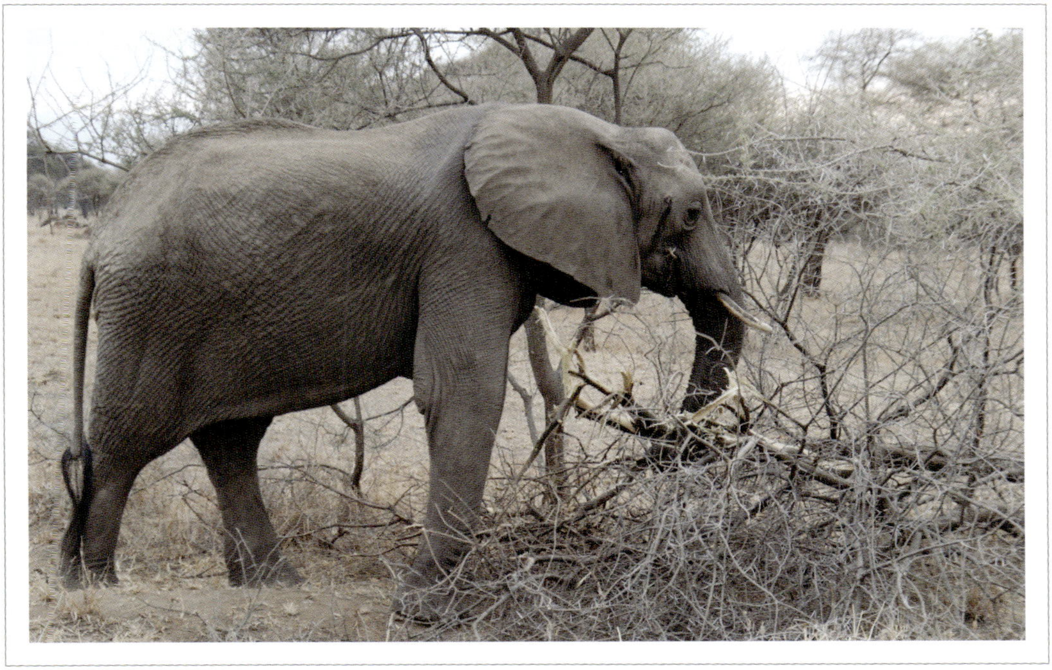

The middle tones of this gray elephant against a similar background make for easy exposure. Even the most unsophisticated cameras should correctly expose this image. *Lisa Ballard*

northern sky. Confronted with a very light or dark scene, the camera attempts to make it middle-toned, yielding overexposed dark subjects (too light) or underexposed light subjects (too dark).

Exposure compensation for these difficult subjects can be achieved in various ways. Most DSLR cameras of reasonable quality have a "spot meter" function where instead of averaging the exposure of multiple segments of the frame, the entire exposure is taken from a specific small portion of the frame. Thus the photographer can meter from a very defined element within the frame, which he or she knows must be properly exposed. For example, my wife and I recently photographed a cottontail rabbit on a snow-covered plain in Idaho. The gray rabbit is a middle-toned subject and should be exposed as such. However,

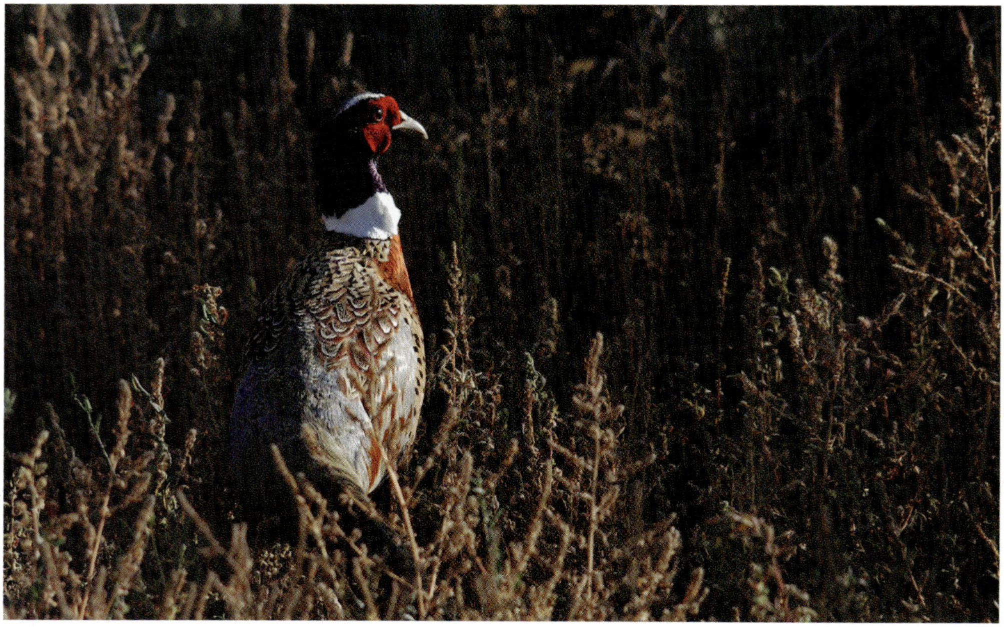

Deep shadows in the background and numerous highlights make the exposure on this male ring-necked pheasant in Colorado difficult. Spot-metering in the middle-toned part of the bird's back in the sunlight rendered a perfect exposure. *Jack Ballard*

the bunny appeared quite small in the overall scene. Letting the camera meter without compensation would have yielded dark, muddy snow (underexposed) and an even darker rabbit. Using the camera's spot meter, we were able to expose directly for the rabbit and ignore its white surroundings. This yielded a properly exposed, middle-toned rendition of the rabbit while retaining the bright whites of the snow.

Lacking a spot meter, exposure compensation can still be made of such a scene by using the camera's exposure compensation. The photographer makes an informed decision about the subject's exposure in relation to the rest of the frame and adjusts accordingly. If the entire frame is out of middle-toned (very dark or light), a similar analysis is used for compensation. For example, in the case of the cottontail, it is obvious that the overall scene will be underexposed by the camera and that an exposure compensation of about +1 or more will be required to properly expose the subject.

The ability to make quick exposure changes based on one's knowledge of exposure and the metering capabilities of the camera is an extremely valuable skill. However, those with less ability can check the exposure of a test frame in the camera's image monitor (assuming the monitor gives an accurate rendition of exposure).

On a final note, it's worth noting that underexposing a subject is preferable to overexposure. Photo-editing software can usually capture the detail lost in dark shadows in a slightly underexposed image. Highlights "blown out" by overexposure are impossible to darken with any detail.

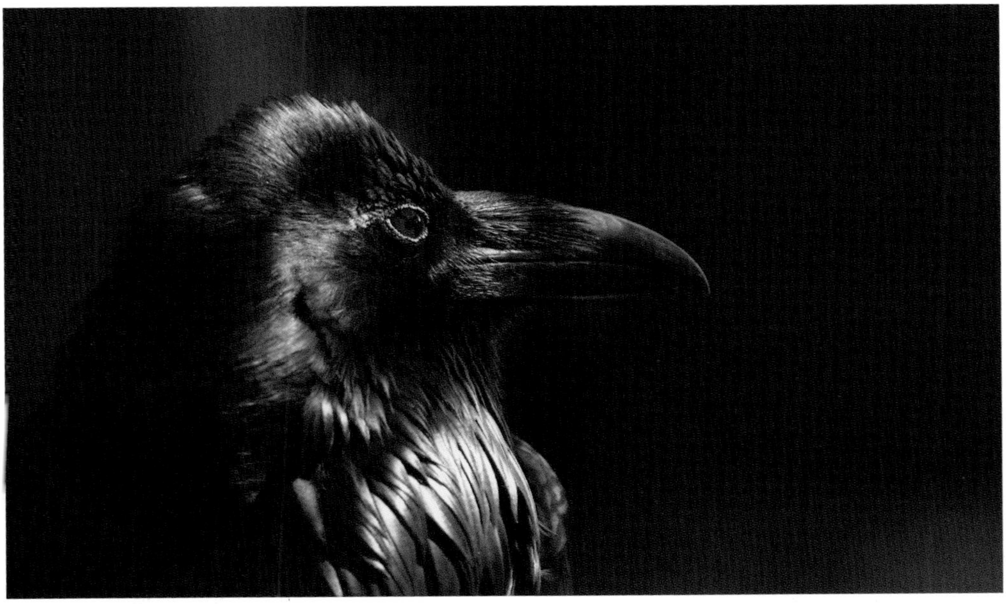

A black subject like this common raven on a dark background can make exposure tricky. When in doubt, it's better to underexpose. Detail in shadows can be regained with editing software, but "blown out" highlights cannot. *Dominic Ballard*

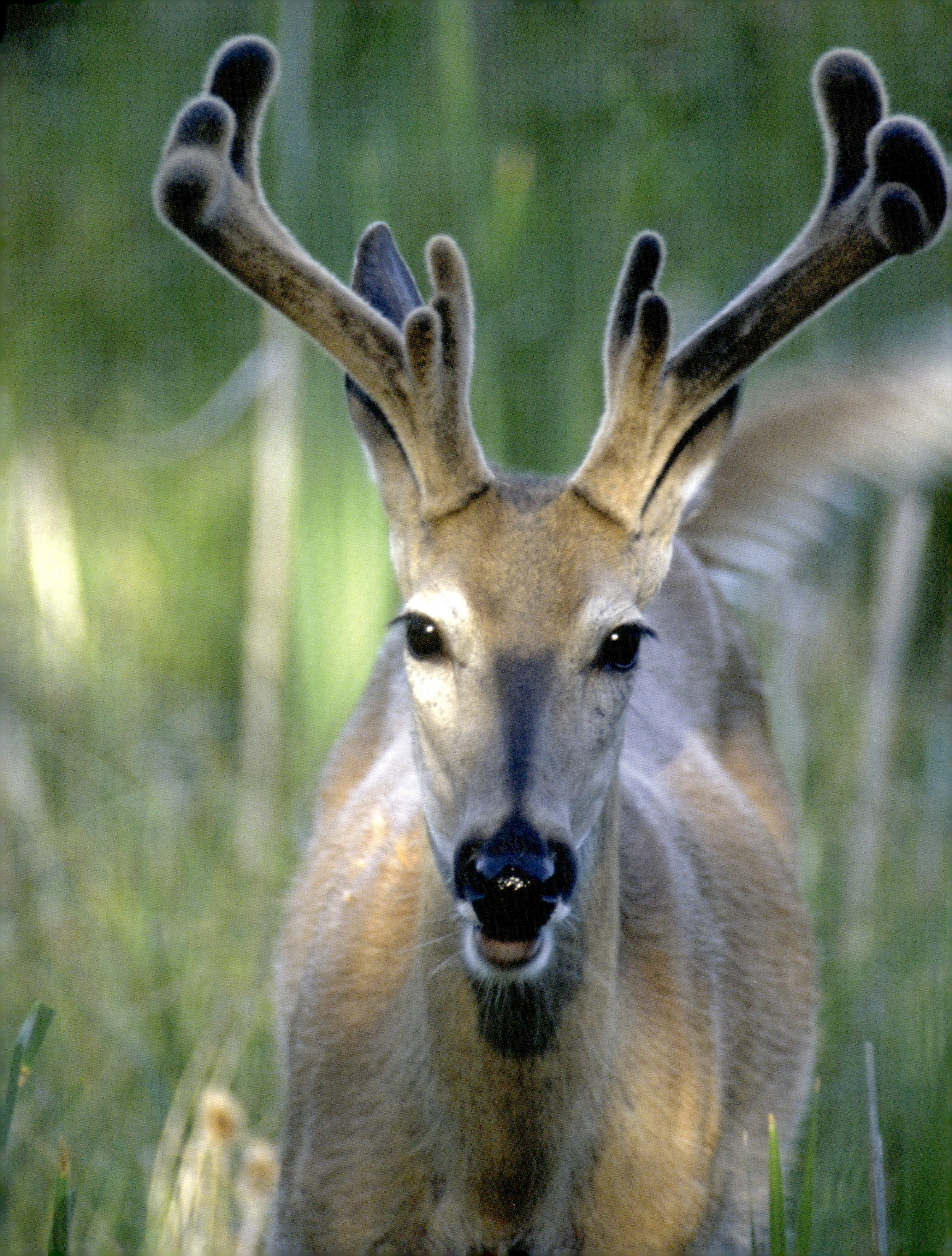

CHAPTER

3

Working with Light

My favorite definition of photography hearkens from the ancient Greek roots of this compound word. The term *photo* descends from the Greek word for "light," and *graphic* has its origins in Greek in terms for "drawing" or "painting." Photography is thus "painting with light." The photographer can be understood as an artist who paints with light.

The subject matter of wildlife photography plays a central role in the creation of mesmerizing photos, but light is equally important. A behavioral photo of two massive bull moose fighting on a sandbar adjacent to a rushing river is an exceptional subject no matter the lighting conditions. But a simple image of one of the contestants framed in the golden light of dawn or dusk, or a silhouette of the animal against a vibrant sunset, requires no drama on the part of the subject. The magic is in the light, and wildlife photographers who wish

Whitetail deer. *Jack Ballard*

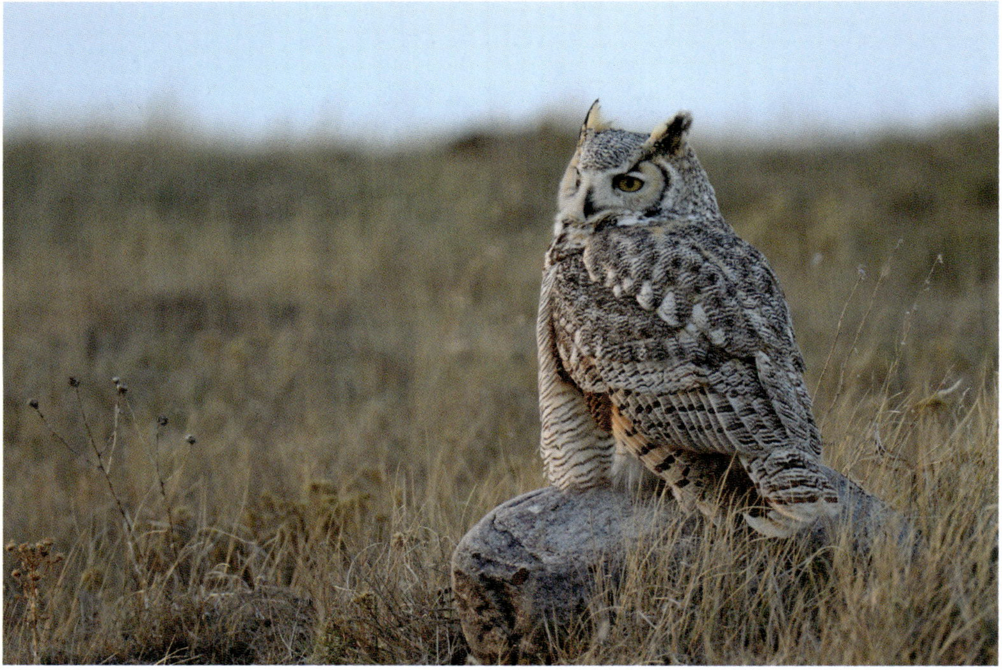

The sun was literally within seconds of being fully set when the author composed this image of a great horned owl in northeastern Montana. The muted sunlight is just enough to subtly accentuate the subject. *Jack Ballard*

to conjure enchantment with their images are as much connoisseurs of light as technical perfectionists.

BASIC LIGHT PATTERNS IN WILDLIFE PHOTOGRAPHY

The sun can't be plucked from the carpet and moved about like a floor lamp in a bedroom, but the way in which a lamp placed at various positions in a room illuminates objects in different ways is an instructive lesson in lighting for outdoor photography. From dawn until dusk, the sun is on the move. A subject cast with light on one side in the morning is lit on the opposite side in late afternoon. Not only does the sun move, but subjects and photographers also change positions, which can dramatically alter the appearance of a photo simply by virtue of how it is lit. However, certain basic, predictable patterns of light are most often available to the photographer. Understanding how they affect a photo's look is a key skill in becoming a master wildlife photographer.

Front Light

A principle of outdoor photography that's been around for decades advises the photographer to shoot with her back to the sun while facing her subject. This

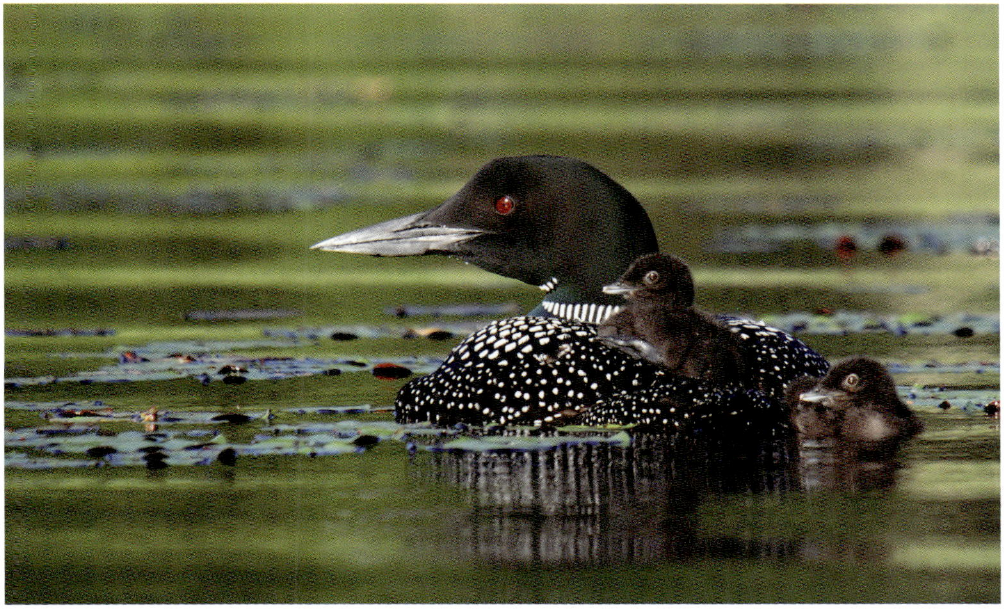

Front lighting provides easy exposure and shows the detail on these fuzzy common loon chicks and their mother on Forked Lake in New York's Adirondack Park. *Lisa Ballard*

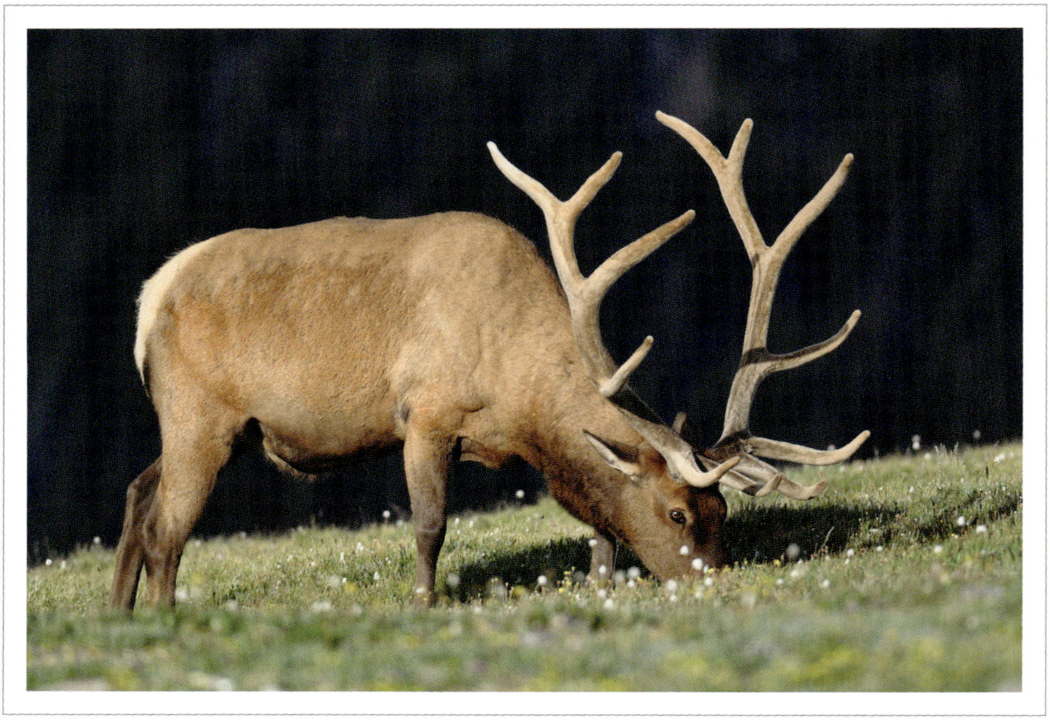

A light subject and dark background in near-front lighting make this grazing bull elk in Rocky Mountain National Park, Colorado, a gorgeous subject. *Jack Ballard*

puts the sun's light directly on the subject in a manner similar to firing a flash from the camera aimed directly at the subject. There are some attractive elements of front lighting that make it the "go-to" angle for most photographers. In most situations, shadows on the subject will be minimized or eliminated. For example, an anhinga (a bird) with its wings spread to dry its feathers in Everglades National Park in Florida is a common but compelling subject. Photographed in front light, the feathers of the darkish bird will be well lit, providing for an image that clearly shows their color and shape without the darkness or distraction of shadows.

Front lighting also makes for easy exposure. Because there are few, if any, shadows with which to contend, the photographer can simply expose for the subject and shoot. It provides for consistent lighting of the background as well. Photographers working in the black-and-white medium are often coached to look for subjects in relation to "light on dark, dark on light." This basic principle also holds true for wildlife photography and works extremely well in creating dramatic photos with front lighting. The photo on the cover of this book is an excellent example of how front lighting and a light subject against a dark background combine to create a stunning photo.

Sidelight

When a subject is lit from the side, the introduction of shadows enhances texture, shapes, and scale in a photo. Professional photographers often shoot

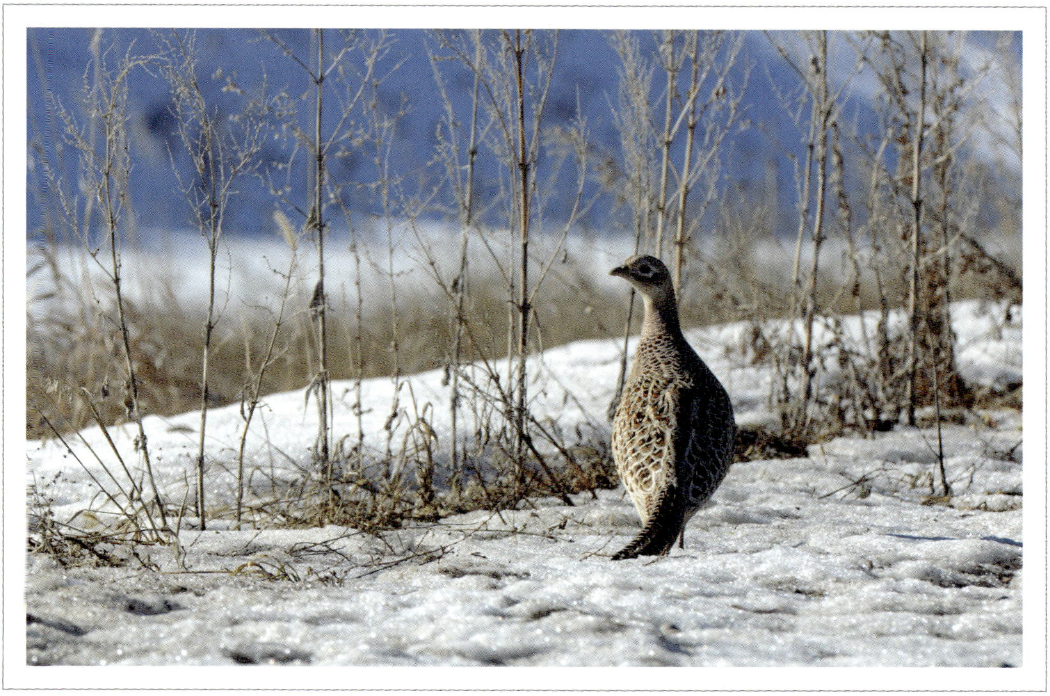

Strong sidelighting creates a dramatic shadow on the feathers of this ring-necked pheasant hen. *Jack Ballard*

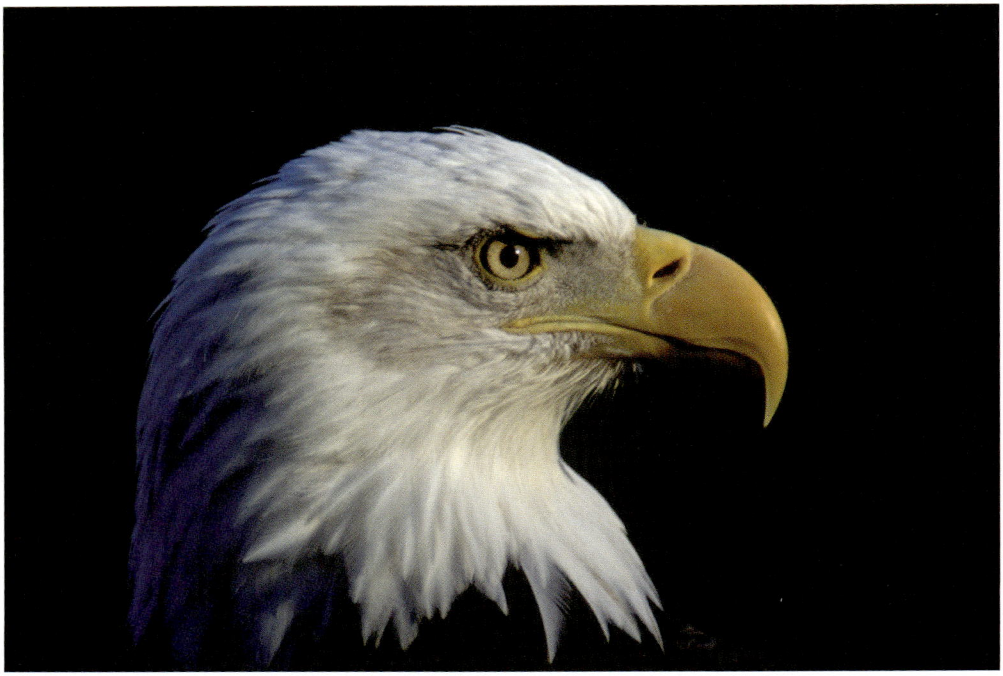

Sidelighting creates shadows in the white feathers of this bald eagle and highlights the curvature of its imposing beak. *Jack Ballard*

portraits of people with a very simple light scheme, with the subject placed in natural light streaming into the room from a window. A classic portrait is created by shooting the model, side-lit in natural light. The interplay of light and shadow allows for many different "looks" within this basic format, created by simply changing the camera angle to the subject or moving the model (sometimes very subtly) in relation to the light.

Wildlife photographers can take a cue from the portrait photographer's esteem for sidelighting. Close-up photos of wildlife shot in sidelight benefit from an enhanced sense of depth and texture. Wide shots of a bird or other animal in its natural habitat become more dramatic due to the long, intense shadows created by sidelighting when the sun is close to the horizon during the early and late hours of the day.

The palette of light and shadows available to the photographer with sidelighting also allows for the creative emphasis of certain elements in a photo. For wildlife photographers, this might include the ability to image a small subject such as a lizard in a shaft of sunlight in a matrix of dark shadows cast by trees. It can also be used to creatively emphasize portions of an animal's body, such as the proverbial eye of a tiger, the ear of an elephant, or the antler of an elk.

Exposure can be a challenge with sidelighting. The extreme tonal difference between very dark shadows and a light subject may result in an exposure where highlights in the frame are overexposed (blown out) and shadows are dingy versus dark. Sidelighting is an excellent time to remember that the most important principle of exposure is to have the main subject of the frame appropriately lit. This may require overriding the camera's metering system with exposure compensation or utilizing a spot-metering function to precisely define a point of exposure (or both). It should also be remembered that details in shadows can most often be brightened with image processing software, but overexposure can be impossible to correct. Thus it is better to err on the side of underexposure.

Backlight

Backlighting occurs when the sun is mostly or directly in front of the photographer, lighting the back or rear of the subject. If the sun is low in the sky, it may be visible in the frame or obscured by the subject or another element in the photo. Backlighting provides a strong emphasis on shapes. It can also create "rim lighting" in which the edges of the subject glow with light illuminating

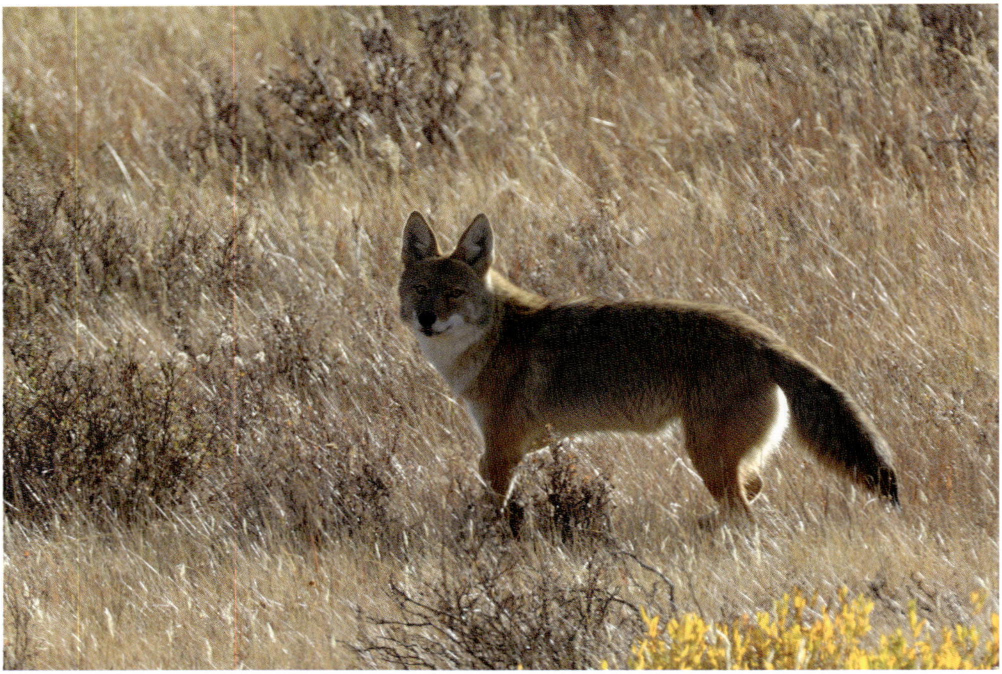

Backlighting on this coyote creates somewhat of a halo effect around its body and emphasizes its shape against the background. *Jack Ballard*

it from the rear. Backlighting can also create extremely dramatic lighting in relation to other aspects of a photo. For example, the breath of a bison in the dead of winter can glow when lit from the rear. Fog rising from a swamp at dawn may take on an ethereal quality when photographed in backlight, powerfully presenting a sense of the place and time of day.

The appealing aspects of backlit photos also create some challenges. Exposure can be difficult unless the scene is evenly lit and of fairly uniform tones. In most cases, the front portion of a backlit subject should be properly exposed and

Right: Backlighting can create exposure challenges. The photographer exposed for the face of this grazing bighorn sheep ewe in Yellowstone National Park, ignoring the bright, harshly lit background. *Dominic Ballard*

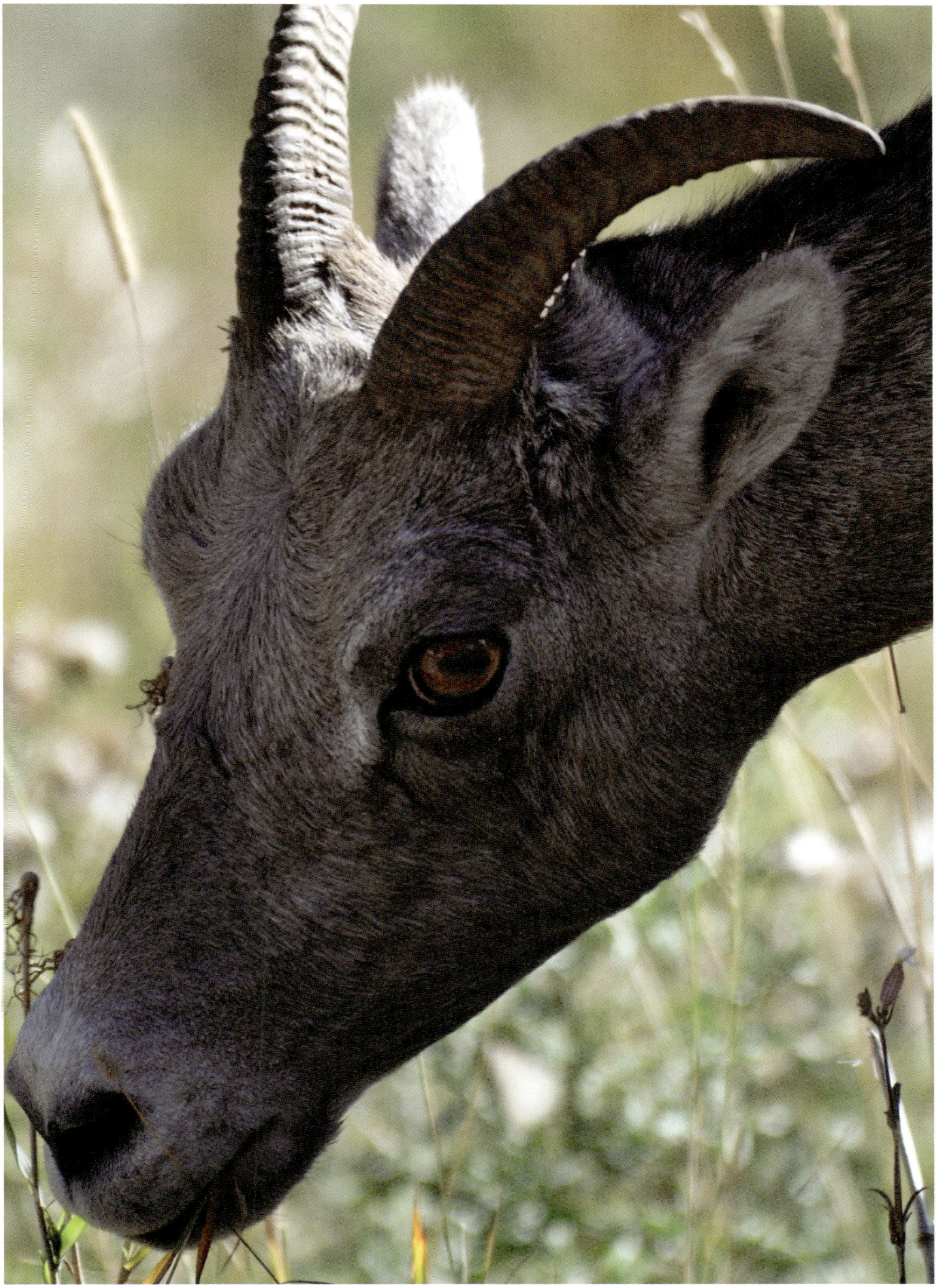

metered as such. Lens flare is another issue sometimes encountered with backlit subjects. If the sun shines directly into the lens, it can cause bright streaks or colored splotches (lens flare) to appear on the photo. This can often be eliminated using a lens hood or by shading the lens with your hand, or both. However, if the sun is directly behind the subject, it may be necessary to shoot from a shaded location behind the trunk of a tree or another object to counteract lens flare.

Overcast (Flat Light)

Some nature photographers bemoan the dawn of an overcast day. Overcast (flat) light provides none of the drama associated with backlighting or sidelighting. A

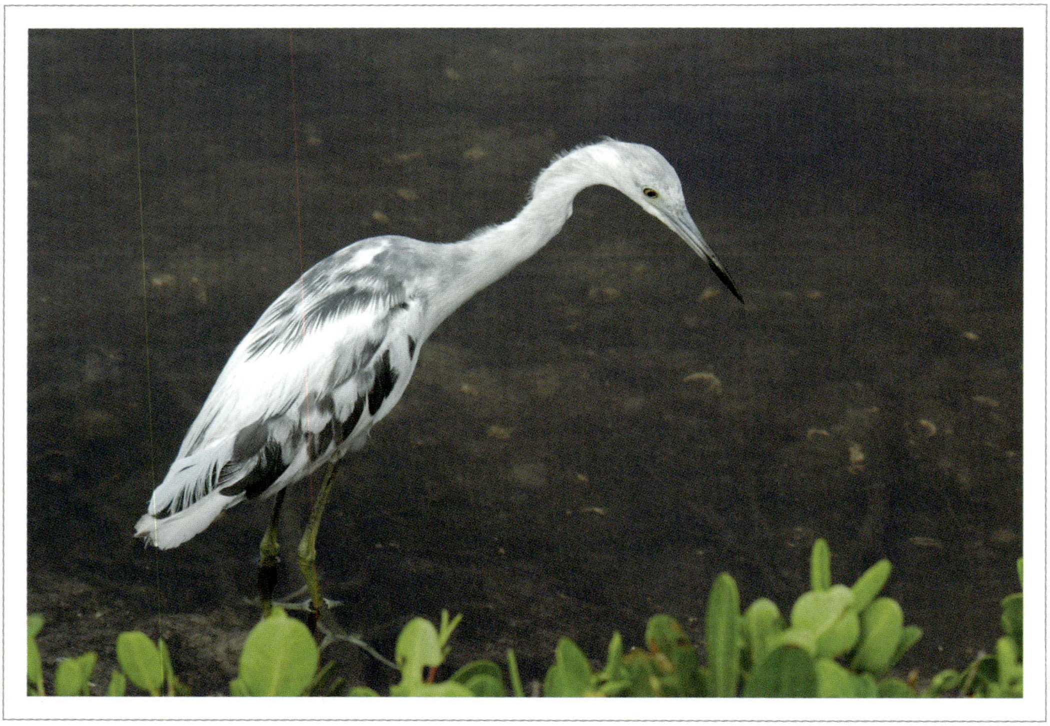

The even character of the bright, overcast light created ideal conditions for imaging this juvenile little blue heron hunting the shallows along Sanibel Island, Florida. *Lisa Ballard*

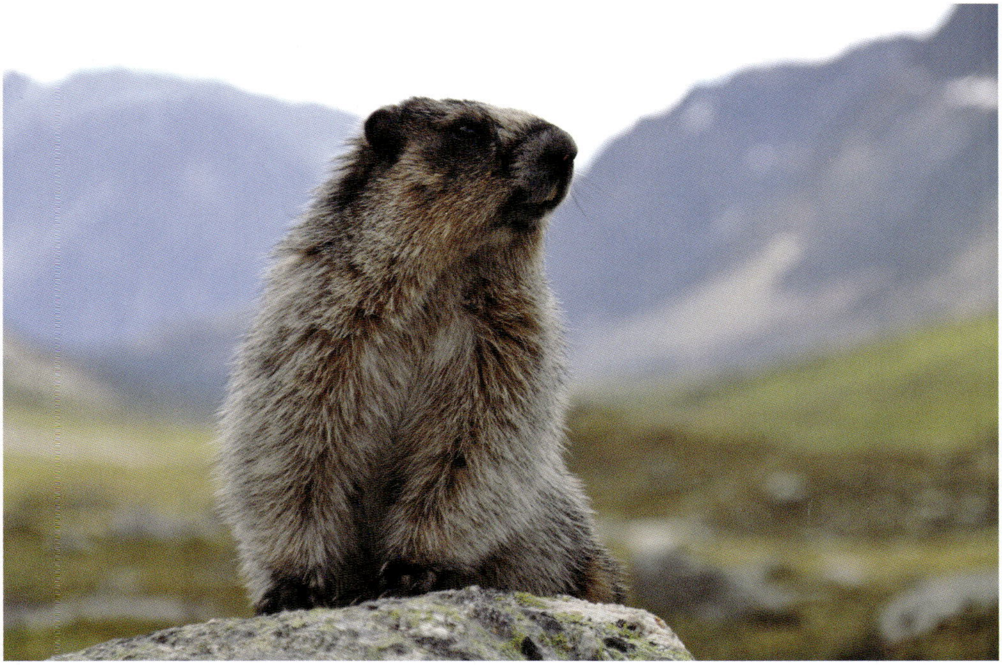

This environmental portrait of a hoary marmot in Jasper National Park, Canada, benefits from even, overcast light. However, the author's preference is to avoid the dead, white sky on overcast days as a background as much as possible. *Jack Ballard*

heavily overcast sky might mean sufficient light for reasonable shooting doesn't occur until mid-morning. However, folks who traffic in wildflower photography love overcast lighting, especially when a thin cloud cover creates "bright overcast," the most coveted light for wildflower close-ups.

Overcast lighting is valued so highly by wildflower specialists because it is soft and consistent. Bright overcast is soft, consistent, and quite warm, perfect attributes for imaging in intimate detail the pastel colors and soft texture of a glacier lily or the bold, contrasting colors of a shooting star. It provides the same consistent palette for wildlife photos, yielding images with true-to-life color and extremely fine detail.

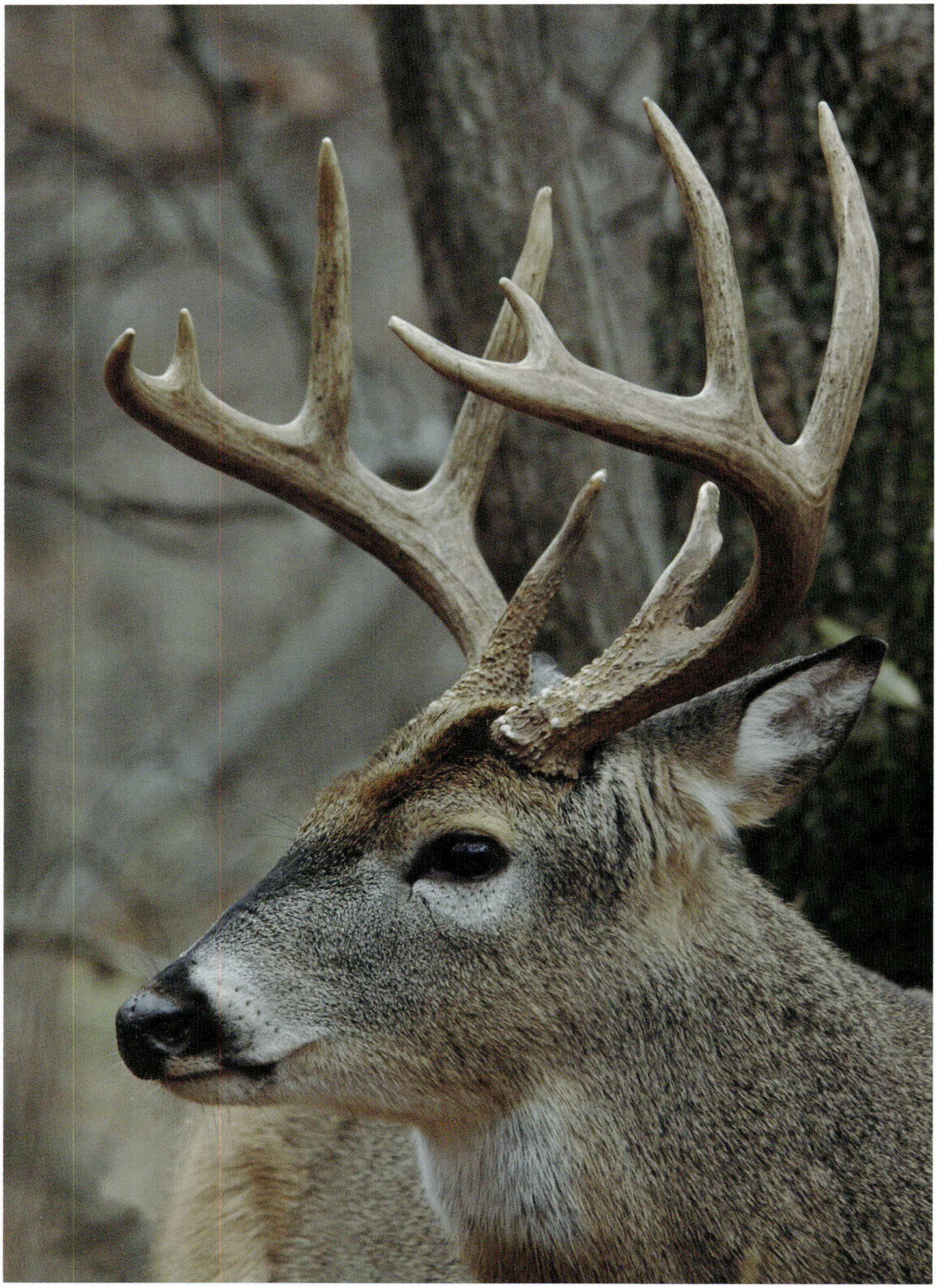

Left: The consistency of overcast light created ideal conditions for this close portrait of a resting whitetail deer buck in Shenandoah National Park, Virginia. *Jack Ballard*

Exceptionally colorful subjects often benefit from photography in overcast light. The iridescent hues on the feathers of a ring-necked pheasant or male mountain bluebird may appear garish when directly lit by the sun. They lose none of their vibrancy in overcast lighting, and achieve an exceptional richness in relation to less intense colors. Close-up images of reptiles in overcast light make it easy to discern the detail and color in their scales. In short, what overcast lighting lacks in drama it more than compensates for in consistency.

Dead, white sky is the downside of overcast lighting. Wildlife photos shot against an overcast sky are generally drab and unappealing. On overcast days I usually avoid taking pictures of animals against a background of sky. Reflections of the sky are similarly dull. I once shot what I believed would be a set of fantastic images of an American dipper (a small waterbird) darting about in Spearfish Creek in the Black Hills of South Dakota. So intent was I upon the antics of the bird, I failed to notice the drab, gray reflection of an overcast sky in the water. Except for a few close-ups, most of the images came to rest in the digital circular file on my computer.

Silhouettes

A silhouette is simply defined as the dark shape or outline of an object against a lighter background. In wildlife photography, silhouettes are most often shot against a colorful sky, typically at sunrise or sunset. Clouds may create a range of colors and textures in the background of a silhouette, or the backdrop may be very consistent, as is the case of a sunset in a clear sky.

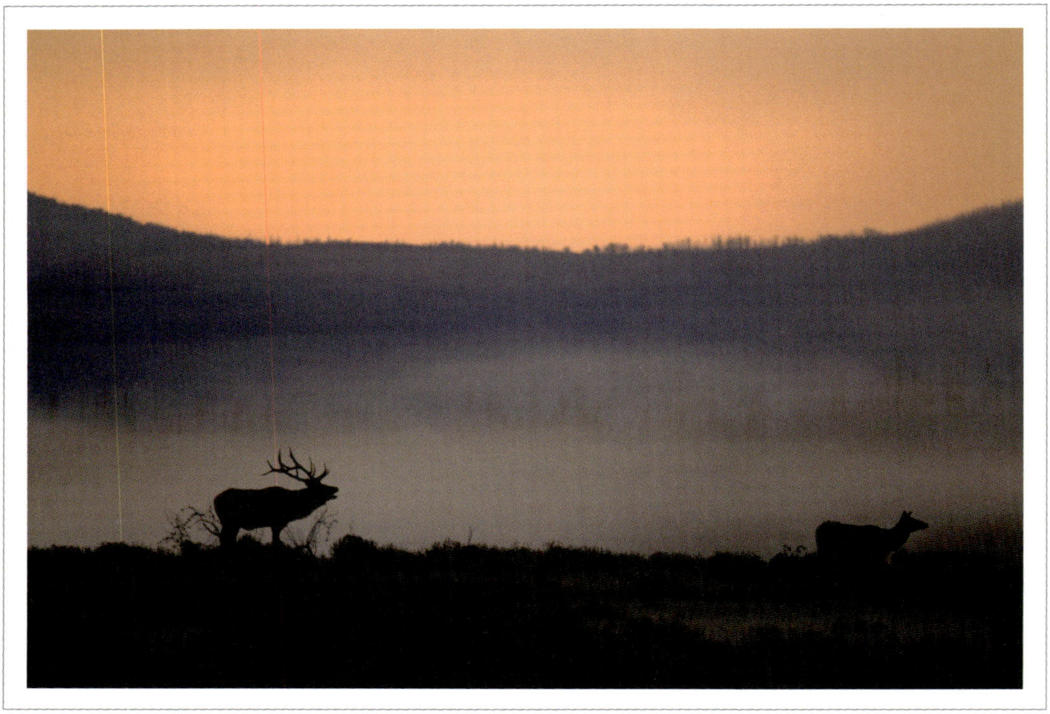

This silhouette has it all: stunning color, interesting texture, and clearly defined subjects. It is among the author's most widely published photos. *Jack Ballard*

Some wildlife subjects make much better silhouettes than others. In general, larger animals and birds are easier to photograph as silhouettes than smaller creatures. The silhouette of an easily recognized subject such as a giraffe gives the viewer a stronger emotional attachment to the image than one of an unrecognizable subject. By the same token, silhouettes are best taken at the angle to the subject that reveals its most characteristic shape. For example, a broadside silhouette of a howling coyote creates a stronger visual image than one taken from a rear angle. Remember that silhouettes are about shape, light, and color, which eliminate details that would otherwise give visual information about the subject.

Exposure is a key element in shooting the wildlife silhouette. Properly exposed, the background colors should be vibrant and middle-toned or slightly overexposed. The subject, by contrast, should be completely dark; otherwise the photo is really a backlit image, not a silhouette.

Another important aspect of the silhouette that's often overlooked is the integrity of the subject's shape. It's not any more desirable to lop the legs from a wading sandhill crane in a silhouette than in a front-lit environmental portrait. Maintaining the integrity of the subject's shape in a silhouette is often as easy as kneeling or lying on the ground to shoot from a low angle.

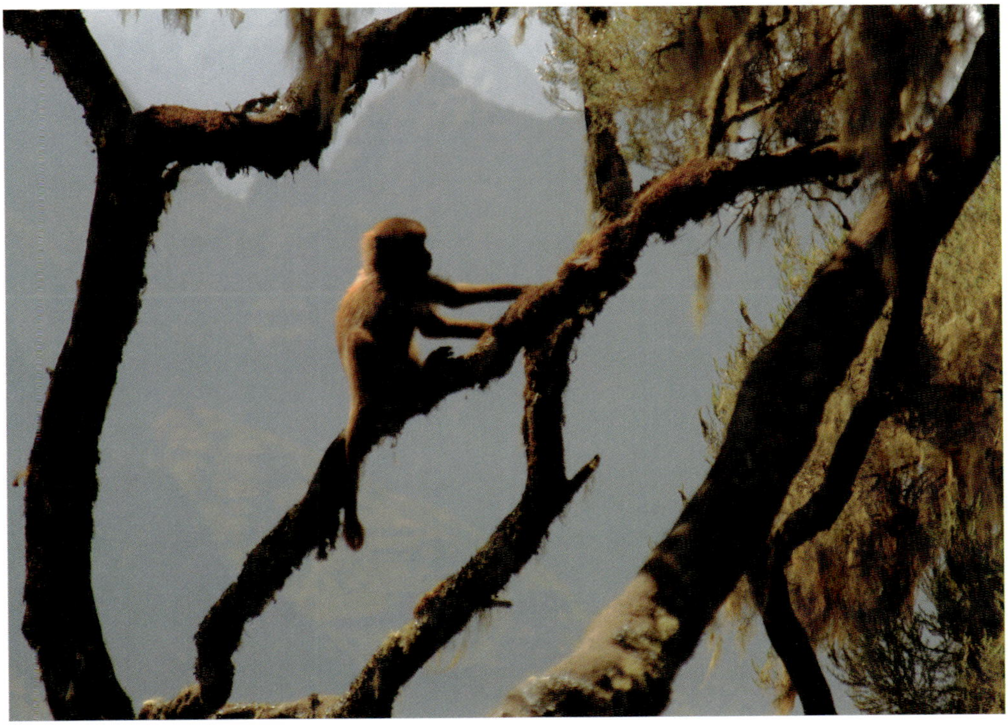

This photo of a young gelada baboon in Simien Mountains National Park in Ethiopia combines elements of backlighting and silhouetting. *Lisa Ballard*

DAILY CHANGES IN NATURAL LIGHT

The sun's movement in the sky creates predictable changes in the quality of light available for photography at various times of the day. For the wildlife photographer, the sixty-minute periods that begin at sunrise in the morning and commences an hour before sunset in the evening are often referred to as the "golden hours" of the day. This moniker has something of a double meaning. The term refers not only to the exceptional photographic opportunities that occur

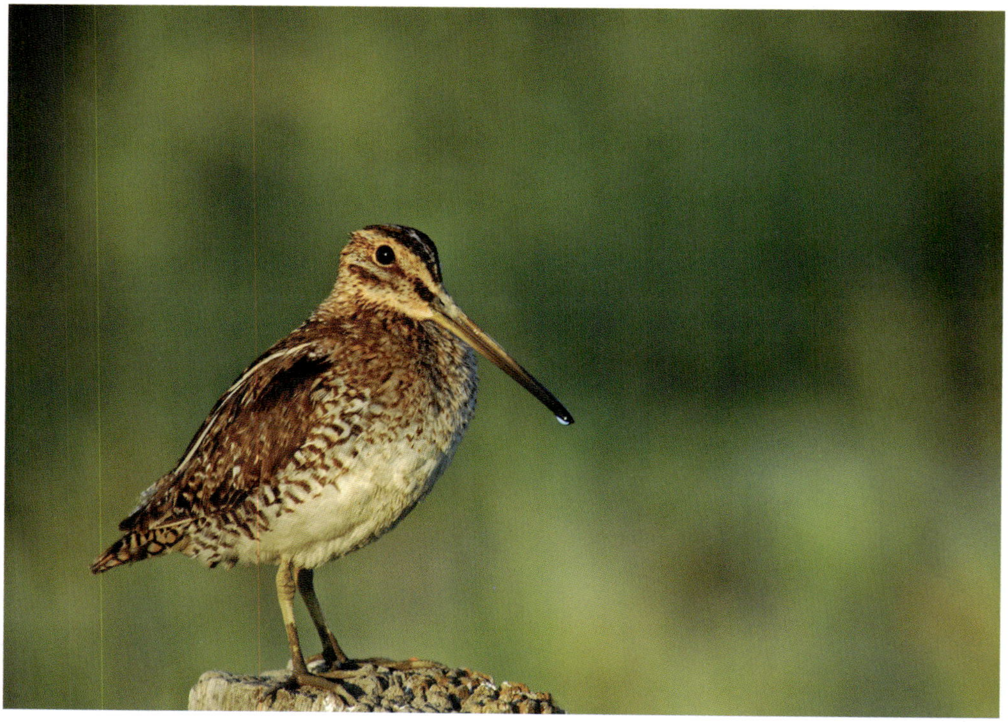

This image of a common snipe with a droplet of water on the end of its bill was captured just after sunrise during a "golden hour" of the day and displays the soft, golden light associated with early morning and late evening. *Jack Ballard*

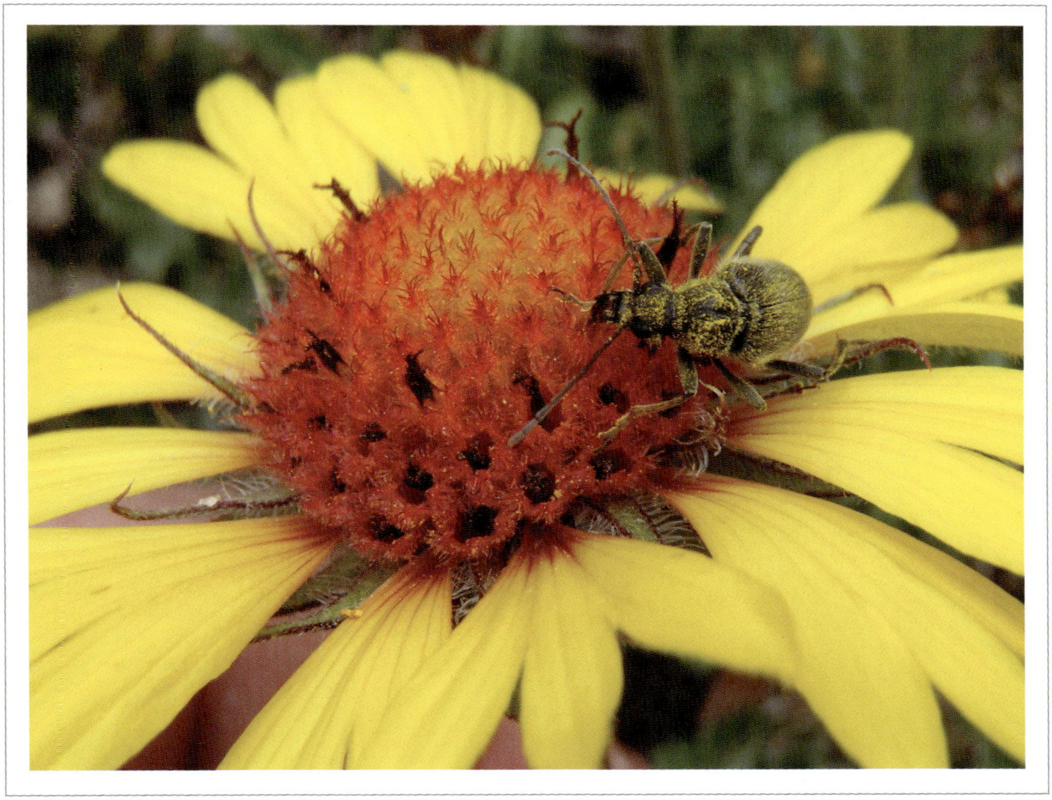

Shot at noon on an overcast day in midsummer, the author took advantage of the even light to photograph a pollen-covered beetle on a wildflower. *Jack Ballard*

during this time, but also to the quality of light that helps create them. During this period, light from the sun passes through more of the earth's atmosphere. This creates lower contrast and filters more of the sun's blue light, creating the warm, honeyed light of the "golden hours."

Although the quality of light is theoretically equivalent at thirty minutes after sunrise and thirty minutes before sunset, wildlife photographers may find very different opportunities at these times of the day. The advantage of morning's golden hour stems from the fact that fewer people are up and about at most

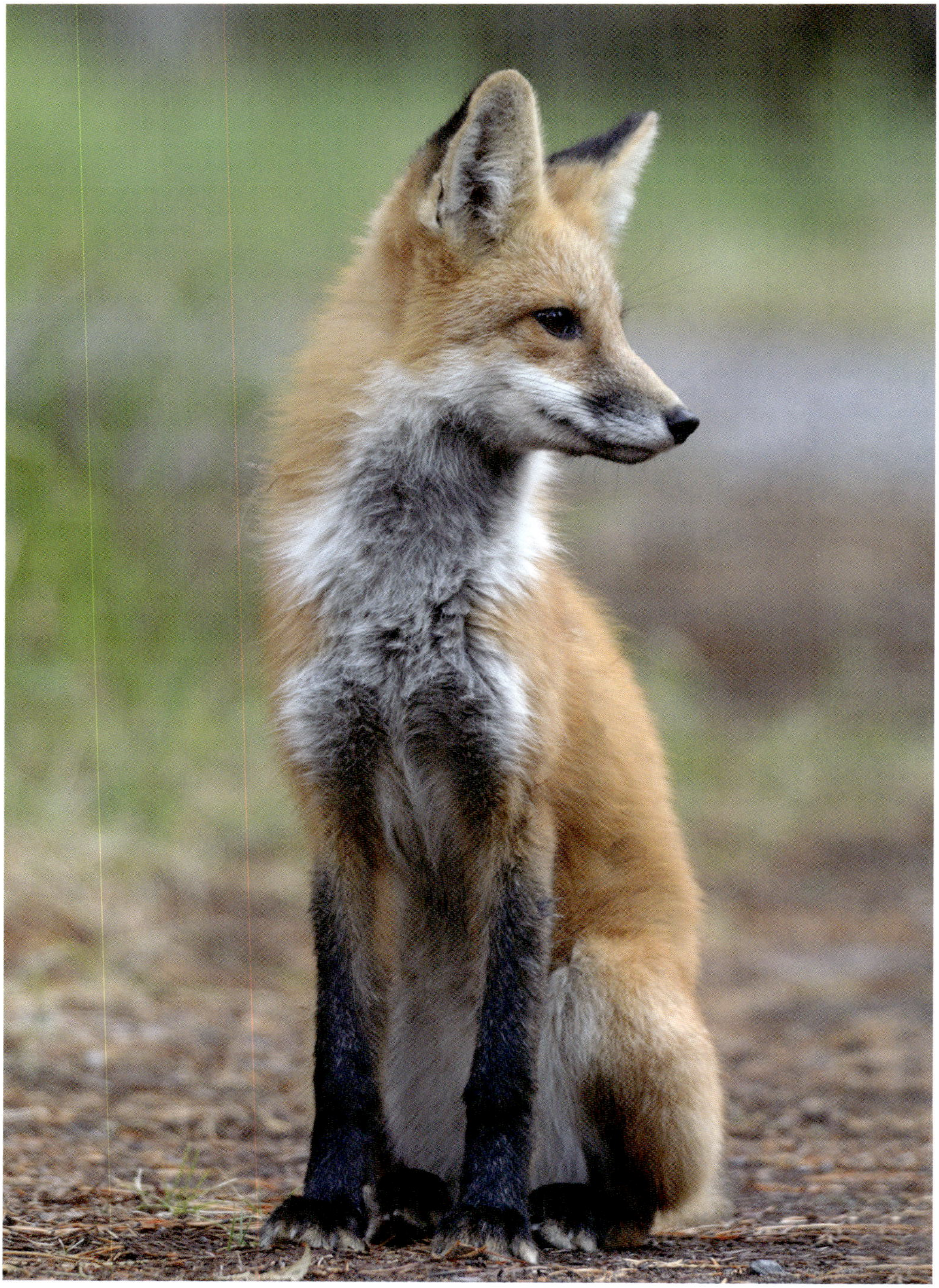

wildlife destinations, reducing the chances of having another person unwittingly scuttle your shot. Additionally, animals enduring tropical heat or midsummer heat in northern locations are more likely to be active at dawn than just before sunset, when it can still be very hot. However, some photographers like the fact that the golden hour before sunset allows more time in the light of day to scout a location and subject, and gives the photographer an amount of security knowing that the quality of the light will only improve with the passing of time.

Midday light is more direct and less filtered, yielding very high contrast and a quality many photographers describe as "harsh" lighting. Wildlife pros on location often use the midday hours for sleep, correspondence, and other tasks away from the viewfinder. The exception occurs on overcast days, when the harsh character of midday light is softened by a filtering layer of clouds.

The amount of the day consumed by harsh lighting conditions is determined by a number of factors, including latitude, the season of the year, and the amount of moisture in the air (humidity). Latitude affects light in relation to the sun's angle on the earth. Farther from the equator, the sun is lower in the sky at midday, creating a longer period after dawn and before dusk in which the light remains ideal for outdoor photos. The sun's angle to the earth is similarly influenced by the seasons. Fall and winter find the sun hanging lower in the sky than during midsummer, allowing wildlife photographers a longer window of opportunity to shoot in good light at the beginning and closing of the day. Humidity also tempers the harsh light of midday, giving moist climates a bit of a boost in relation to the length of the golden hours.

Left: Experienced wildlife photographers are capable of creating satisfying images in nearly any lighting conditions, like the one of this red fox on an overcast day in Glacier National Park, Montana.

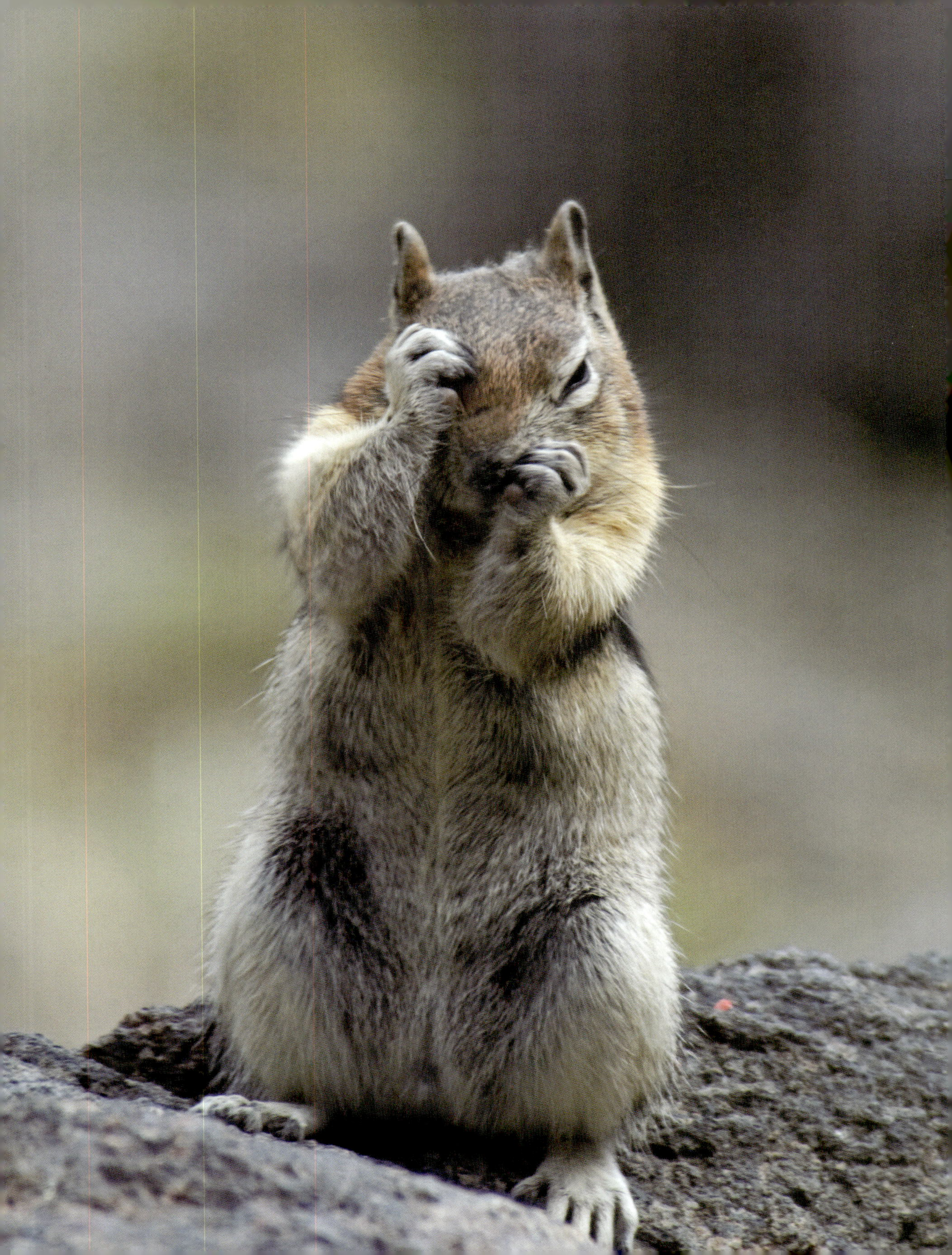

CHAPTER 4

Composition

COMPOSITION DEFINED AND EXPLAINED

As I write this sentence, I am composing. A college class in English composition concerns itself with writing, the manner in which words, sentence structure, and their organization combine in the completion of some form of written communication. Photographers have similar choices. Subjects can be placed at various locations in the frame, and a change in the magnification of the lens alters the perspective of the subject within the frame. A focused background versus one that is blurred may profoundly modify the overall texture of the image and the visual emphasis placed upon the subject. Photographers capable

Left: Golden-mantled Ground Squirrel. *Jack Ballard*

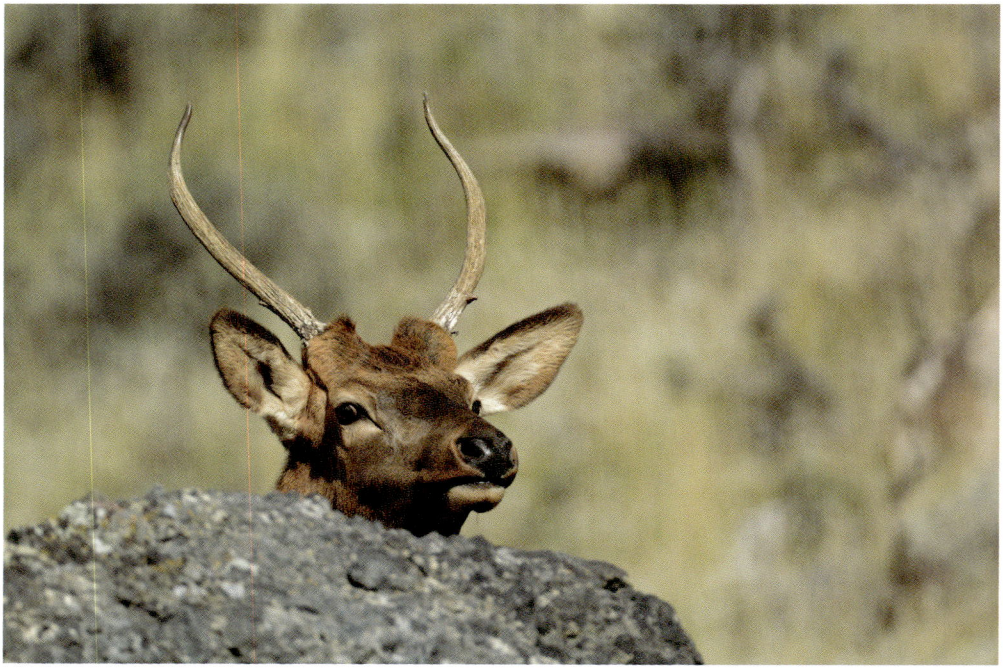

Composition refers to the way a photographer arranges visual elements in the photo. In this case, the elk, its eye and antlers, the rock in the foreground, and a mottled background of stones and grass all contribute to the final composition. *Jack Ballard*

of consistently producing artful wildlife images are masters at quickly making and implementing choices in relation to composition.

For the purposes of this book, we will define composition as the way in which a photographer combines the available visual elements of subject and background in a photograph. The term "available" is an important aspect of the definition because photographers often encounter situations where visual elements perceived by the human eye are necessarily excluded from a photo due to limitations of equipment or location.

For example, suppose a wildlife photographer is imaging waterfowl on a placid segment of the Madison River in Yellowstone National Park. Looking up, he notices a black wolf trotting along the far bank of the stream and its image perfectly reflected in the water. He recognizes an extremely rare opportunity to capture an image of the canine and its reflection. However, the wolf is on the move and there won't be time to switch his tripod-mounted 500mm lens for something shorter, and the long lens allows a photo of the wolf or its reflection, but not both. There's a compositional decision to be made, but unfortunately the most desirable composition is not an option. Thus the wildlife photographer is sometimes confronted with situations in which time or equipment profoundly limits the compositional equation.

BASIC COMPOSITIONAL RULES

A number of time-honored compositional "rules" are utilized by seasoned photographers to quickly capture images in time-sensitive situations. In other circumstances, there's enough time to experiment. While it's tempting for novices to "break the rules" to capture a more artistic or compelling image, in the vast majority of situations, it's wise to start with a classic arrangement then try more unusual compositions once the image is safely recorded to the camera's memory.

Rule of Thirds

Perhaps the most useful compositional tool used by professional photographers is the "rule of thirds." This simple maxim asserts that the strongest place to locate the subject in the frame is at one of four points created by the division of the frame in thirds, both horizontally and vertically. Think of the frame as having two lines that divide it into thirds from left and right and two more lines

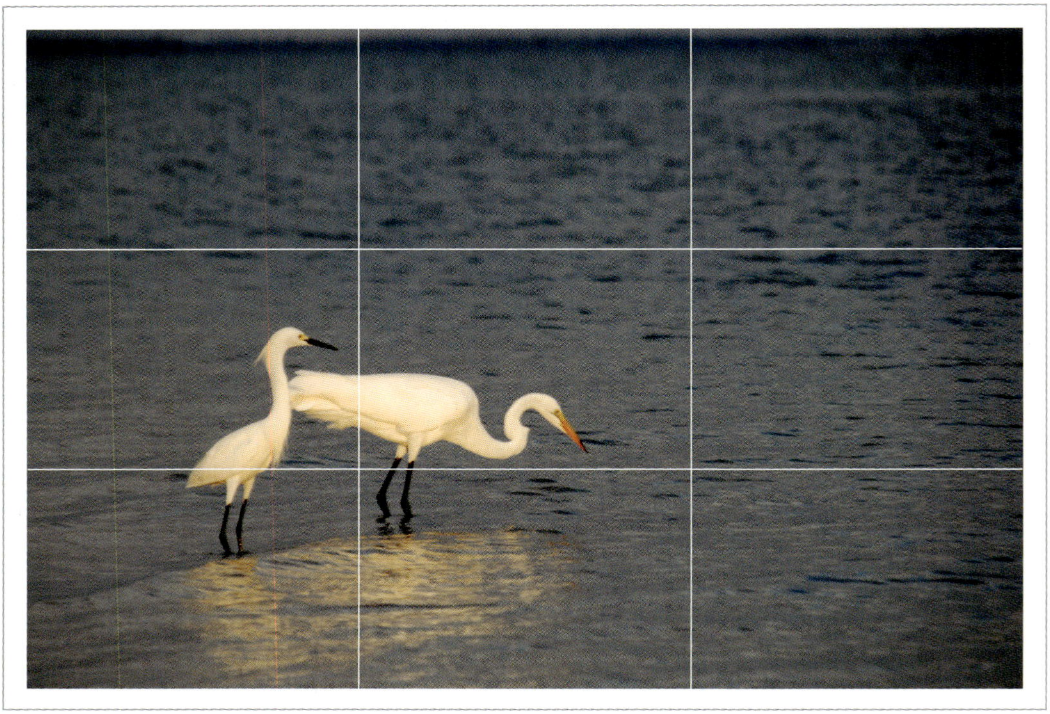

The rule of thirds indicates that the strongest compositional placement of the subject is at one of the four intersections when the frame is divided into thirds. *Lisa Ballard*

that divide it from top to bottom. This yields a grid like the game of tic-tac-toe, where the vertical and horizontal line cross in four places. In most situations, an image in which the subject occupies one of the four intersections of thirds results in a pleasing composition. Some cameras even allow this simple grid to be viewable in the viewfinder or screen as a compositional tool.

The rule of thirds applies to photos of animals in their environment, but it is also a useful compositional tool when shooting more intimate photos of a creature, such as a portrait of an elk's neck and head or a close-up of a bird. In

The rule of thirds can be applied to close-ups. In this case, the author used the eye of this long-billed curlew as the focal point of the photo following the rule of thirds. *Jack Ballard*

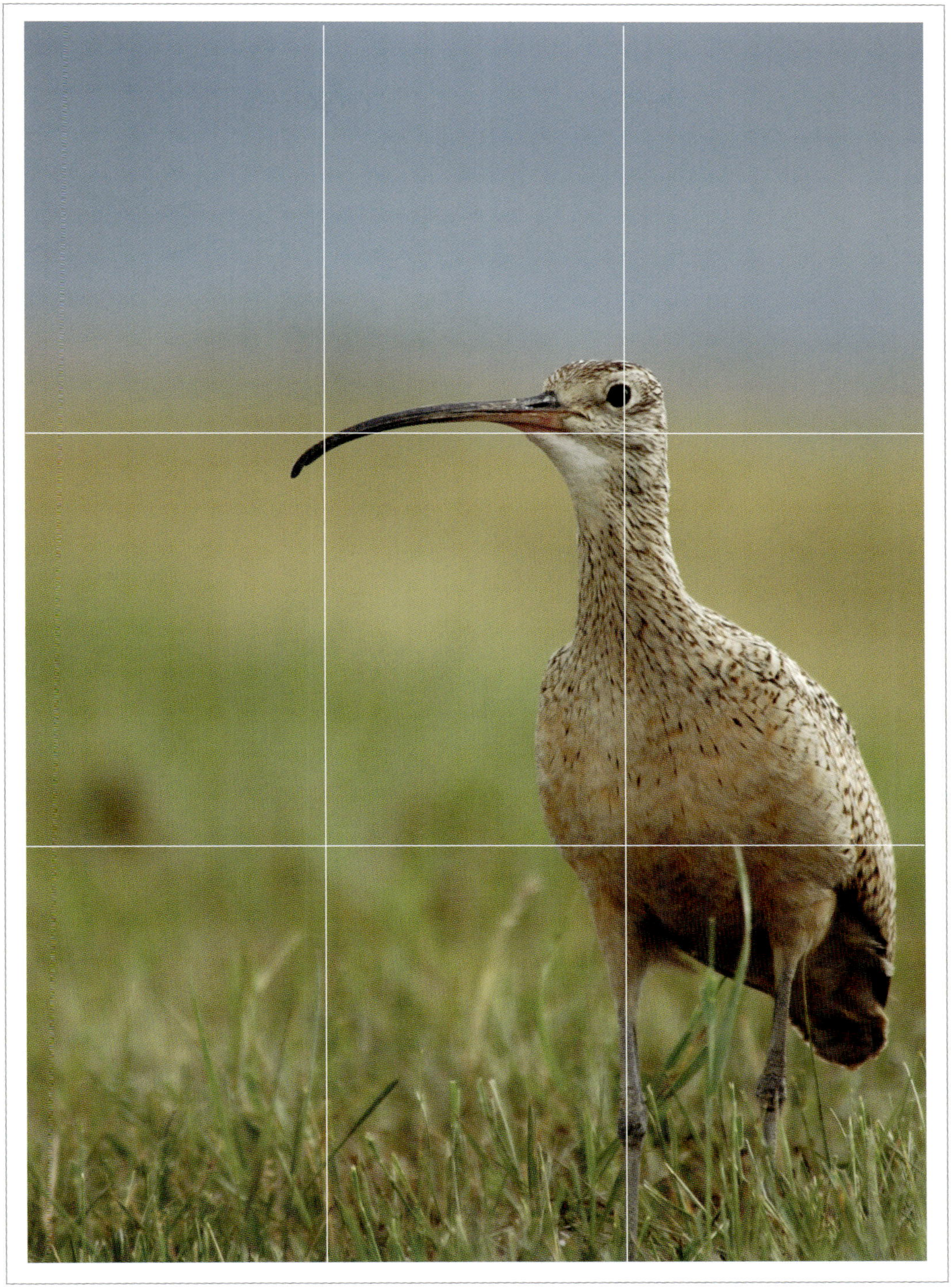

such photos, the eye of the subject becomes the focal point and is located at the intersecting lines of the rule of thirds. Some subjects lend themselves to a composition located more centrally in the frame, but in most cases, the rule of thirds allows for a quick, pleasing composition of wildlife subjects that offer but a fleeting moment in which to capture their image.

Level Horizons

Water does not flow from the upstream side of a lake nor do aspen trees grow sideways from the flank of a mountain. Landscape photographers are extremely careful to compose their photos on the level, which means framing the images with the camera on the level. This can be accomplished by leveling the tripod (some tripod heads include a level indicator), but a wildlife photographer shooting a handheld camera or reacting rapidly to a momentary opportunity doesn't have that luxury. Nonetheless, tilted images of animals look as odd as similarly botched landscape shots.

Several framing cues are helpful in achieving a level composition. Photographers shooting with a high-quality camera and lens are advised to widen their framing to allow the image to be slightly rotated and cropped with image-editing software. I use this trick on a regular basis, especially when photographing moving subjects. For example, when shooting an osprey in flight, it's natural to try to keep the bird's image level in the frame. However, when panning to follow its flight, you may be unaware it has banked slightly. If there's a water body such as a lake or bay in the background that should be level, the picture will look very odd with the water tipped in the frame. The proper composition demands that the surface of the water is level, an easy-to-achieve computer fix if you've left enough room to rotate and crop.

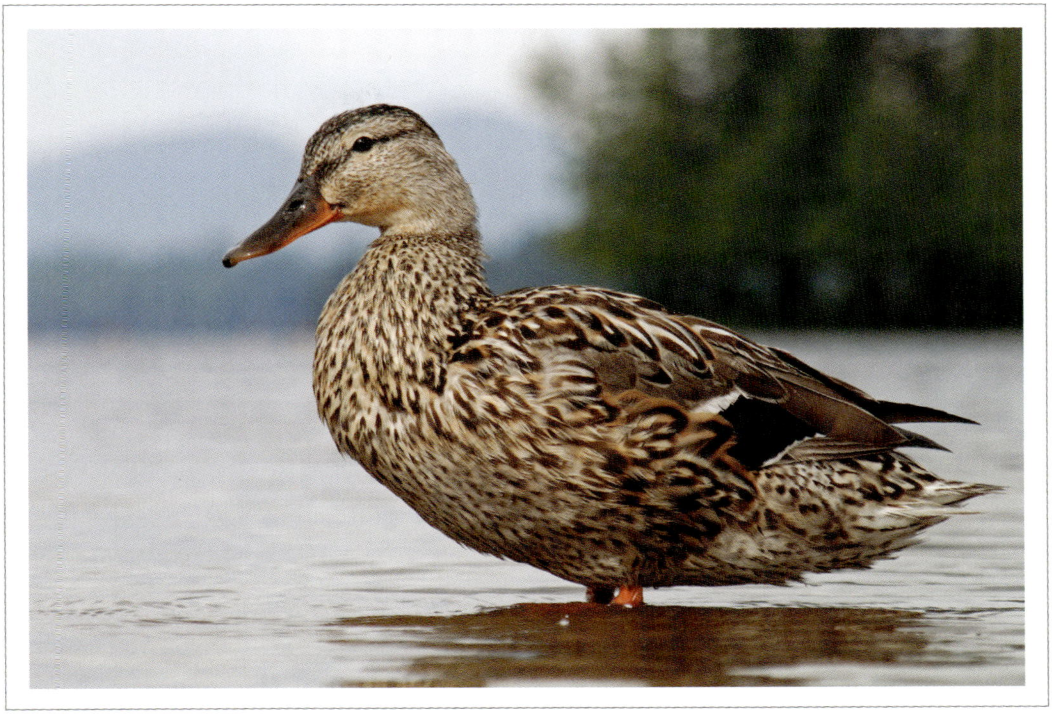

This simple, close-up photo of a mallard hen in her environment on a lake in New York's Adirondack Park demands that the shoreline in the background appears level in the frame. *Jack Ballard*

Professional wildlife photographers with years of experience also take framing cues from the environment and can do so very quickly. There is the occasional tree that grows at an angle, but for the most part tree trunks can provide a rapid indicator of what should be the vertical axis of a photo. Cattails and other vegetation that grow vertically also provide cues. The front and rear feet of a mammal grazing on level ground should appear at roughly equal distances from the bottom of the frame. This cue is especially helpful when dealing with creatures such as bison that do not have a level back.

Subject Framing

The rule of thirds provides a basic framework for locating the subject within the frame, but other considerations are also important. One of these is giving the subject space to hypothetically move forward in the frame or view its surroundings. Suppose you're photographing wading birds in shallow-water mangrove habitat along the Gulf of Mexico. A white ibis catches your eye as it probes about for a morsel. The rule of thirds gives you four compositional options, but two of those find the bird placed as if it's moving out of the frame, with more space behind it than ahead of it. A more natural and pleasing composition finds the bird located as if it's moving into the frame, with plenty of space ahead of it to theoretically look and walk.

Decisions must also be made in relation to placing the subject toward the top or bottom of the frame, even when utilizing the rule of thirds. In some cases it's wise to do both, as the same subject might yield two very different but compelling compositions. Suppose you're photographing a mountain goat perched atop a promontory of rocks in Montana's Glacier National Park or imaging a hawk perched upon a fencepost. Framing the subject higher in the frame emphasizes the habitat beneath it. It underscores the height of the goat above its surroundings and the ground beneath the hawk, which it might be scanning for prey. Locating the subject low in the frame calls attention to the sky overhead that may include attractive compositional elements such as a pale moon or billowing clouds. It also suggests the hawk has a great space in which to fly and the goat lives at the top of the world. Given time, the seasoned photographer will shoot the photo with both compositions and may ultimately decide they are equally pleasing.

Right: This photo follows the rule of thirds. Placing the leaping mountain goat kid in Glacier National Park high in the frame shows where it will land and gives a sense of the height from which it is jumping. *Lisa Ballard*

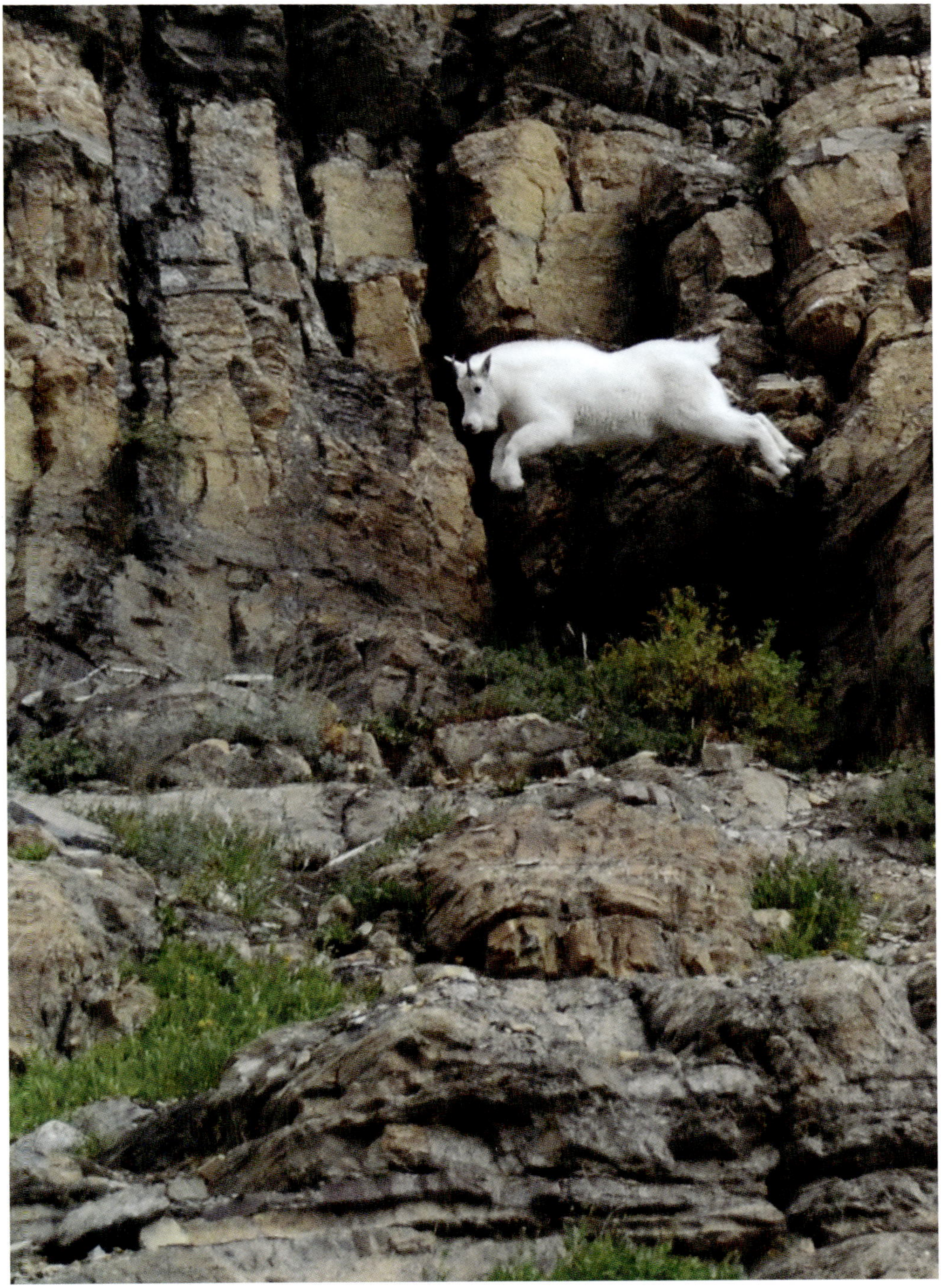

There are times when basic subject framing rules can be tossed to the wind to achieve particular goals with a photo. For example, I once entered a photo contest at an Outdoor Writers Association of America (OWAA) conference. For one of the subjects, I composed an image of the eye of a great horned owl at a zoo. Several compositions were recorded, most honoring the rule of thirds. However, the image that seemed to most strongly emphasize the bird's intense yellow eye was one in which the orb was framed dead-center in the photo. The judges must have agreed, because the photo won a top award in its category.

Focus

An oft-quoted maxim among professionals asserts that a photographer's portfolio is only as good as its weakest shot. Three decades ago as a budding pro, I took this principle to heart. Film was the photographic medium of the day, leaving no room to correct, crop, or sharpen "almost good enough" photos. Slides with even minor imperfections all found the same destiny, a resting place in the trash bin beside my desk.

Exposure was sometimes a problem, but oftentimes otherwise perfectly good photos were reduced to rubbish because they were slightly out of focus, or "soft" in the vernacular of photography. A good photo has the subject in focus, but exactly what to focus upon is not always obvious to the fledgling photographer.

A nearly sacred rule of thumb in wildlife photography commands that the eye of the subject be in focus. This perhaps stems from the fact that eye contact and the expression of the eye are such important parts of nonverbal communication among humans. Thus professional wildlife photographers routinely first focus on a creature's eye and then frame the image as desired.

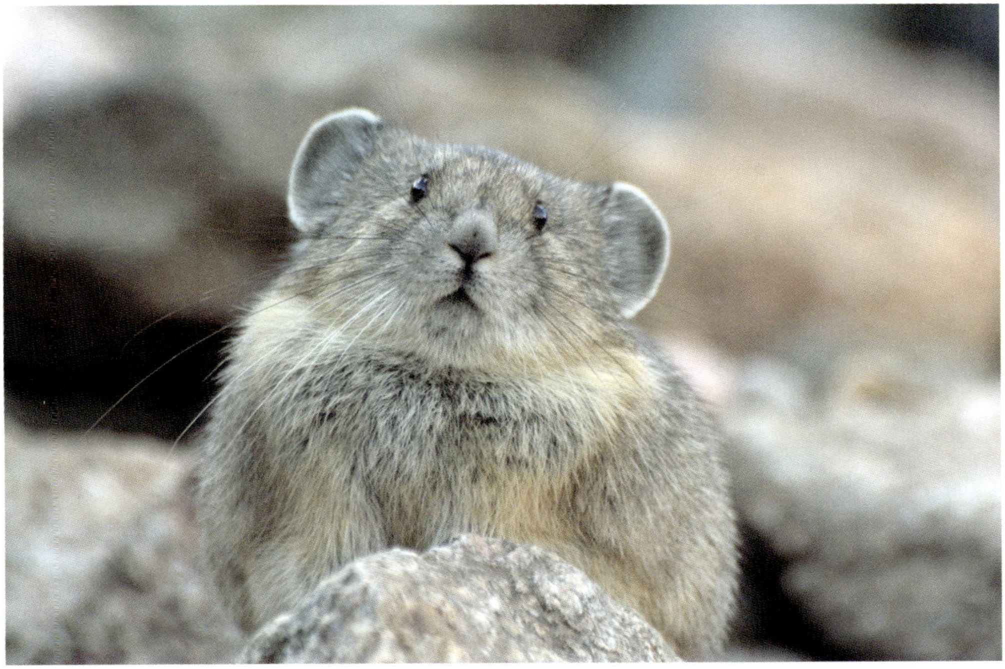

A nearly sacred rule of composition in wildlife photography asserts that the eye of the subject should be in focus, as is the case with this pika photographed along the Beartooth Highway in Wyoming. *Jack Ballard*

Exceptions to the "focus on the eye" rule exist, usually as a means of creating a wildlife photo for a specific purpose. I once submitted photos to a magazine that was searching for pictures of an elk to illustrate *wapiti*, the Cree and Shawnee Indian term for elk, which translates to "white rump." A photo of an elk facing away at an angle seemed perfect for the illustration. Instead of focusing on the slightly visible eye, I put the animal's rump in sharp relief to emphasize the source of the term *wapiti*. Photographers might also choose a different focal point for other specific reasons. For example, a close-up image of a bull bison's horn might also include the eye. If the shape, texture, and curvature of the horn are the primary subject, the eye may be out of focus. However, in the vast majority of situations, the eye of an animal, if apparent, becomes the point of focus.

Photographing groups of creatures, whether a flock of snow geese rising from a grain field or a herd of pronghorn resting on the prairie, also entails choices in focus. Groups a considerable distance from the photographer bunched tightly together might all easily be kept in focus. Multiple animals in a herd at varying distances from the photographer, however, usually require a choice regarding which one to focus upon. In general, focusing on the animal or animals nearest the camera is the safest point of focus. Choosing a critter in the middle of the herd is more risky, as out-of-focus subjects in the foreground of the photo are often distracting.

However, there are times when the observant photographer deliberately focuses upon a subject at the middle or even in the rear of the flock. Species of migrating waterfowl sometimes intermingle in odd ways. A single gray Canada goose might be spotted in a large flock of snow geese. Focusing on the former places a clear emphasis on this anomaly. A flock of resting shorebirds might see one toward the back of the bunch rising and stretching a wing. A quickly composed image that focuses on the active bird at the rear of the flock may yield an exceptional photo. Such opportunities for creative composition in relation to focus often require the photographer to react within seconds. Wildlife photographers with the ability to recognize and capitalize on these unique opportunities are among the best in the business.

When photographing multiple subjects, focusing on animals in the foreground is generally preferable to focusing on those toward the rear or center of the frame. These western painted turtles were photographed at the National Bison Range in Montana. *Lisa Ballard*

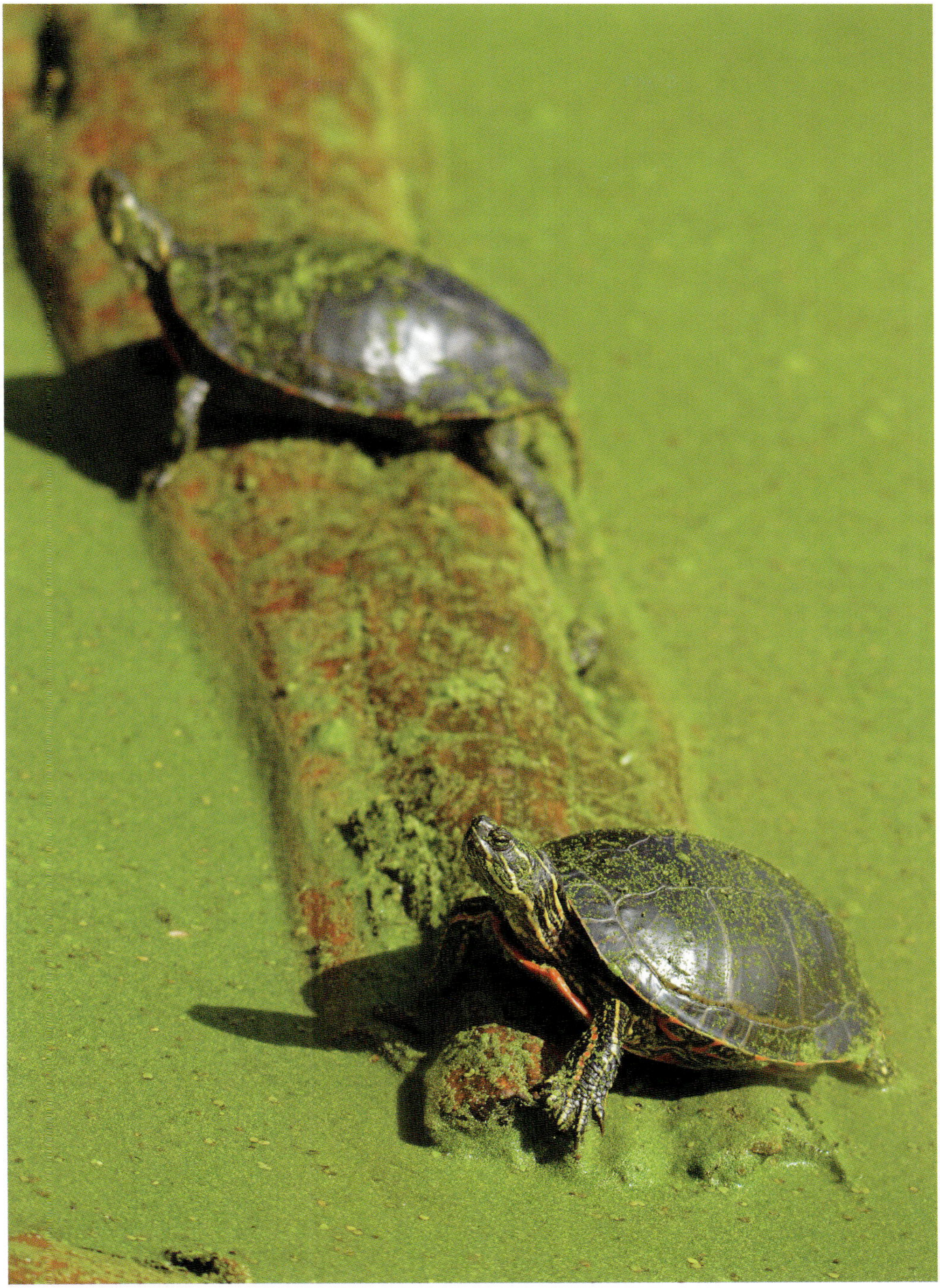

Depth of Field

As noted in chapter 2, depth of field is one of the three elements that affect a photo's exposure. It is also an important aspect of composition. Depth of field refers to what portion of the photo remains in sharp focus in relation to the rest of the frame. A shallow depth of field achieved by using a wide aperture (e.g., f/2.8) may see only objects in the range of 20 to 21 feet away from the photographer in focus, while an extended depth of field achieved by a more closed aperture (e.g., f/22) may see everything from 10 to 1,000 feet away in focus. Shallow depth of field is often favored for animal portraits because it places the entire emphasis on the subject and renders the background as a

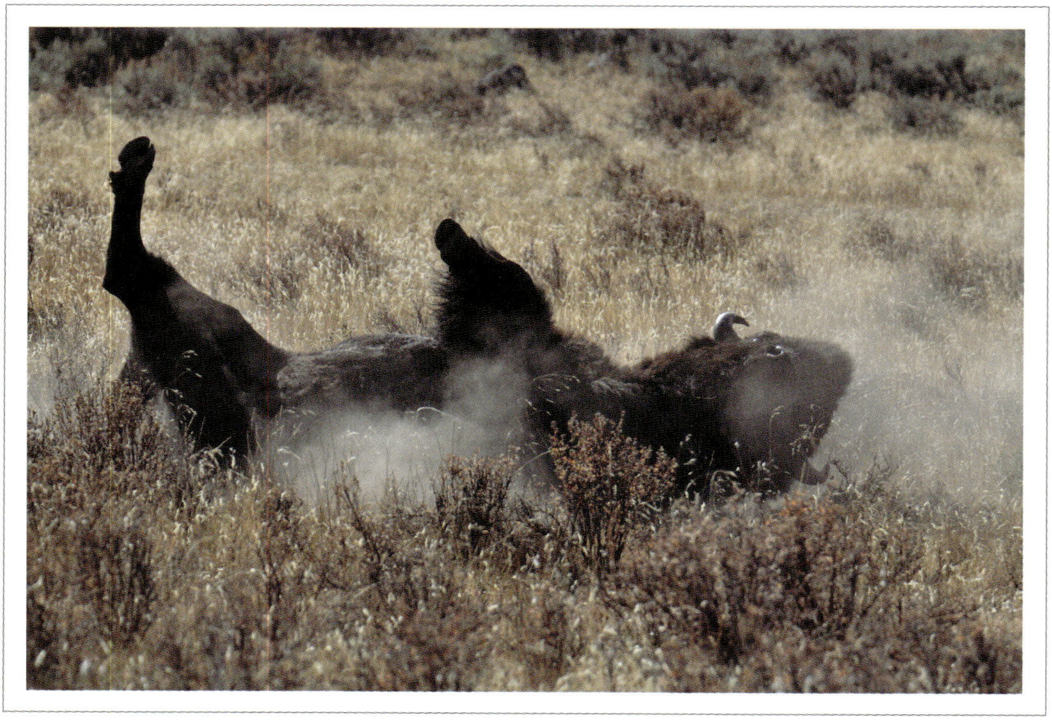

The shallow depth of field on this image of a bull bison rolling in Yellowstone National Park renders a soft foreground and background, emphasizing the subject and its behavior. *Dominic Ballard*

blur of color. However, an extended depth of field may clearly show specific elements of habitat in focus, yielding a picture that gives the viewer a clear sense of the creature's environment.

Although most photographers tend toward a shallower depth of field, choosing an aperture is a matter of personal preference. Some wildlife photographers start with their lens wide open (smallest number on the f-stop), while others opt for a different point of beginning. I tend toward a setting a stop or two above the maximum opening (e.g., f/5.6 or f/8 on a lens with maximum aperture of f/4), which gives a little more "fudge" factor on focus and yields slightly sharper images, as most lenses are sharper at the midrange of their aperture than the extremes. The aperture is adjusted from there to achieve compositional effects requiring more or less depth of field.

Perspective

Photos of certain wildlife subjects are dramatically altered by changing the position of the camera up or down by just a few inches. A bumblebee pollinating a flower looks very different when shot on its level versus elevating the camera a foot to shoot down on its back. A walrus sacked out on the seashore appears very differently when photographed head-on from the sea than from the rear looking out toward the ocean. These compositional decisions have to do with perspective, with changing the distance, angle, or physical location from which the photo is made.

Many photographers take wildlife pictures from the same perspective time after time. That's the perspective of a standing human photographing at her eye level with a tripod-mounted camera. While superb images can be created from this position, using it as your primary perspective is a mistake. Better images are

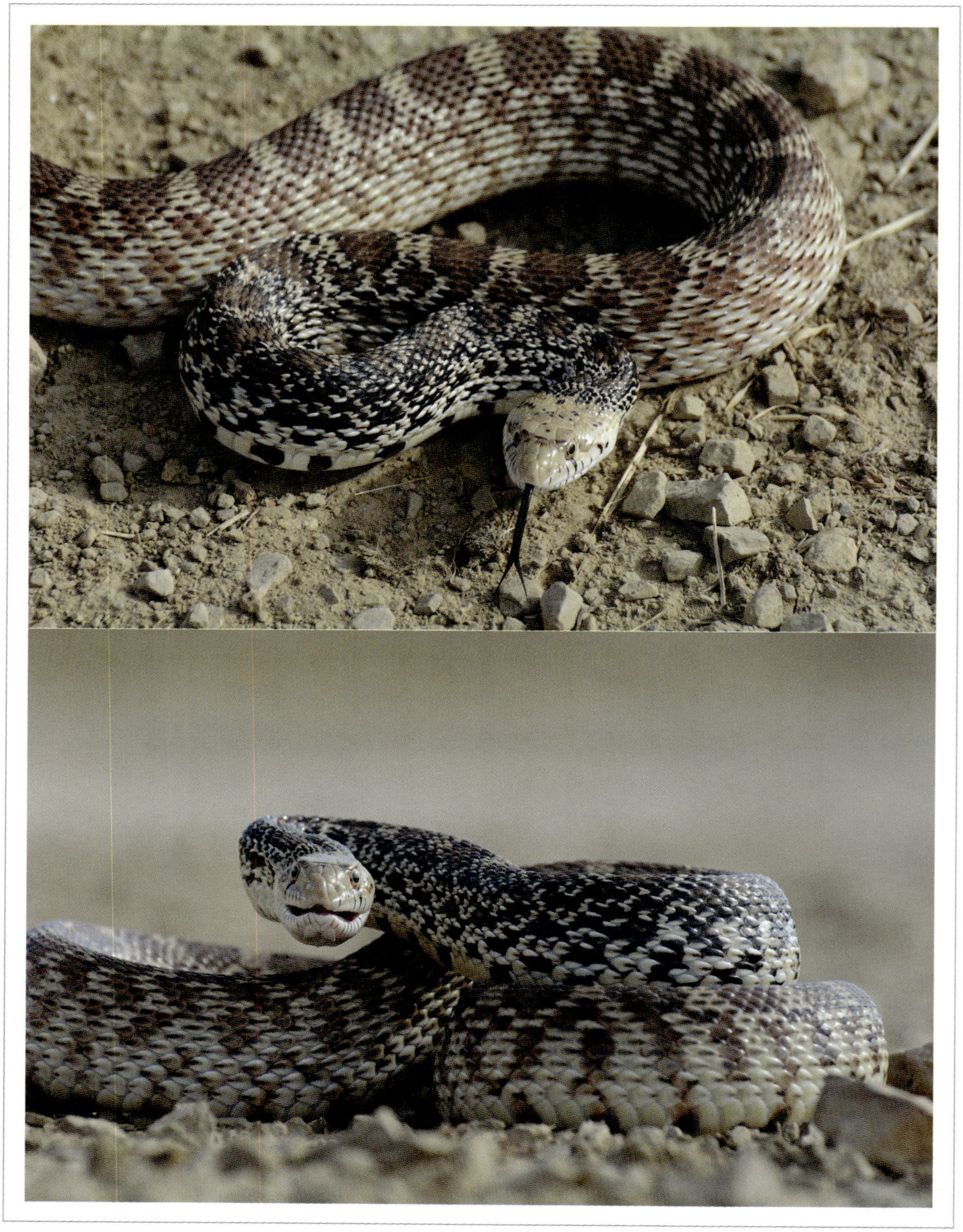

These photos of a bullsnake taken on a county road in Montana amply illustrate the dramatic difference between taking a photo from the perspective of a standing human versus eye level with the subject. *Jack Ballard*

created when the photographer is eye level with the subject, not shooting from her own eye level. Photos taken at subject eye level give an impression of seeing the world as the subject sees it and emphasize the subject's size and shape against the larger background. They also emphasize the eye-to-eye contact that suggests stronger emotional connection in human communication.

This is especially true for small creatures. A photo of a ground squirrel taken by a photographer lying on the earth is almost always a far better image than one taken from 5 feet above the subject. Photographers shooting with a handheld camera can easily squat, kneel, or prostrate themselves to get at subject level. A low-level perspective is also possible with a tripod. The legs of my primary tripod are hinged and can be rotated outward to flatten the support to within less than a foot from the ground. Some photographers also carry a beanbag that serves as a functional camera support when photographing at ground level.

While shooting at the subject's eye level is the best starting point in relation to perspective, other angles make for creative images. A low-angle view of a larger subject (think of a moose photo shot from ground level, from a distance of course) can emphasize its size. On a photo safari in Tanzania, I was once scheduled to take a hot-air balloon ride at dawn to view and photograph wildlife on the Serengeti. A stomach issue found me confined to the bathroom in our room at the lodge while my companions took the opportunity to photograph animals from the perspective of a soaring vulture or perhaps a leopard lounging in an acacia tree. The aerial perspective from the platform of the balloon allowed for an intriguing view of common African wildlife.

Another composition decision related to perspective is whether to shoot horizontally (camera held level to the earth) or vertically (camera tipped 90 degrees). There's a simple way to make this decision, at least initially. Shoot

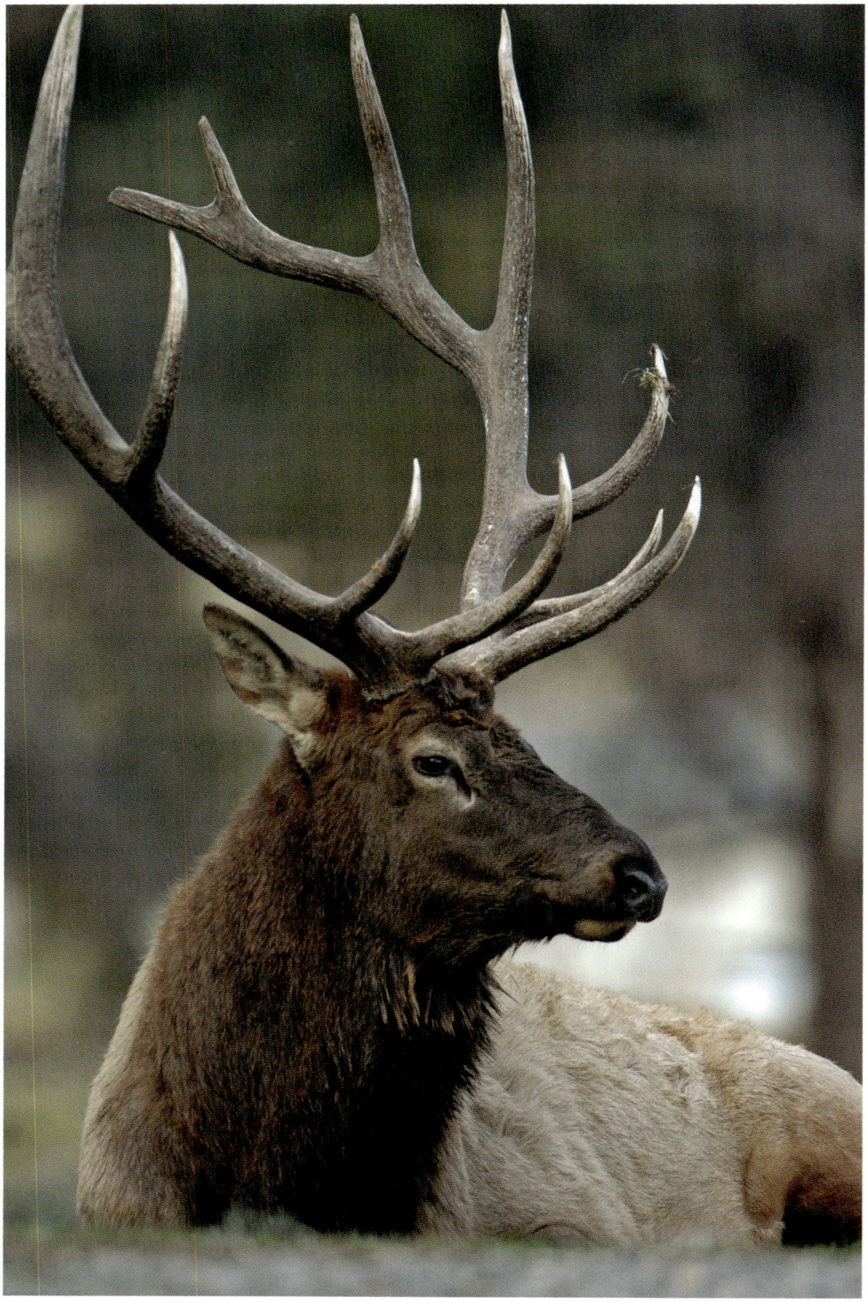

The low-angle perspective of this photo of a resting bull elk in Yellowstone National Park accentuates the size of its magnificent antlers. *Jack Ballard*

tall or narrow subjects vertically; shoot broad subjects horizontally. Sometimes a vertical and horizontal image can be made of the same subject. A grazing bull elk offering a broadside view from the road in Theodore Roosevelt National Park in North Dakota is probably best shot horizontally. If the animal turns to face the photographer, it transforms itself into a narrower subject, begging for a vertical composition.

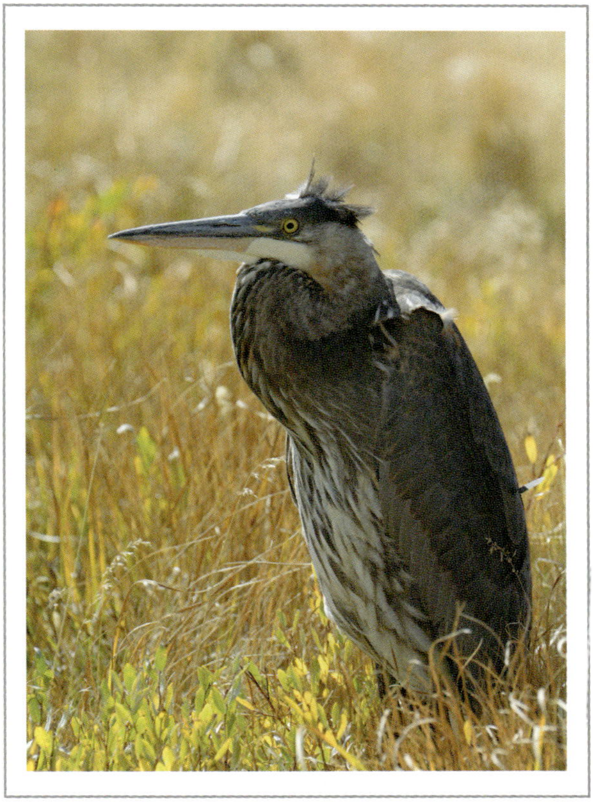

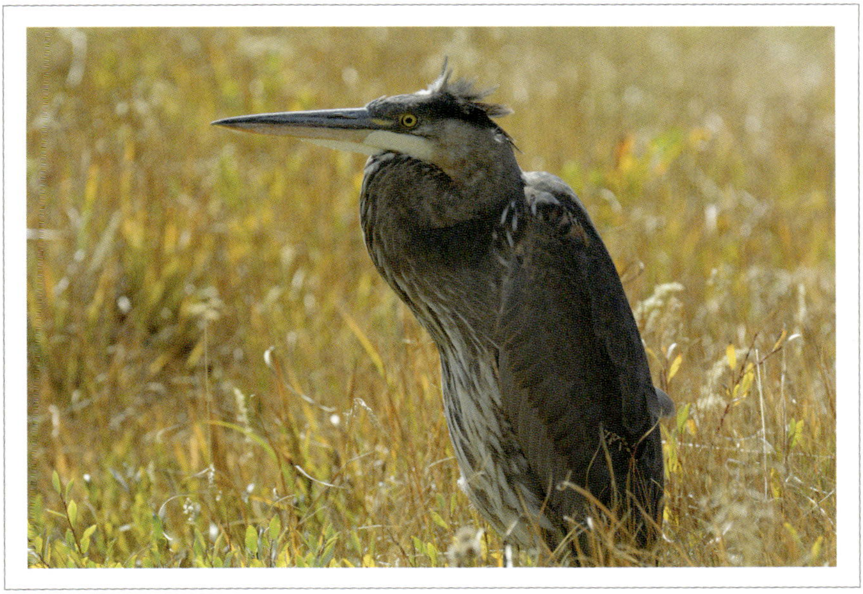

The images of this great blue heron, taken in Wyoming, demonstrate that some subjects can be photographed vertically and horizontally, depending on the intended purpose of the image. The vertical in this case would make a fine magazine cover, while the horizontal might be perfect for a calendar.
Jack Ballard

COMPOSITION KILLERS

A number of compositional errors, "killers" we might call them, are common to novice photographers. The first of these is continually shooting a "bull's-eye" composition, where the subject is centered in the frame. While it's true that many budget cameras only focus in the center of the frame, most allow the photographer to partially depress the shutter button to trigger the focus. If pressure is kept on the button, the image can be recomposed using the rule of thirds or a different composition. The button is then pressed completely to trigger the shutter and capture the image.

Another common problem is failing to recognize a vertical subject as such and shooting it horizontally, or vice versa. This usually happens on the horizontal side, because most beginning photographers seem to forget that their camera will function in the vertical position. Choosing the wrong perspective for the subject essentially wastes the majority of space in the frame and severely limits the amount of magnification available for the subject.

Failing to detect extraneous objects in the frame is a composition killer that plagues experienced photographers as well as beginners. This occurs when some unintended object encroaches in the frame, typically a branch or blade of grass that creates an exceedingly annoying, out-of-focus smear across the frame. One pro I know thinks of this in terms of "weed-eating" around the perimeter of the frame as she composes images to look for unintended objects jutting into the picture. This also applies to other elements in the frame that can intrude on the subject or distract the eye of a person viewing the photo. A limb in the background jutting from the head of a perched bald eagle in an otherwise clear sky is one such example. Very light or dark objects in an otherwise middle-toned background create tonal

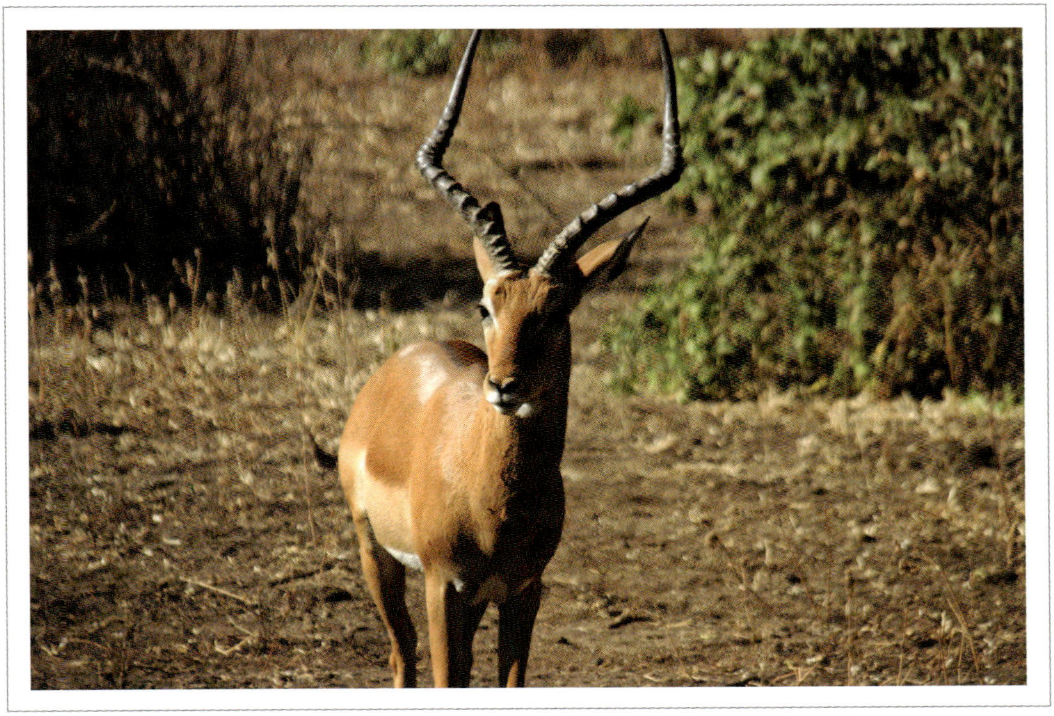

This photo of an impala ram illustrates three composition killers in one image. The subject is bull's-eye in the frame, the tips of the horns and feet are cut off, and what is most logically a vertical photo was shot horizontally. *Jack Ballard*

aberrations that distract the photo viewer's eye from the main subject. Choosing a slightly different camera angle is often all it takes to avoid such distractions.

"Unintended surgery" is another composition killer. In an attempt to achieve a tightly framed image of the subject, it's easy to accidentally lop one (or more) of its appendages from the frame. This plagues me when shooting antlered ungulates. Intent on including all of their antlers in the frame I have successfully removed all of their hooves in some photos due to unintended surgery. Tails, wings, and feet of birds are also at risk, as are the antennae of insects. It is, of course, perfectly acceptable to selectively crop portions from an animal when framing a portrait of its head or another part of its body. For full-body photos, though, unintended surgery is an error. It does have a simple solution, back off on the magnification.

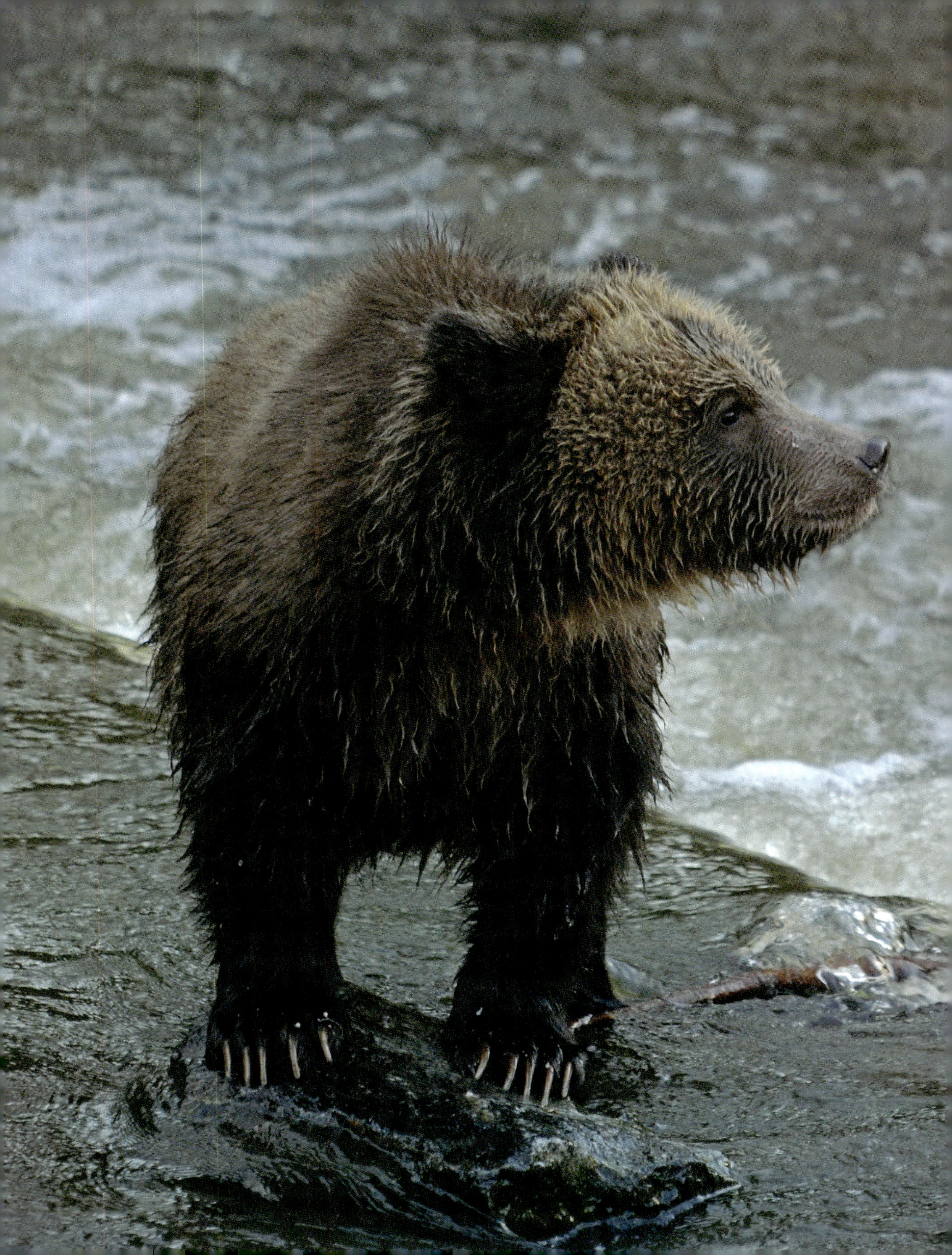

CHAPTER

5

Finding Wildlife

Wildlife photography on a faraway continent or at a heralded domestic destination such as Yellowstone or Great Smoky Mountains National Park is the dream of those fascinated with capturing the images of wild creatures. But wildlife exists almost everywhere, from the skyscrapers of New York City to the burning deserts of Death Valley. Residents of urban areas and small towns with an intimate knowledge of their surroundings often capture gorgeous and gratifying wildlife photos, often within a mile of their home. Photographers in the United States are blessed with copious locations for wildlife photography. The question for most pros is not locating a nearby or far-flung destination at which to shoot, but choosing a location from the myriad of options.

Grizzly bear. *Lisa Ballard*

URBAN AND BACKYARD WILDLIFE

Numerous wildlife species are as at home in the suburbs as they are in rural areas or the wilderness. These include birds, reptiles, and small mammals, but larger creatures such as deer, elk, foxes, and coyotes are found in some urban areas as well. Mountain lions and moose are also associated with certain cityscapes, though the former are seldom seen during daylight hours.

Within the "city" limits of Red Lodge, Montana, my hometown, I have photographed dozens of different bird species along with cottontail rabbits, jackrabbits, whitetail deer, and moose. Trips to visit relatives in the metro area of Denver, Colorado, have yielded outstanding images of waterfowl, eastern fox squirrels, red foxes, and raccoons.

Although many creatures have become "naturalized" in urban areas to the point where a dozen generations or more of a species have shared human habitat, most photographers prefer a natural background when imaging wildlife. Fortunately, most urban centers have swatches of natural habitat in the form of green spaces, creek

ETHICS AND ETIQUETTE

FEEDING WILDLIFE

Urban wildlife such as ducks and squirrels are sometimes fed by folks assuming the animals need a handout. Oftentimes the meal is horrible from the standpoint of nutrition (e.g., feeding white bread to geese), but creatures gobble it just the same. Many parks and wildlife areas strictly prohibit the feeding of wildlife. Urban coyotes and foxes habituated to human handouts can become aggressive and my need to be removed by wildlife managers. For these reasons, avoid feeding an animal in public urban areas to obtain a photograph. Managing a bird feeder in your backyard is considered an acceptable practice by most wildlife photographers. Tossing a piece of bread to a mallard behind a Do Not Feed the Ducks sign at a park is not, even if others are doing it.

Right: This comical short-eared owl was photographed from a county road. Wildlife photographers with local knowledge often shoot their best photos close to home. *Jack Ballard*

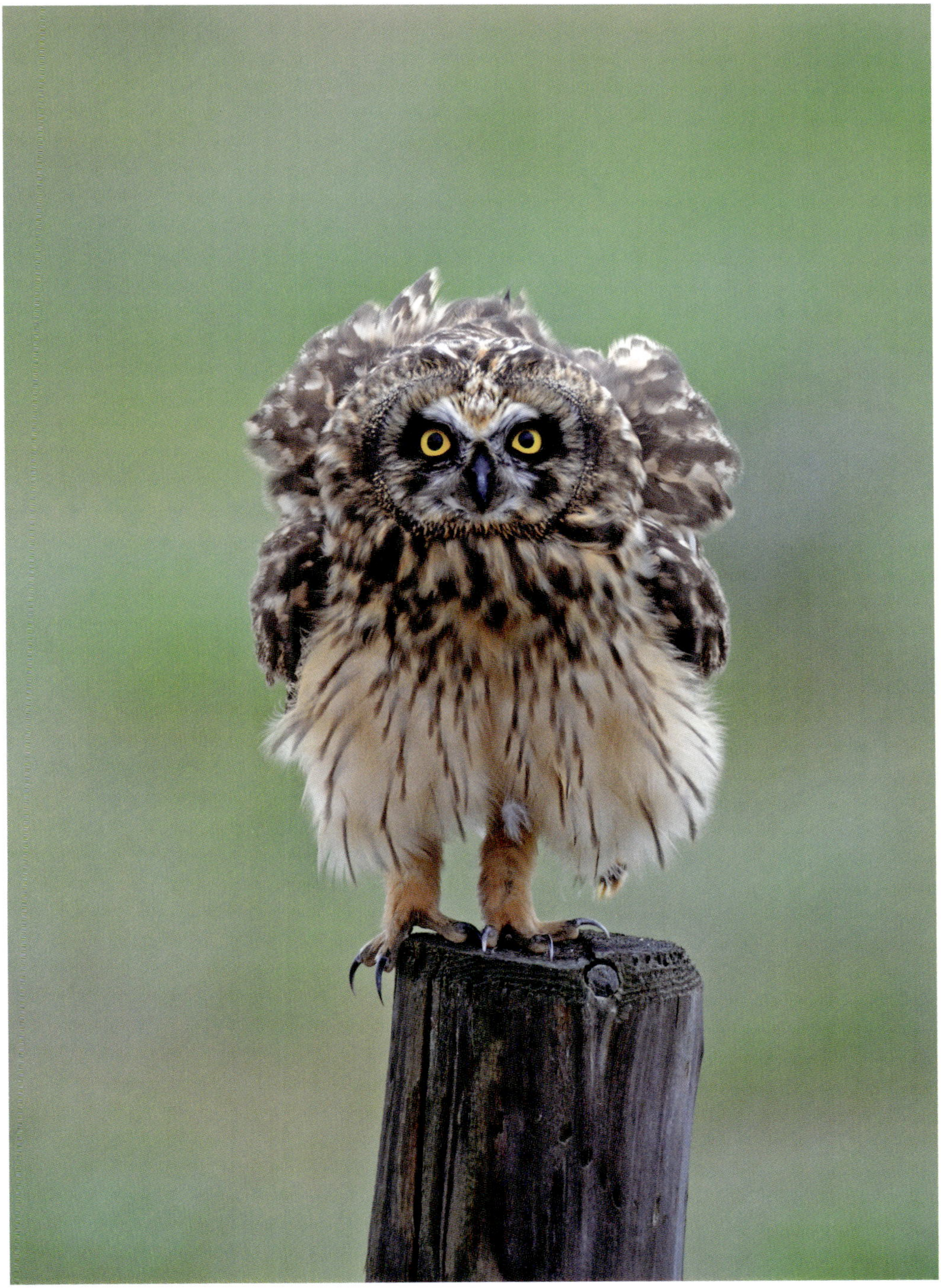

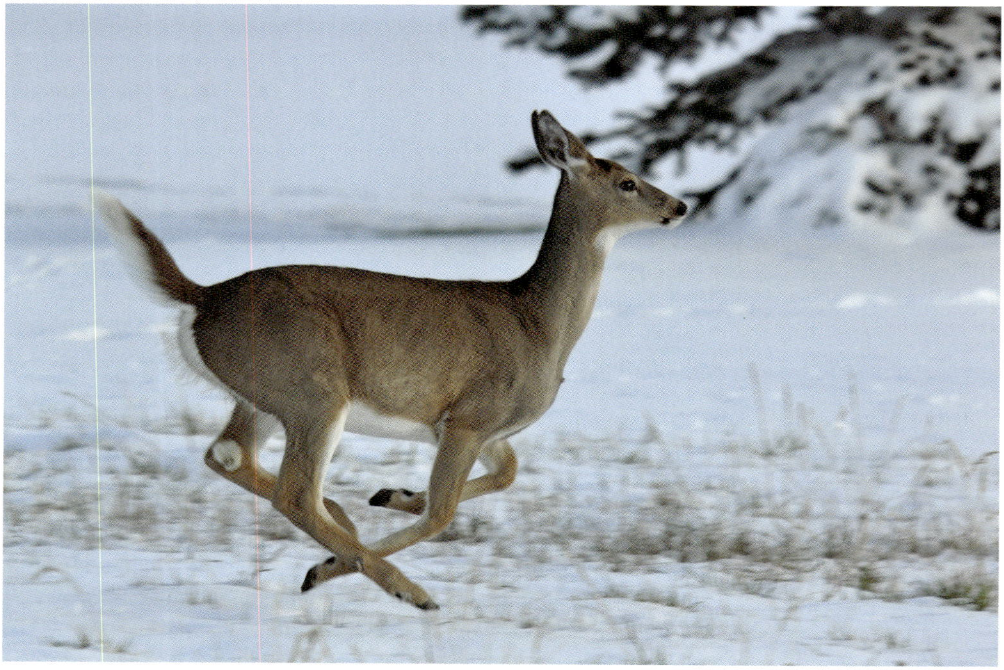

This picture of a running whitetail deer was taken when the animal crossed a vacant lot just down the street from the author's home. Swatches of natural habitat are available in many urban areas and sometimes yield excellent wildlife photos. *Jack Ballard*

corridors, parks, and trees that provide a natural setting for wildlife. Property owners can create natural habitat in a portion of their backyard to achieve a desired background for photos as well.

Once discovered, photographers can take several steps to increase their prospects of photographing urban wildlife in a natural setting. Early morning is usually the best time to be about on a greenbelt or creekside walking path. Animals tend to be most active at dawn and dusk. Fewer visitors are out at this time, decreasing the chance of another person disturbing your subject. Morning light is soft and pleasing, lending a superior aesthetic element compared to photos shot at midday.

ZOOS AND OTHER FACILITIES

Zoos exist for the purpose of holding and displaying animals to the public, and sometimes maintaining the existence of species that are extinct or severely threatened in the wild. Animals that have sustained injuries prohibiting their release back into the wild are cared for at some zoos. Some professional wildlife photographers absolutely refuse to shoot in zoos, while others use the facilities to capture wildlife portraits or hone particular techniques. For example, exposure on polar bears can be tricky. One photographer I know visited a zoo to practice exposure on captive polar bears with his camera setup before embarking on an expensive photo tour to Canada to photograph the creatures in the wild.

Several challenges confront photographers attempting to obtain natural-looking photos in a zoo or other wildlife holding facility. Catching the animal against a background that doesn't look man-made is difficult in many zoos. This can be overcome by shooting with a very shallow depth of field that throws the background out of focus. Many zoos are increasingly attempting to hold animals in habitat that resembles their natural surroundings in the wild.

ETHICS AND ETIQUETTE

ZOOS

Photos of wildlife taken in a zoo for one's own pleasure or posted to a noncommercial site on the Internet are of little concern to professional wildlife photographers or the editors of publications dealing with wildlife. However, when photos taken in a zoo or other captive facilities are portrayed as "wild" images by a photographer or a publication, most wildlife pros feel an important ethical line has been crossed.

When shooting in a zoo, remember you are not the only person anxious to view the animals. A busy facility demands that the courteous photographer take his turn at the best places to see the creatures, just like everyone else.

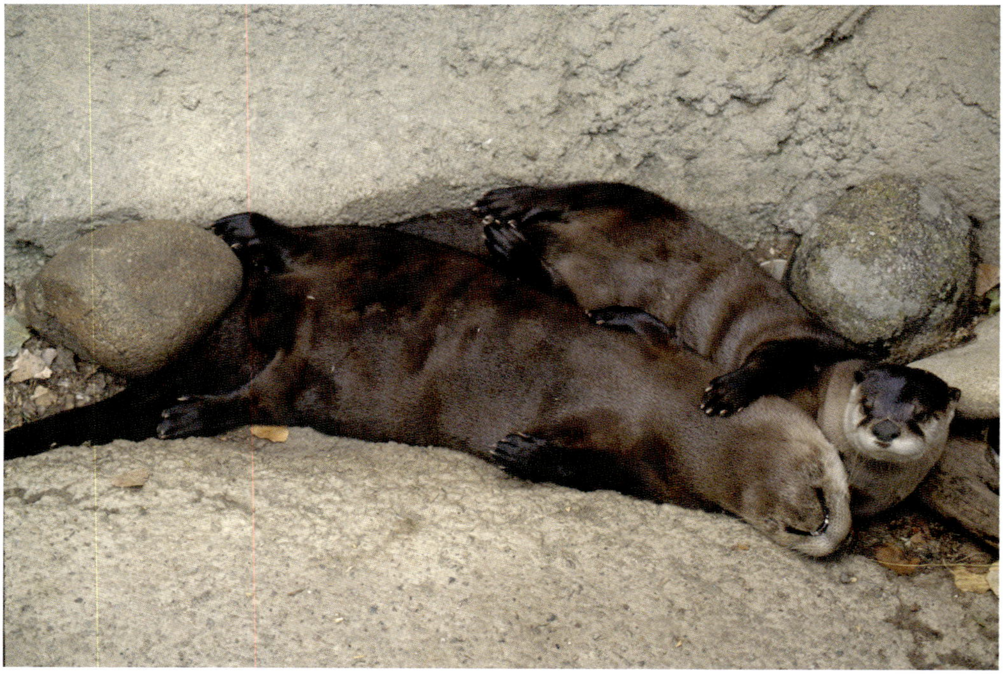

This cute photo of a pair of river otters was taken at ZooMontana in Billings, Montana. The background isn't perfect but is quite representative of their natural environment in some places they live in the wild. *Jack Ballard*

Shooting in such a facility ups the chances of capturing a pleasing image. Tight compositions of an animal's face or other portions of its body that minimize the background are another means of acquiring a photo that doesn't have the look of captivity about it.

Fences and barriers at zoos sometimes make it difficult or impossible to photograph certain creatures. However, it's possible (where allowed) to shoot "through" the woven mesh of a chain-link fence by getting a small-diameter lens as close as possible to the mesh.

Right: Facilities for the rehabilitation and conservation of wildlife sometimes offer superb photo ops. This black crowned crane (native to Africa) was photographed at the International Crane Foundation near Baraboo, Wisconsin. *Jack Ballard*

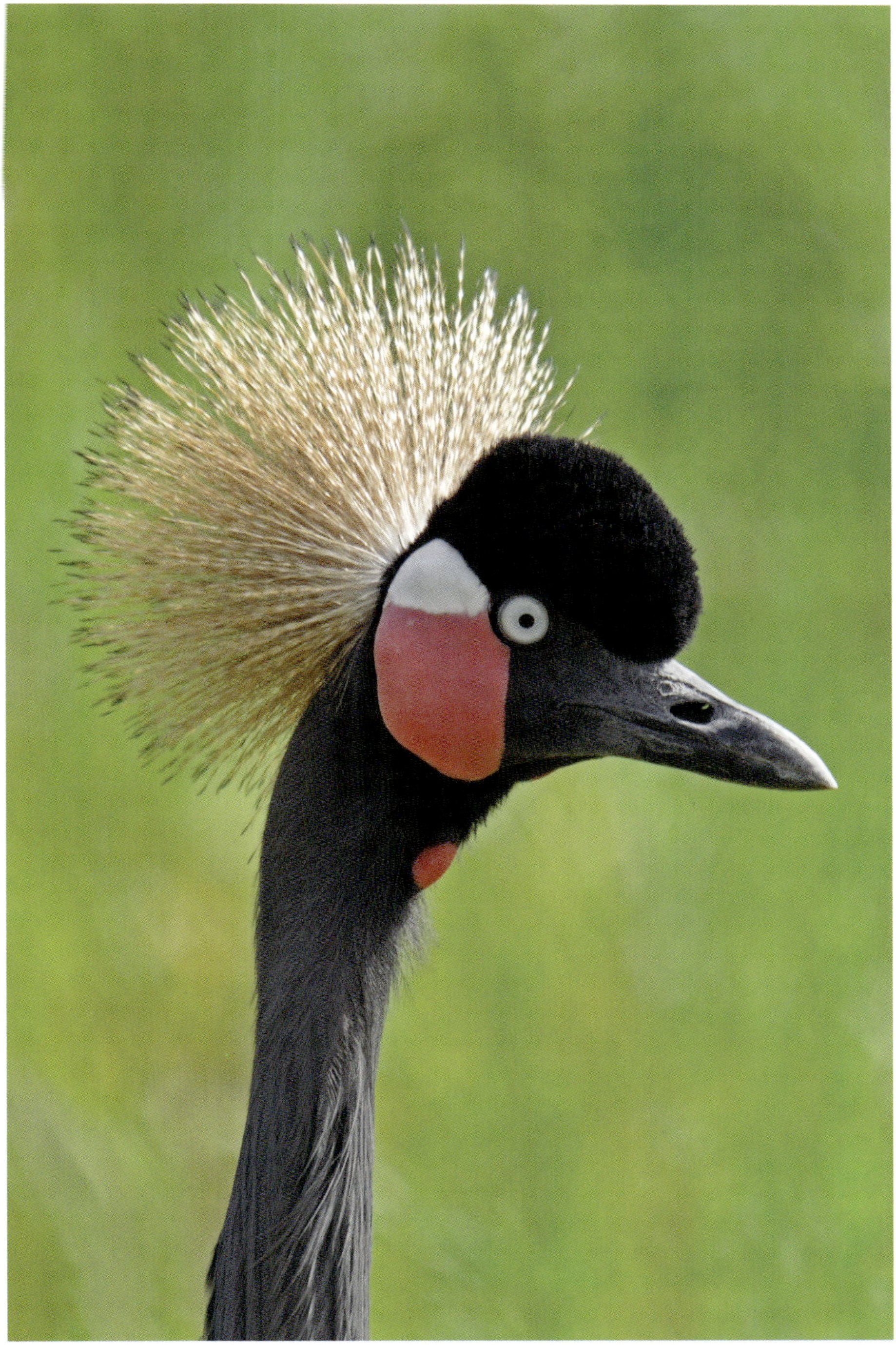

Zoo animals often follow a daily schedule similar to their wild counterparts, being active early and late in the day, while lounging in the shade or sleeping indoors at midday. The best opportunities for photographers (especially in the summer) usually occur in the hour immediately after the facility opens in the morning.

Sometimes wild birds mingle with captive species in zoos, especially wintering waterfowl who seem happy to enjoy the company of captive ducks and geese on a pond in a zoo. Early in my career as a nature photographer, I photographed wild waterfowl and other non-captive species at the National Zoo in Washington, DC. The grounds of some expansive zoos are home to other creatures that roam outside the pens, such as rabbits, birds, and squirrels.

Along with facilities formally designated as "zoos," other locations hold captive wild animals of interest to photographers. Some of these include creatures that are used in movies and advertising photos, such as grizzly bears, mountain lions, and wolves. For a fee, a photographer or group can "rent" an animal for photos with the assistance of a handler who directs it to desired backgrounds. The vast majority of published mountain lion photos have been obtained in this manner, as these elusive cats are seldom seen and rarely photographed in the wild. Other facilities house wild animals with injuries from automobile collisions or other accidents that prohibit them from returning to their natural habitat. Still other organizations keep animals for breeding or conservation purposes. One such group is the International Crane Foundation in Baraboo, Wisconsin. A leading force in the conservation and restoration of crane species worldwide, their facility houses cranes of every species in the world and provides excellent opportunities for photography.

STATE AND NATIONAL PARKS

State and national parks are among the crown jewels for wildlife photographers in both the United States and Canada. Wildlife conservation is typically one of the objectives of these parks, making them home to numerous species of mammals, birds, reptiles, amphibians, and fish. What's more, animals that live in the protected environment of a park are usually much more tolerant of human activity and approachable for photos.

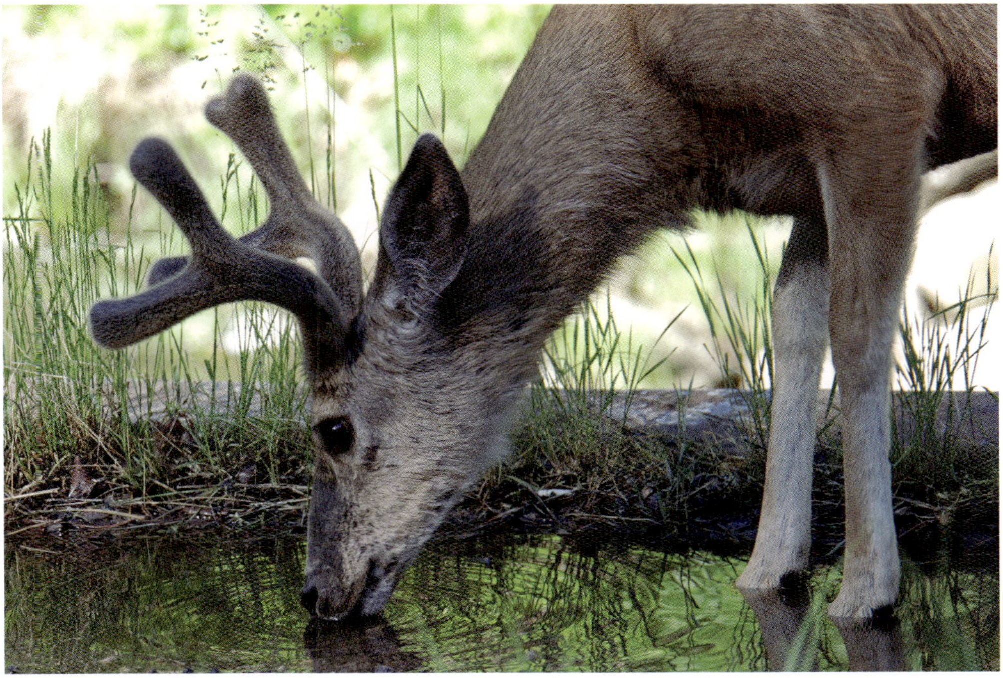

State parks can be fantastic destinations for wildlife photography. This mule deer buck drinking from a pool was taken in Custer State Park, South Dakota. *Jack Ballard*

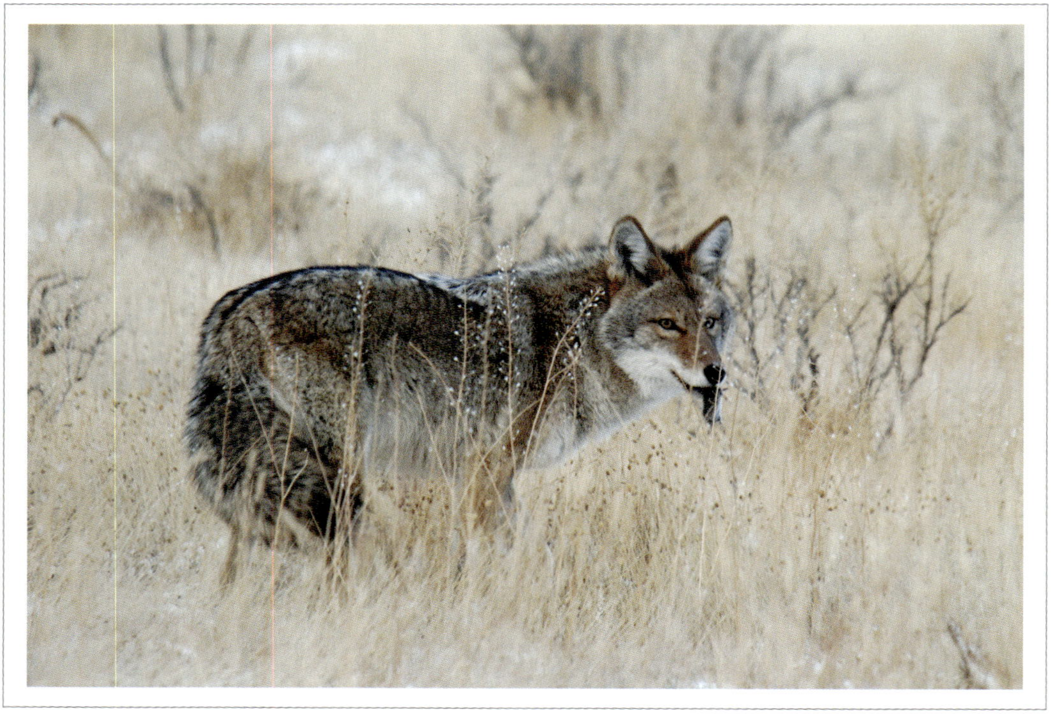

Coyotes are among the creatures predictably photographed in Yellowstone National Park in autumn. This one had just nabbed a mouse when the author clicked the shutter. *Jack Ballard*

Locating subjects in a park is often a matter of driving the roads, usually in the morning and evening when animals are most active. A light foot on the gas pedal makes it easier to spot wildlife. Working in a team where one person drives and one or more passengers look for animals is a great way to increase safety and success by keeping the driver's eyes on the road and having multiple eyeballs scanning habitat for wildlife.

Certain subjects are strongly associated with various national parks, giving a photographer very high odds of success for photographing those creatures in

Right: Wildlife often frequent campgrounds and picnic areas in national parks. This inquisitive red fox was found adjacent to a campground in Glacier National Park, Montana. *Jack Ballard*

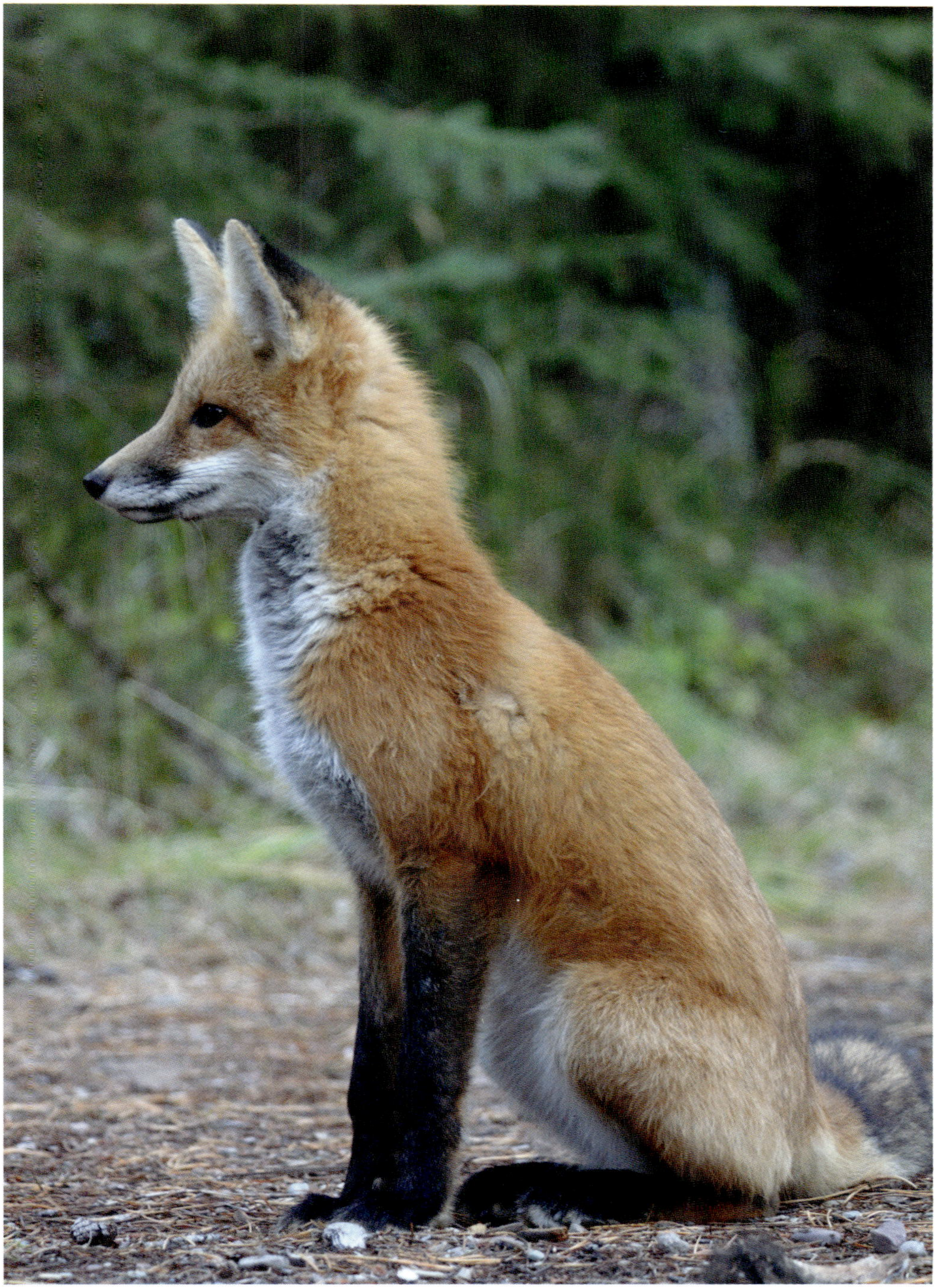

season. For example, grizzly bears can usually be photographed in Yellowstone National Park (Wyoming) in May. Elk are readily found in Rocky Mountain National Park (Colorado) in September and October. Whitetail deer make a beautiful fall subject in Shenandoah National Park (Virginia) during their mating season in November. Many state parks offer similarly predictable opportunities to photograph certain species at various times of the year.

While some photographers never venture beyond the pavement of national or state parks, those willing to hike often find more unique opportunities. A bull elk with a harem of cows near the landmark Mammoth Hotel in Yellowstone may literally be photographed over a hundred thousand times in a single autumn. However, a mobile photographer who encounters its counterpart on one of the park's many hiking trails may capture much more precious images of a unique subject in a completely different background. When I first started marketing wildlife photos to magazines, I mostly avoided the readily available subjects adjacent to the roads in popular national parks. I took to the trails instead, believing I may capture far fewer photos but acquire one-of-a-kind images that would set my work apart from the competition, a practice I continue to follow decades later.

ETHICS AND ETIQUETTE

KNOW THE RULES

The first principle of etiquette for photographing in state and national parks is knowing and following the rules. Different parks have different guidelines for how closely animals may be approached and other regulations pertinent to photographers. Photographers should also conduct themselves in a manner that does not inconvenience other visitors. If you're driving slowly to look for wildlife, pull over to let other motorists pass. A tripod can effectively block a pathway, so be aware of how your equipment might impede other visitors. If other people are photographing an animal, politely ask to take space near other guests toting a camera. Avoid being the obnoxious, under-gunned individual with a low-magnification lens who barges closer to an animal than other photographers and scares it away.

The areas around campgrounds in national parks are often reliable places to find wildlife. Some species (most notably small mammals and birds) are attracted to the crumbs inadvertently left by campers and picnickers, though it is illegal to feed animals in a national park. Others include the campground as part of their territory and are typically quite tolerant of humans.

WILDLIFE REFUGES AND WILDERNESS AREAS

From a wildlife management perspective, the purposes of wildlife refuges and federally designated wilderness areas are different from state and national parks. Wildlife refuges exist for animals, not human visitors. Some portions of wildlife refuges may be seasonally or permanently closed, and some animals in wilderness areas and wildlife refuges may be hunted. However, certain refuges and wildernesses provide superb opportunities to photograph wildlife.

Most wildlife refuges publish information regarding what species are present and at what times of the year. A good number of refuges in the middle and southern states were established to protect migrating waterfowl and other birds. While all of these contain year-round wildlife subjects, the best opportunities often occur at various times during the migration or in relation to wintering birds. Some wildlife refuges have permanent blinds that can be reserved and used for wildlife photography.

Wildlife photography in wilderness areas is not for the faint of heart, but some outstanding opportunities await the adventurous. A sprawling wilderness area, the Absaroka-Beartooth, lies just west of my home in Montana. Several

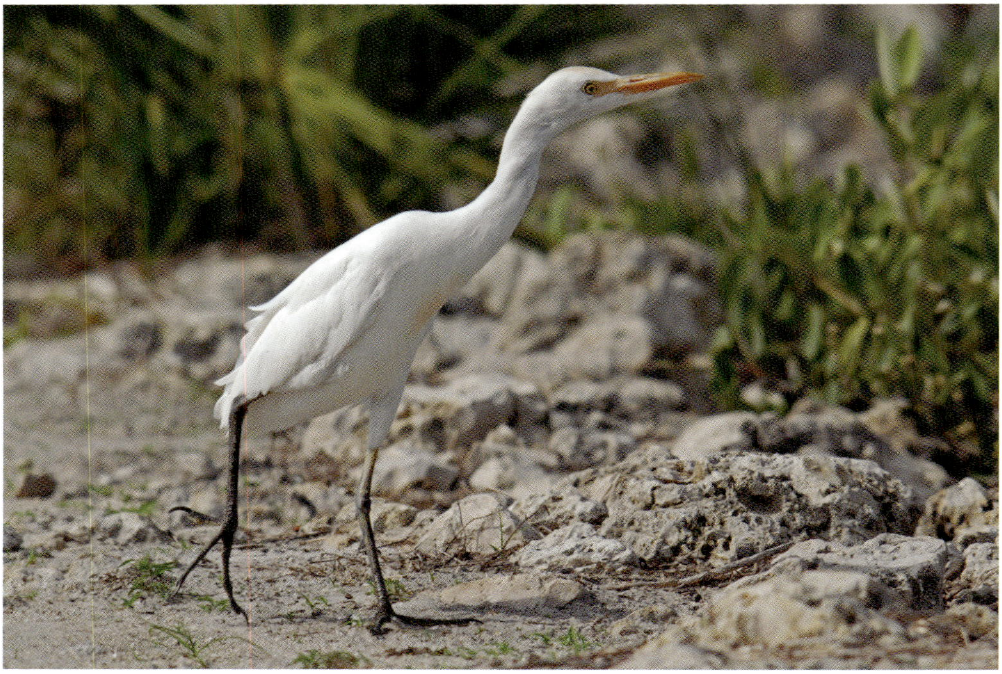

National wildlife refuges are often excellent destinations for wildlife photographers. Refuges with regular human visitation usually hold animals quite habituated to people, such as this cattle egret at a refuge in Florida. *Lisa Ballard*

locations boast very high odds of photographing mountain goats, and I've also captured images of numerous small creatures including golden-mantled ground squirrels, pikas, white-crowned sparrows, dusky grouse, snowshoe hares, and American martens. Penetrating a wilderness area usually involves some hiking. Lightweight gear allows the photographer to go further and encounter more opportunities than those burdened with weighty equipment. My standard outfit for photographing in wilderness includes an 80–400mm lens with vibration reduction for wildlife portraits and an 18–105mm lens for scenics and photographing animals in their larger habitat.

Right: Wilderness areas sometimes offer unique opportunities for wildlife photography. This white-crowned sparrow with a beak full of insects was chasing bugs on a willow in the Absaroka-Beartooth Wilderness in Wyoming. *Jack Ballard*

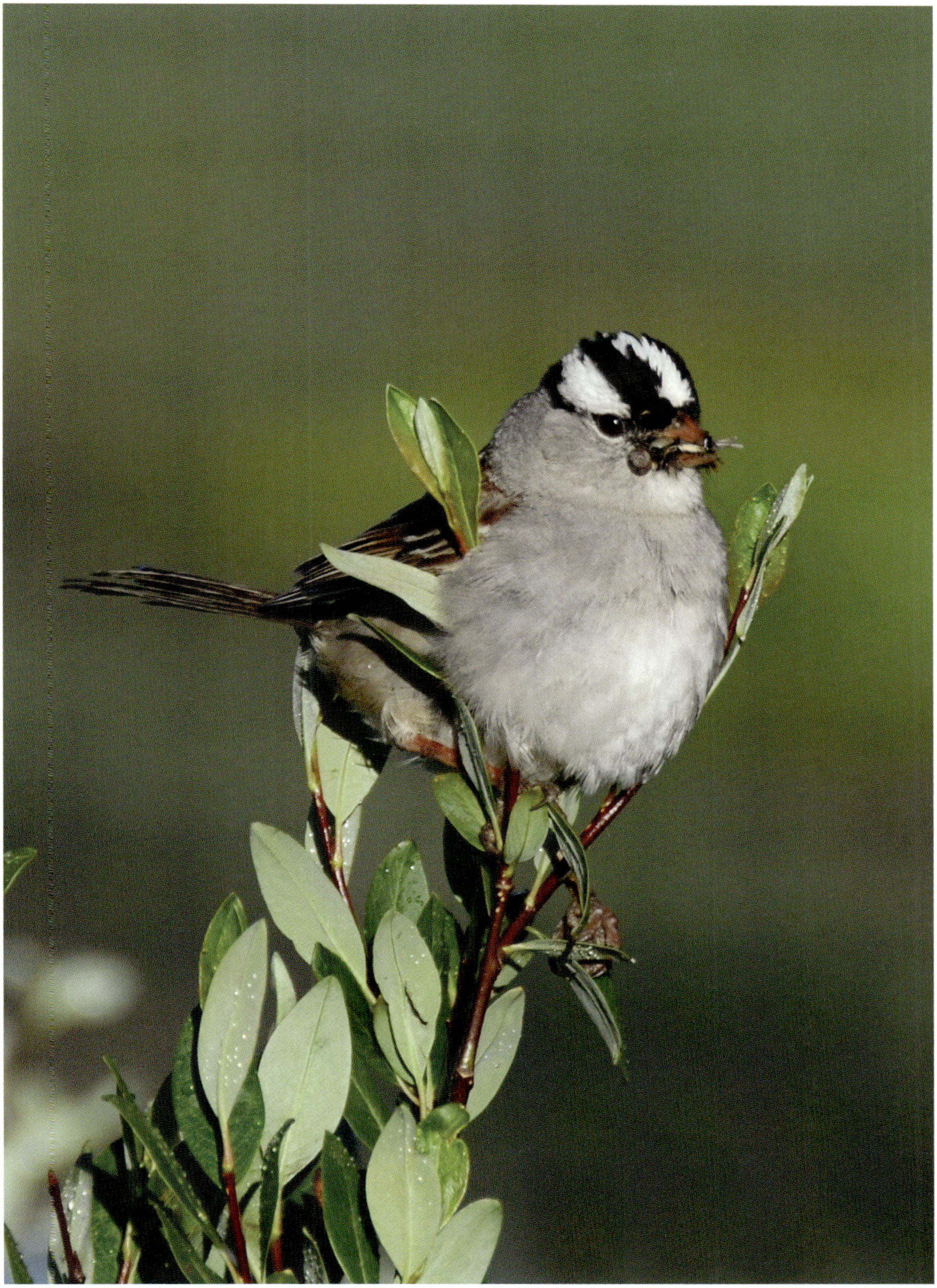

LOCAL HOT SPOTS

Parks and refuges are perennially popular with wildlife photographers, but outstanding images are often made by individuals with knowledge of local opportunities. For example, a herd of pronghorn frequents a suburban/rural interface in Billings, Montana, where I formerly lived for two decades, and some of my best pronghorn photos were taken of these animals. Some thirty minutes west of town, a fairly large, shallow lake is a favored nesting location for various shorebirds, including lovely American avocets and spindly black-necked stilts. The major catch to photographing at this location is the fact that there's only water in the lake during wet years.

Local landowners may be another source for wildlife photos. An active beaver pond on private property might host the engineering rodents along with many other creatures. A blind located at the edge of a beaver pond is an ideal way to document the many ways in which wildlife use such habitat.

ETHICS AND ETIQUETTE

PRIVATE PROPERTY

It should go without saying that a photographer should always obtain permission (written is best) to photograph on private property. Permission should also be granted to erect a permanent or portable blind. If livestock are in the area, discuss their presence with the landowner. Not only is a bad-natured bull a hazard to the photographer, but some farm animals are happy to trample a blind left in a pasture as well. One of the best ways to thank a landowner is to compose a pleasing photo of his rural residence or a scenic portion of the property. Print and frame it, then offer it as a token of your appreciation.

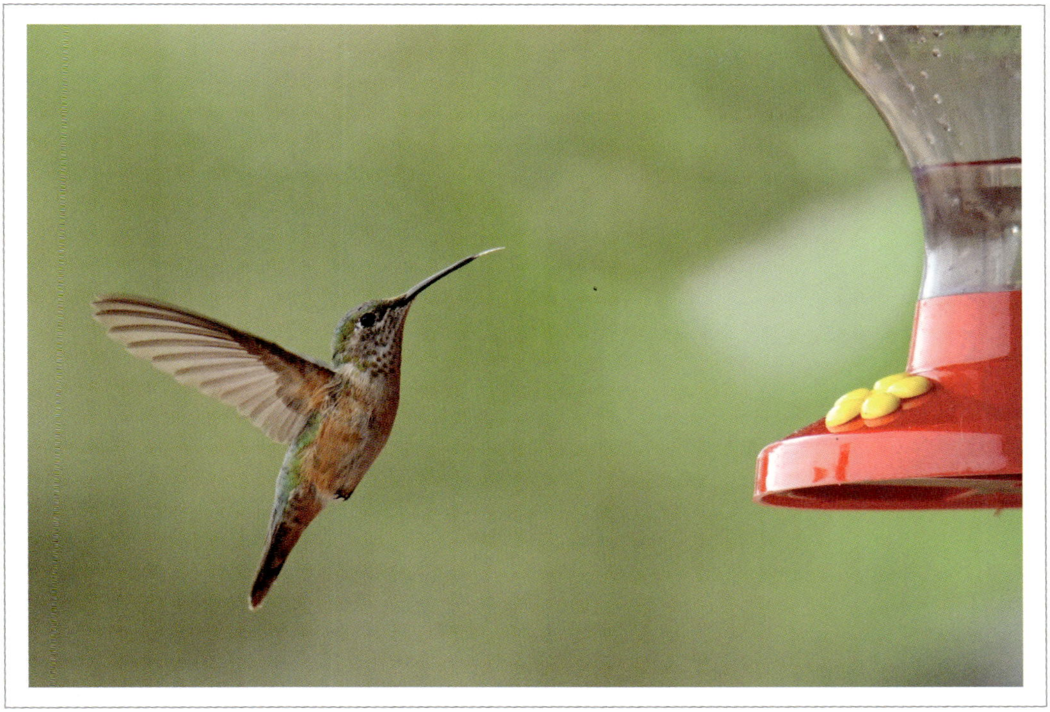

The author and his wife stumbled on a local hot spot, a coffee shop/general store in Allenspark, Colorado, that kept hummingbird feeders on its patio. This image of a female broad-tailed hummingbird is one of dozens shot at the location. *Lisa Ballard*

PHOTO TOURS AND SAFARIS

A seemingly countless number of photo tours and safaris are available for wildlife photographers who have the cash to join them. Tours to national parks in the United States are a popular way to obtain photos of high-profile wildlife species such as wolves and grizzly bears, while expeditions to faraway destinations in Africa, Antarctica, and the jungles of South America are also available. Arrangements range from single-day excursions costing around $100

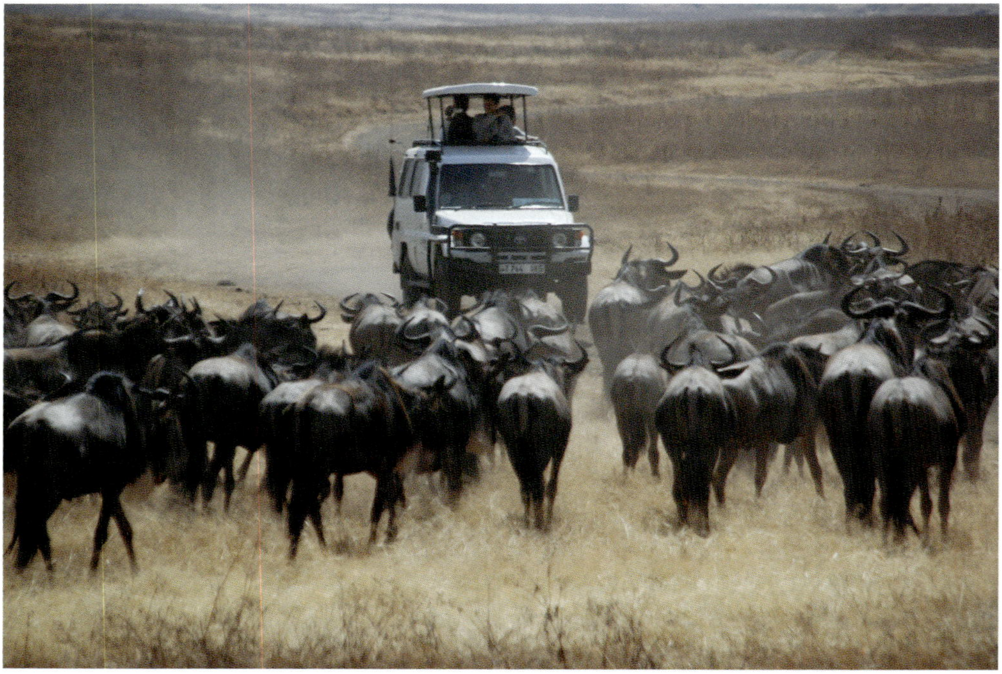

Photo tours and safaris are a reliable (but expensive) way to garner wildlife images in exotic locations. Here a tour vehicle confronts a herd of blue wildebeests in the Ngorongoro Conservation Area, Tanzania. *Jack Ballard*

at domestic locations to extended international itineraries demanding a price tag of $20,000. Some national associations organize wildlife photo tours, as do local camera clubs. These can be an affordable alternative to pricey private tours.

It's also possible to arrange do-it-yourself photo safaris, saving substantial amounts of money in the process. However, these normally require many hours of planning ahead of time and a certain amount of flexibility. A number of years ago, I and two companions completed a wildlife photo safari to several national parks in Tanzania. We arranged our own lodging and a private driver. Our driver was exceptional, and the trip yielded thousands of wildlife photos and a lifetime of memories. We also saved a bundle in relation to booking a private, photo-specific tour. That said, many, many hours were involved in planning the expedition, and any glitches in the itinerary would have been ours to overcome.

A wildlife photo tour can be a great way to capture desired photos, but given the substantial financial investment involved with most tours, it's imperative to know exactly what to expect before booking. Customer satisfaction is an important clue. Look at online reviews. Many tour operators will provide a list of references from previous customers. Ask to communicate with someone who was dissatisfied as well as those who left positive references.

Guides can make or break a photo safari. A good tour operator should be able to tell you exactly who will be guiding your tour and their credentials as photographers and teachers. The teaching skills of the guide are actually more important than traveling with a "big name" photographer. Working with a skilled teacher who's less well known is preferable to shooting with a celebrity unable to effectively communicate his knowledge to others. The ratio of guides to participants should also be discussed. If you're very confident in your photographic technique and comfortable in the environment you'll be shooting, a higher participant-to-guide ratio is okay. Think of this in terms of time. At a 10:1 participant-to-guide ratio, the average group member receives only six minutes of individual time from the guide per hour.

A frank discussion about equipment with the tour operator or guide is critical. If you show up with a 400mm lens when everyone else in the group has a 600mm, chances are you'll be frustrated as your needed distance from subject to lens is different from the rest of the group. Find out what the typical participant brings in the way of equipment and assess how yours stacks up. Tour guides that allow a high degree of independence of participants will be a better

ETHICS AND ETIQUETTE

PHOTO TOURS

Etiquette on photo tours runs the gamut of dealing with other participants to adapting to social customs in a foreign country. Basic courtesy goes a long way with other photographers. Don't cut in front of another's lens when they're shooting. Take turns when appropriate. Avoid attempting to converse with someone who is preparing or taking photos.

Occasionally groups include hyperaggressive individuals who attempt to dominate the best opportunities. This is an issue for the guide. Everyone in the group has presumably paid the same money for the experience and should receive equal opportunity. If you feel there's inequity in this aspect, discuss your concerns with the guide and firmly push for a solution.

Tipping expectations vary from tour to tour and country to country. The best approach is to have a conversation with the tour operator (not the guide) regarding tipping practices. Adjust from there. I am a firm believer in the idea that tips are a gratuity, not a requirement. However, there are parts of the world where the "tip" is actually a portion of a guide or driver's wages and failure to tip is equivalent to depriving the individual of his or her wages.

bet if you're a little "under-gunned." Discuss how much flexibility you'll have in choosing your own subjects and shooting perspectives.

Finally, make sure you thoroughly understand the demands the shooting environment will place on you and your equipment. Will biting insects be a problem? What about dust? (We encountered more of that than I care to remember in Tanzania.) Does the mode of transportation potentially lead to motion sickness? How cold will it be, and how will my gear function in severe temperatures? The answers to such questions may eliminate certain destinations from your list of potential itineraries. They will also allow you to successfully prepare for the trip of a lifetime.

OTHER TRAVEL

Our work frequently takes Lisa and me to various locations around the globe when pursuing writing assignments, photography projects, and other opportunities. Although some of this travel is not wildlife photo specific, we are always on the lookout for chances to take pictures of local wildlife. This readiness has yielded images of endangered walia ibex in Ethiopia, Andean condors in Chile, and a host of other species (including lots of birds) in the Czech Republic, England, Russia, and other locations.

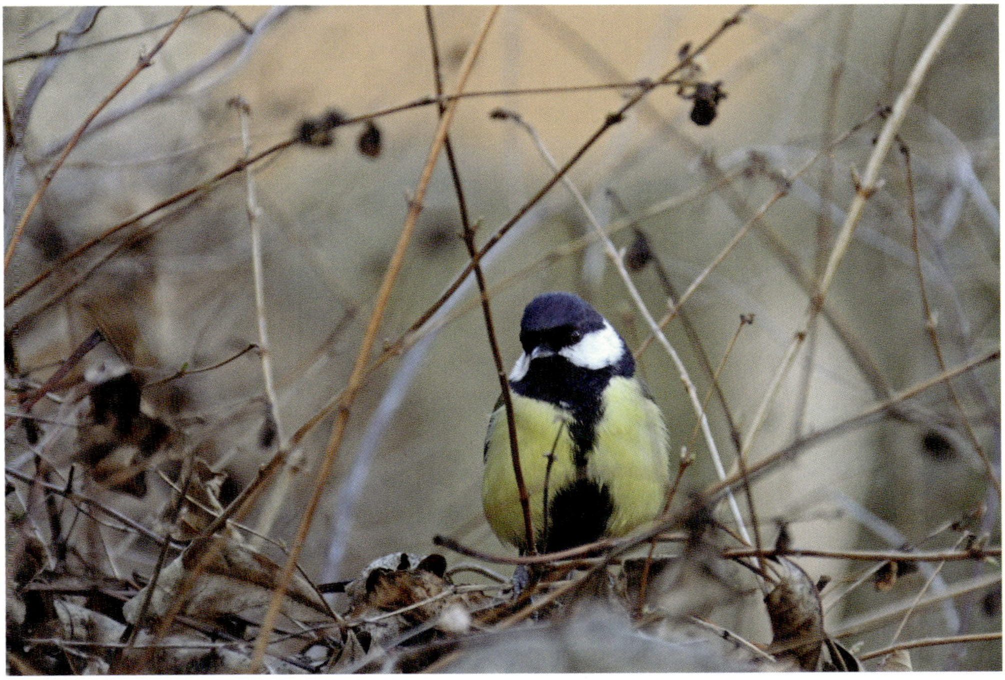

General travel can yield otherwise unavailable chance for wildlife photos. This picture of a great tit was taken in the Old Jewish Cemetery while touring Prague, Czech Republic. *Lisa Ballard*

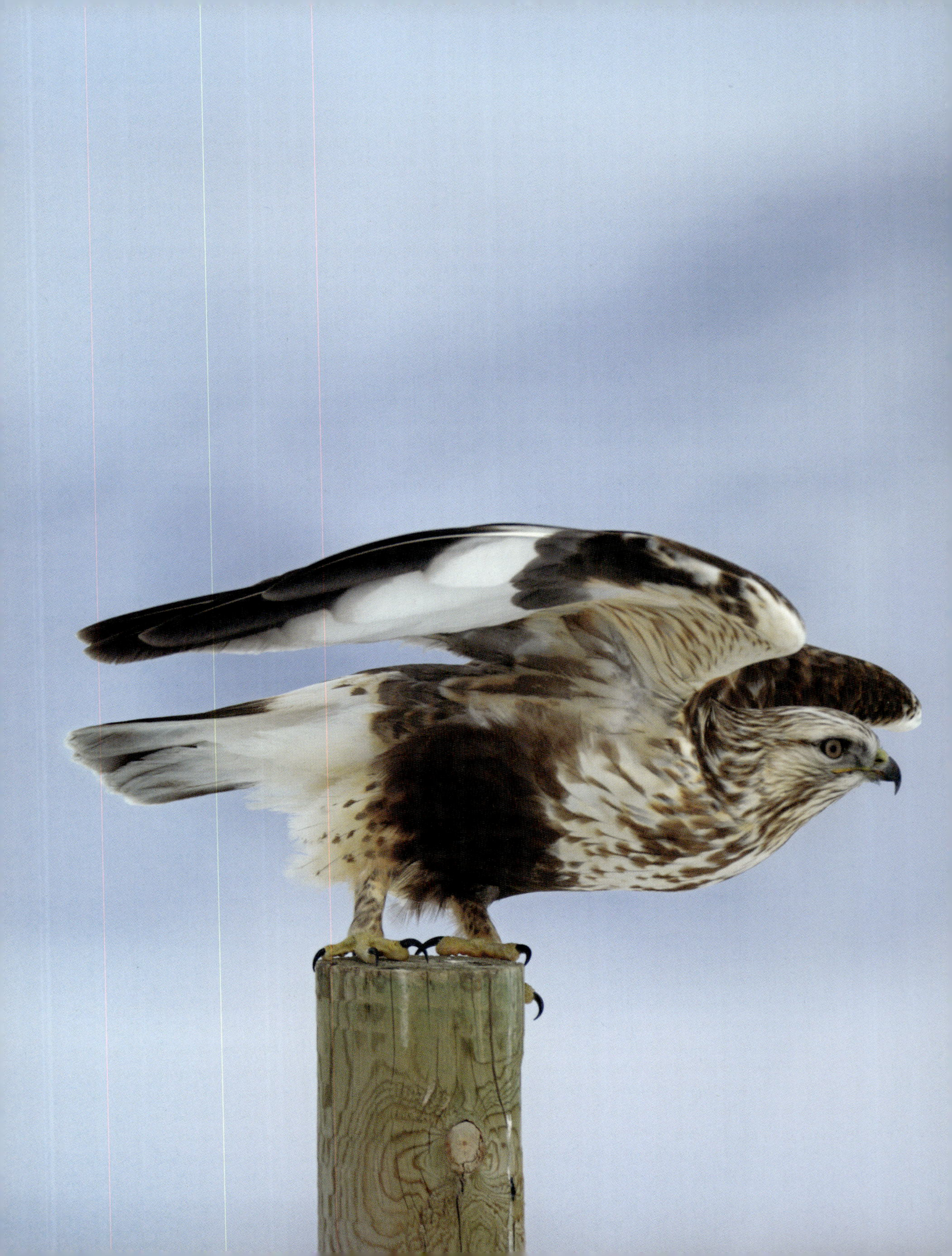

CHAPTER 6

Photographing Birds

Some 1,154 species of birds occupy North America in Mexico, the United States, and Canada. Of those, 914 species are found in the United States and Canada. Birds range in size from the ponderous California condor with a maximum wingspan of 9.5 feet and weighing 23 pounds to the tiny calliope hummingbird that weighs just 0.1 ounce and has a wingspan of slightly over 4 inches.

For sheer diversity and abundance of opportunity, there is no class of animals more attractive to the wildlife photographer than birds. Various species thrive from mountaintops to seashores, from the arctic tundra to southwestern deserts. Some birds are reclusive and exceedingly difficult to photograph. Others, such as the American robin, are quite tolerant of humans, even in locations where their contact with people is minimal.

Rough-legged hawk. *Jack Ballard*

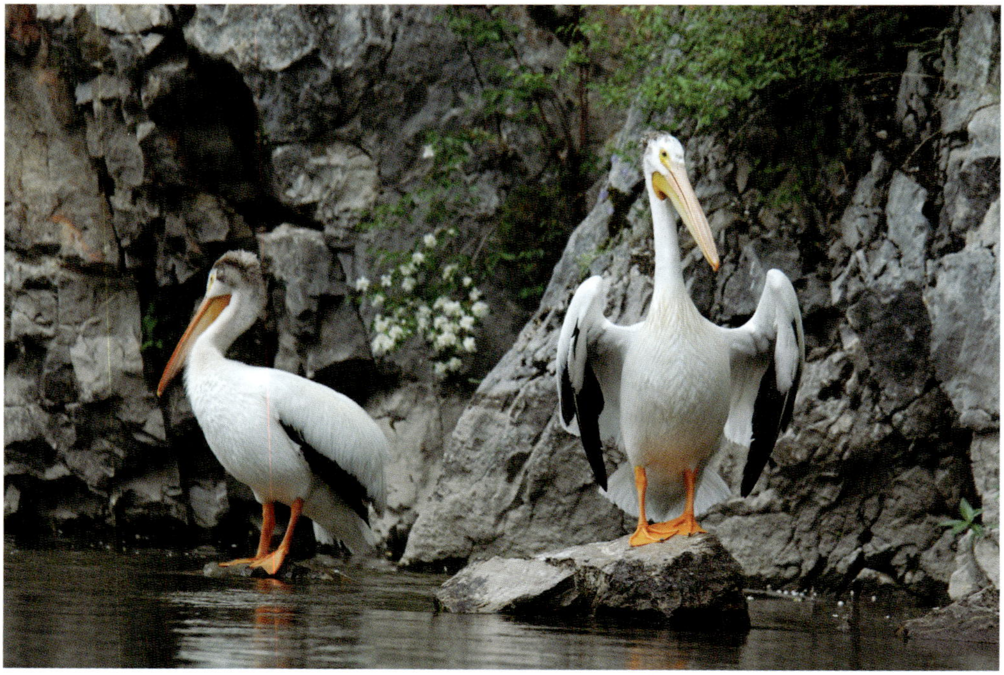

Of the 914 species of birds found in the United States and Canada, American white pelicans are among the largest and are generally easy to photograph. These were photographed from a canoe in Montana. *Jack Ballard*

BIRD BEHAVIOR BASICS

Birds, like other creatures, follow predictable behavioral patterns based on daily routines and seasonal activities. Outstanding bird photographers are ardent students of bird behavior. Understanding the behavioral peculiarities of a particular species or an individual bird allows the photographer to anticipate action and acquire the most compelling images.

Movement Patterns

Seasoned bird-watchers appreciate several general rules of bird movement that are extremely helpful to photographers. One of these is the notion that the smaller the bird, the less time it remains in one place. Observation of birds at my backyard feeders lends credibility to this maxim. Sprightly chickadees flit quickly to nab a sunflower seed, then often retire to a nearby branch to hastily peck through the shell. Red crossbills, a larger species, are more apt to camp out on the feeder or perch for a minute or two on a twig.

When dealing with little birds that are maddeningly capable of departing the frame just as you're about to click the shutter, up your odds for getting

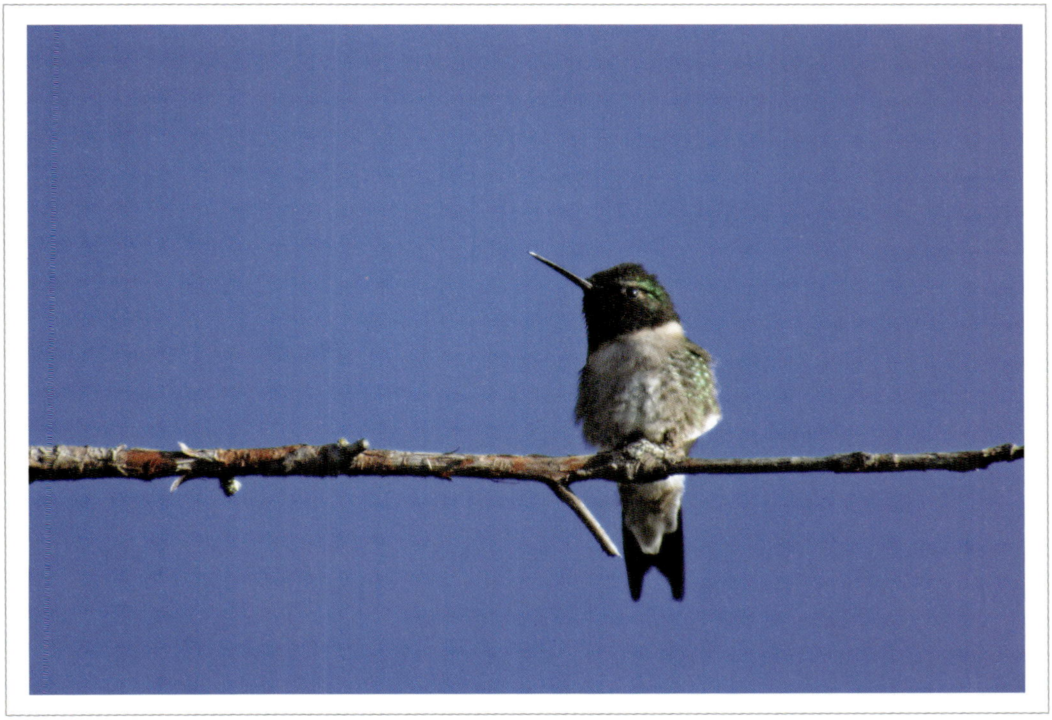

The smaller the bird, the less time it spends in one place. This black-chinned hummingbird in the Adirondack Mountains of New York perched just long enough for the author to shoot three frames. *Jack Ballard*

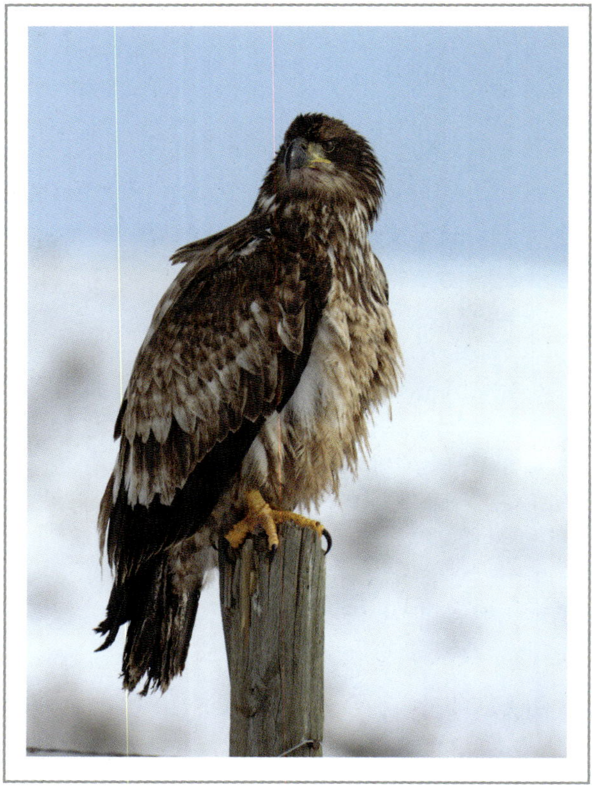

the shot by having all camera adjustments made beforehand. It's also helpful to prefocus your camera on an object at about the distance you expect the subject to appear. This reduces the amount of time it will take the camera's focus to lock on the subject.

If the bird is returning frequently to the same place (such as a chickadee using the same perch to crack its sunflower seeds), prefocus on that spot. When the subject

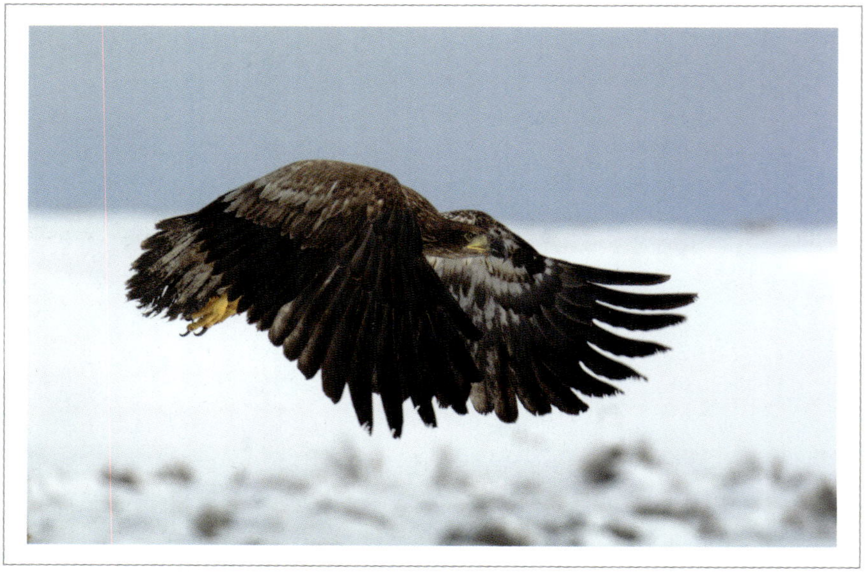

This immature bald eagle sitting on a post in central Idaho (top) lifted its tail and defecated. The author knew this was a signal it was about to fly and was able to prepare for a flight shot (bottom). *Jack Ballard*

returns, you'll be able to compose the image and shoot without wasting time focusing at all. It's also possible to frame the image as desired, lock the camera down on a tripod, and disable the auto-focus after focusing directly on the perch. This allows the fastest reaction time but gives less predictability, as birds returning to a favored perch don't always land and orient their bodies in exactly the same way.

Another less savory movement pattern known to experienced birders is the fact that birds often defecate just before flying. This behavioral aspect is extremely valuable in anticipating a bird's takeoff from a perch. On a recent trip to Idaho, I happened across an immature bald eagle perched on a fencepost near a deer that had been killed in a vehicle collision. I pulled the car off the road at an angle beyond the eagle, dropped the window, and composed several frames. When the raptor raised its tail and pooped, I knew it was showtime. It lifted from the post seconds later. Even though I was shooting a hefty 500mm lens (not the best for flight shots), I was able to successfully garner a half-dozen nice images of the eagle in takeoff.

Seasonal Activities

The lives of many birds are governed by daily rituals. Most also follow a yearly cycle of activity: nesting, molting (replacing feathers), mating, and sometimes migrating. Astute wildlife photographers are in tune with the seasonal activities of the species they endeavor to photograph and use this understanding to capture better images.

The males of most species have more vibrant plumage than females. Colorful males achieve their showiest feathers in preparation for the mating season, an adaptation thought to attract females. Thus the best time to capture an image of most male ducks in their best plumage is from fall to spring. They are rather dull in appearance in late summer during a phase known as "eclipse plumage."

Seasonal activities can also be related to food sources. The ripening of berries may predictably bring birds to an area. At one of my former residences, crab apples remaining on a tree in late winter invariably attracted cedar waxwings. Along the coastlines, seasonal arrivals of small fish or other prey may provide a feeding boon to wading birds.

The mating season of birds is another important part of the seasonal behavioral cycle of keen interest to photographers. Courtship among many bird species involves fascinating rituals such as dancing, acrobatic flight, and

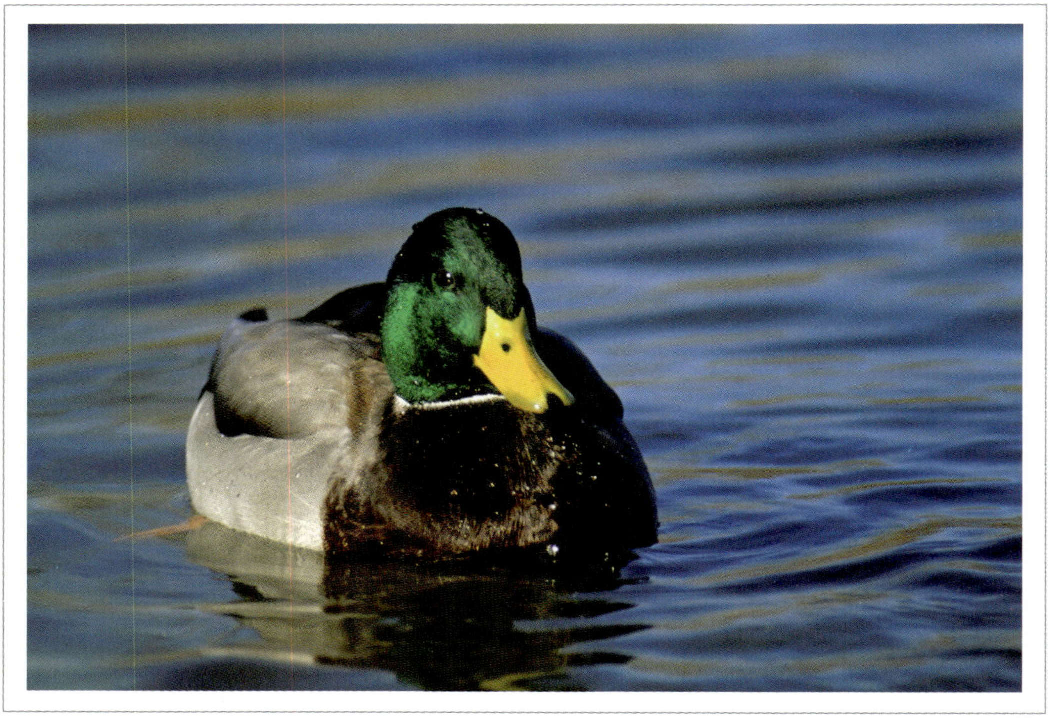

Male birds carry their brightest coloration during the mating season. This classic image of a mallard drake was taken in very early spring in Colorado. *Jack Ballard*

sometimes violent clashes between males seeking the attention of the same female. Males of numerous migratory species return to nesting grounds before the females to claim a territory they defend from other males. When the females arrive, the suitors attempt to entice a mate into their territory, often with songs (that are sometimes not melodic at all, such as with yellow-headed blackbirds) and elaborate displays that may involve ruffling feathers or spreading wings. These mating behaviors provide opportunities for some of the most dramatic photos of the year and underscore the principle that the better the photographer understands the yearly cycle of birds in an area, the greater his or her opportunity.

Migrations

Hundreds of species of birds, from hawks to hummingbirds, engage in yearly migrations, some covering thousands of miles. A common migration pattern among birds is nesting during the summer in the north and wintering at warmer locations in the south.

Many of these migrations entail regular stopover points or terminate in known locations, bringing species within range of local photographers for just certain months (or days) of the year. In my area, rough-legged hawks arrive from northern

ETHICS AND ETIQUETTE

STRESSED BIRDS

Irruptions of birds during a tough winter create rare opportunities to photograph species not typically found in one's area. However, it's imperative to understand that these events arise due to unusual wintering conditions that create stress for birds. The arrival of a northern species such as a snowy owl might create quite a buzz among local bird-watchers and photographers. Dozens of people attempting to view or photograph the visitor may push it from perch to perch or disrupt its hunting if they get too close. Take your pictures from a distance. If the bird flushes due to your presence, back off. Unnecessary activity further stresses an already disrupted creature. Its survival is more important than acquiring its photograph.

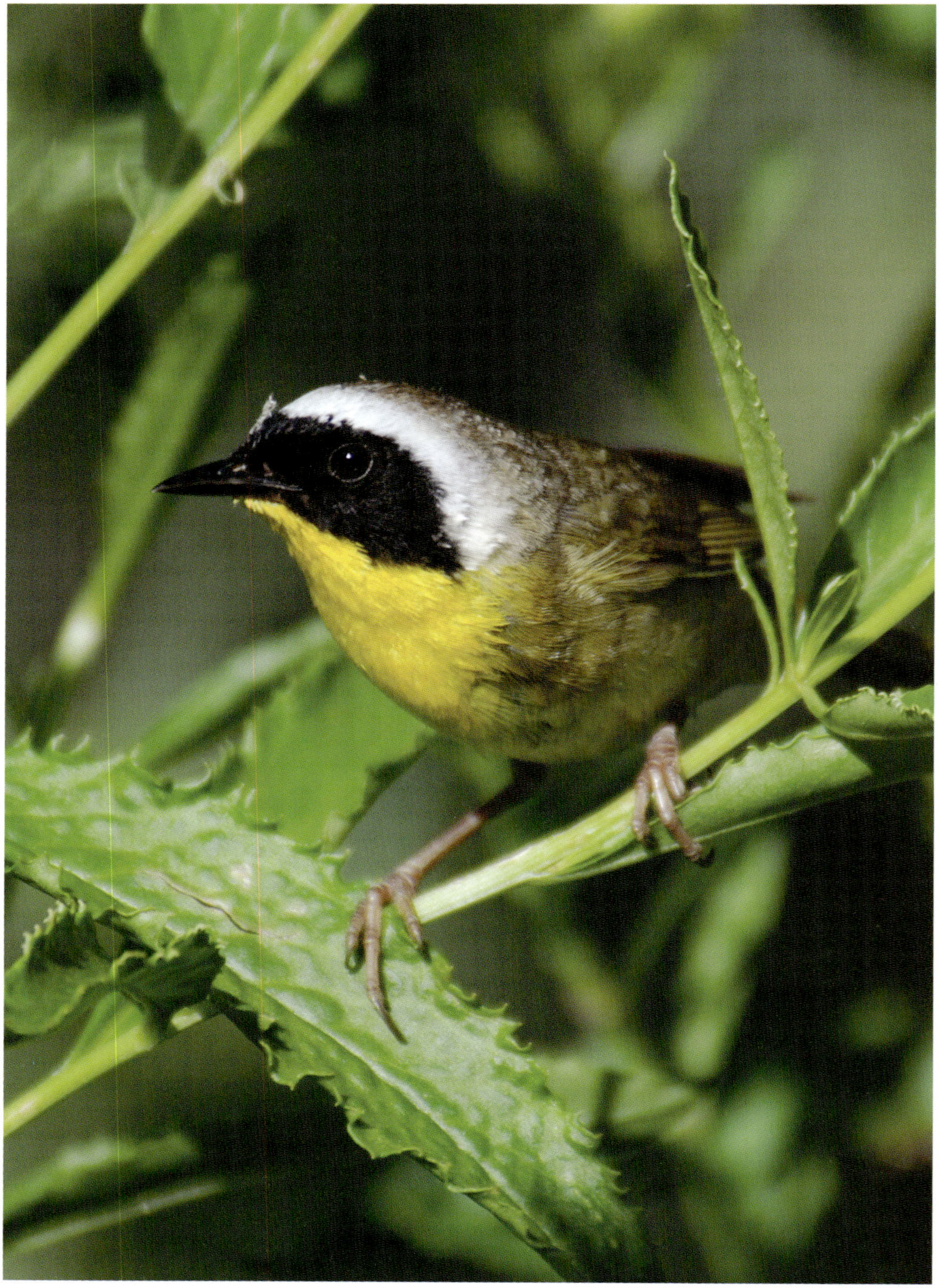

locations, their numbers especially high during severe winters. Winter "irruptions" of many species occur when a particularly severe winter moves birds to areas much farther south than their normal wintering areas. Local irruptions can also occur. During one exceptionally snowy winter, I photographed a great gray owl on a creek bottom in the foothills of the Absaroka Mountains, at an elevation much lower than normally preferred by this mountain-loving species.

BACKYARD BIRD PHOTOGRAPHY

Several professional photographers with whom I'm acquainted have invested hundreds of hours of labor and considerable resources creating designer habitat on their property for birds. This has involved developing water resources, planting trees and shrubs with flowers and/or fruit that attract birds, and creating winter cover. They also maintain nest boxes and provide forage, from sunflower seeds and oranges in feeders to planted grains in small plots, to bring birds within camera range. The payoff is opportunities to create superior bird photos with a high degree of certainty and a broad array of species at which to point a camera.

However, backyard bird photography can be rewarding almost anywhere and with a more modest investment of time and resources. For nearly a decade, I lived in a suburban neighborhood in Billings, Montana. My home had a large backyard with a variety of trees and shrubs. I enhanced the habitat with a few plantings (berry bushes and sunflowers) but mostly upped its attractiveness to birds with feeders, a year-round birdbath (kept ice-free in the winter with a heater), and nest boxes. My reward was hundreds of memorable images of our feathered

Left: Common yellowthroats nest in northern states (this male was photographed in Montana) but winter in southern locations. Local photographers have access to this species only at certain times of the year. *Jack Ballard*

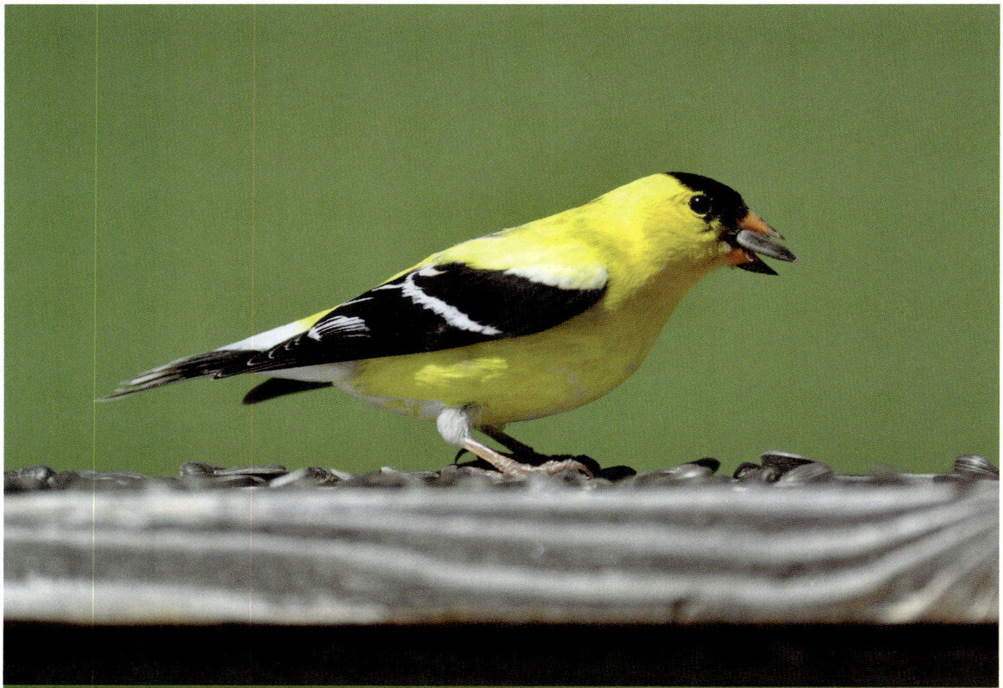
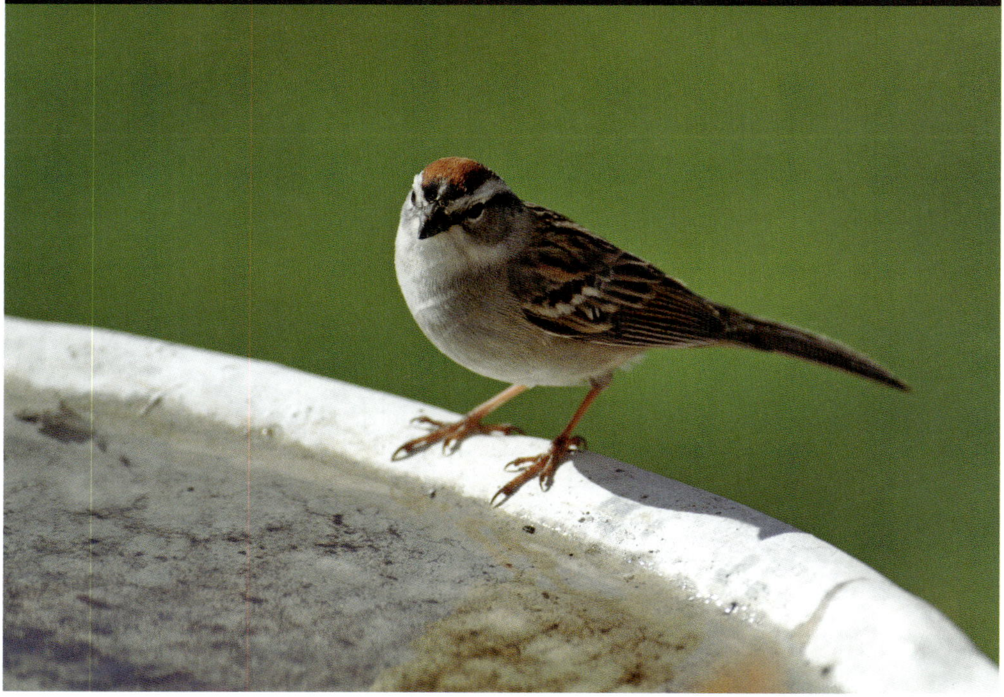

visitors, including northern flickers, downy woodpeckers, red-breasted nuthatches, American robins, yellow warblers, house wrens, eastern screech-owls, dark-eyed juncos, cedar waxwings, and a Cooper's hawk (looking to nab other birds for a meal).

Nest boxes and feeders were placed so most of my photos could be shot from an open window in the house. Others were taken from the window of my children's backyard playhouse. Strategically placed perches near feeders provided expected places for the birds to alight, providing a desirable background and lighting. I have since moved to Red Lodge, Montana, where similar efforts have yielded comparable opportunities for bird photography with a different mix of species.

Compared to birds unhabituated to humans, backyard birds are often more easily approached. This allows photographers with more modest equipment to acquire pleasing pictures. A 300mm lens is often sufficient for backyard

ETHICS AND ETIQUETTE

PROVIDING FOOD AND WATER FOR BACKYARD BIRDS

Feeders, nest boxes, and water sources placed by photographers provide backyard birds all the necessities of life: something to eat and drink, and a protected place to rear their young. Although most wild birds are flexible and opportunistic in their diets, experts warn that birds habituated to a food source may have a difficult time if it is suddenly withdrawn, especially during a period of vulnerability such as nesting or in winter. It is thus imperative to be consistent in providing food. Nest boxes should be cleaned after each brood to prevent diseases and parasites. Water sources must be cleaned regularly for similar reasons. A variety of organizations provide information regarding bird-feeding and backyard bird habitats. Respect for the creatures we photograph demands the highest standards of care for their well-being.

Left: Providing food and water is a predictable way to draw a variety of species to one's backyard. Shown are an American goldfinch at a simple platform feeder (top) and a chipping sparrow at a birdbath (bottom). *Jack Ballard* photography. Zoom lenses in the 70–300mm range add flexibility in composition. Cameras with remote-control capabilities allow a high level of creativity and experimentation in backyard photography. For example, a tripod-mounted, remotely triggered camera can be prefocused on a perch at close range. This technique allows close-ups or wide-angle compositions at ranges unachievable to a photographer on foot or even in a blind.

PHOTOGRAPHING FROM A BLIND

A blind, or "hide" (as it's known in European circles), is simply a place of concealment for a hunter or photographer. Blinds, often in the form of a small hut, are permanently erected at some wildlife refuges and other public management areas for birds and may be open to photographers. Many professionals use portable blinds for bird photography. Some store-bought blinds are specially designed for photography, but blinds made for hunters can be used as well. The advantage of photo-specific blinds is the placement of openings for the lens. A good photo blind has lens openings at ground level for the photography of ground-dwelling birds, while hunting blinds typically do not. However, most blinds can be modified with a knife, fabric, and tape to accommodate lens openings wherever you'd like them.

Odds are extremely high you already own one of the best bird photography blinds in existence, your automobile. It's the proverbial "rare bird' that hasn't seen a car. In fact, most birds encounter autos on a regular basis. Early in my career as a photographer, I once parked a pickup near a tiny wetland on the family ranch in western Montana to photograph red-winged blackbirds. I left

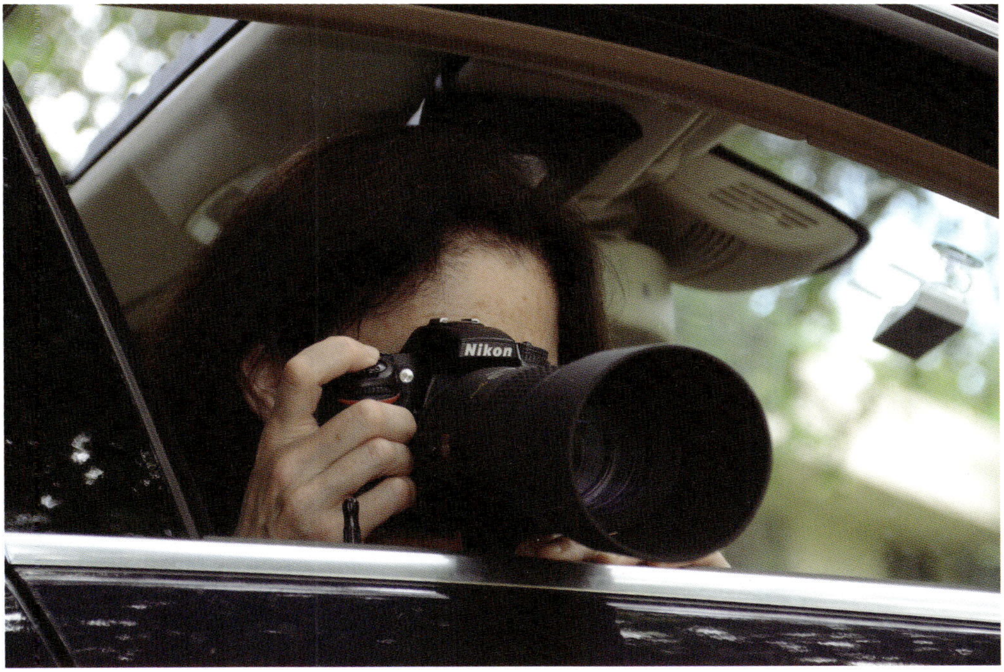

A vehicle makes a very good blind. Many birds will quickly accept a parked car as a part of the environment.
Jack Ballard

the old pickup there for several days with a piece of cloth draped over an open window, a slit for my camera's lens cut into the fabric. It worked perfectly.

Birds flushed from a roadside pond by a vehicle will often return quite quickly in the presence of a parked car, as long as you stay inside. For lighter equipment, braces that attach to a car window with a tripod adapter make fine stabilizers. Large lenses can be braced against the door frame with good results. Depending on the seating configuration, a tripod can sometimes be used from inside the vehicle. If your vehicle has mirrors that fold in, collapse them before shooting, as birds have an uncanny ability of posing for photos behind automobile mirrors.

No matter what type of blind is used, good field techniques will result in more photo opportunities. Movement is what usually alarms birds. Fight the temptation to rapidly move your lens in the direction of a newly arrived subject. When possible, orient your lens in the direction the birds you're targeting are most likely to arrive to minimize the distance you must move the camera to take a photo. Take care not to touch the sides of the blind. Be quiet. While the human voice doesn't seem to bother some birds, it can be alarming to others. If using a blind that's in continuous use or will remain in place for a period of time, enter and exit the blind before and after birds are active if possible. The

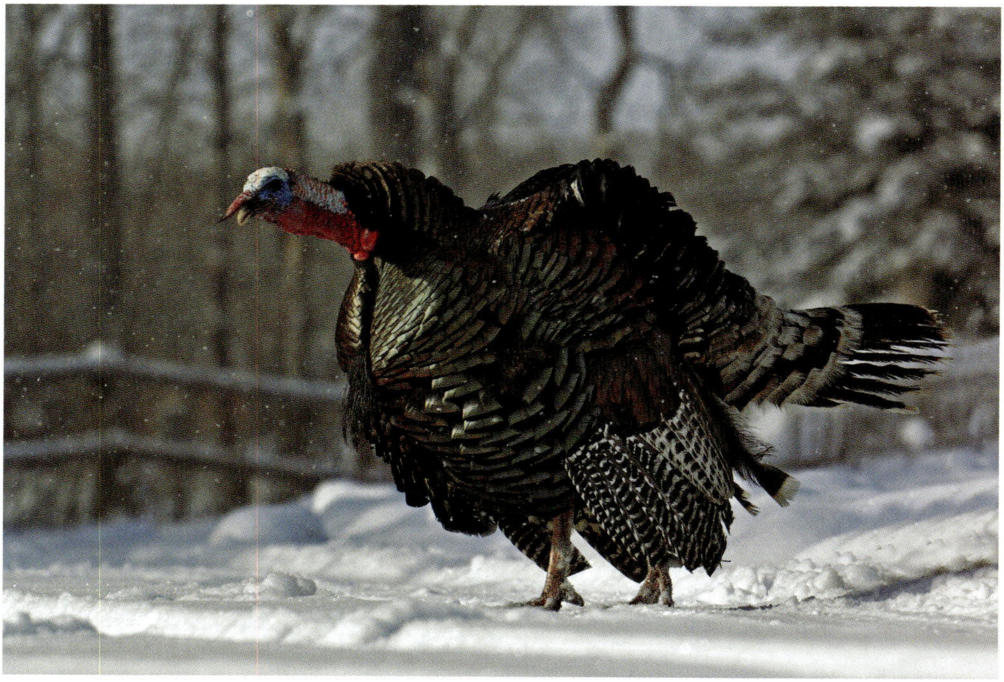

The author waited behind his car (pulled off the side of a rural road) to capture this unusual image of a strutting wild turkey gobbler in a spring snowstorm. *Jack Ballard*

Right: This portable blind was used on a photo project in Nebraska and put in place a week before use to give birds and other wildlife time to accept its presence. *Jack Ballard*

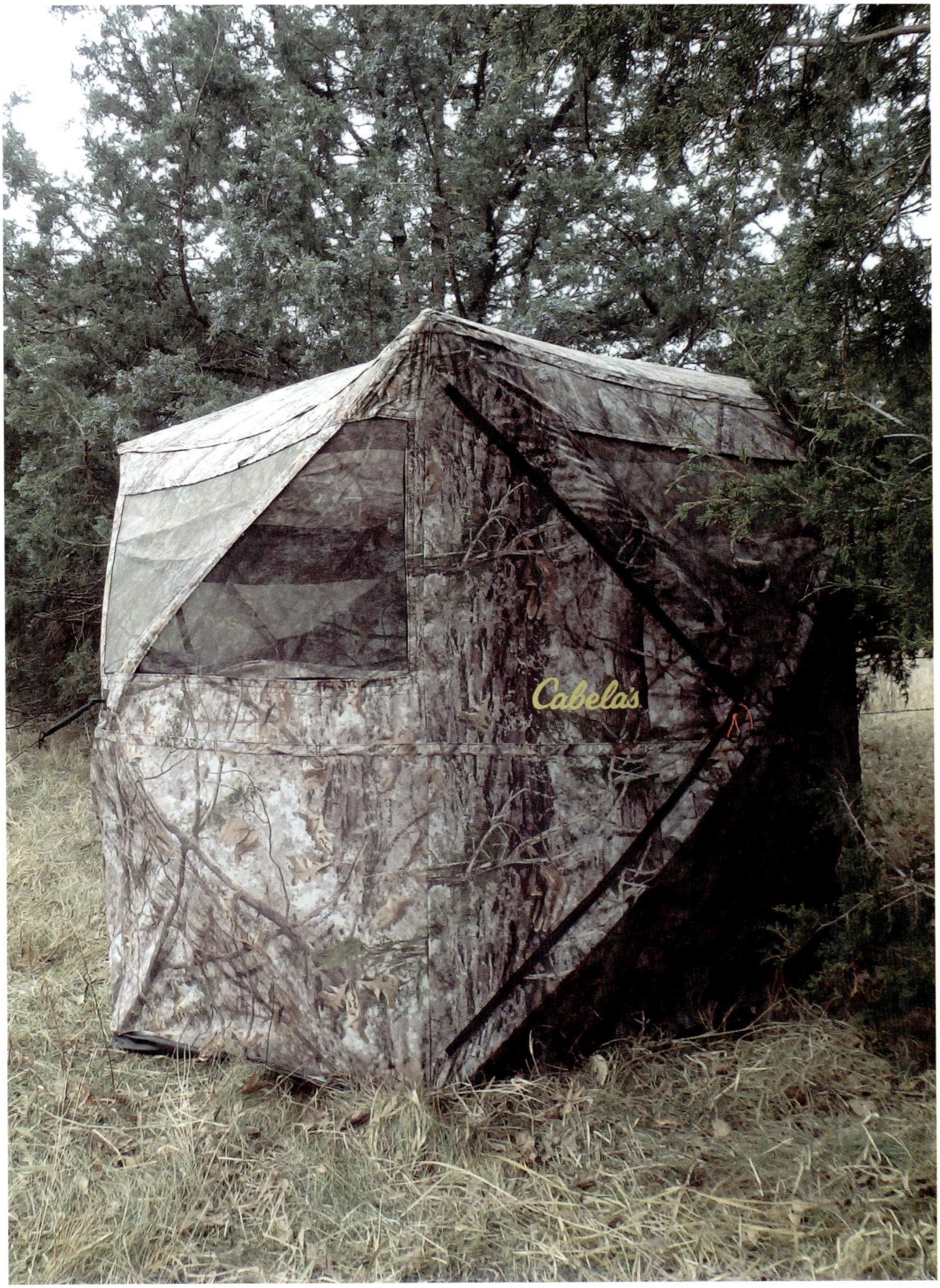
Cabela's

ETHICS AND ETIQUETTE

KNOW THE RULES

When photographing from a car, be sure to pull completely from the road to insure your own safety and that of other motorists. Pay attention when exiting the vehicle on the side facing the road.

Some wildlife refuges and parks have blinds available to the public. Many of these require advance reservations or a "sign in" with the governing agency if the blind is vacant. Know and follow the rules. Regulations regarding the placement of portable blinds on refuges or other public lands vary from agency to agency and location to location. Some places allow daily placement of blinds, while others may allow them to be left overnight.

less wary birds associate your blind with other creatures, the greater their acceptance of it as part of the natural environment.

Blind placement and camera equipment choices should be dictated by the subject. Blinds placed several days (or weeks) before use offer the greatest rewards as birds become accustomed to their presence. Raptors are typically very skittish and often take flight at the slightest movement. Photographing raptors from a blind often requires a long telephoto lens (500mm or longer) and placement of the blind well away from the subject. By contrast, some birds become very tolerant of blinds in a short period of time and may land within feet (or inches) of a lens poking from the hide. I therefore like to have a variety of lenses available when shooting from a blind, if space allows, to afford more framing options and be able to photograph when birds are very close. Long telephoto lenses have relatively lengthy focusing distances. If that's all you carry to the blind, you may find yourself frustrated by subjects too close for the focusing capabilities of your lens.

PHOTOGRAPHING NESTING BIRDS

The photography of nesting birds is as much a subject of ethics as one of equipment and technique. (I have thus chosen to discuss ethical considerations directly instead of communicating them in a sidebar.) Some ornithologists and wildlife photographers believe nesting birds should never be photographed. Their reasoning is simple: The presence of a photographer, they believe, inevitably creates stress for the parent birds. It also may broadcast the presence of the nest to predators, both wild animals and domestic threats such as dogs and especially house cats.

As a word of caution, photographing rare or endangered species while nesting is strongly discouraged and sometimes illegal. The risk of these birds abandoning a nest or losing offspring due to stress or predation is simply too high to justify photography under any circumstance.

However, many respected bird photographers photograph some nesting birds, albeit with an exceptionally high degree of care. The key to ethical photography of nesting birds, they believe, is a highly tuned sense of behavior and a commitment to cease photography when the nesters give any indication of disruption, including a lengthening of time a bird stays away from the nest due to the presence of a photographer. Eggs and very young hatchlings can perish due to cold or malnutrition quite quickly. Extended absences of parent birds increase the odds of both.

The toleration for humans of an individual bird or pair of parents (with some species both parents are involved in rearing the young; with others only one parent does the rearing) is key to photographing nesting birds. For example,

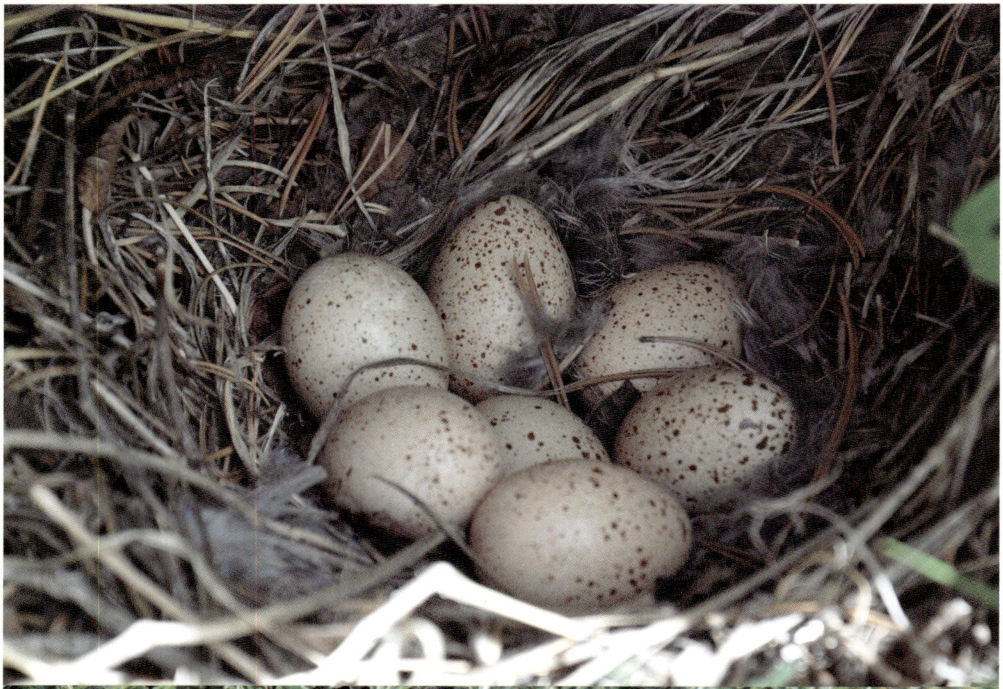

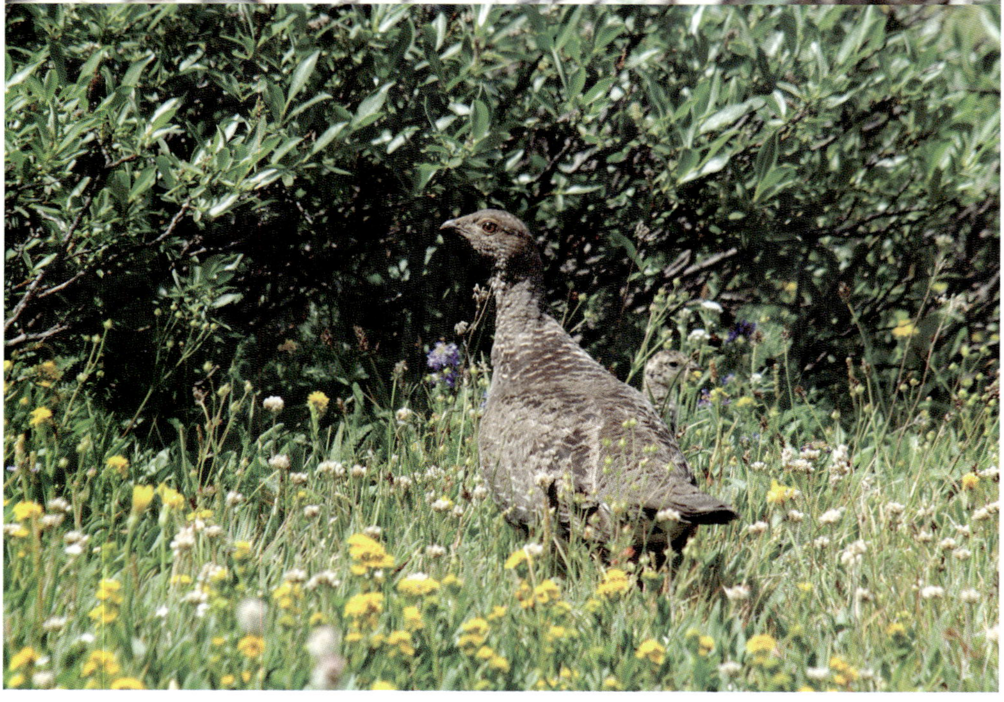

nesting American robins are often very tolerant of people, especially if the observer is a frequent and benign visitor to the nesting area, but on some occasions I have encountered robins that are very skittish around the nest and unsuitable for ethical photos.

From the standpoints of both ethics and effectiveness, the best way to photograph birds is from a blind established at a known nesting site before it is claimed by the subject. For example, I have often placed nest boxes within camera range of the windows of my house to allow photography of cavity nesters such as chickadees and nuthatches from a bedroom window. I've similarly placed portable blinds at known nesting sites prior to the nesting season to photograph waterfowl.

Photographing from a preestablished blind is often the best way to photograph nesting birds, but what about situations where the photographer stumbles upon a nest during a hike or while paddling a canoe? Is it okay to photograph birds in those situations?

Some would say "no," but many photographers take advantage of such situations. The key is to carefully gauge the reaction of the nesting female or the parent(s) caring for the young. Flushing a female that's incubating eggs on a nest and delaying her return by your presence probably dooms the hatch. Disrupting the care of newly hatched young likewise dramatically reduces their prospects for survival. If you decide to photograph a nesting bird you've sighted, approach very slowly and with frequent, long pauses. The first indication of alarm from the bird is a signal to back off.

Left: The author accidentally flushed a female blue grouse from her nest while hiking in the Absaroka Mountains of Montana. He left the area immediately to avoid keeping her from the nest. Weeks later his wife was rewarded with this photo of the mother and one of her young. *Jack Ballard and Lisa Ballard*

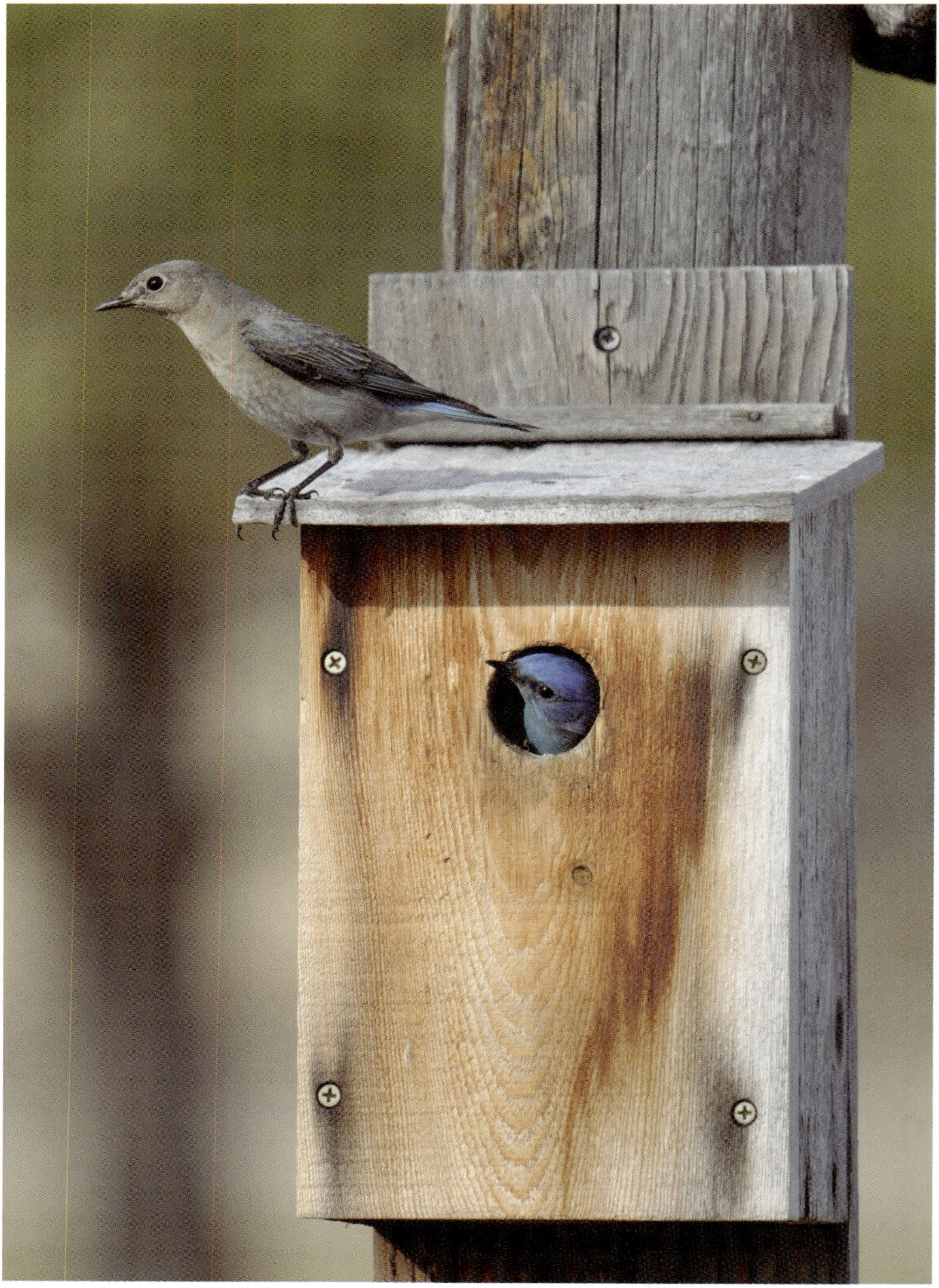

However, some nesters are very tolerant of humans, especially if they're introduced to people at comfortable distances over time. The late Tom Ulrich, one of the outstanding wildlife photographers of my generation, once befriended a female grebe nesting on a pond near his home. The mother became so tolerant of his presence over the course of the year that she completely accepted him to the point of allowing him within inches of herself and her offspring.

Shooting eye level with the subject is the most desirable camera angle for the bulk of wildlife photography, and this principle is doubly true photographing nesting birds. Shooting up at a nest yields pictures of a bird's head and the nest, but acquiring a level or slightly elevated position gives better portraits showing the whole subject and the nest environment. Although this is difficult

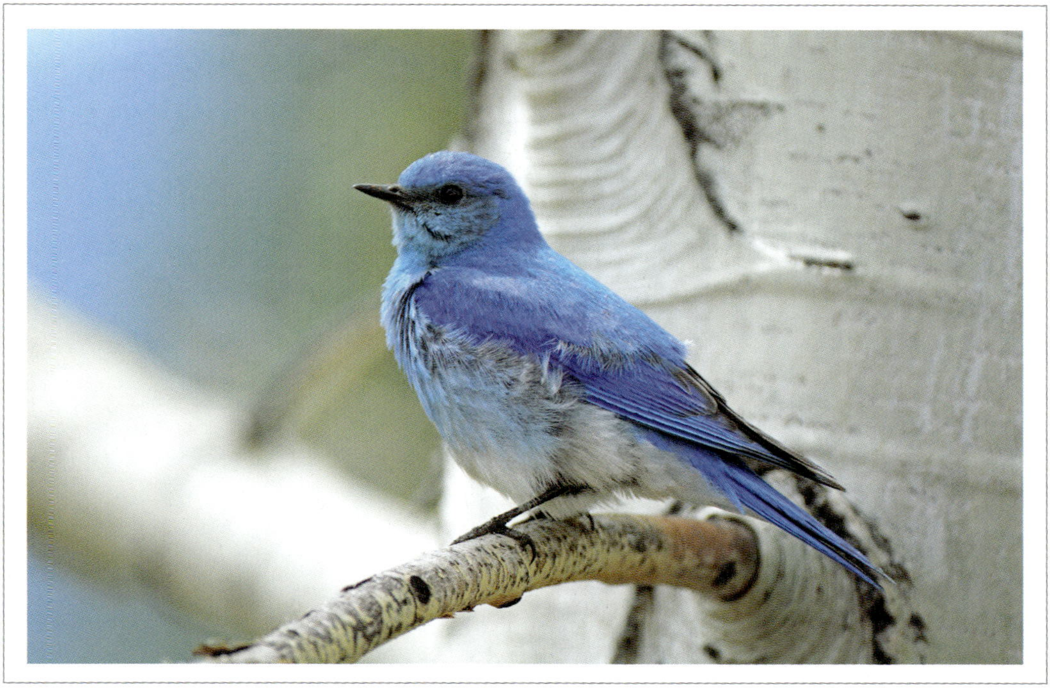

These mountain bluebirds at a nest box in the author's backyard (left) became extremely tolerant of his presence, allowing hundreds of eye-level photos of the nesting habitat and portraits of the individual birds (right). *Jack Ballard*

to achieve with birds nesting on high platforms, such as an osprey on a power pole, topography sometimes allows a photographer (usually with a very high-magnification lens) to shoot down toward such a nest or at eye level. Nests of accepting backyard birds can often be photographed on the level by using a step ladder. Introduce the ladder as an object in the bird's world from a distance. Once "okayed" from a safe buffer, it can be moved closer. Be especially vigilant of the bird's behavior, as a step up a ladder seems to trigger a predator-aversion response in some birds, possibly akin to a cat starting to climb a tree.

FLIGHT PHOTOGRAPHY

Flight photos are some of the most treasured yet difficult to acquire images of our feathered neighbors. Some birds, such as soaring bald eagles or turkey vultures, are quite easy to photograph, though often it is challenging to find them within camera range. Others, such warblers and sparrows, move so quickly and erratically that planning flight photos is nearly impossible, although it never hurts to hazard a flight photo even when the odds are low.

The photographer's equipment is highly determinative of his or her consistent success with flight photography. Lenses that focus quickly and cameras with accurate focusing-tracking capabilities and high frame rates greatly improve one's potential for success. Technique is also important. The art of following a moving subject (panning) while keeping it in the frame takes much practice to achieve. This is equally as difficult with a handheld camera as one mounted on a tripod, but is a critical skill for reliably producing focused, nicely composed flight pictures.

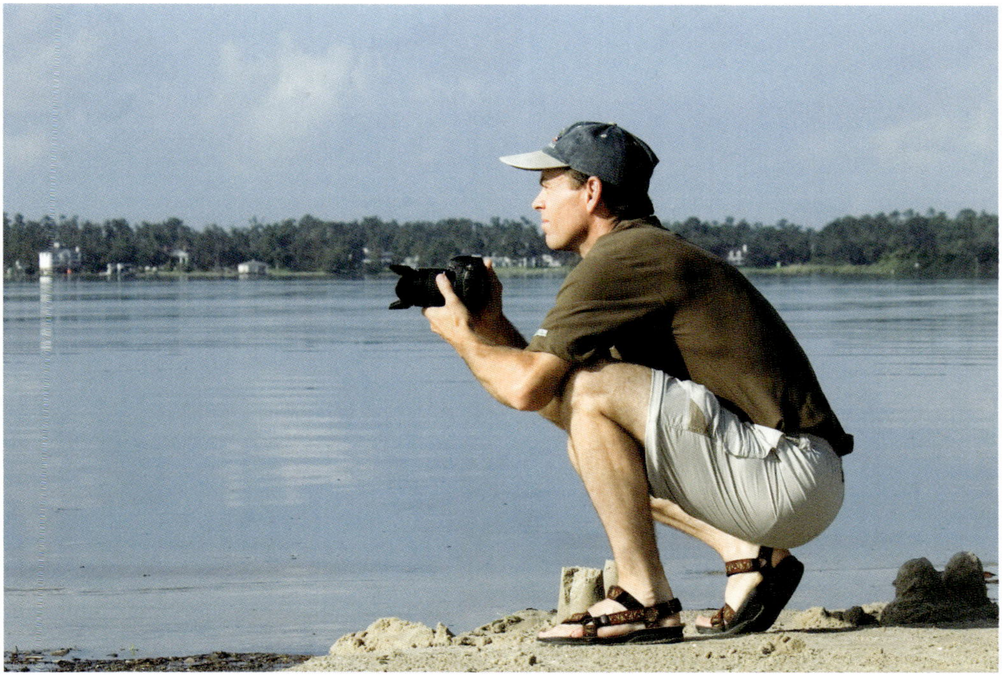

Short zoom lenses are easy to handle and ideal for flight shots of birds habituated to humans. Here the author prepares to photograph shorebirds at Lake Charles, Louisiana. *Jack Ballard*

Camera settings are also critical to flight photography. The relationship between depth of field and shutter speed at a particular ISO setting is especially important. More depth of field may yield sharp images without pinpoint focusing, as there is more margin for error with focus. However, greater depth of field requires lower shutter speed, which may yield blurred images, especially with fast-flying birds or species with rapid wingbeats (small waterfowl species such the green-winged teal fit both categories).

Another technical issue relates to the type of image the photographer wishes to achieve. The gliding image of an eagle or osprey is generally most pleasing when the entire bird is sharply focused. However, a slight blurring of the primary (longest) feathers on the wings suggests movement and may be preferable when an eagle is just launching from a perch. The blinding speed of one of these raptors diving for a fish may be more forcefully suggested with the head and eye sharply focused but the rest of the body and background noticeably blurred.

The shutter speeds required to achieve such effects vary considerably among species and situations. As a very broad rule of thumb, shutter speeds slower than 1/250th of a second are too slow for flight photography, except for panning soaring birds or creating a blurred effect. Shutter speeds of 1/1000 or higher are preferable for tack-sharp images of flying birds. However, the best way to analyze shutter speed is to take careful notes in relation to your own equipment and technique. The effectiveness of past attempts is the greatest predictor of future success, and perhaps nowhere in wildlife photography is this principle more appropriate than in relation to flight photography.

For example, suppose you are photographing bald eagles on an Alaskan river where they have congregated to catch spawning salmon, or shooting flying gulls at the J. N. "Ding" Darling National Wildlife Refuge on Sanibel Island, Florida. Both destinations should yield multiple opportunities for flight photography. After shooting a number of images, analyze the results in terms of sharpness or blurring of the action, and adjust the shutter speed up or down in relation to what you see. Want an image with no blurring? Increase the shutter speed. Looking to experiment with an artistic blurring of the wings and background? Dial back the shutter speed to achieve the desired effect.

Right: Shutter speeds required for non-blurred panning shots of birds vary with species. The rapid wingbeats of these chukar partridges in Wyoming see a slight blurring on the wing tips even at 1/1500th of a second (top). These soaring great egrets above Sanibel Island, Florida, can be sharply photographed at slower shutter speeds (bottom). *Jack Ballard and Lisa Ballard*

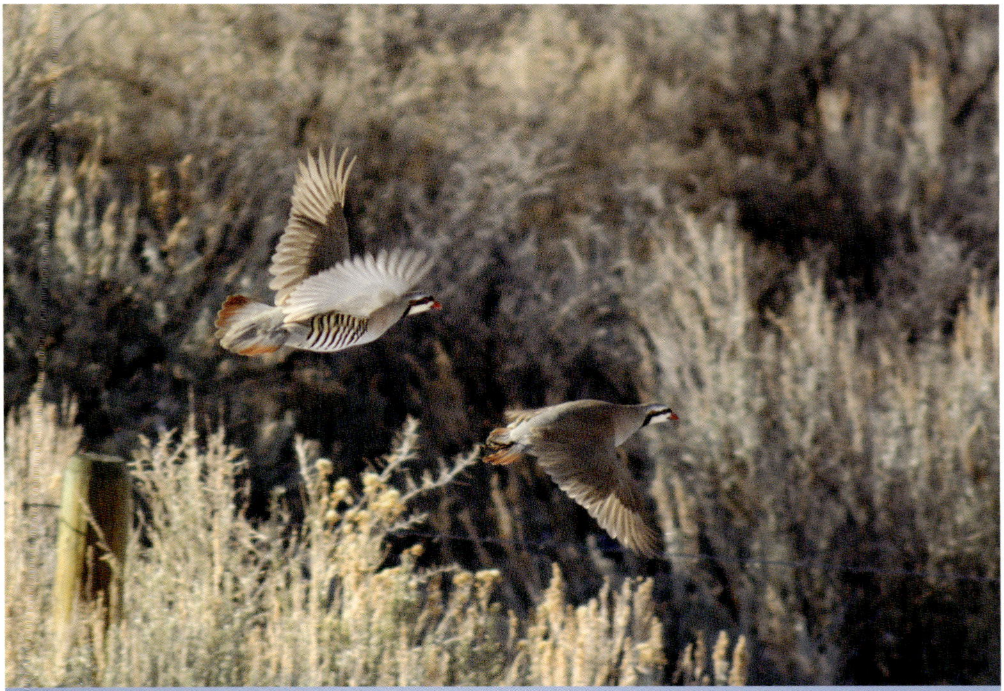

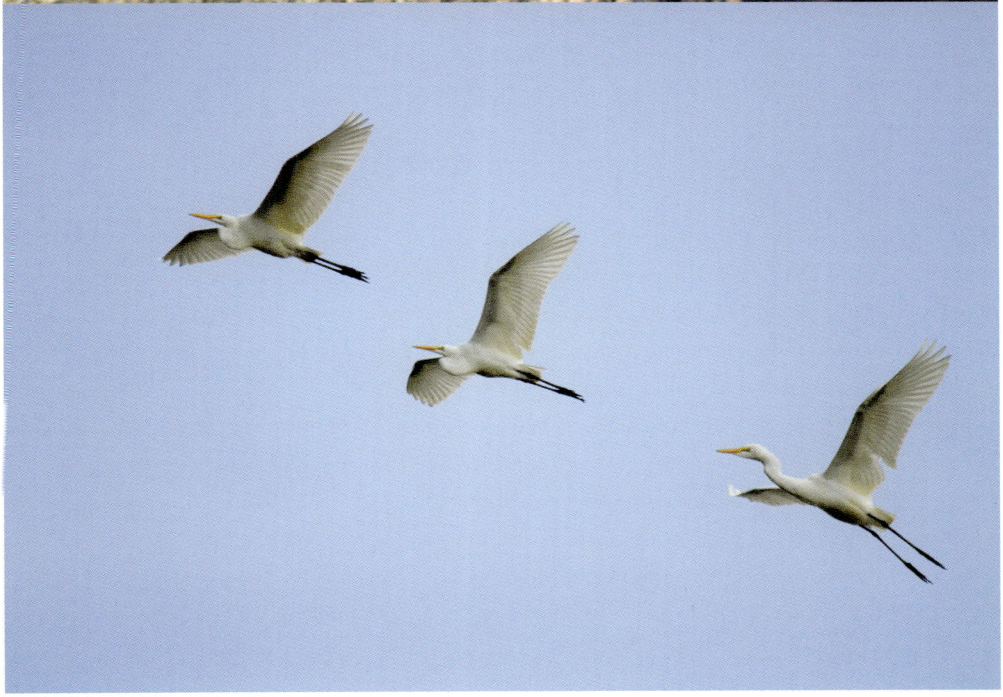

Birds can be photographed from three basic angles in flight: from the side (panning), head-on (flying toward the photographer), or departing (flying away from the photographer). Panning shots are the most difficult in terms of technique, but are also the most usual opportunity for flight photography. The biggest mistake when panning is failure to keep the entire subject in the frame. When tracking a bird through the viewfinder, it's easy to crop a wing or the head or feet of a subject that may be moving both horizontally and vertically through the air. When using a zoom lens on a quality camera, loosen the framing. It's easy to crop photos from cameras that produce high image quality with your editing software, but impossible to re-create those wing feathers lopped from a flying mallard.

Head-on shots are typically easier to execute but harder to anticipate. The focusing system on your camera should readily lock onto birds coming straight toward the sensor, and you won't need to move the camera too much to follow

ETHICS AND ETIQUETTE

BAITING RAPTORS

In recent years the practice of baiting raptors to achieve flight photos has come to the forefront as an issue in the ethics of wildlife photography. Raptors, especially owls, can sometimes be enticed to swoop in upon bait (typically a mouse or gerbil) offered by a photographer. The practice of baiting wintering owls in such a way has become disturbingly common in northern states during the winter. It commonly takes place along rural roads, which photographers cruise in hopes of spying an owl.

From an artistic standpoint, flight shots of raptors gained this way tend to trivialize the skill and persistence required to capture what should be a rare image. The fact that these images are often passed off to the press as truly "wild" situations by some photographers is one ethical issue. The welfare of the birds is another. Captive rodents may carry diseases that could potentially threaten wild raptors. Perhaps potentially more fateful is the fact that the practice encourages raptors to hang around roads, where collisions with vehicles may occur quite frequently. Owls hunting at night or in the dim hours of daylight and dawn are especially vulnerable when crossing a vehicle's path.

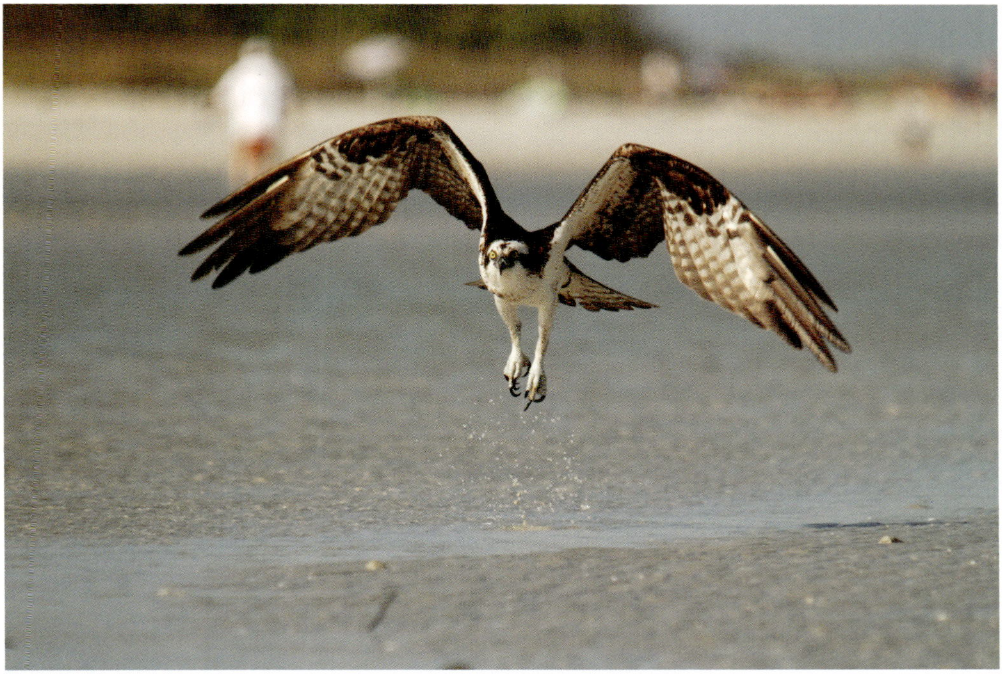

Lisa Ballard realized this osprey was about to be disturbed into flight by a beachcomber on Sanibel Island, Florida, and set up for an easy head-on flight photo. *Lisa Ballard*

the action. Head-on images are easiest to achieve in places where birds are regularly landing at a particular location. Waterfowl photographers can take a cue from hunters when desiring flight photos, especially head-on images. Ducks and geese will often alight next to decoys placed on the water, allowing a well-hidden photographer the chance for multiple flight opportunities, sometimes in the space of an hour. Some birds return to a favored perch for hunting or preening, yielding a similar chance to "set up" for a head-on flight shot.

Departing flight photos aren't normally favorite flight shots, but they can be quite compelling, especially if the bird turns its head slightly. These images are one situation where shooting the subject on its own level is usually not the best angle.

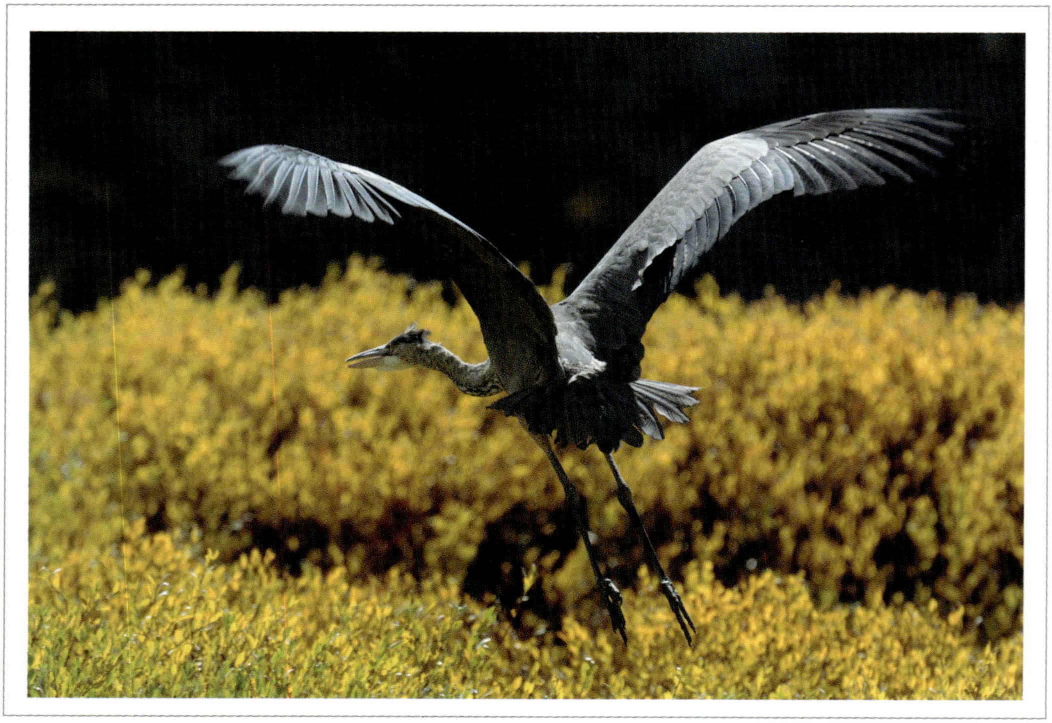

The slight angle of this departing shot of a great blue heron in Yellowstone National Park, Wyoming, creates a unique perspective on the bird's outline and plumage. *Jack Ballard*

Departing flight shots of birds overhead or beneath the plane of the photographer tend to yield superior results. From these angles the image will display more of the bird's plumage and outline than photos taken from directly behind the subject.

Whether captured in flight or at rest, the perfectly composed image of a bird is among the most cherished wildlife images in a photographer's portfolio. Photographers in America are fortunate to have such a dizzying array of feathered subjects and should be among the nation's most ardent advocates of habitat conservation programs ensuring the continued existence of our many birds.

Right: Winter irruptions may bring owls, such as this great gray in Montana, into locations to the south or at lower elevations than their normal range. Baiting or continually disturbing them in an attempt to acquire a photograph may threaten their survival. *Jack Ballard*

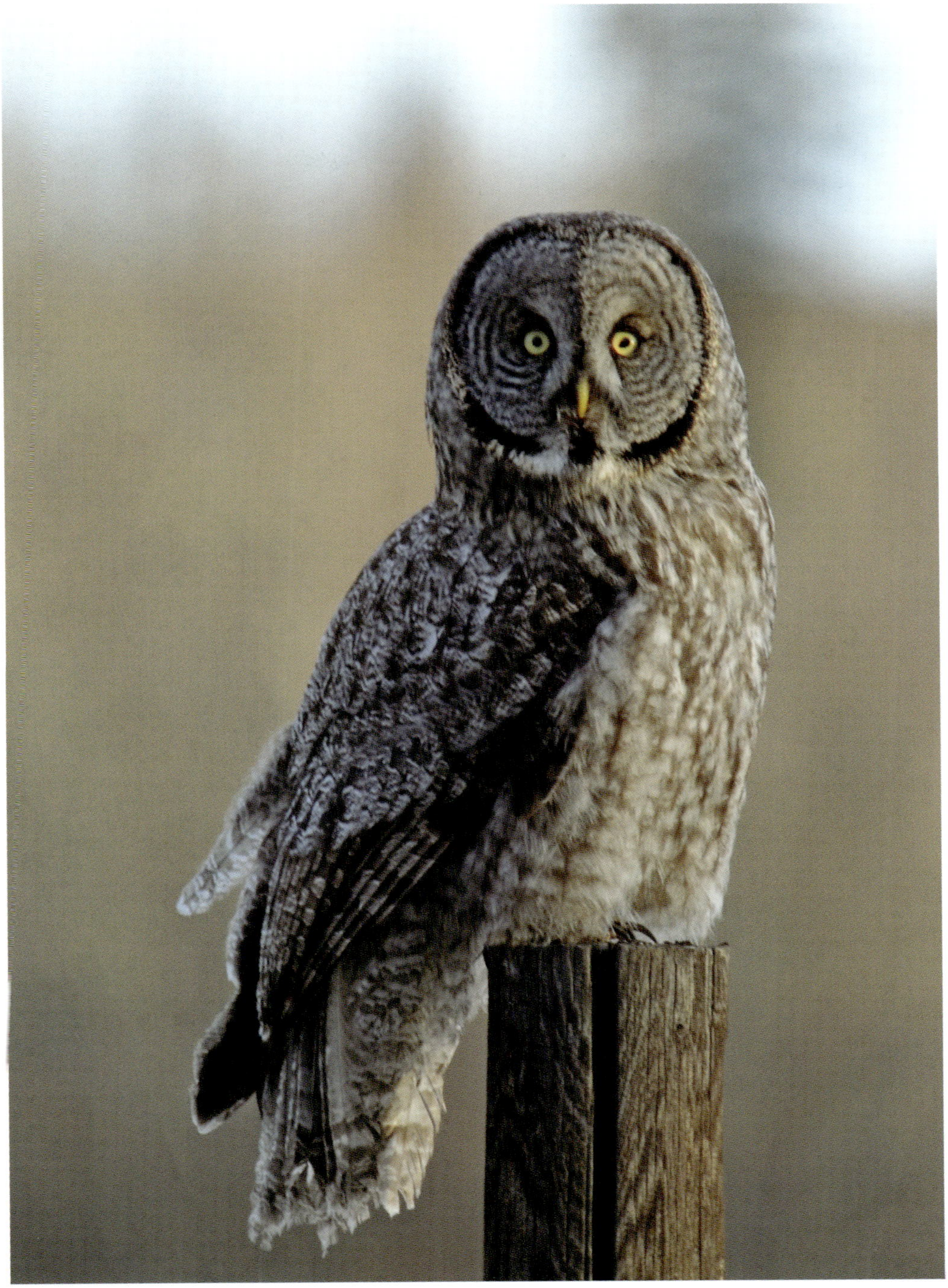

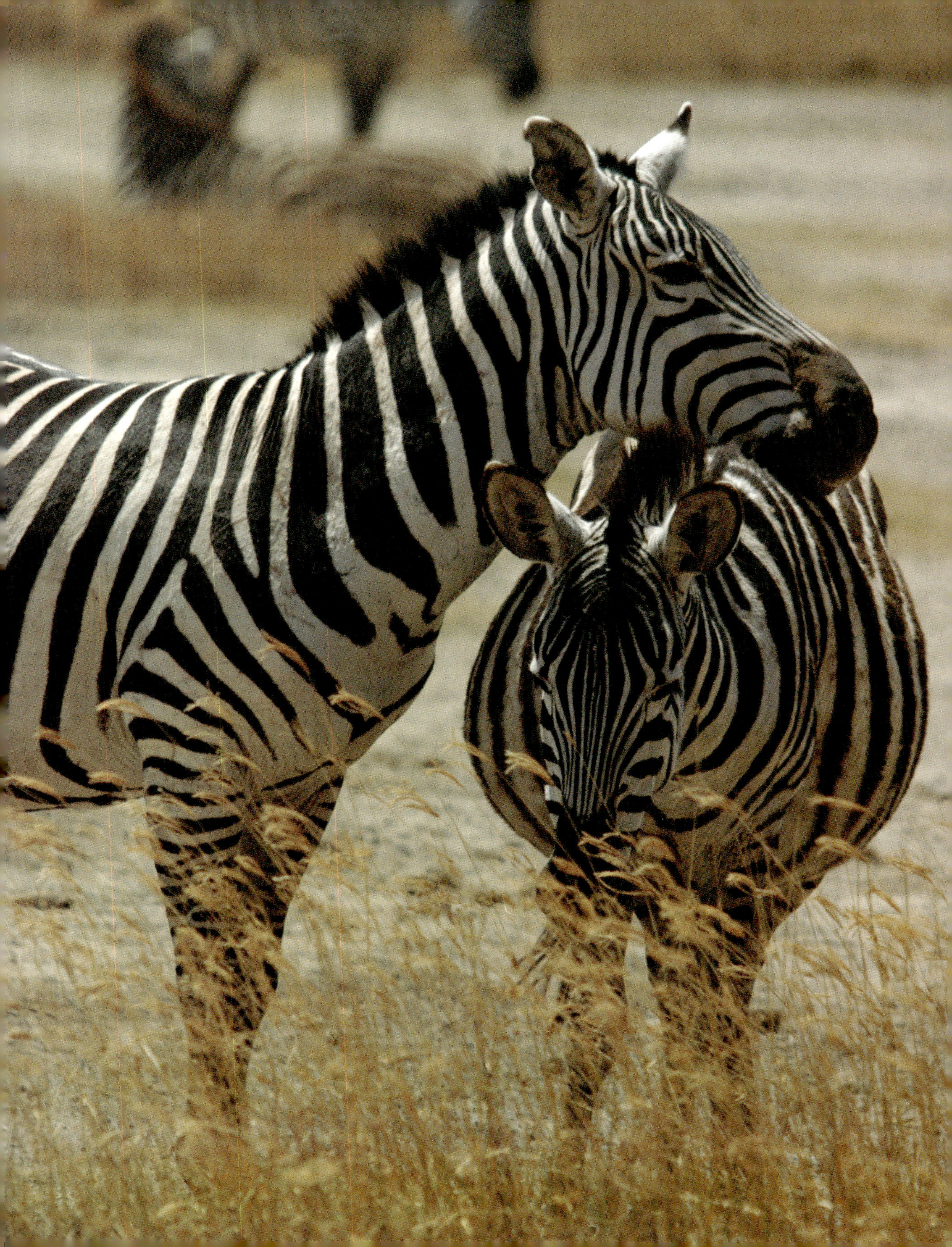

CHAPTER

7

Photographing Mammals

The array of mammals in North America and the opportunities they afford to photographers is truly remarkable. A wildlife photographer at Custer State Park, South Dakota, may have her lens trained on a massive bull bison weighing 2,000 pounds while one of the creature's prairie neighbors, a 6-ounce 13-lined ground squirrel, peers from its burrow nearby. A similar, immense disparity exists in the size of the continent's carnivores. The paws of a massive male grizzly bear prowling the Alaskan coast may be propelling 1,500 pounds of bone, muscle, hide, and fur while a tiny but fierce least weasel hunting in the forest nearby could be marked as an outsized representative of its species at 2 ounces.

Zebra. *Lisa Ballard*

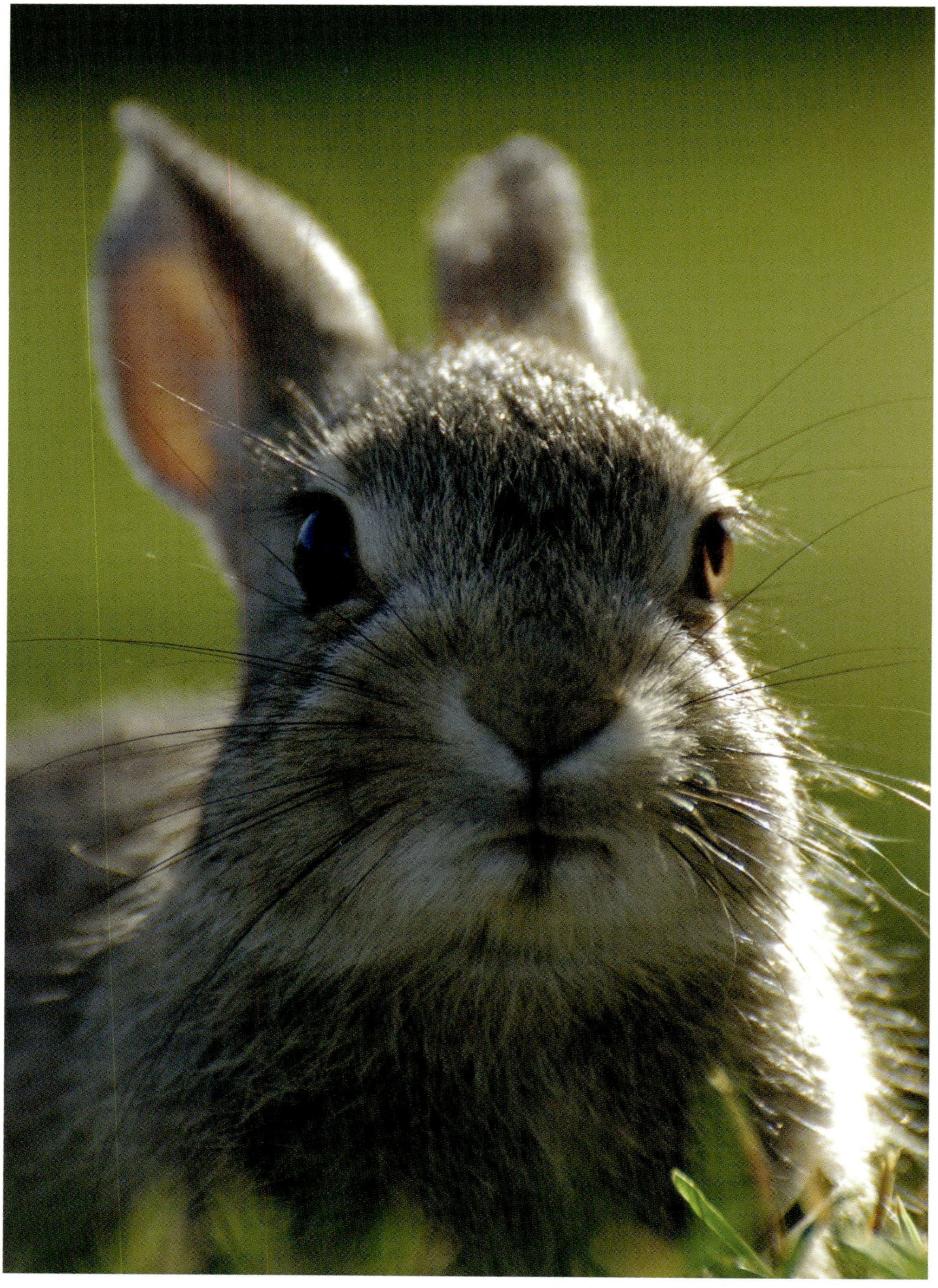

Although the Smithsonian National Museum of Natural History lists 740 species of mammals as native to North America, even the most avid amateur naturalist is lucky to view half of them in a lifetime. For wildlife photographers, attaining iconic portraits of common mammals or capturing images of those seldom seen are among the primary attractions of wildlife photography.

MAMMAL BEHAVIOR AND HABITAT BASICS

The list of North American mammals includes whales, sea lions, bats, bears, felines, canines, rodents, and deer, among a host of other species. Mammals are even more diverse than birds in their range of habitat and behavior. Some species spend much of their life underground. Others, like bats, pass extended periods of time in caves. Predators such as mountain lions may be primarily nocturnal. Whales are creatures of the oceans and may move thousands of miles throughout the year. Thus there is no single formula that describes the basics of mammal behavior.

However, mammal behavior is often quite predictable within various families or types of animals. For example, grazing and browsing mammals such as bison and elk follow a basic pattern during the summer months of filling their stomachs in the early morning and late evening while resting at midday to chew their cud (food that's regurgitated for more chewing). Burrowing mammals follow a similar routine but may be more active at midday, except during the height of the summer when they retreat underground to beat the heat.

Small mammals such as this baby cottontail rabbit can be as interesting a subject as larger species. *Jack Ballard*

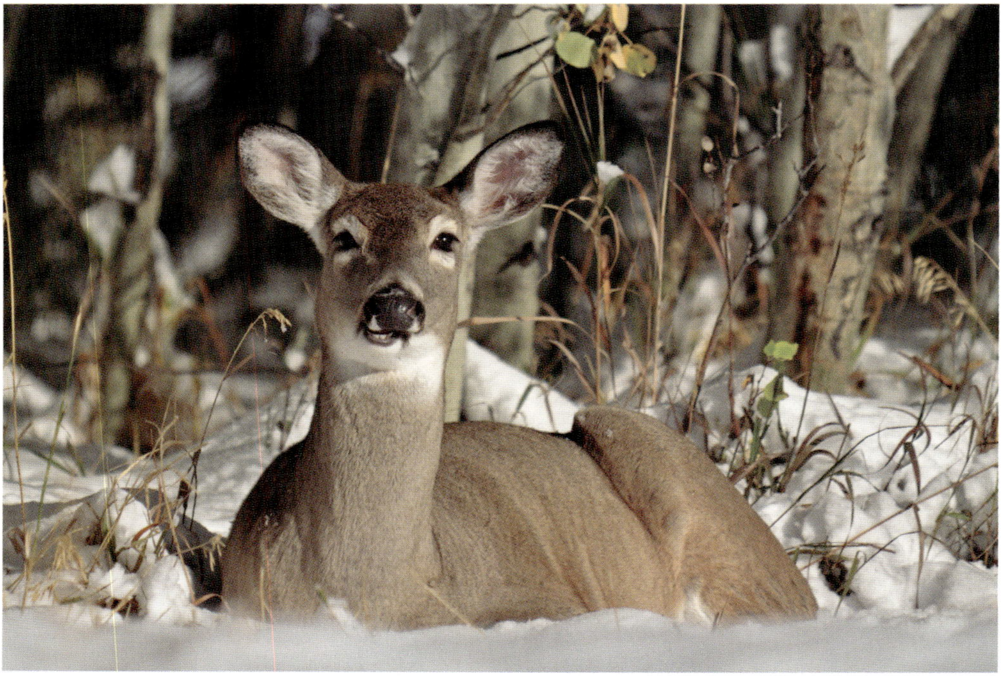

Browsing and grazing animals like this whitetail deer doe usually lie down and chew their cud at midday, limiting photographic opportunities. *Jack Ballard*

Photographers desiring images of a specific species are advised to learn all they can regarding the creature's habitat preferences and behavioral patterns. For example, suppose a wildlife photographer undertakes a weeklong excursion to Yellowstone National Park in September. He's already checked wolves and grizzly bears, the park's two marquee predators, from his photo bucket list, having completed a successful guided photo safari the previous year. This time around, he hopes to collect images of coyotes and black bears.

While driving a highway across an open meadow at mid-morning, he spies a coyote leaping in the grass, apparently hunting mice. The animal is within camera range of the road, but by the time he pulls over, the coyote has wandered away. Around the next bend he confronts a backup of two dozen cars parked alongside the highway. A quick inquiry to a lady returning to her vehicle indicates a black bear was seen feeding on a cache of pinecones stashed at the base of an evergreen tree by a squirrel, but it had retreated into the shade of heavier timber.

What are the odds of either creature reappearing at the same location in the morning? Knowing the hunting patterns of coyotes are nomadic and not too predictable, the photographer decides to check for the bear. Sure enough, the calorie-craving carnivore has returned to the cone cache to glean what nutrition he can from the squirrel's efforts before hibernation. Wildlife behavior is never

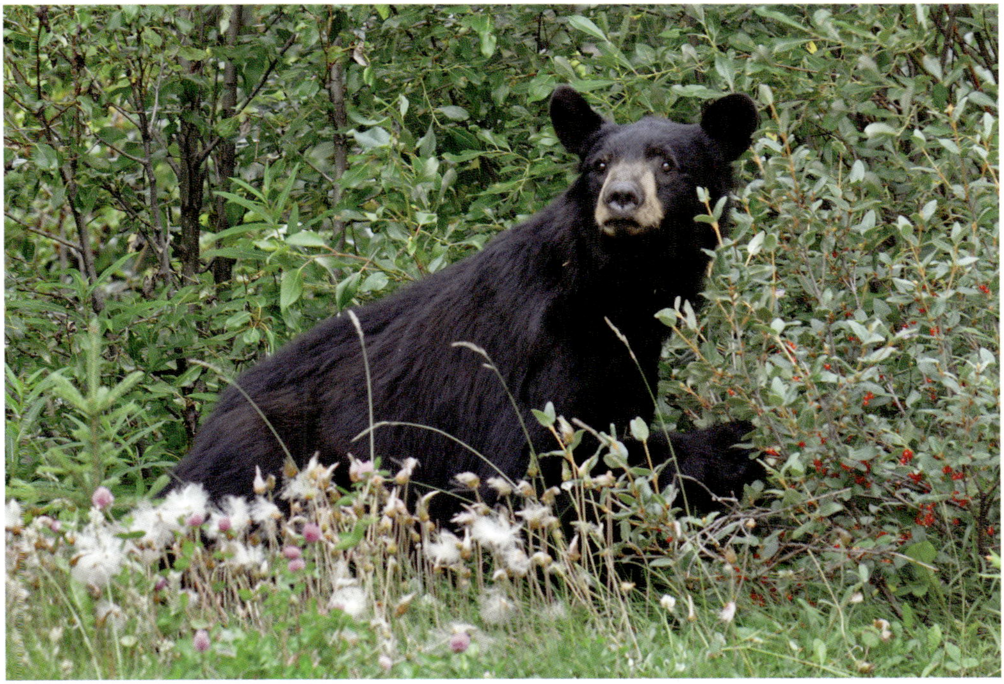

A black bear looks up from feeding on berries in Canada's Banff National Park. Odds are high it will stick around until the berries are gone. Knowledge of feeding habits of various species is invaluable for wildlife photographers. *Jack Ballard*

completely predictable, but in this case the photographer was able to use his understanding of basic species behavior to up his odds of a photo-worthy encounter.

Photographers with an intimate understanding of creatures' habitat preferences also increase their odds when attempting to photograph mammals. Elk, for example, are one of the primary attractions for wildlife photographers at Colorado's Rocky Mountain National Park. Late July finds the animals at high elevation, commonly spotted at over 10,000 feet along Trail Ridge Road in the alpine zone. Two months later, the animals are found at much lower elevations in the park's valleys. Successful photography of the continent's mammals is as much about understanding their habitat needs and behavior as having the latest camera equipment and technical proficiency as a photographer.

Movement Patterns

Male grizzly bears and mountain lions often control extremely large territories covering 150 square miles or more. Within that homeland they have certain favored areas and travel routes, but predicting their movement patterns is still a near-impossible task short of attaching some tracking device to the animal. Other creatures follow more established routines, with predictable patterns of behavior allowing a photographer high odds of acquiring a photo at a particular place and time of day.

For example, for several years a white-tailed jackrabbit frequented a vacant lot adjacent to my home. The hare had a long split in one of its ears, making it easy to identify. A patch of weeds on one corner of the lot was our leggy neighbor's favorite resting place in late afternoon. Over the course of the summer, my son and I frequently wandered near the area, as much to habituate the big-eared

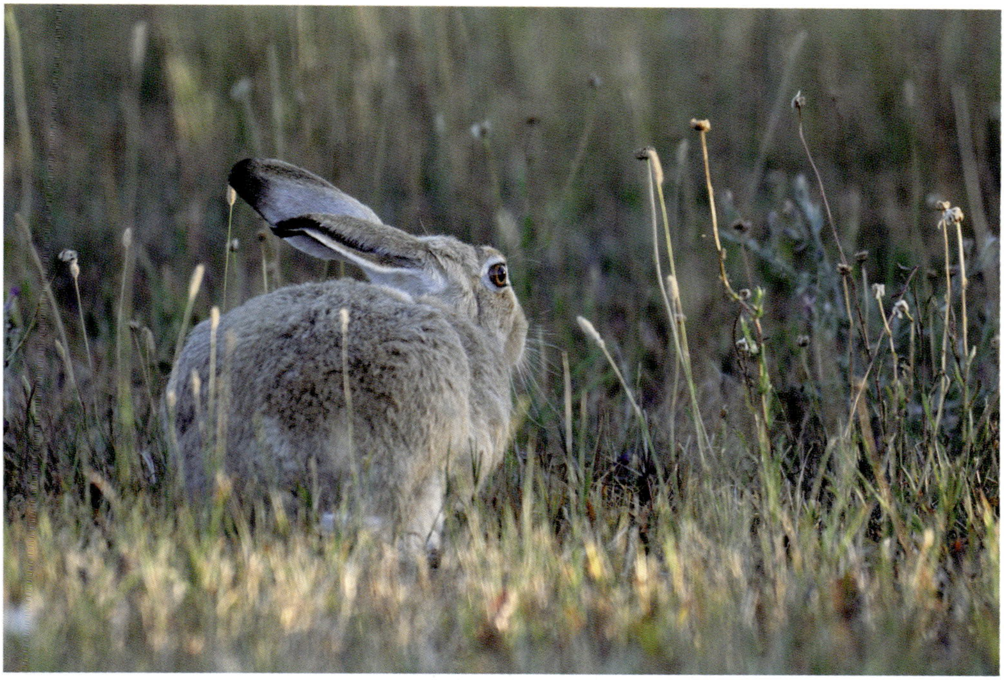

Learning the daily routine of this white-tailed jackrabbit and habituating it to his presence allowed the author's son to record its image when conditions were optimal. *Dominic Ballard*

bunny to our presence as to check on its whereabouts. Its daily routine, along with our "friending" efforts, led to a situation where we could easily shoot frame-filling photos of a normally skittish species with a 300mm lens.

As noted previously, land mammals, especially herbivores (plant-eaters), tend to be most active in the early and late hours of the day. This behavioral trait corresponds nicely with the most favorable lighting conditions for photography. However, beyond this biological basic, other aspects of mammal movement can greatly aid the efforts of the wildlife photographer.

One of the consistent challenges of photographing mammals is finding animals within range of the camera. This is not a difficult proposition for certain

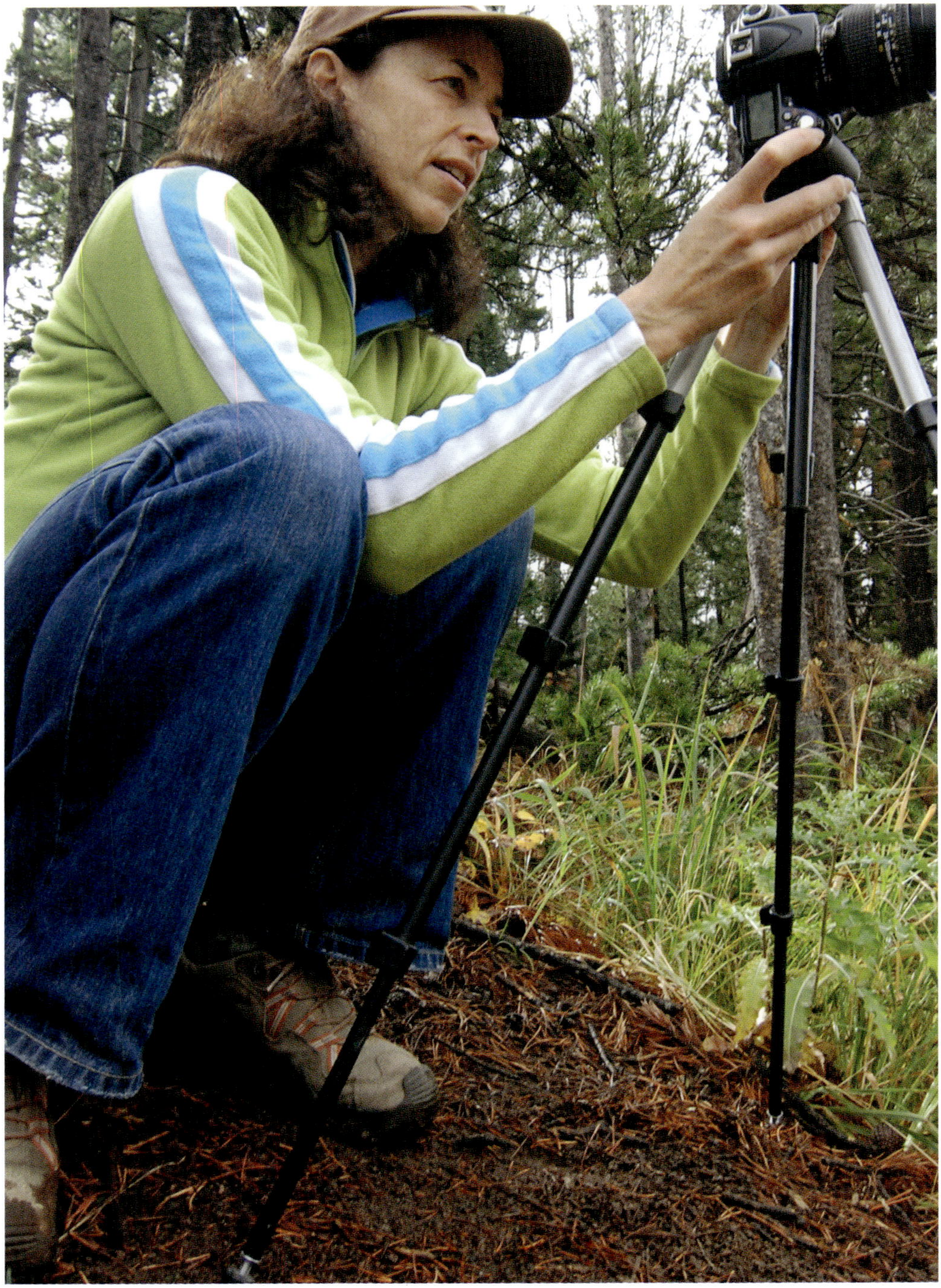

species habituated to humans in parks, refuges, or urban areas, but with creatures not so accustomed to people or those species with a naturally wary disposition, simply getting within camera range can be one of the photographer's greatest obstacles. Equipment constraints also play into this equation. A 600mm f/4 lens makes photographing large mammals from a considerable distance quite doable, but new lenses of this type from major camera companies come with a price tag exceeding $10,000. Wildlife photographers utilizing more budget-friendly equipment often find themselves in situations where getting within ideal shooting range is a challenge.

Two behavioral patterns of mammals (also applicable to other wildlife) are important to understand for closing the range on photo subjects. The first relates to the fact that most animals are more at ease approaching a visible, stationary photographer than having a moving human coming at them from the rear. Attempting to overtake a walking whitetail deer from behind puts the photographer's behavior in the category of a stalking predator and will most likely stimulate the animal's pace or lead to outright flight.

A better strategy in this situation would be to note the deer's direction of travel and set up ahead and to the side of it, allowing the subject to come to the photographer. Sitting quietly within eyeshot of a moving animal allows it to make a decision about your intentions. If the creature decides you're not a threat, it may stroll within easy range of a telephoto lens. If not, no amount of chasing or stealth will bring a photographer within range of a mammal that has decided it doesn't want a human's company.

An additional nuance of this foundational principle is exceedingly important. A photographer who has positioned herself adjacent to some environmental

Left: Getting within range of mammals is one of the biggest challenges for wildlife photographers without long telephoto lenses. *Jack Ballard* attractant and a mammalian subject that's approaching it has an even higher chance of finding herself within camera range. Food sources, mates, and novel objects may all stimulate the approach of mammals.

My first serious excursion as an aspiring professional outdoor photographer occurred in Yellowstone National Park. Elk were my chosen subject, and I was delighted to find a herd of animals with a majestic stag in residence in a meadow not far from the campground serving as home base for the trip. I hiked from the campground at dawn to discover a bugling bull elk, his breath exhaling in giant puffs of sunlit frost, and his harem of some two dozen cows and their calves. Unfortunately, I was under-gunned. A gaggle of professional photographers, some of whom I recognized from books and magazine articles, were banded along the road at the meadow's edge, their 500mm and 600mm lenses trained on the elk. My longest telephoto at the time was a 400mm f/5.6, just lacking enough magnification to obtain the stunning portraits of individual animals for which I'd hoped.

Crouched behind my tripod, considering my options, I noticed a young cow elk drifting from the herd. Her path took her closer to the road, well within range of my camera. I knew bull elk are extremely territorial during the mating season, repelling rival males but also prohibiting females from abandoning their herd. Tripod folded, I hustled along the shoulder of the highway to take position within camera range of the unconcerned cow. Within minutes of getting set, the bull noticed the wanderer and came charging to goad her back toward the herd. I feverishly burned a roll of film, yielding several superb photos. By positioning myself so the bull came toward a desirable element in his environment (the cow), I was able to collect photos otherwise unattainable.

Right: This whitetail deer has been "spooked" by the photographer. Chasing it in an attempt to get more images will almost surely be futile. *Jack Ballard*

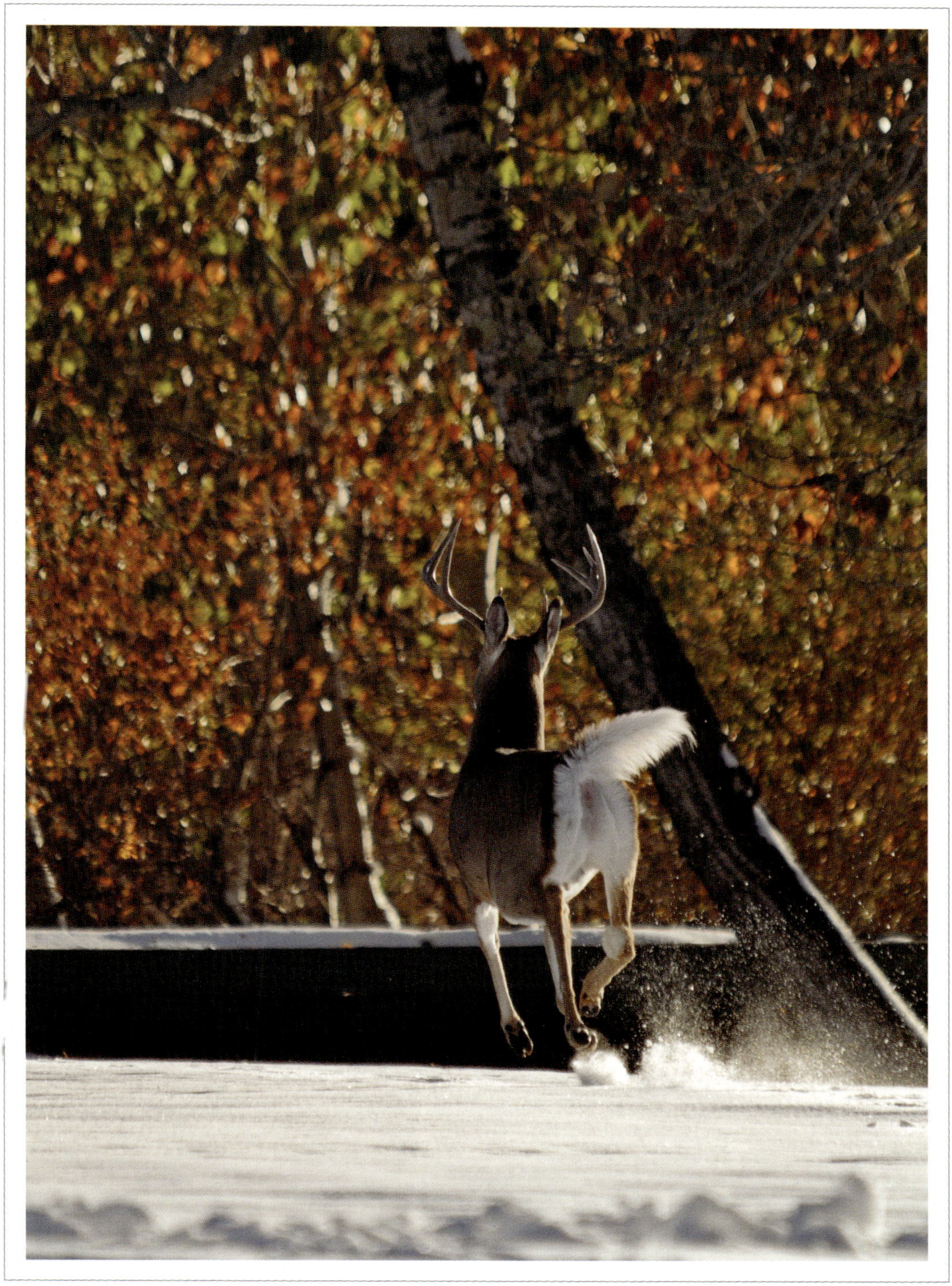

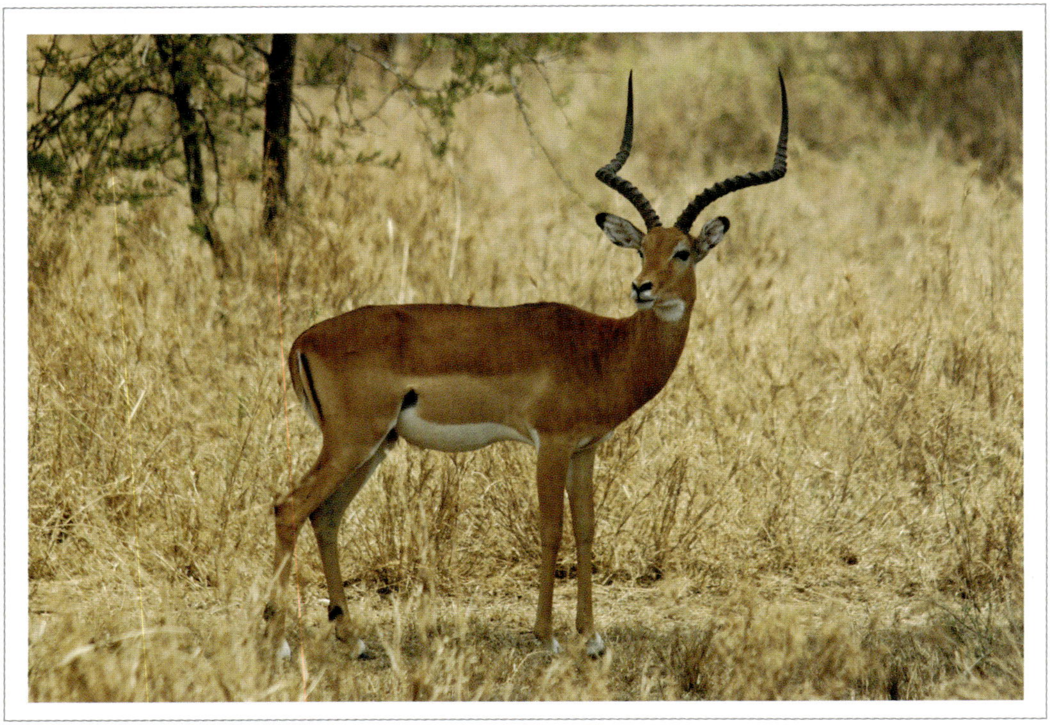

This elegant impala ram was photographed from a vehicle parked and positioned between the subject and a water source, bringing the impala within easy range of the author's camera. *Jack Ballard*

A similar situation occurred when my wife and I were photographing in Tanzania's Tarangire National Park. Noticing an elegant impala ram on the move, I realized its destination was a water source on the opposite side of the road our vehicle was driving. Our driver stopped the Land Rover, allowing us to photograph the knurl-horned beauty as he paused on a rise above us en route to a drink.

Photographing an animal approaching some desirable element in its environment is an excellent strategy for wildlife photographers to capitalize on the natural movement patterns of mammals. However, some situations require the photographer to move toward the subject. What's the best way to get close?

For the most part, attempting to stalk or sneak up on a mammal is a poor tactic. Most mammals have excellent eyesight that is highly sensitive to movement and a sense of smell many times more acute than a human's. Those factors make it very difficult to sneak within camera range. Furthermore, the movement required to focus a handheld or tripod-mounted camera on a subject once in range creates greater odds of being detected.

Most mammals, like other creatures, have what might be described as a "flight zone" in relation to people. This is the range at which an approaching human will cause the animal to flee. An alarmed fox might simply trot away from a photographer who gets too close. A foraging squirrel might zip up a tree, while a disturbed beaver often slaps the water with its tail and then dives and swims to the opposite side of a pond. In each of these cases, the flight is triggered when a person penetrates the critter's flight zone.

The flight zone of a mammal can change drastically over time. A photographer who pops over a rise on a trail to encounter a snowshoe hare might see the soft-footed herbivore hop away at a distance of

ETHICS AND ETIQUETTE

PROXIMITY

Approaching a mammal for photography or stationing oneself by something the subject is approaching should be governed by some simple considerations for safety and the welfare of the animal. The space directly between a subject and its mate or young should be left alone. Males of many species such as whitetail deer may become very aggressive during the mating season and possibly attack a photographer in the vicinity of a mate. A similar situation occurs with adults tending young, such as a coyote returning to a den. When using an environmental attractant as "bait" for an approaching subject, set up to the side of it with plenty of space to back off if the animal shows any signs of aggression.

If a creature is repeatedly disturbed by your attempts to get close to it for photos, leave it alone. Further trials won't alter the fact that its flight zone is too large for photography. Reduce its stress and your frustration by finding another subject.

50 yards if he continues forward. However, if he stops and allows the bunny to settle, it might be possible to patiently close the distance to 20 yards, perhaps less.

Successfully approaching mammals for photos is a product of reading behavioral cues and patience. Various species have different ways of displaying discomfort. A grazing mammal that raises its head to stare at a photographer is assessing the potential danger. A deer might swish its tail or stamp its foot, both behaviors indicating greater arousal. If it drops its head to feed or begins grooming itself, it has dismissed the threat of the photographer at her current distance and will probably allow a closer approach. Pushing toward a creature that's displaying anxiety behaviors is almost certain to trigger its flight.

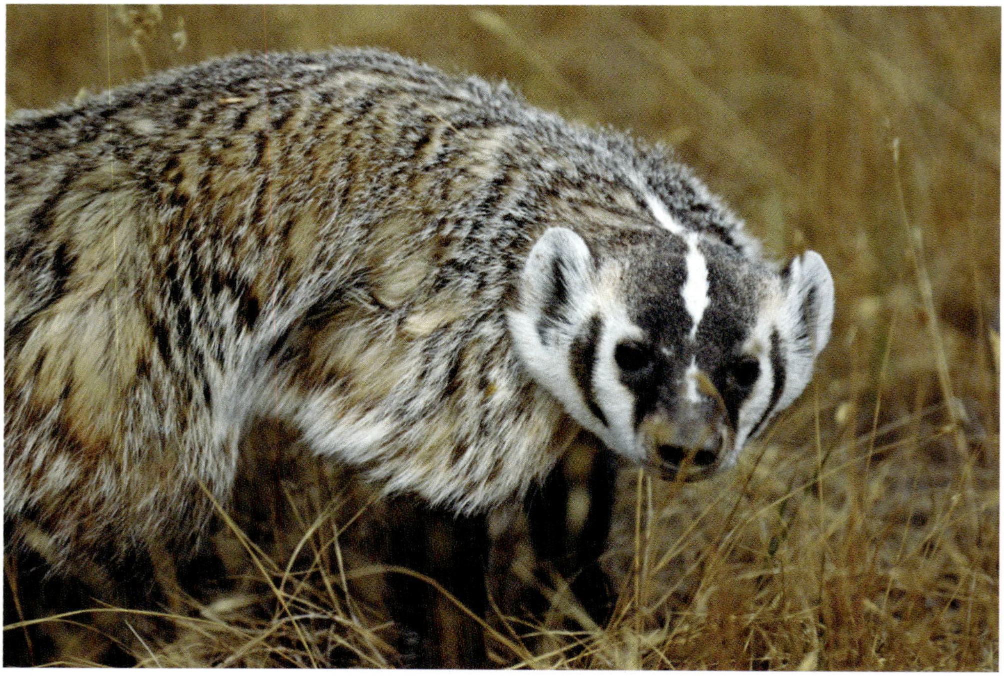

This Wyoming badger is staring directly at two photographers, gauging them as potential threats. Its next move will likely be determined by their behavior. *Jack Ballard*

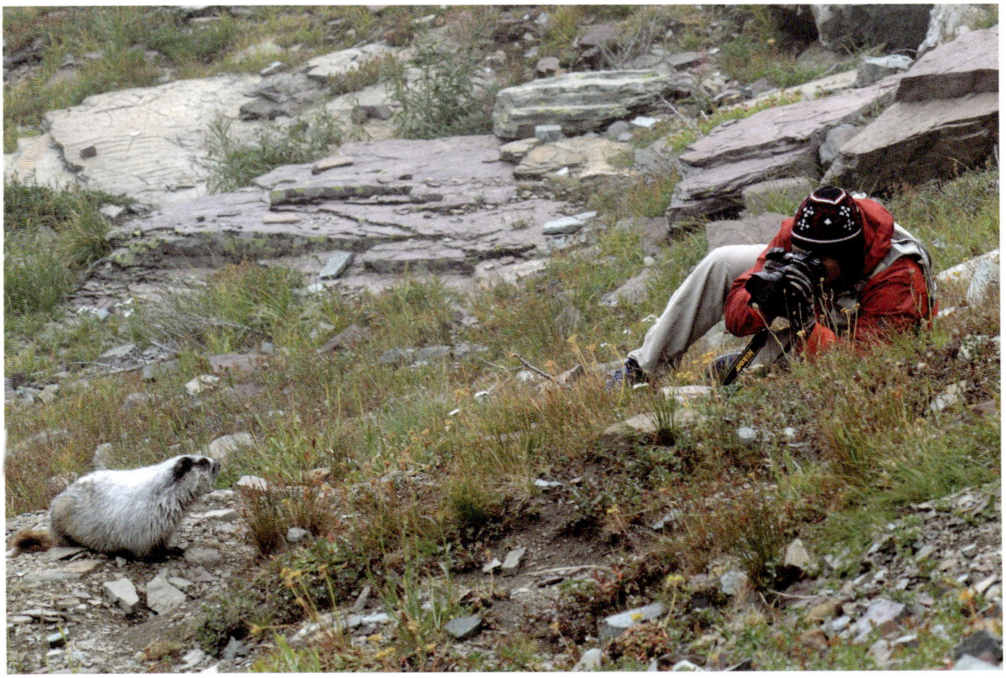

The author used slow, patient movements to get within rather close range of this hoary marmot. It is alert, watching him. A sudden move at this point will probably send it into its burrow. *Lisa Ballard*

Reading a mammal's behavioral cues of anxiety and attempting to decrease the distance between subject and photographer only when the animal is relaxed is one key to getting closer. Another involves the behavior of the photographer. Slow, fluid movements are less likely to cause alarm than quickly walking, abruptly standing, or jerkily raising an arm. Animals are also more comfortable with humans who don't come directly toward them. Several of my professional wildlife photographer friends think of their approach toward a mammal in terms of "enjoying the wildflowers." This refers to a slow, circuitous approach toward a creature in which it appears the photographer has no interest in the subject but is instead fascinated by flowers on the ground. After staring at the earth for a few minutes, the photographer moves to view another "flower" a few feet away. Her path takes her on a zigzagging, diagonal approach to the subject, which never involves moving rapidly or directly toward the animal. This movement pattern makes it appear as if the photographer is uninterested in the subject and simply going about her business in the same area.

In addition to an indirect approach, avoiding eye contact with the subject also increases the chances of successfully coming within the desired camera range. Staring directly at a mammal is typically interpreted as having a predatory intent (in the case of prey species) or aggression (in the case of predators). In either case, direct eye contact further alarms an already alerted subject. A direct look at the subject may eventually be required to frame and focus the photo, but even those movements should be slow and involve as little eye contact as possible. Once a mammal has thoroughly accepted a photographer's presence, eye contact is usually tolerated.

Along with avoiding eye contact, minimizing the noise of a camera's focusing system and shutter also ups the odds of a successful approach. Triggering the shutter from a distance gives the animal the opportunity to become accustomed to the sound of the camera before shooting at the desired range.

Seasonal Activities

The annual cycle of life for mammals includes mating, the birth of young, and rearing offspring. It might also involve migration and seasonal shifts in habitat. These activities determine where a species is to be found and what types of behavior a photographer can expect to record at various points on the calendar.

The mating season is a dramatic time of the year for most mammals. Dominant, photogenic males of ungulates such as moose, pronghorn, and bighorn sheep

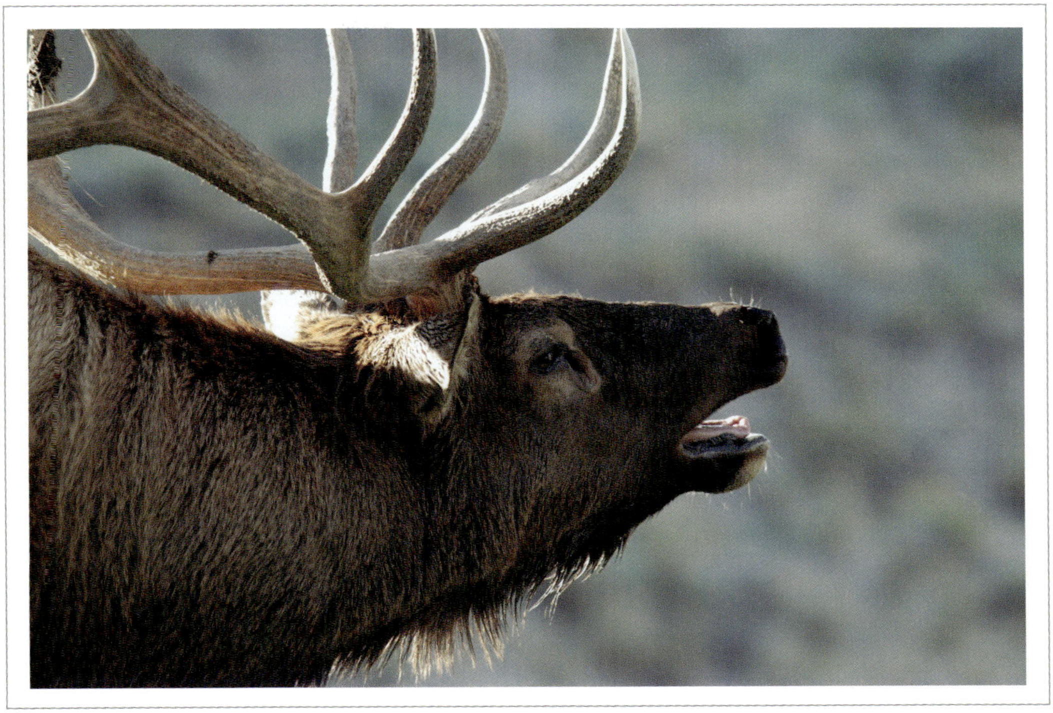

This bull elk in Yellowstone National Park is bugling, emitting a loud whistling noise associated with the mating season. Mating behaviors provide intriguing fodder for wildlife photos. *Lisa Ballard*

engage in unique posturing and occasionally fight to secure mates. Photos of these fascinating activities against an autumn backdrop rank high on the list of coveted images for most wildlife photographers. Predators normally mate in late winter or spring, as do a host of their prey species such as burrowing rodents and rabbits. Knowing when the mating season occurs and the preferred habitat of a species during this time is requisite to imaging this behavior.

Cute, fuzzy mammal babies are perhaps the most endearing wildlife photo subjects in the world. The majority of mammal species in North America birth their young in the spring. Young are born to grizzly and black bears in the den in the depths of winter, but emerge with their mothers as tiny cubs in most

ETHICS AND ETIQUETTE

NEWBORN ANIMALS

The first weeks or months of life are typically the most perilous in terms of survival for many mammals. In some places, predators may kill the majority of young born to ungulates such as elk or deer. Mothers of these species hide their young in cover for the first few weeks of life, returning to them but a few times a day to nurse. A photographer who incites a baby ungulate to flee creates chaos between it and its mother and ups the odds of it being found by a predator that sees its movement or detects it in a different, inferior hiding place. Baby mammals absent the presence of their mothers should be photographed with the greatest of care. When they're a bit older and can keep up with their mother, their survival is much less likely to be compromised by the actions of a photographer.

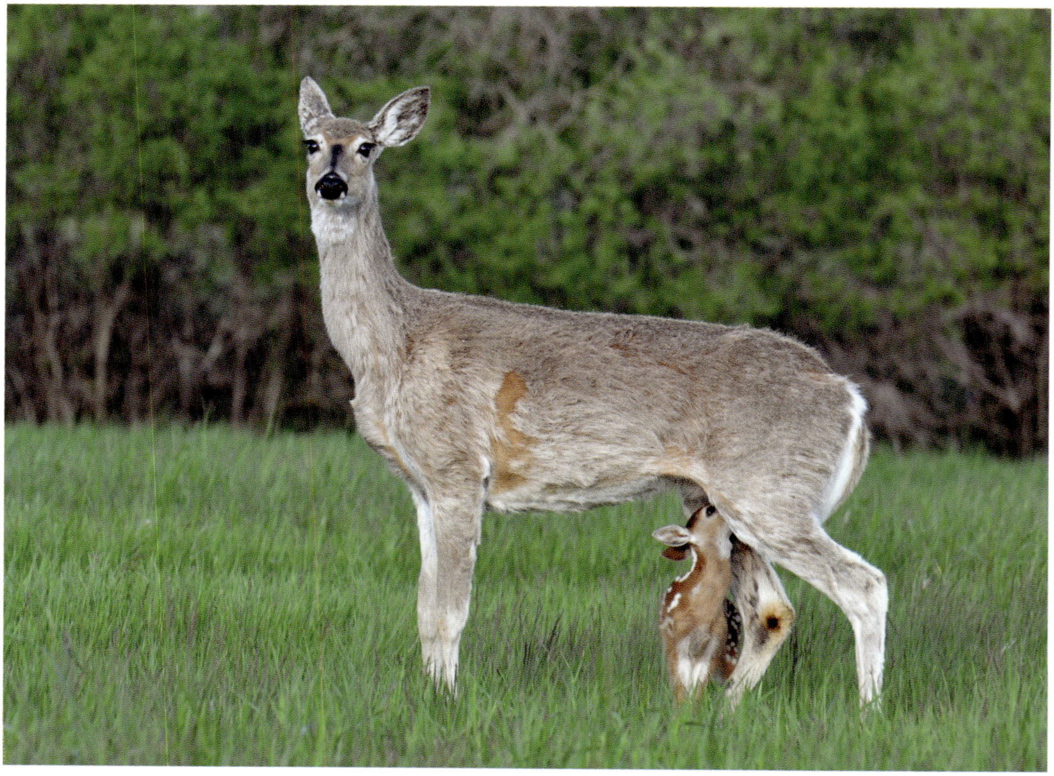

This nursing baby whitetail deer is as cute as can be. Baby mammals make super photo subjects, but should be photographed with the utmost care. *Jack Ballard*

places in early spring. Fox kits, baby skunks, deer fawns, and numerous other mammal babies first follow their mothers in the spring as well. Mammal mothers habituated to humans usually tolerate people around their offspring as well. It should be noted that some species (bears, moose, wolves, elk, etc.) are often fiercely protective of their young and should only be photographed with great caution.

Pelage Transitions

Mammals, by definition, are creatures with hair. The yearly routine of many species involves transitions from summer to winter pelage. Winter hair is longer and denser than the summer coat, and may also be marked by subtle or extreme differences in color. Several species of weasels, for example, are brown in the summer but completely white in the winter except for a black tip on the end of the tail. Snowshoe hares and jackrabbits also transition from a darker summer coat to an overall white mantle in the winter.

Common species of hooved animals, including deer and elk, also see changes in their overall coloration from summer to winter. Summer coats tend to be more reddish, while winter pelage softens to more muted tones of tan, brown, and gray. The coats of young deer and elk are spotted at birth. The spots disappear when the offspring begin to grow their first winter coat in autumn.

Other variations in seasonal pelage don't involve much change in color but still dramatically change the appearance of some species. The short, slick summer hair of a mountain goat transitions in the fall to an incredibly long, dense, luxuriant winter coat. Coyotes, foxes, wolves, bobcats, and other predators also grow fur that is heavier and more regal in the winter.

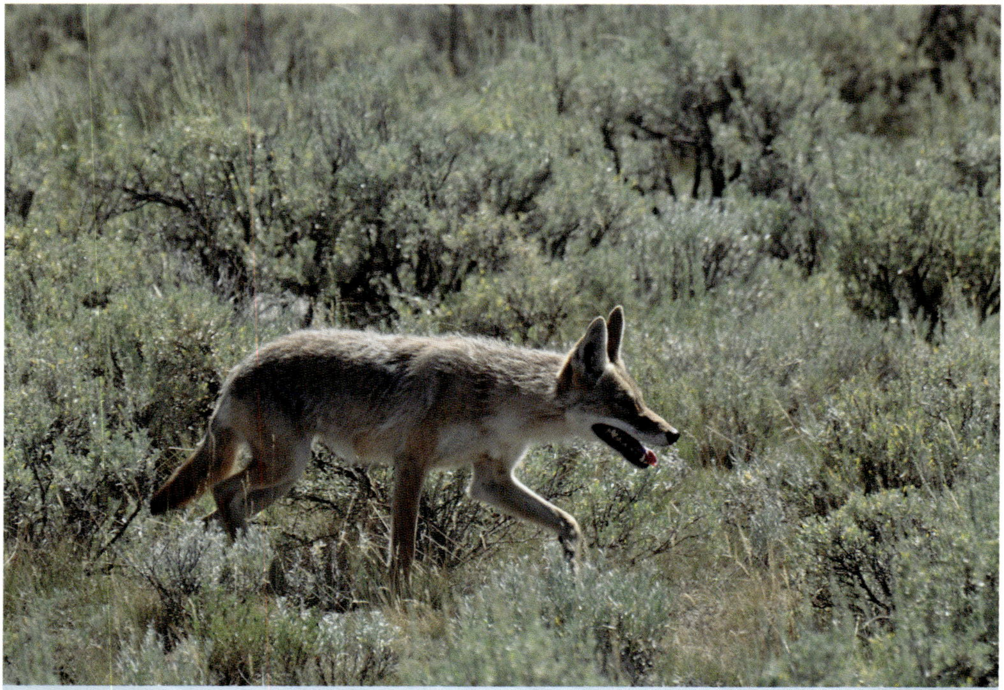

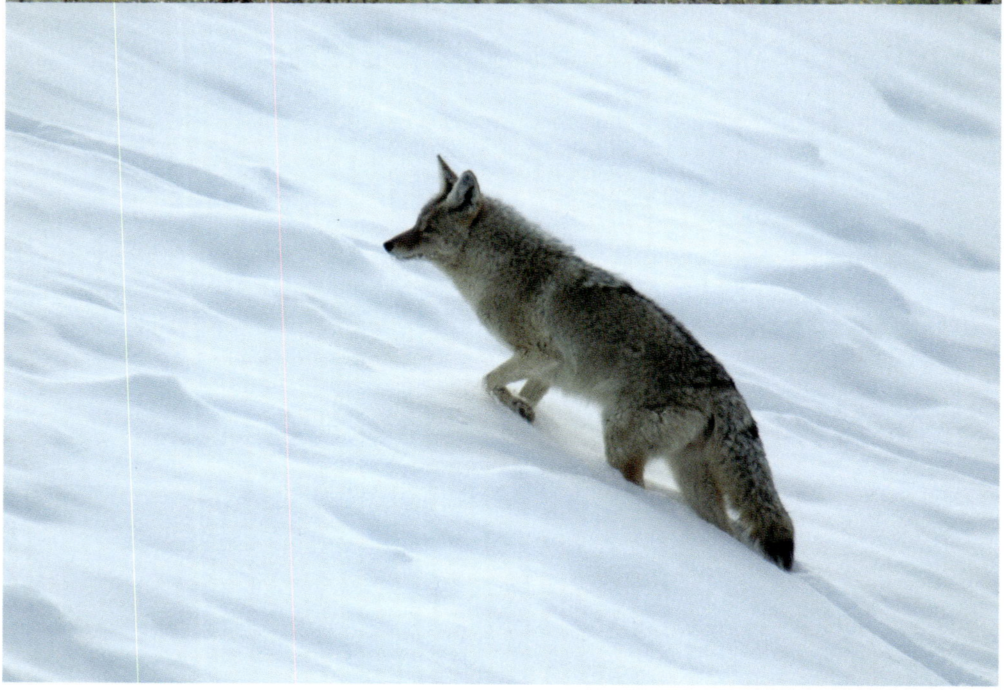

Left: The length and appearance of an animal's coat can vary dramatically through the seasons. Notice the difference on these coyotes photographed in August and January. *Jack Ballard*

Photographing a species through pelage transitions is a fascinating project for the wildlife photographer. However, it should be noted that most mammal species don't look very appealing during the molting of winter hair. Toward spring, the winter coat fades. When shedding begins, it takes on a patchy, ratty appearance until replaced by summer hair. Most professional wildlife photographers in northern latitudes look elsewhere for subjects during the molting period of winter hair.

URBAN MAMMAL PHOTOGRAPHY

Some species of mammals have occupied urban areas since the origin of the city. The past few decades, however, have seen an upsurge in the number of mammals that have adapted to living in proximity to high numbers of humans. Coyotes, foxes, mountain lions, deer, elk, and even moose are increasingly showing up in cities and towns across the continent. These animals often live on the outskirts but may also roam the interior of large cities. Other smaller mammals, including squirrels, raccoons, cottontail rabbits, mice, moles, and skunks, are frequently found in urban locations.

Most wildlife photographers prefer natural habitat as the background for their subjects. One of the primary challenges of shooting mammals in urban locations is finding or suggesting such a background. While living in Billings, Montana, I discovered a small population of white-tailed jackrabbits occupying a cemetery near the center of town. I took a few photos of these oddly placed creatures among the tombstones for documentary purposes, but couldn't get too enthused about creating portraits of the jacks against a background of lawn grass and headstones.

That all changed in the winter. Every fresh snow tempted me with a cemetery visit. Catching a jackrabbit hopping about or resting in a coverlet of snow created the opportunity to photograph the confiding creatures against a background that might just as well be natural habitat on a shortgrass prairie.

Along with the jackrabbits, I have hundreds of photos of other mammals taken in urban environments in natural habitat. These were mostly shot at the edge of town, in parks, green spaces, or vacant lots, or are portraits of critters such as raccoons and squirrels in trees. Keeping an eye out for urban mammals and thinking creatively about how to photograph them is a challenging way to engage in wildlife photography without leaving the city.

PHOTOGRAPHING DANGEROUS MAMMALS

It is foolish to assume that all mammals view *Homo sapiens* as lords of the earth and will flee from a human. It is equally absurd to think of wild mammals as peaceful cohabitants of nature who will live and let live. Many species of mammals pose serious physical danger to wildlife photographers. Polar bears, mountain lions, hyenas, and some other predators may see humans as prey. Other mammals pose a threat when they become aggressive due to mating or protecting young or in defense of themselves or their social group.

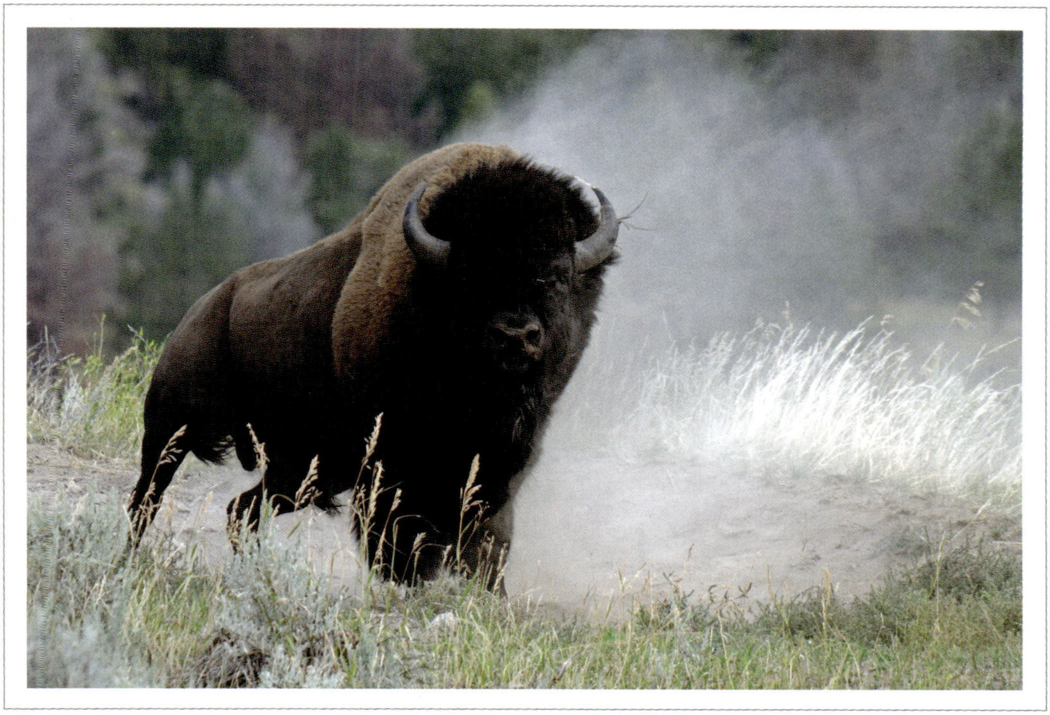

Bison don't always strike such an intimidating pose as this bull rising from a dust wallow. Like their Cape buffalo cousins in Africa, they are always dangerous when people get too close. *Lisa Ballard*

The foundational principles for safely photographing dangerous mammals are really quite simple. Photograph from a vehicle, an impenetrable enclosure such as a building or permanent blind, or from an extreme distance. Most instances of photographers being mauled, gored, or trampled by mammalian subjects involves carelessness or error on the part of the photographer.

In North America, wildlife photographers should show a healthy respect for bears, no matter how placid the subject seems to be. This applies to black bears as well as grizzlies. Black bears kill more humans in an average year than grizzly bears. Photographing moose requires caution as well. Moose can be unpredictable at any time of the year. Cows with calves are notoriously aggressive in some cases, as are bulls during the mating season. Bison might appear as gentle, unconcerned creatures but account for more injuries to humans in Yellowstone National Park than any other animal. Bull elk, buck deer, and other male ungulates are known to charge people during the mating season. I have personally witnessed heart-stopping incidences of photographers being chased by bison and bull elk in more than one national park.

A very cautious approach and a discerning eye for animal behavior are critical for safely photographing dangerous mammals. For example, wildlife experts realize that bison sometimes display behavioral cues of discomfort and aggression, but may charge a perceived threat without any warning whatsoever. They also understand that male and female ungulates may be extremely different in the extent to which they will protect their young or mates from apparent danger with an attack of their own. No matter the mammal in question, a simple rule applies when photographing potentially dangerous species: Risk increases with every step taken closer to the animal. Jealous male ungulates aren't out to injure people, nor are mothers protecting their young. Penetrate their "fight zone," however, and they will mount an aggressive attack.

ETHICS AND ETIQUETTE

DANGEROUS MAMMALS

The uppermost concern in the mind of the average photographer when photographing dangerous mammals is his own safety. However, inciting a charge from a bear or bull elk by venturing too close also has repercussions for the animal. Aggressive elk are sometimes tranquilized and have their antlers removed. This essentially ends their mating season and might render them more vulnerable to predation. Bears that maul humans are sometimes relocated to unfamiliar territory where they must adapt to new surroundings (and other, possibly dangerous bears) and in some instances may be euthanized. The ethical photographer thus realizes that his behavior in relation to dangerous mammals has consequences not only for himself, but for the subjects he admires.

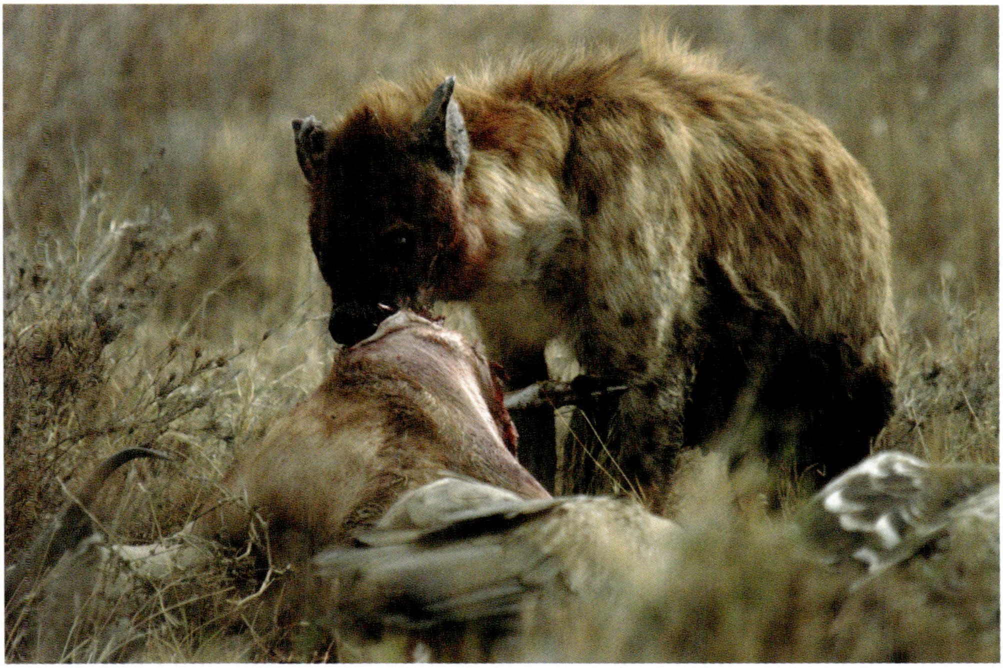

A predator on a carcass, such as this hyena feeding on a gazelle, is always dangerous. This photo was taken from an enclosed vehicle from a distance. *Jack Ballard*

Outlining strategies for handling aggressive behavior from all the various species of dangerous mammals is beyond the scope of this book. However, a couple of principles are helpful to remember in dealing with North American species. Bear pepper spray, a powerful irritant designed to repel attacks by grizzly bears (somewhat similar to teargas), is carried by most professional wildlife photographers when shooting in areas containing potentially dangerous mammals. The spray canister must be carried where it can be reached quickly (not buried in a backpack). Spray is directed at a charging animal at close range. While normally very effective, it is considered a last resort when dealing with a belligerent mammal.

The majority of situations involving aggressive or protective ungulates (moose, bison, elk, deer, etc.) can be handled by simply fleeing. A cow moose with a calf that chooses to charge or a whitetail buck with its antlers lowered and ears flattened during the mating season are both seeking the same goal, ejecting a perceived threat from the vicinity. If you have enough space to run or can quickly climb a tree (if available) in such a situation, do so. Predator attacks are handled differently. Biologists recommend fighting an attack from a mountain lion or black bear. They advise people to "play dead" if charged by a grizzly bear, which involves dropping to the ground in the fetal position and wrapping arms around the head and neck for protection.

If you plan to photograph where potentially dangerous mammals are present, it is imperative that you research procedures for dealing with aggression from various species. It is also critical to become competent in interpreting their body language that might indicate an impending confrontation. The best advice? In the presence of dangerous mammals, always stay inside a vehicle or sturdy enclosure and keep your distance.

PHOTOGRAPHING FROM A BLIND

Photographing mammals unaccustomed to humans or those inhabiting regions where they're hunted is a real challenge. Remotely fired or motion-sensing cameras set up at some attractant or along trails can yield photos of such creatures, but photographers seeking the higher predictability of a "hands-on" approach often shoot from a blind. Even in ideal circumstances, photographing wary mammals from a blind might involve sitting inside an entire day to garner a few frames, or none at all.

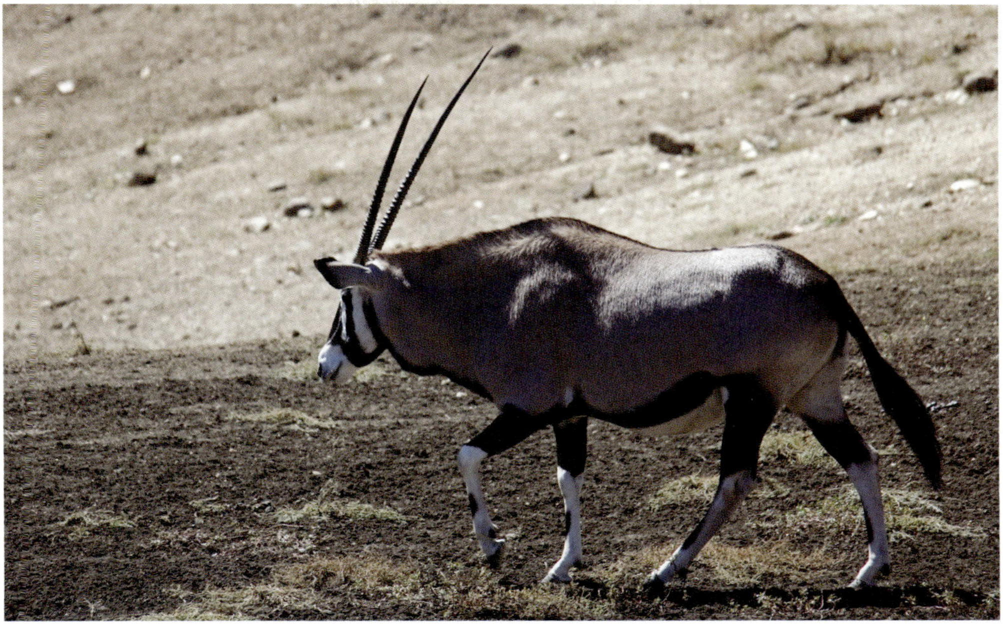

This gemsbok was photographed from a permanent blind near a waterhole in Namibia. In arid environments, blinds placed near water sources are a reliable way to photograph wary mammals. *Jack Ballard*

Blind placement is a critical factor in creating opportunities. Erecting a blind along a known travel route or in proximity of an environmental attractant (primarily food and water) offers the greatest odds of success. I once photographed a variety of mammals while working on a property in Namibia where animals were hunted. A permanent blind near a waterhole provided exactly the kind of concealment I needed to get within range of skittish species including gemsboks, warthogs, and waterbuck.

Shooting from a blind in such situations demands a photographer's best technique. Camera movements should be very slow and occur when the subject is looking away. Silence every possible camera function. Minimize activity in the blind. Photographing truly wild mammals from a blind is difficult, but may yield the most prized images in a wildlife shooter's portfolio.

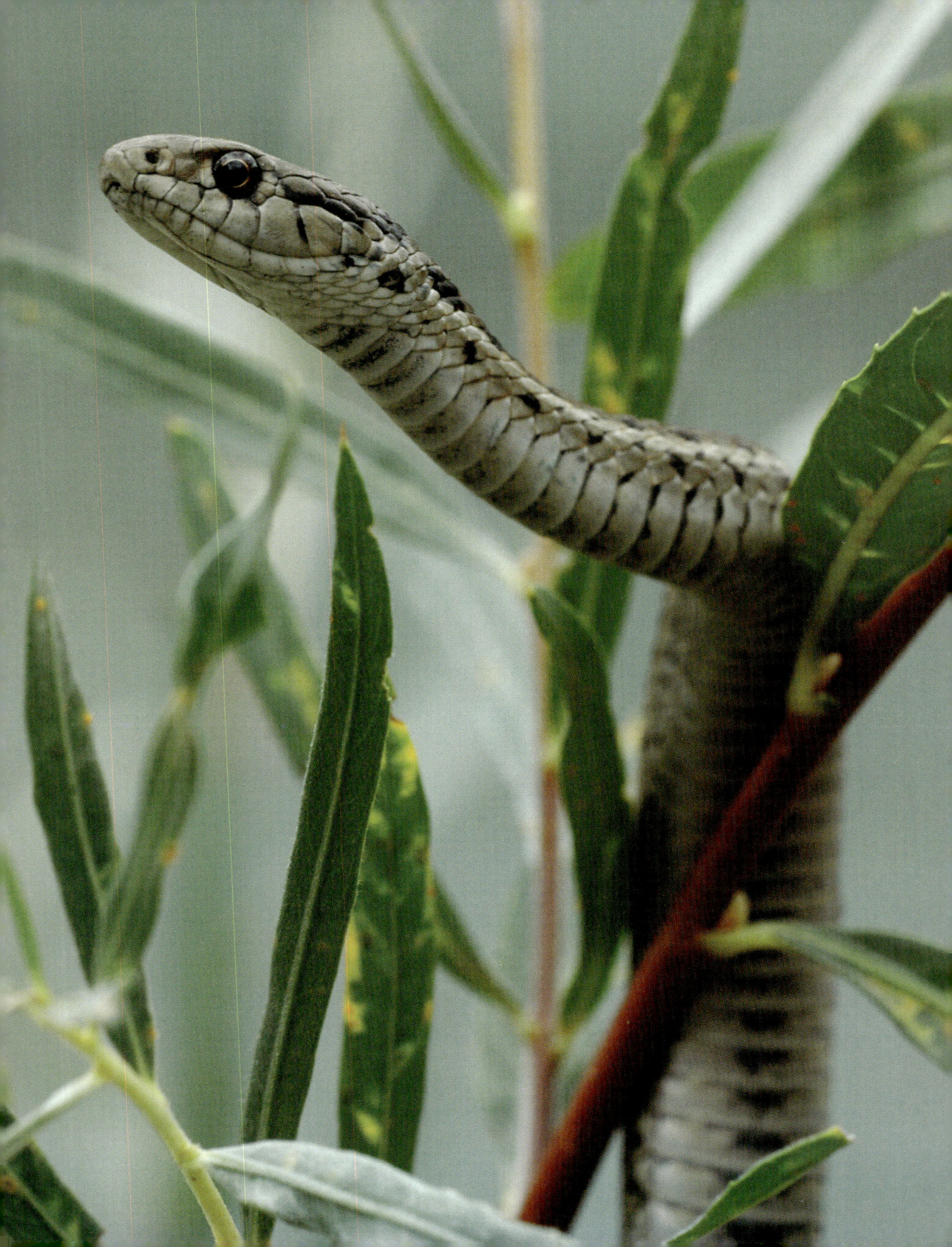

CHAPTER

8

Photographing Reptiles and Amphibians

Snakes. Lizards. Toads. People seem to love them or hate them. While numerous wildlife photographers overlook these categories of animals as subjects, a handful actively seek them. While I can't say I've ever embarked on an excursion to specifically shoot reptiles or amphibians, I'm happy to photograph them when the opportunity arises, as it frequently does. My photo files include hundreds of photos of reptiles and amphibians. Among these are images of lizards taken while floating the Colorado River in the Grand Canyon; several species of snakes from my home state of Montana; alligators around Lake Charles, Louisiana, and Everglades National Park in Florida; and numerous frogs, toads, and salamanders in New York's Adirondack Park.

Common garter snake. *Jack Ballard*

REPTILE AND AMPHIBIAN BEHAVIOR BASICS

Although some are skittish, many reptiles and amphibians can be closely approached by a photographer, making them attractive subjects for individuals lacking high-magnification telephoto lenses. The physical characteristics and behaviors of reptiles and amphibians are highly diverse. Photographers desiring

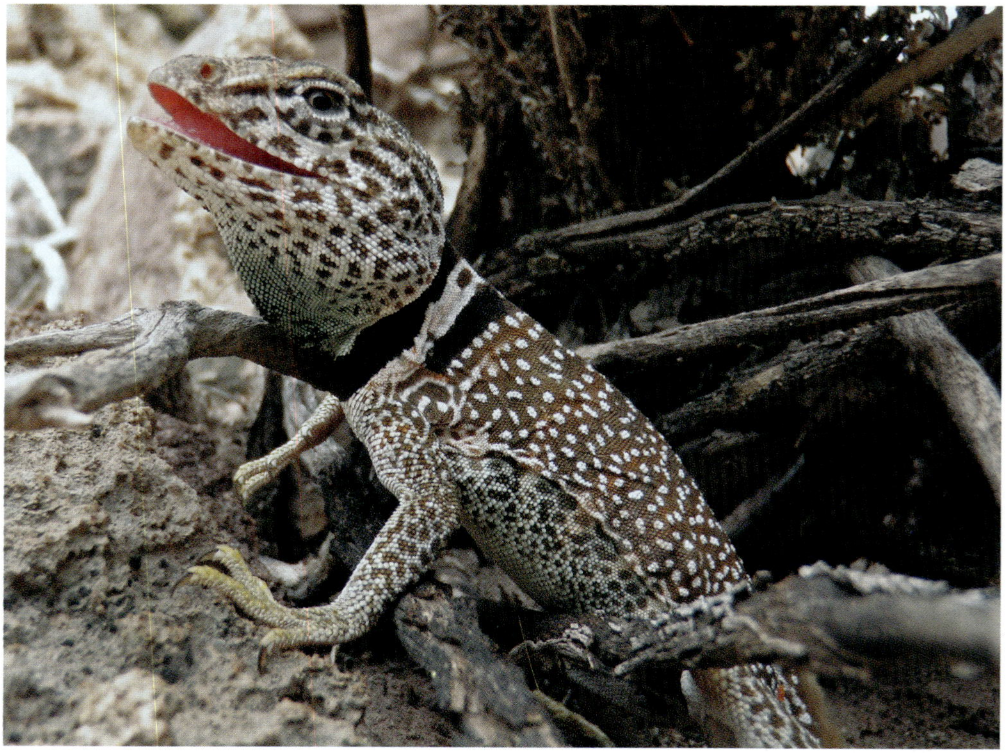

Some reptiles and amphibians can be approached quite closely. The author photographed this collared lizard from a couple feet away on a float trip on the Colorado River in Grand Canyon National Park, Arizona. *Jack Ballard*

Right: Snakes such as this common garter snake can detect ground vibrations and may be alerted by the footfalls of an approaching photographer. *Jack Ballard*

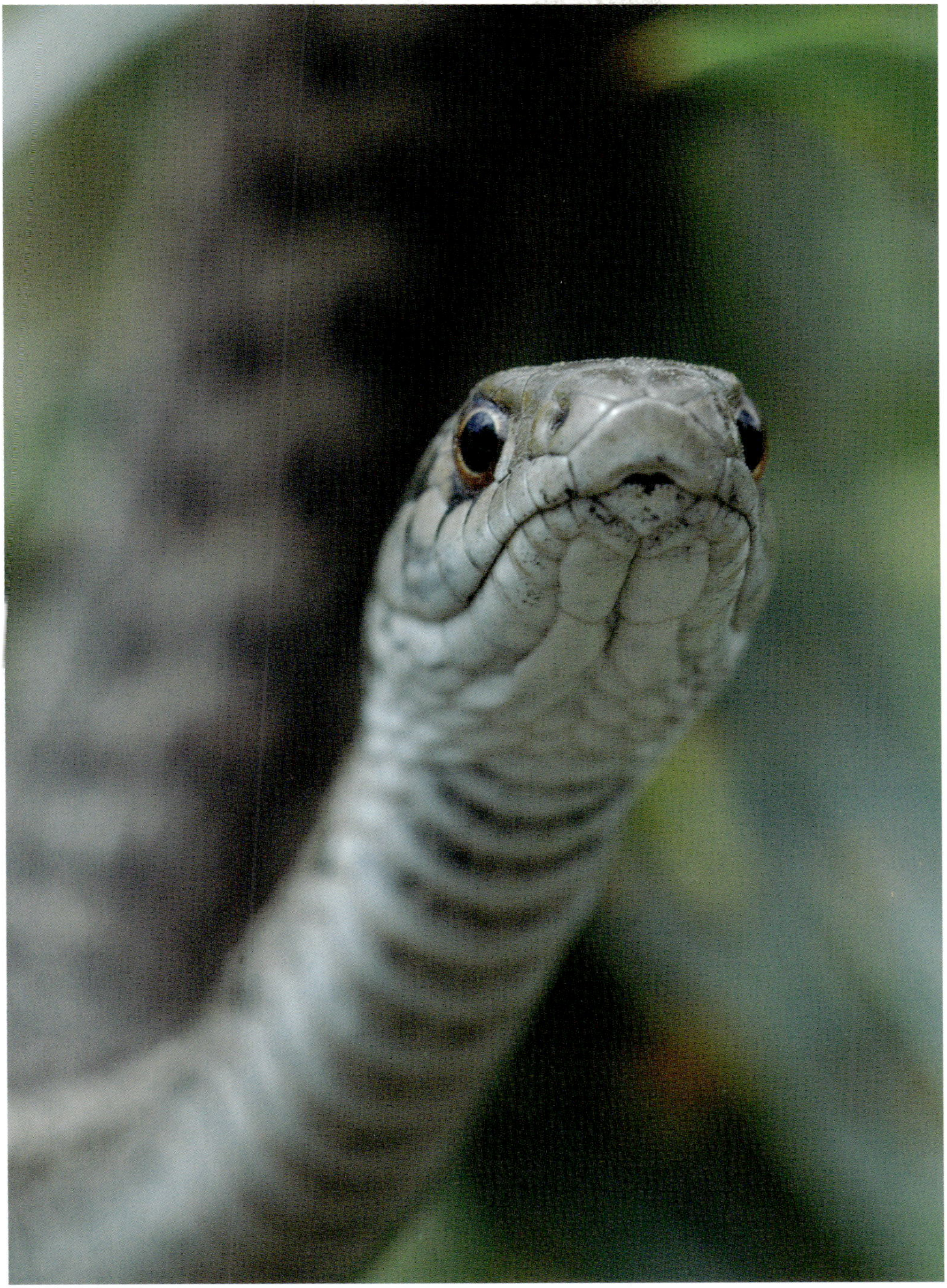

images of such creatures are advised to learn as much about the behavior and habitat of a species before attempting to photograph it.

The sensory mechanisms of amphibians and reptiles can be quite different from those of birds and mammals. Snakes, for example, do not have eardrums and are essentially deaf to airborne sounds. They can detect ground vibrations with ease, such as the footfalls of an approaching human. Their sense of smell is good, coupled with the ability to "taste scent," which involves capturing scent particles on an outstretched tongue and then "tasting" them via specialized organs inside their mouths. Snakes are thought to be quite short-sighted, relying on other senses to inform them of danger or discover prey.

Some amphibians, on the other hand, have excellent eyesight that they rely upon to detect environmental threats and the smaller creatures they eat. The eyes of frogs are located on the top of their head, which allows them to submerge their body in water but still clearly view their surroundings. Frogs have acute depth perception and excellent night vision. Despite the fact frogs can easily see the movement of an approaching human, some species will allow a slowly moving photographer to get very close.

Given the wide variation of sensory capabilities and behaviors, the astute wildlife photographer understands that interacting with reptiles and amphibians may pose a different set of challenges than working with other types of creatures.

Movement Patterns

Perhaps the greatest factor affecting the movement patterns of reptiles and amphibians is their cold-bloodedness. These animals do not regulate their body temperature through internal forces of metabolism and heat dissipation. Their body temperature is instead determined primarily by the temperature of their surroundings. Lizards and snakes are thus quite active on warm summer days. Their movement is curtailed when it gets very hot, however, and they often retreat to shady locations. The preferred temperature varies from species to species, a factor of interest to photographers seeking to photograph a particular species. American alligators, for example, are most active between 82 and 92 degrees Fahrenheit.

Reptiles in most locations in the United States typically become dormant during the winter. In the spring and fall, they seek locations that retain heat, such as the warm asphalt on a paved road. Amphibians are also cold-blooded, but some, such as the Cascade frog, tolerate quite cold temperatures. Cascade frogs live at high elevations and surface from hibernation while ice and snow

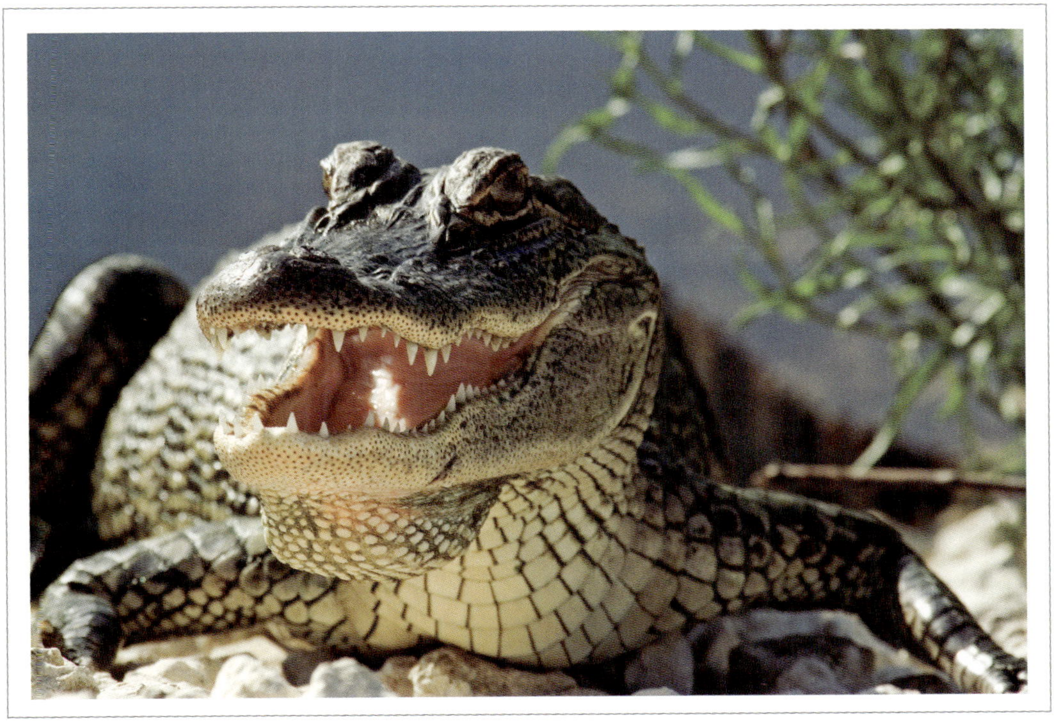

Amphibians and reptiles, like this American alligator photographed at Cameron Prairie National Wildlife Refuge, Louisiana, have a preferred temperature range where they are most active. *Jack Ballard*

may still be clinging to the ponds in which they live. Desert-dwelling species sometimes undergo the opposite of hibernation. Estivation occurs when very high temperatures and/or aridity cause cold-blooded creatures to burrow into the earth or retreat below ground to escape extreme conditions.

The extent to which reptiles and amphibians tolerate humans and allow a photographer to come within camera range varies widely from species to species. I've had entire populations of frogs dive into a pond at my approach, but at other times had frogs allow the lens of my camera within inches of their eyeballs. The same is true for lizards and snakes. Both reptiles and amphibians seem much less alarmed by a photographer who moves toward them with a low

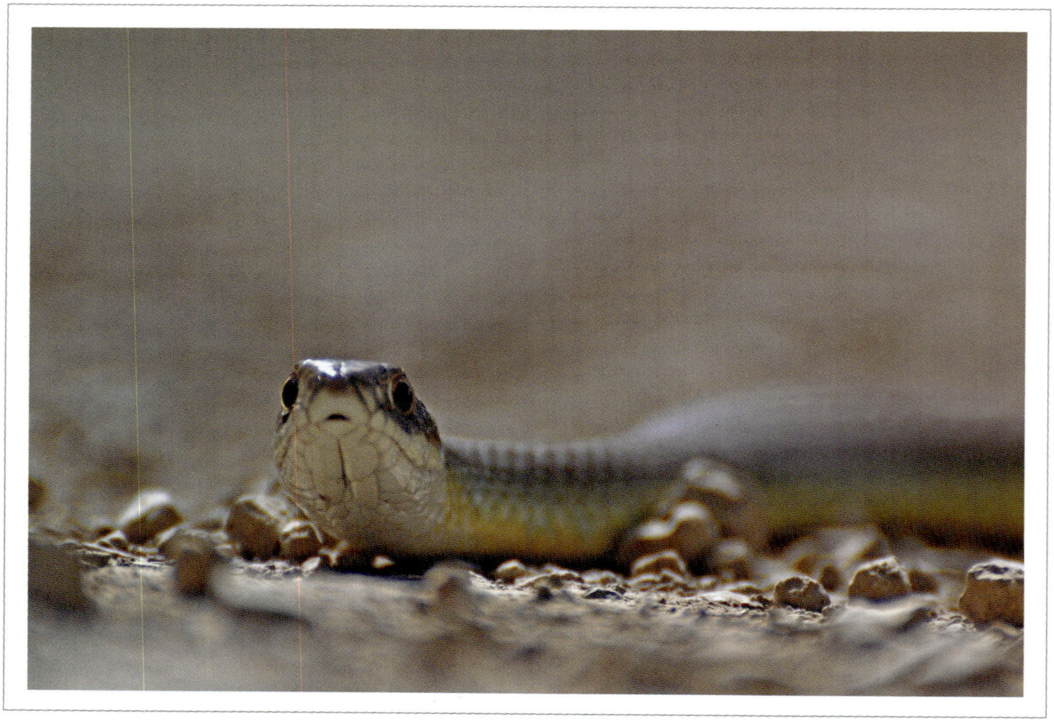

The author crawled within range of this western yellow-bellied racer in southwestern Colorado using a 300mm telephoto lens. It allowed but two frames before "racing" away. Some snakes allow photographers quite close; others are wary. *Jack Ballard*

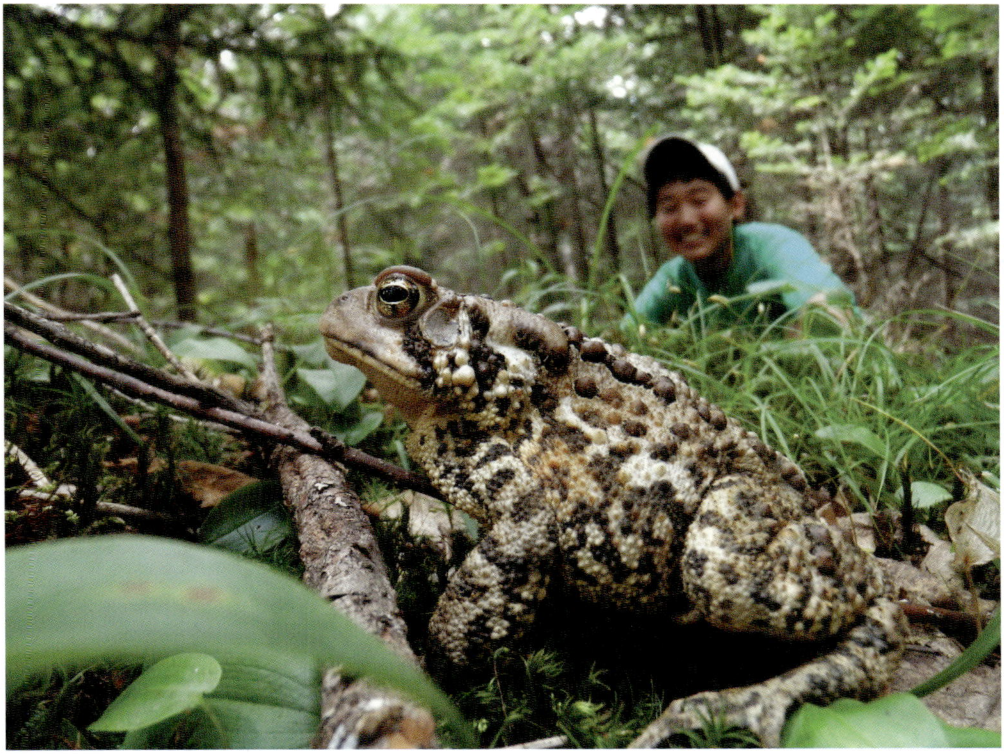

This American toad, with a fascinated young hiker in the background, was photographed at a distance of a few inches with a compact camera. Knowing the minimum focusing distance of a lens helps to eliminate focusing errors on such confiding subjects. *Jack Ballard*

profile (crouching or crawling) than a person standing erect. As is the case with mammals, an indirect, very slow approach yields the best odds of achieving the desired camera range.

While some lizards can move very rapidly (a handful of species can run over 20 miles per hour), many reptiles and most amphibians can be overtaken by a walking human on land. Evasion strategies of these animals involve hiding, climbing trees, retreating to dense cover, or disappearing into holes, crevices, and burrows. Frogs and some species of lizards elude people by diving into water and swimming away. As is the case with fleeing mammals, it is generally futile to pursue a lizard on the run or a swimming frog. A better tactic is to patiently wait for a frog to return to land or a lizard to emerge from the temporary refuge of a hole.

The fact that some reptiles and lizards will allow photographers to get quite close makes it imperative to understand the minimum focusing distance of your lens. When a creature allows a photographer to get within close range, it's tempting to reduce the distance as much as possible. However, it's often possible to get closer to reptiles and amphibians than a telephoto lens will focus. Rather than be forced to back off, know the minimum focusing distance of your lens and don't get too close.

Seasonal Activities

Reptiles and amphibians follow a yearly cycle of reproduction and growth, just like birds and mammals. Some types also undergo appearance transitions at certain times of the year. These aspects of the life cycle create unique opportunities for wildlife photographers in tune with the seasonal activities and transformations of the species they intend to photograph.

Most amphibians require freshwater for reproduction and produce young in the springtime. Exceptions to this general rule are mostly found in the tropics, where amphibians may reproduce year-round. Frogs are probably the most readily available amphibian for most photographers in North America and begin their life cycle in the spring. Male frogs croak and call to attract mates. Some species inflate an air sac under their chin when vocalizing, a behavior creating distinctive and sometimes comical fodder for photos. Frog eggs transform into tadpoles, which eventually metamorphose into mature frogs. Photographers with access to a frog pond who are willing to devote several weeks to the project can record this entire life cycle in photos.

Late spring and early summer are also excellent times to be on the lookout for salamanders. Salamanders live in moist environments and in many places are most likely to be seen in damp areas before the heat of midsummer dries them up.

Seasonal behaviors of reptiles may also create unique opportunities for wildlife photographers. American alligators mate in June, with females laying their eggs in July. Hatchlings emerge from the nest in September, under the watchful eye of the female. Photographers who are lucky enough to record the

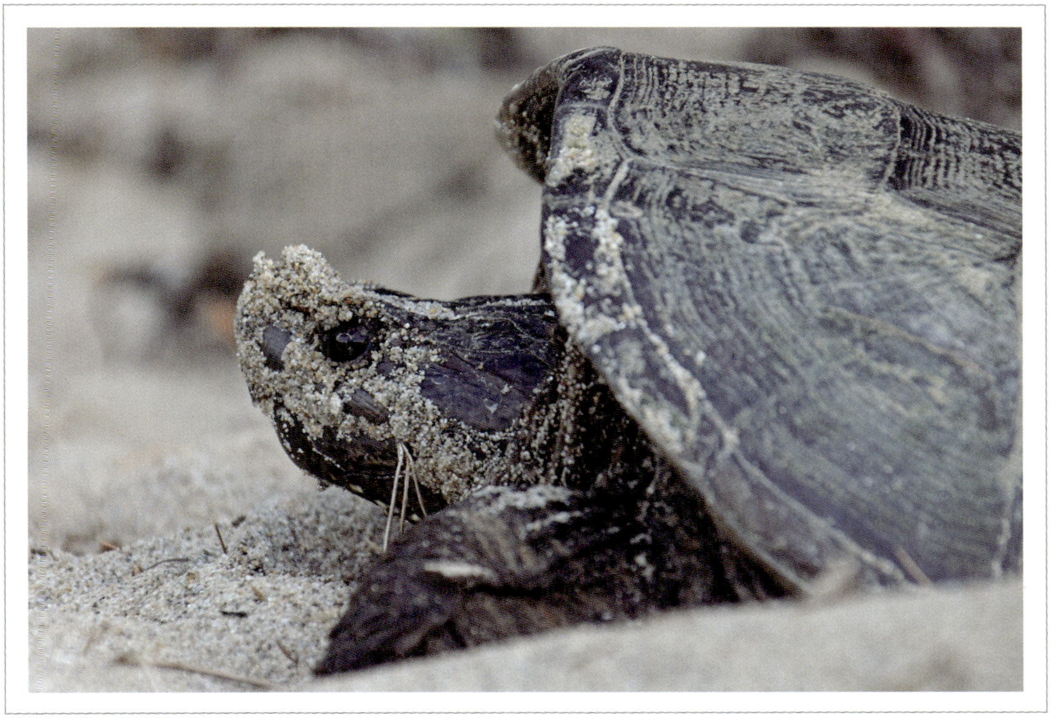

Life-cycle behaviors of reptiles and amphibians create unique photo opportunities, such as this image of a female snapping turtle taken while she was laying eggs. *Lisa Ballard*

ETHICS AND ETIQUETTE

TOUCHING REPTILES AND AMPHIBIANS

To touch or not to touch? That's a question confronting wildlife photographers in relation to reptiles and amphibians. It's always foolish for anyone but authorized wildlife management personnel to handle dangerous species. But what about grabbing a garter snake or gently relocating a sluggish toad to a better background for a photo?

Some states have laws governing the harassment of wildlife that might directly or indirectly prohibit the handling of wild reptiles and amphibians. A first question to ask concerns legality. Other issues pertain to the safety and welfare of both the subject and the photographer.

Nonpoisonous snakes, including common garter snakes, will occasionally bite a handler, sometimes with enough force to break the skin. These wounds tend to be superficial, similar to getting jabbed in the thumb with a small thorn. Although the wound itself isn't an issue, there is some risk of infection associated with such bites, including tetanus. While researching this issue, I also found multiple warnings of frogs being potential hosts of salmonella, a bacteria that can cause serious illness in humans. Most of the warnings involve the handling of domestic frogs, with particular emphasis on keeping them away from young children, but some of the cautionary statements also applied to frogs in general. The skin and secretions of some amphibians are highly toxic to humans. Unwittingly handling a species with toxic properties and then inadvertently contacting one's mouth with the toxins poses potential danger to photographers.

The welfare of the subject is also a matter of concern. The skin of amphibians is very porous compared to most other creatures. Oils, soap residue, perfumes, and other chemicals on the skin of a person might easily be transmitted to an amphibian, as these creatures can absorb substances (such as water) directly through their skin. Little specific information is available on the subject, but some biologists theorize such substances could possibly be toxic.

Give the current state of information, to touch or not is an issue without clear guidance from wildlife professionals. At least in the case of rare species, it's best to leave them alone. Regarding the others, minimal or no handling is probably the best decision, due to the fact that amphibian populations worldwide are declining, with numerous species becoming extinct.

Right: Handling this garter snake isn't likely to harm the boy or the snake. However, photographers are advised to exercise caution if handling reptiles and amphibians for their own safety and that of the animals. *Jack Ballard*

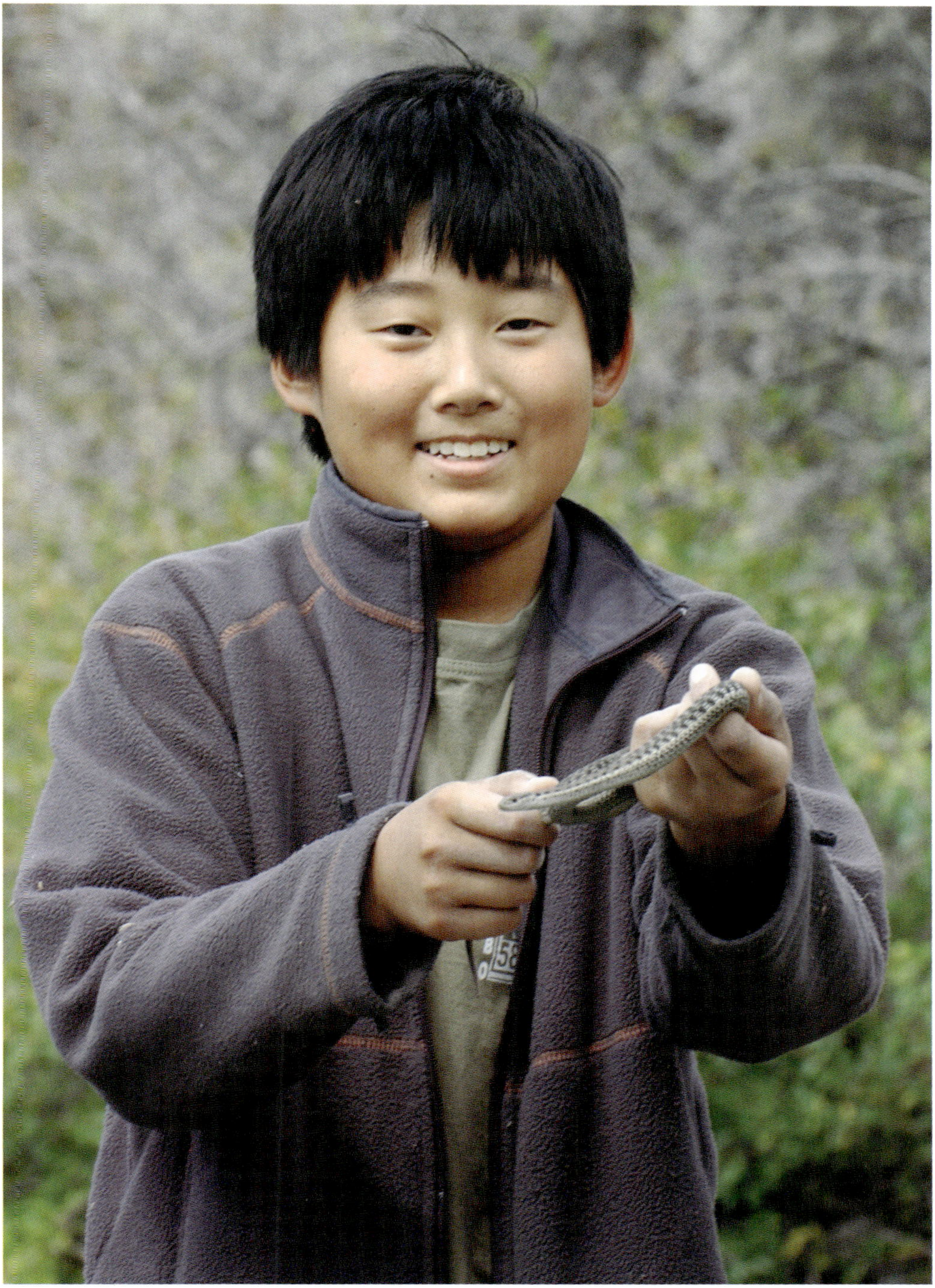

interactions between a female alligator and her tiny young (baby alligators are only 6 to 8 inches long when they hatch) have documented one of nature's magical moments. The life cycle of turtles also offers singular chances for photography. One of the more memorable moments of my wife's wildlife photography career was an early morning in late June when she happened upon a snapping turtle laying eggs in the sand on a beach at Long Lake in Adirondack Park.

Appearance Transitions

Both reptiles and amphibians shed their skin. While some species, such as snakes, abandon their cast-off skin, others eat it to recycle nutrients. Skin is generally shed more often among growing members of these species as opposed

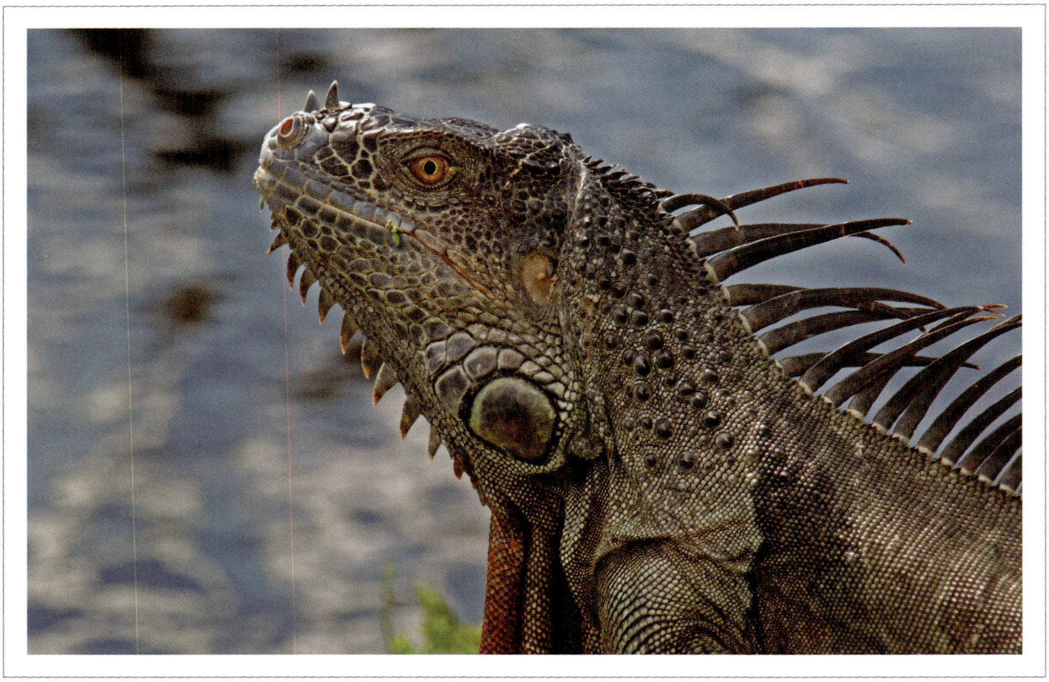

Younger reptiles and amphibians shed their skin more often than fully grown specimens. New skin is more colorful and exhibits more intense patterns than the old. The skin on this very large iguana in southern Florida is in good shape for photos and isn't likely to be shed any time soon. *Lisa Ballard*

to those who have reached their maximum size. For wildlife photographers, skin-shedding itself offers the prospect of recording intriguing images of this unique phenomenon. Other odd biological aspects sometimes accompany skin-shedding. For example, the eyes of some species of reptiles bulge substantially from their head just prior to shedding their skin. The appearance of a creature's skin also changes in relation to shedding. Old skin tends to exhibit duller colors and more subdued patterns. The new skin on a reptile or amphibian that has just molted exhibits brighter colors and more distinct patterns.

Some species of reptiles and amphibians undergo changes in color in relation to their life cycle and environmental conditions. Chameleons, lizards native to portions of Africa, Europe, and Asia, are the most famous for their color changes. The hue of their skin can change dramatically in relation to the color of the background environment, but also alters as a means of regulating body temperature and displaying social signals. Photographers able to capture the color changes of a chameleon in images have documented one of nature's seemingly miraculous transformations.

While alterations in chameleon color are among the most widely recognized, other species of reptiles and amphibians also change colors. Some species of frogs alter the hues of their skin between the juvenile and adult state. Others don't change their basic color, but display lighter or darker tones in relation to environmental surroundings and heat. Frogs may develop a lighter appearance when it's hot, as lighter colors reflect more heat than darker hues. From a photography standpoint, this sometimes means the color of an individual frog changes slightly in relation to temperature swings at various times of the day. Some snakes also experience appearance changes. Juveniles of numerous species are much more highly patterned (thought to aid their camouflage) than adults.

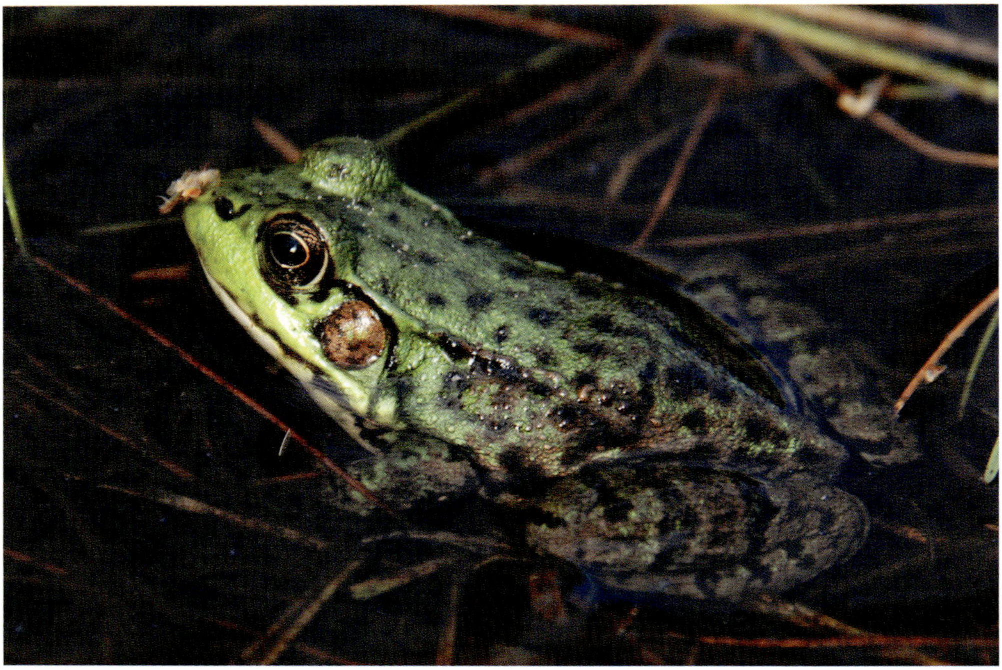

Some frogs may change their color and tone in relation to temperature. *Lisa Ballard*

PHOTOGRAPHING DANGEROUS SPECIES

It should be noted that some species of reptiles and amphibians, including poisonous snakes and large constrictors, should be photographed from a distance and with the utmost care. Large reptiles such as alligators, crocodiles, and Komodo dragons are also potentially dangerous, especially if approached too closely. Some amphibians, including a number of brightly colored frogs and salamanders, have skin that contains highly toxic substances and shouldn't be handled. A thorough understanding of the particular risks and behaviors associated with a perilous species is requisite to safely photographing it. For example, the maximum striking distance of snakes is about one-half their body length. A photographer who keeps a full body length away from a dangerous snake won't get struck, but should remember that some snakes move quickly. Unless cornered, even venomous snakes are happier retreating from a human than confronting it.

A rule of thumb uppermost in my mind when photographing potentially dangerous reptiles (amphibians are pretty much harmless unless handled) is that where there's one, there are often more. A photographer intent on capturing images of a rattlesnake might inadvertently back into its mate. If you choose to photograph dangerous reptiles, it's wise to have another person act as a "spotter" to watch for other hazards.

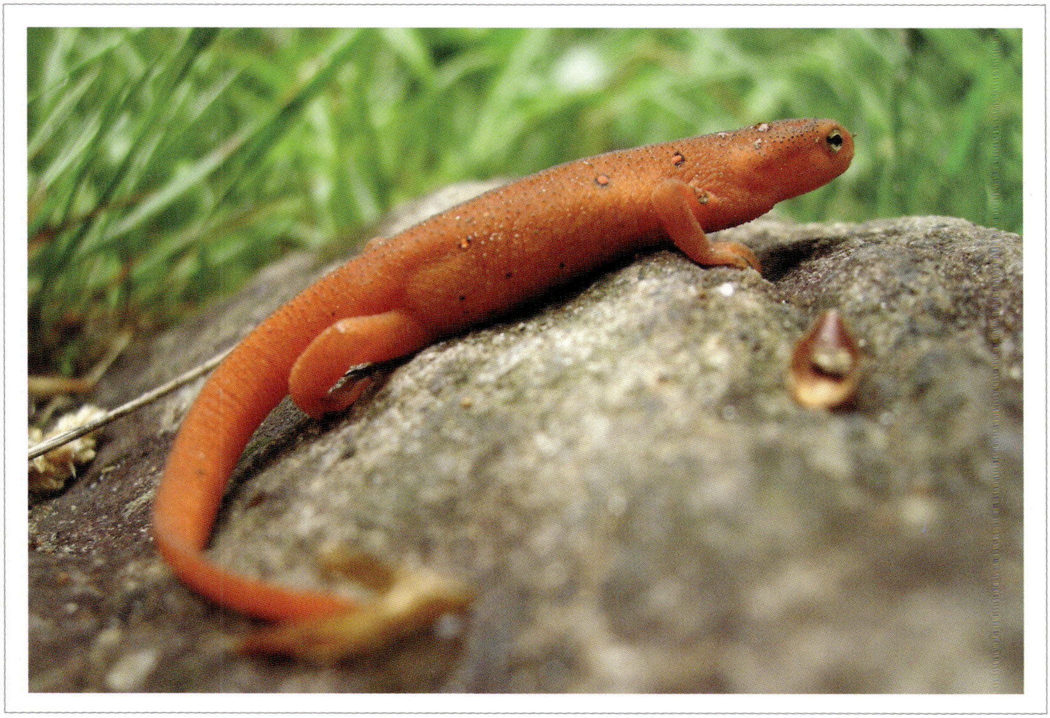

The skin of many salamanders is toxic, especially brightly colored species. This juvenile (red eft) form of the eastern salamander is somewhat toxic and shouldn't be handled. Knowing the specific dangers posed by various species of reptiles and amphibians is important for photographers. *Jack Ballard*

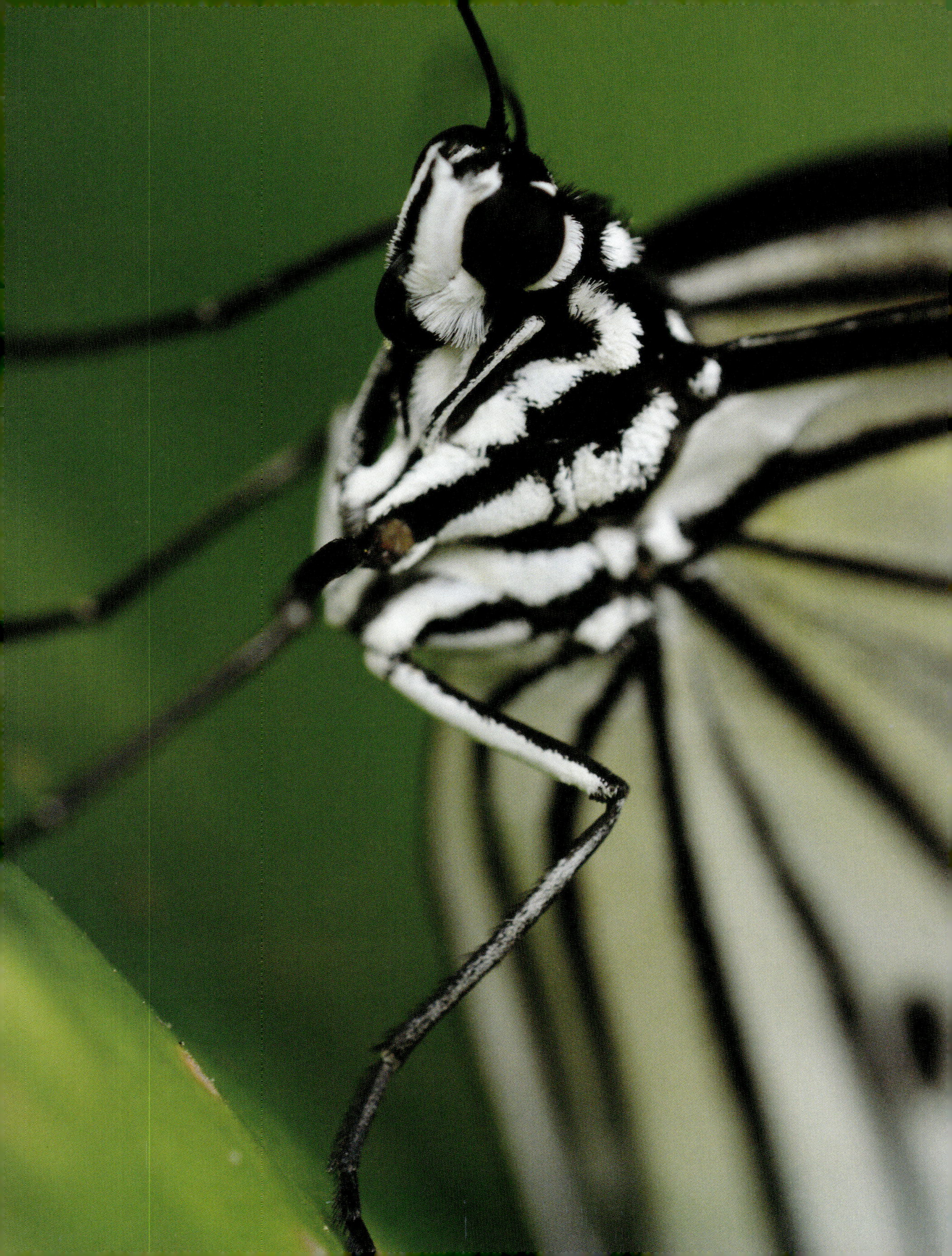

CHAPTER 9

Photographing Small Subjects and Macro Photography

Tiny hummingbirds, cheery chipmunks, miniature lizards, and a seemingly infinite number of insect species all hold promise as engaging subjects for wildlife photos. Specialized equipment can also be employed to capture images of even smaller organisms such as amoebas, though we'll forgo that discussion as I don't know any photographers who would classify these single-celled critters as "wildlife." However, the world of itty-bitty creatures commonly encountered in the natural realm has enormous potential for wildlife photographers. Some require specialized equipment to successfully photograph on a regular basis. Others aren't so difficult provided the photographer can get close enough to record their images with everyday equipment.

Butterfly. *Jack Ballard*

SPECIALTY EQUIPMENT FOR SMALL SUBJECTS

There are essentially two ways to make the subject appear larger in a photograph. The first is to photograph it at a closer distance. The second is to use a higher-magnification lens. Each approach has its advantages and drawbacks.

High-Magnification Lenses

High-magnification lenses operate no differently when photographing a small subject such as a tiny lizard as they do when imaging an immense hippopotamus. A common estimation of a lens's power of magnification in relation to human eyesight assumes that a person's normal vision is equal to a 50mm lens on a film camera body or a digital body with a full-frame sensor. Thus a 100mm lens approximates a magnification factor of 2X. A powerful 500mm telephoto enlarges the subject times 10 (10X).

While the length of a lens determines its magnification factor, that's not the end of the story when photographing small subjects. Its minimum focusing distance (the point closest to the subject the camera can maintain a sharp image) is equally important. For example, suppose the minimum focusing distance for 500mm lens A is 15 feet, and the minimum focusing distance for 500mm lens B is 10 feet. Because small wildlife subjects such as insects are often photographed at a distance of 10 feet or less, lens B has far superior capabilities.

Right: This butterfly was photographed with a high-magnification 80–400mm zoom lens at the 400mm focal length. It would not tolerate a closer approach by the author. *Jack Ballard*

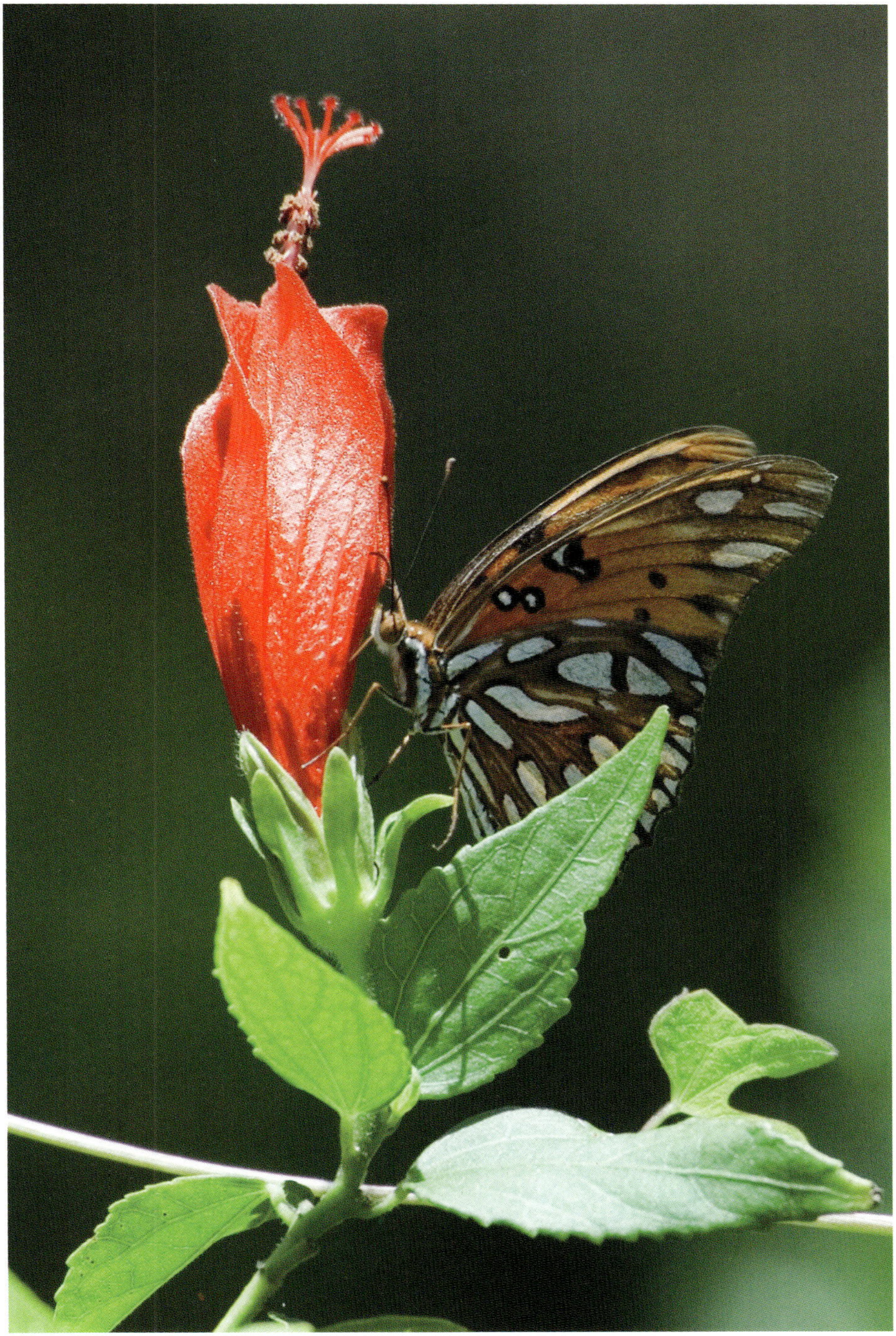

Wildlife photographers often use high-magnification zoom lenses, and many of these have excellent capabilities for tiny creatures. While it's easy to assume that the optimal magnification of such a lens occurs at its maximum length, such is not always the case due to the fact that the minimum focusing distance can change in relation to how much the lens is "zoomed." For example, one 50–500mm zoom lens popular with wildlife photographers has a minimum focus distance at 500mm of 9.8 feet and at 200mm of 3.6 feet. A bumblebee on a flower will thus appear larger in the frame if the photographer can get within 3.6 feet with the lens at 200mm than it will at 9.8 feet at 500mm (provided the photographer can get within 3.6 feet of the subject). This difference is expressed in what is often referred to as the "magnification ratio" of a prime lens or a zoom lens at a particular focal length. A lens with a 1:1 magnification ratio can magnify the subject so that its size as captured by the image sensor (or on film) is the same as in real life. A lens with a 1:2 magnification has the ability to magnify the subject up to 50 percent of its life size on the sensor or film. In the above case, the 50–500mm lens at 200mm has a magnification ratio of 1:5.2 and a ratio of 1:6.8 at 500mm.

Macro Lenses

In its classic understanding, macro photography is defined as photographing subjects at a 1:1 magnification ratio or larger. A "true" macro lens thus has 1:1 magnification ratio capabilities. However, in its more popular sense, macro photography is often understood the same as close-up photography. What's the definition of close-up photography? Unfortunately it's similar to an illicit image—it's almost impossible to define, but you'll know it when you see it.

Whether defined as "close-up" or "macro" photography, lenses with high magnification ratios are very important for the best results. Although a true macro

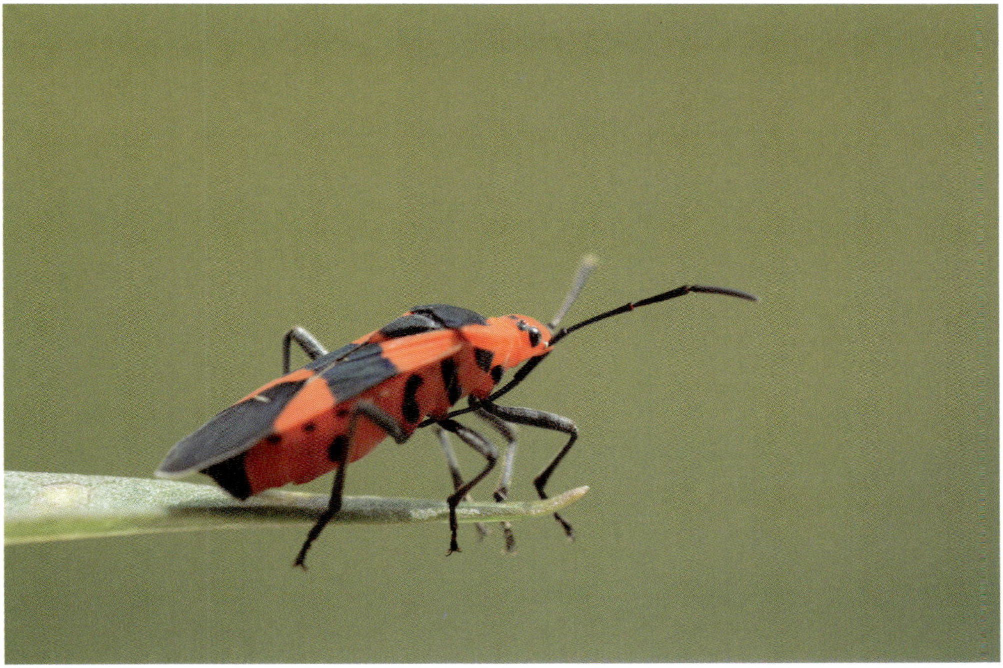

With a true macro lens, the size of the subject captured on a camera's recording medium is the same as its size in real life. This nonnative firebug (about a half inch long) was photographed in Florida with a 1:1 macro lens. The photo has not been cropped. *Jack Ballard*

lens has 1:1 capabilities, many camera and lens manufacturers classify lenses with lower magnification ratios as "macro." While there is no standardization in this area, a number of companies classify lenses that have 1:2 or higher magnification ratios as macro lenses. Some also tout close-focusing telephoto lenses as having macro capabilities. What's crucial is not how the lens is labeled or marketed, but its actual magnification ratio. Suffice it to say that a lens with a 1:2 ratio has better small-subject capabilities than a lens with a 1:3 ratio, even though the latter might be advertised as "macro" while the former is not. When selecting lenses for macro photography or the photography of tiny subjects, evaluate them on the basis of their magnification ratios, not how they're classified by the seller.

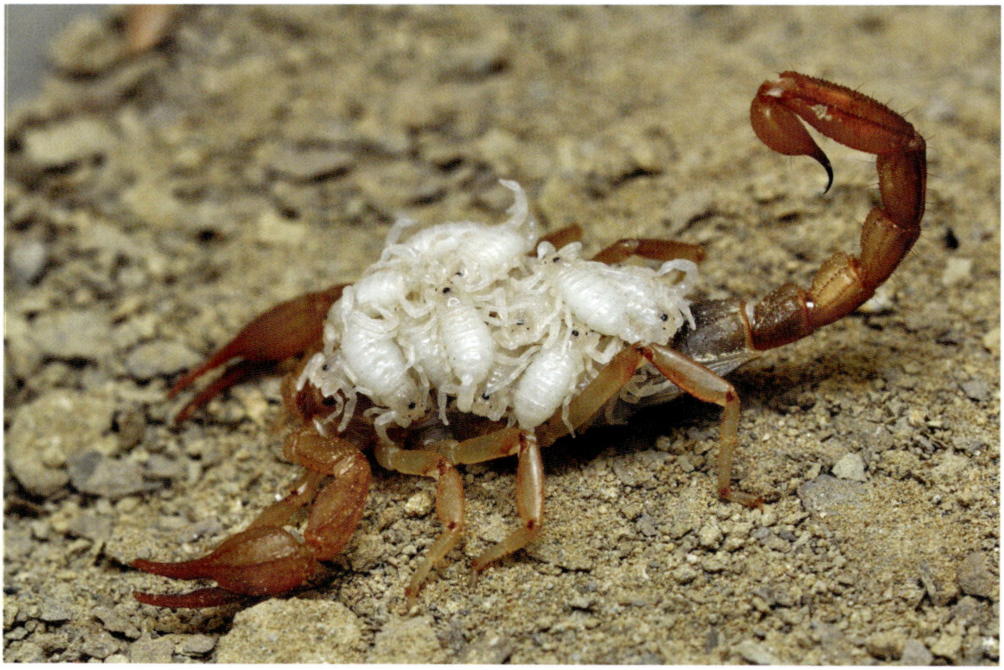

Short macro lenses require the photographer to shoot a very short distance from the subject. The author used a 180mm macro to photograph this northern scorpion with babies clinging to her back at a distance of around 18 inches in a controlled setting for an article project. *Jack Ballard*

True macro lenses tend to be expensive and have rather short focal lengths. Producing a lens with macro capabilities that minimizes distortion and other problems associated with extreme close-up photography is technologically challenging. A 200mm lens with a 1:1 magnification ratio is on the long side. Most 1:1 lenses range from around 40mm to 105mm in focal length. However, a longer macro lens has some advantages. While a 50mm macro lens may require a minimum focusing distance of 8 inches to achieve 1:1 magnification, the 200mm lens may stretch that to around 20 inches. That may not seem like much, but when photographing a stinging or skittish insect, being an extra foot away is sometimes invaluable. Furthermore, a 200mm macro lens will maintain a fairly high magnification ratio a few feet from the subject. A 50mm macro lens will not.

Adaptable Cameras

Some compact cameras (point-and-shoot) offer surprisingly good macro capabilities. I often carry a compact camera when trail running, skiing, or in other situations where the bulk of a full-size DSLR is impractical. My compact camera, like most others, has limited capabilities for normal wildlife photography due to the constraints of its focal length. It's pretty useless for photographing

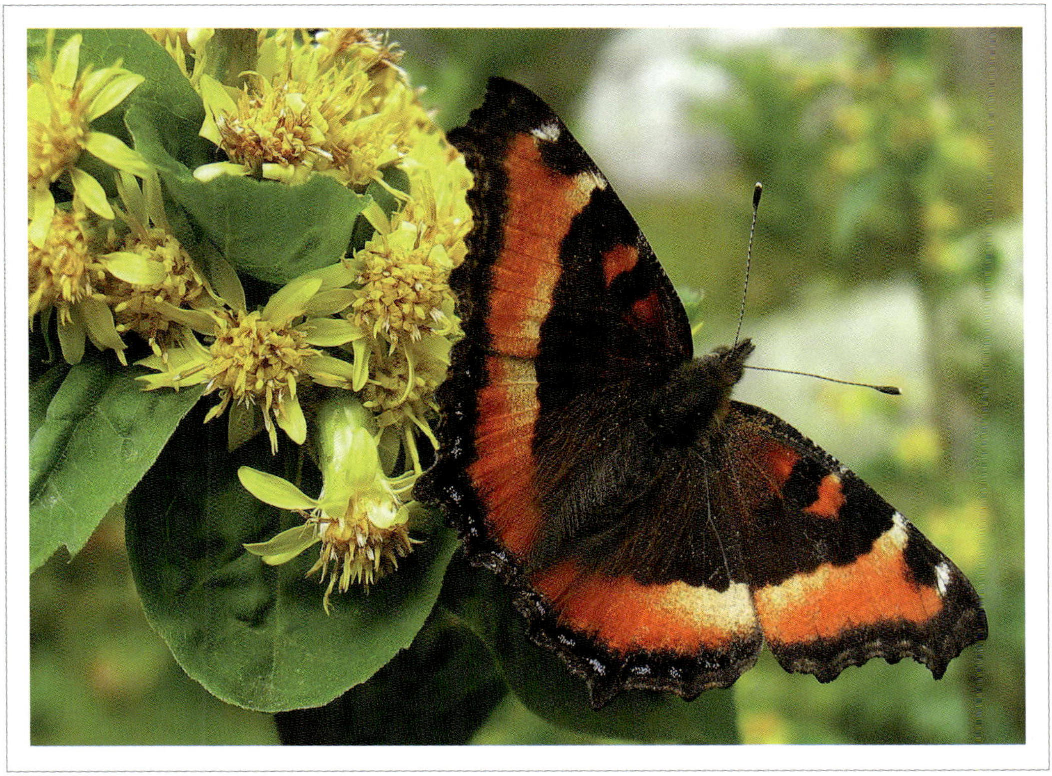

Some compact cameras have very good macro capabilities. This photo of a butterfly on alpine goldenrod was photographed with a compact camera on a hiking trip in the Presidential Range of mountains in New Hampshire. *Lisa Ballard*

even the largest mammals at a distance. On the opposite end of the spectrum, photographing tiny subjects at close range, it shines.

Reviews of compact camera macro capabilities by competent sources will help narrow your search for such a camera. Despite their excellent capabilities, using compacts for macro photography has some disadvantages. First, you'll need to get extremely close to the subject, perhaps as close as a couple of inches away, to get a true macro (1:1 magnification ratio) photo. I've sometimes found frogs, lizards, and insects that will allow the camera within such a close range, but many subjects won't have it, even with the most patient approach. Second, the flash on the camera will need to be disabled (if it functions in the macro mode) in most cases, as the addition of camera-integrated flash at such close range usually ruins the exposure. Finally, much of the appeal of a compact camera stems from its small size and portability. For the best macro results, however, the camera will need to be supported to avoid the reduction in image quality associated with vibration or movement. The ground or natural objects can sometimes be used to stabilize the camera, but the best macro results with a compact camera will require use of a small tripod, which takes some of the "compact" out of the camera equation.

BASICS OF MACRO PHOTOGRAPHY

For our purposes, this section will deal with macro photography in the popular sense, which includes extreme close-ups of wildlife subjects that may not fit the 1:1 magnification of true macro photography. The discussion will thus include the use of relatively close-focusing telephoto lenses in addition to macro lenses as designated by manufacturers.

While some macro specialists look down their nose at any gear beyond that with true macro capabilities, using a relatively close-focusing telephoto lens to photograph small wildlife subjects has several attractions. The first is the ability to keep a longer distance away from easily disturbed or potentially dangerous subjects. A second has to do with a phenomenon known as "telephotic compression." This refers to the fact that at high magnification the lens not only magnifies the subject, but creates the perception that features in the background are closer together than they are. This effect, for example, can minimize the fore and aft distance of a butterfly pollinating a flower, while a true macro shot of the same subject may create the perception that the flower is much larger than it actually is.

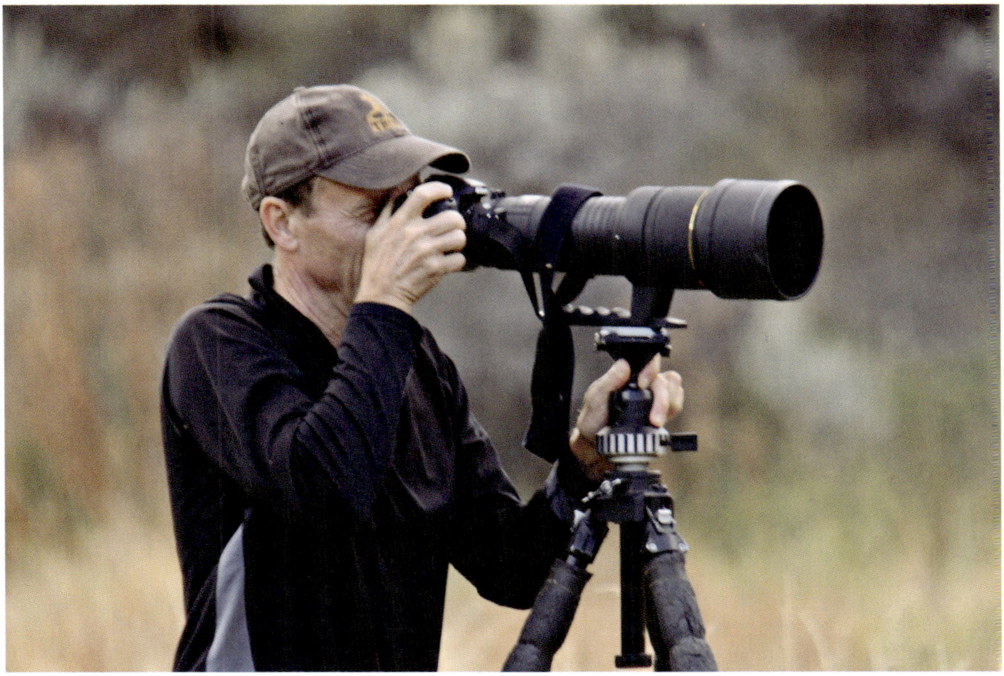

Long telephoto lenses create more depth of field when photographing small subjects at wide apertures versus macro lenses, allowing the photographer to create increased depth of field at higher speeds. This, along with other characteristics, make them superior to macros for close-up photography in many situations. *Lisa Ballard*

Another advantage has to do with depth of field. Most true macro lenses, because of the near distance needed to the subject, create an exceedingly short depth of field. Shot at a maximum aperture of f/2.8, when trained on the head of a dragonfly, a macro lens may only render a tiny sliver of the eye in focus. To achieve more depth of field, the f-stop needs to be increased dramatically, creating a correspondingly slow shutter speed. Slow shutter speeds up the odds of blurred images due to slight movements of the camera or the subject. A close-focusing telephoto lens shot at an aperture of f/4 allows a snappy shutter speed and creates a soft focus on the background when photographing a small subject from several feet, both desirable when shooting extreme close-ups. Additionally, a camera's pop-up flash or an on-camera external flash can be used to add fill-light to extreme close-ups with a telephoto lens but do not typically work well when using a true macro lens.

To increase the macro capabilities of close-focusing telephotos, wildlife professionals sometimes add a teleconverter. (See chapter 1 for a detailed discussion of these.) The converter increases the size of the subject in the frame by the magnification of the converter (1.4X and 2X are most common), nudging the image further in the direction of a true macro photo. However, it's critical to remember that converters also decrease the maximum aperture of the lens and cause some degradation of image quality, especially when paired with zoom lenses. On the positive side, they slightly decrease the minimum focusing distance of the lens due to the extension created between the camera body and the lens.

No matter what lens is used, certain principles of macro photography should be kept in mind when creating such intimate images of wildlife subjects. One of these has to do with background objects. Most macro photographers aim for

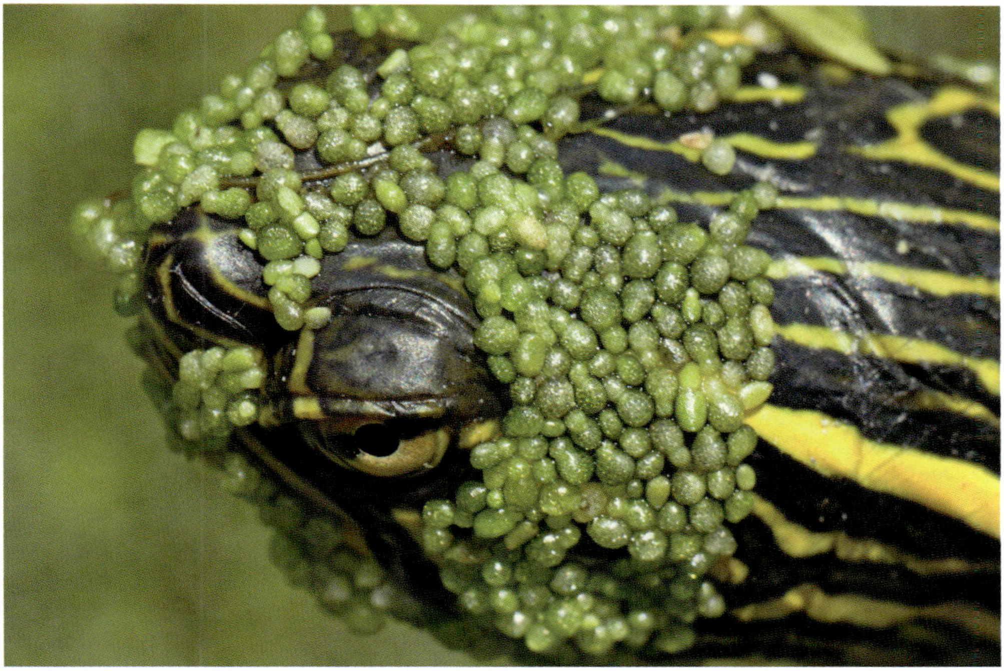

A shallow depth of field and clean background emphasize the eye and tiny globules of duckweed clinging to the head of this painted turtle in a pond at the National Bison Range in Montana. *Jack Ballard*

images in which the background is completely softened due to shallow depth of field. This renders background objects unidentifiable except for basic shape and color. The presence of a light object in an otherwise middle-toned or dark background, even when completely blurred, will create a light spot that will draw the viewer's eye from the subject of the photo. (The same is true for a dark object in a light background.) Consistent background tones normally produce the best macro photos, as they minimize distraction from the subject.

Along with watching for light or dark aberrations in the background, choosing a camera angle allowing a background color that complements the subject (if possible) is another skill cultivated by adroit macro photographers. For example, a damselfly resting on a tall blade of grass may allow for several backgrounds. One might be the deep greens of foliage at eye level. Another could include the azure tones of the northern sky slightly above the subject. A third could be the brown trunk of a massive tree angled just a few feet behind the subject. Many damselflies are light blue, but others are red, brown, or another color. A light blue subject against a blue sky won't stand out in the same way it will against an intense green background. Because macro photography often takes on something of a studio effect in the sense of a completely soft background, choosing background colors that accentuate attributes of a wildlife subject is similar to a portrait photographer pairing a background with her subject's wardrobe and physical features.

Another critical aspect of macro photography is remembering that an extreme close-up of the subject is necessarily an extreme close-up of every other element in the frame that is also in focus. The tiny bit of spiderweb on a cattail, the damaged petal on an otherwise perfect flower, and an errant pine needle jutting next to a tiny mushroom may all create horrid distractions in an otherwise perfect macro shot. My wildlife photo files include a nice close-up of a spring peeper in lakeside foliage in upstate New York. The gentle little fellow had hopped from the sandy lakeshore into the grass. It allowed me to position my compact camera within inches of its head, yielding some delightful images. However, a few tiny globs of sand clung to its head. While it doesn't kill the photo, it's definitely a distraction. A gentle brushing with a twig would have removed the glob from the placid peeper, but I failed to notice it until the images were transferred from memory card to computer.

Right: A low angle and clean blue sky create a sense of loftiness to this dragonfly's perch on a marsh reed. The color of the sky also serves as a fine complement to the black and white hues of the bug. *Jack Ballard*

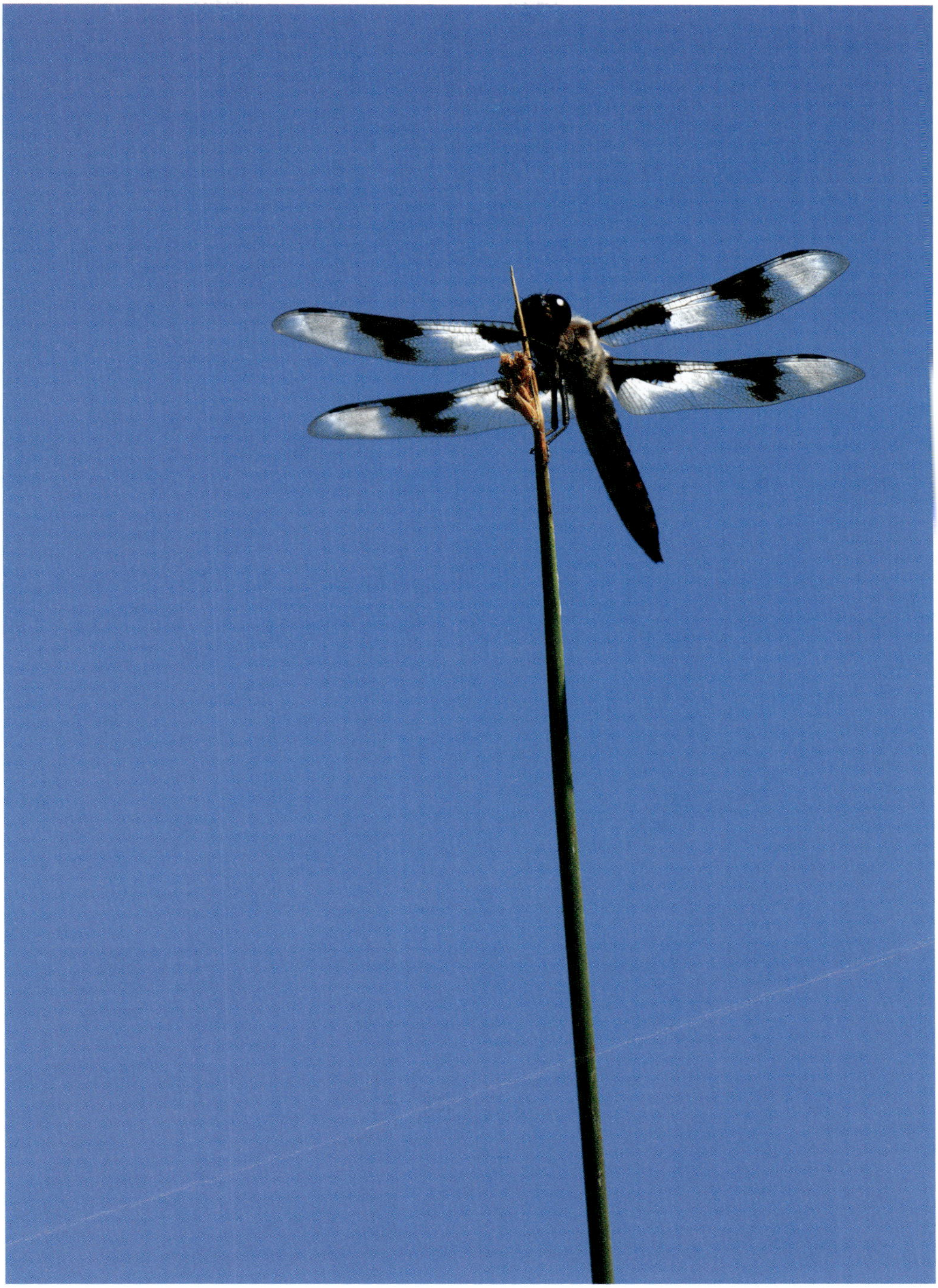

A final basic aspect of extreme close-up photography when using macro lenses is depth of field. Many new users of macro lenses attempt to shoot macro photos with the lens set at or near maximum aperture. Remember that because of the very close distance to the subject, the depth of field will be much shallower than at a greater distance. An aperture setting of f/4 might nicely isolate the subject against a fairly soft background at a distance of 30 feet. At 18 inches it will render but a tiny slice of the frame in sharp focus. Many macro lens users opt for settings at the mid or minimum aperture more often than shooting with the lens wide open. Before using a macro lens to photograph wildlife, test it in a controlled setting that allows you to analyze the images for satisfactory depth

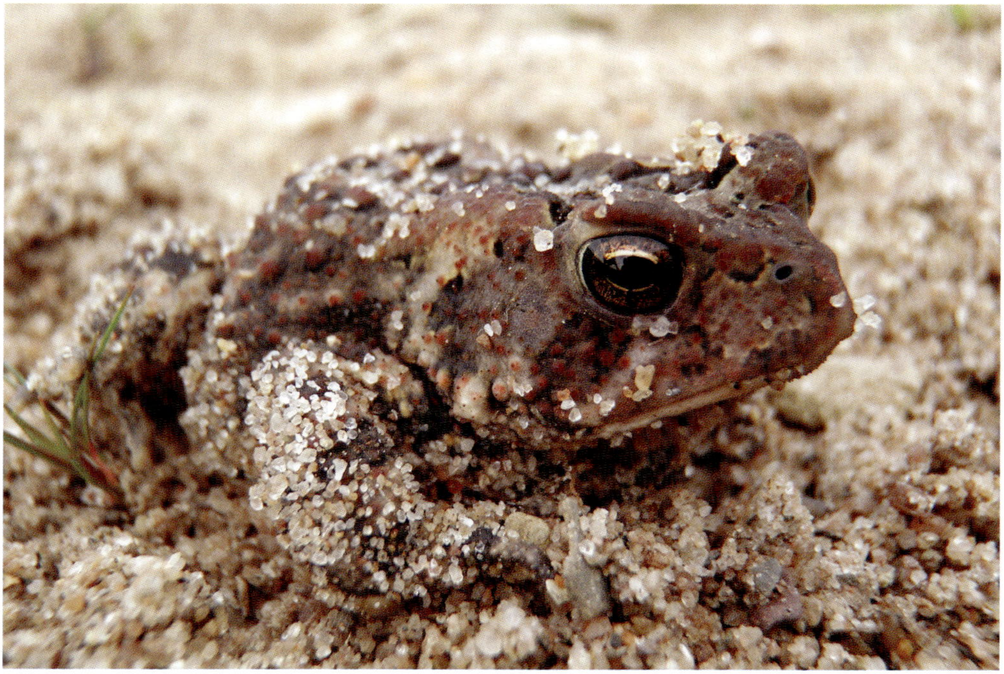

Close-up images magnify every distracting element in the frame as well as the subject. The grains of sand clinging to the nose and head of this spring peeper are distracting (in the author's opinion) and illustrate this hazard in macro photography. *Jack Ballard*

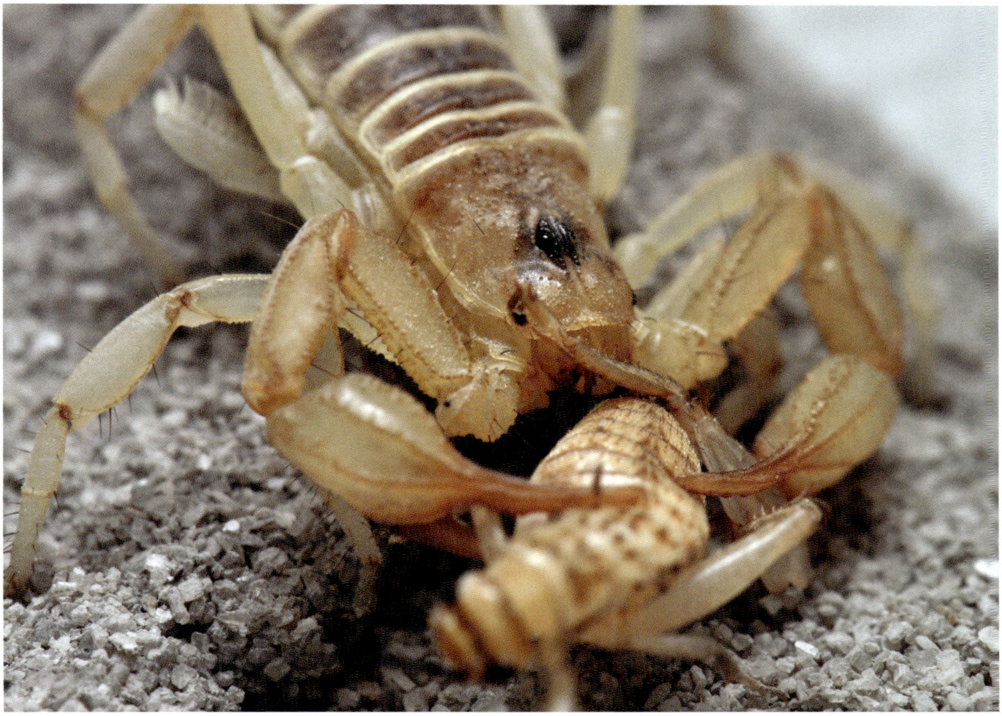

This close-up of a northern scorpion preying on a cricket in a captive environment was shot at f/10 with a macro lens but still yielded a quite shallow depth of field due to the close distance to the subject. *Jack Ballard*

of field at various focusing distances. When shooting with a macro, I generally err on the side of extra depth of field when in question.

PHOTOGRAPHING INSECTS

The 1998 computer-animated movie *A Bug's Life* is anything but an accurate description of the natural history of insects. However, the title is quite fitting for artfully composed images of insects going about their daily life. From pollination

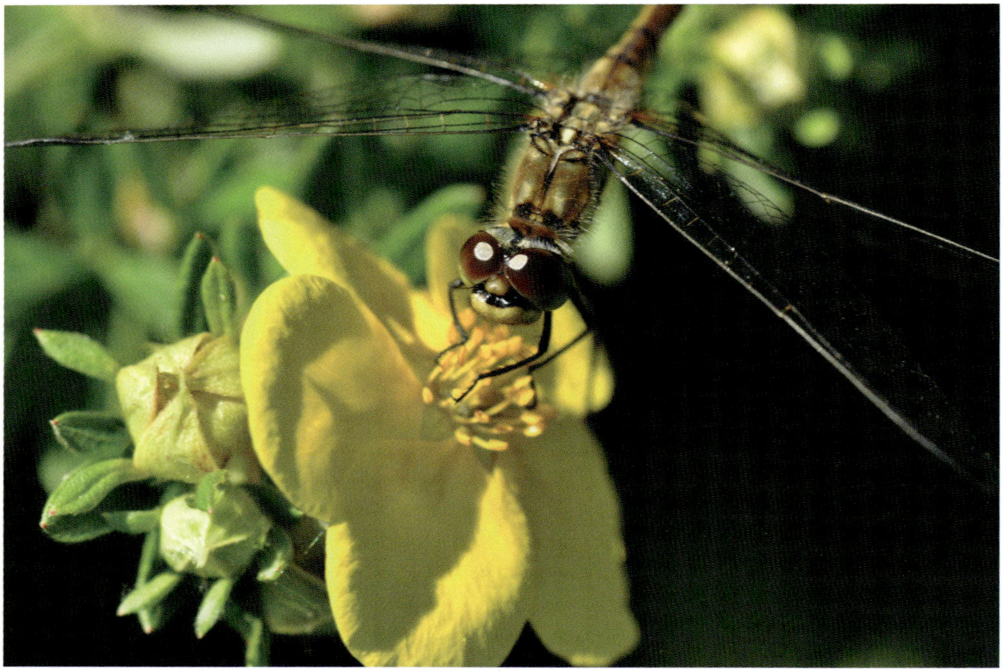

Insects can be found almost anywhere, and many can be photographed without specialty equipment. The author's son found this dragonfly on a photo walk around his neighborhood and captured the image with a 70–300 lens. *Dominic Ballard*

to metamorphosis to predation, the world of insects holds a world of fascination for photographers who choose to document it.

Some larger insects, such as butterflies, bumblebees, and grasshoppers, can often be nicely photographed with a telephoto lens without any specialized equipment. However, the ability to really zoom in on the features of these and smaller bugs normally requires a very close distance between the subject and lens.

Crawling bugs can usually be photographed by carefully moving the camera within range when they're stationary. Insects that use their legs or bodies for

Right: The author noticed this monarch butterfly returning to a favorite flower. He moved close, waited for several minutes, and composed this macro shot from scarcely a foot away. *Jack Ballard*

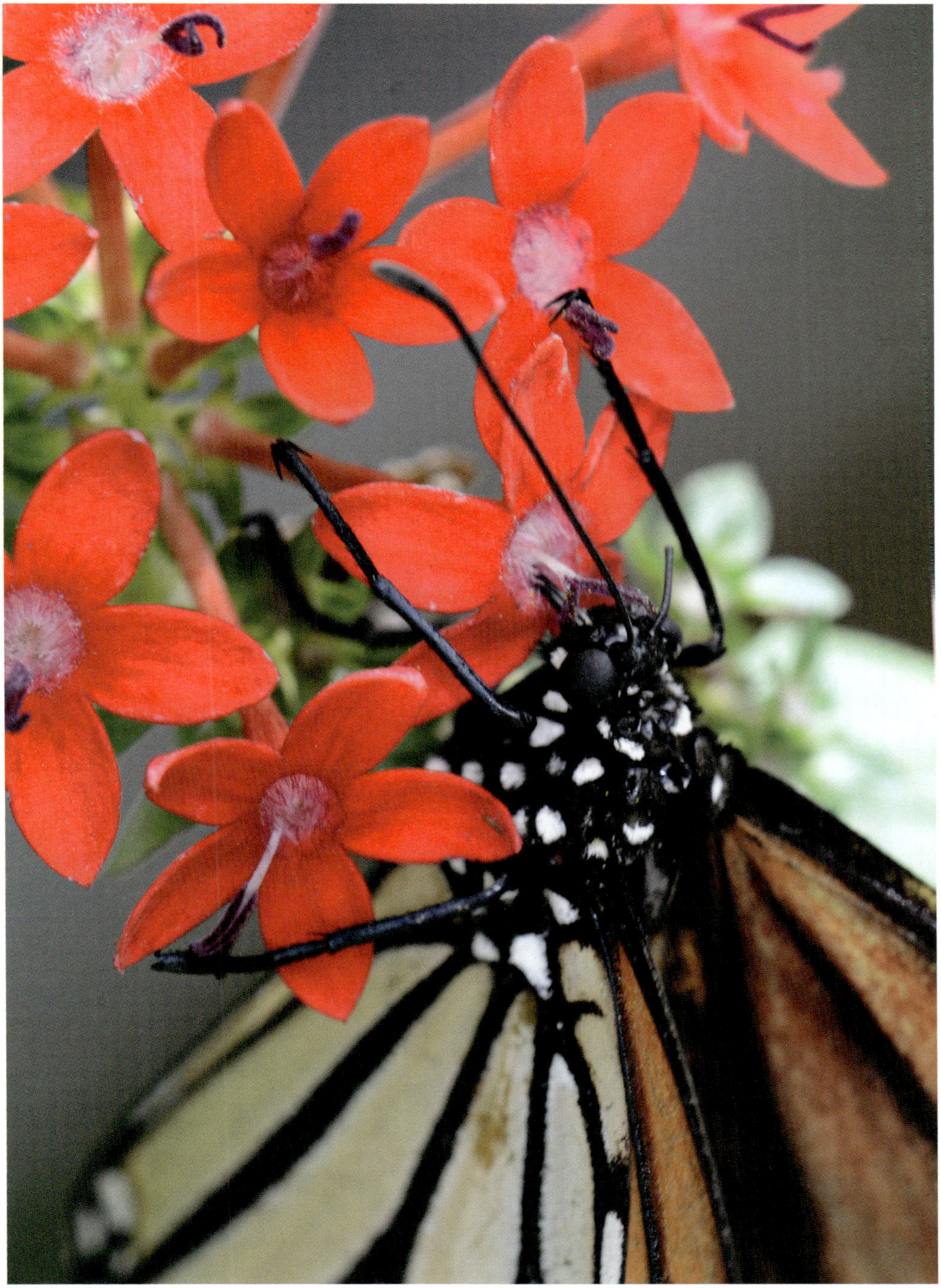

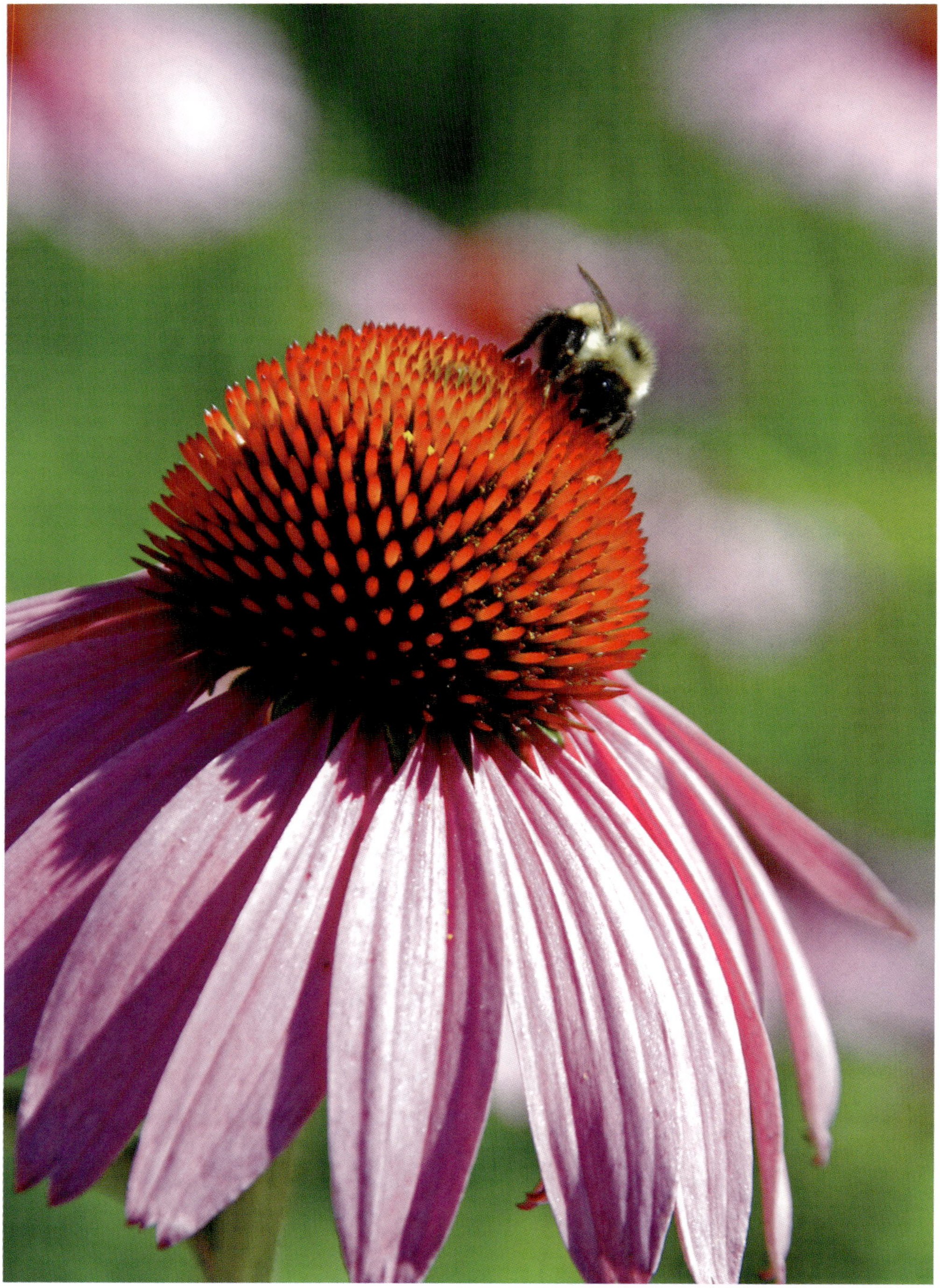

locomotion can also be moved or directed toward a desirable background. Flying insects are most easily photographed when they alight on some attractive element in the environment. This might be a flower for a nectar-collecting butterfly or a piece of rotting meat in the case of a wasp. Similar to photographing birds and mammals, staking out a favored attraction is a good way to photograph insects. If you notice a butterfly returning to a particular flower, compose a photo with the posy and let the insect flit into the frame.

Along with the adult forms of insects, don't forget about other stages in the life cycle. Colorful butterflies and moths are a favorite subject among generalist wildlife photographers, and these vibrant adults may develop from caterpillars that are equally intriguing subjects. Some caterpillars sport flamboyant colorations, while others are colored and shaped to provide camouflage against an environmental object such as a leaf. Documenting all stages of a winged bug's life (egg, pupa, larva, and adult) is a challenging photography project that may hold real value for teachers and students of biology.

The author photographed this bumblebee on a purple coneflower with a close-focusing telephoto lens, an ideal choice for skittish or potentially harmful insects.

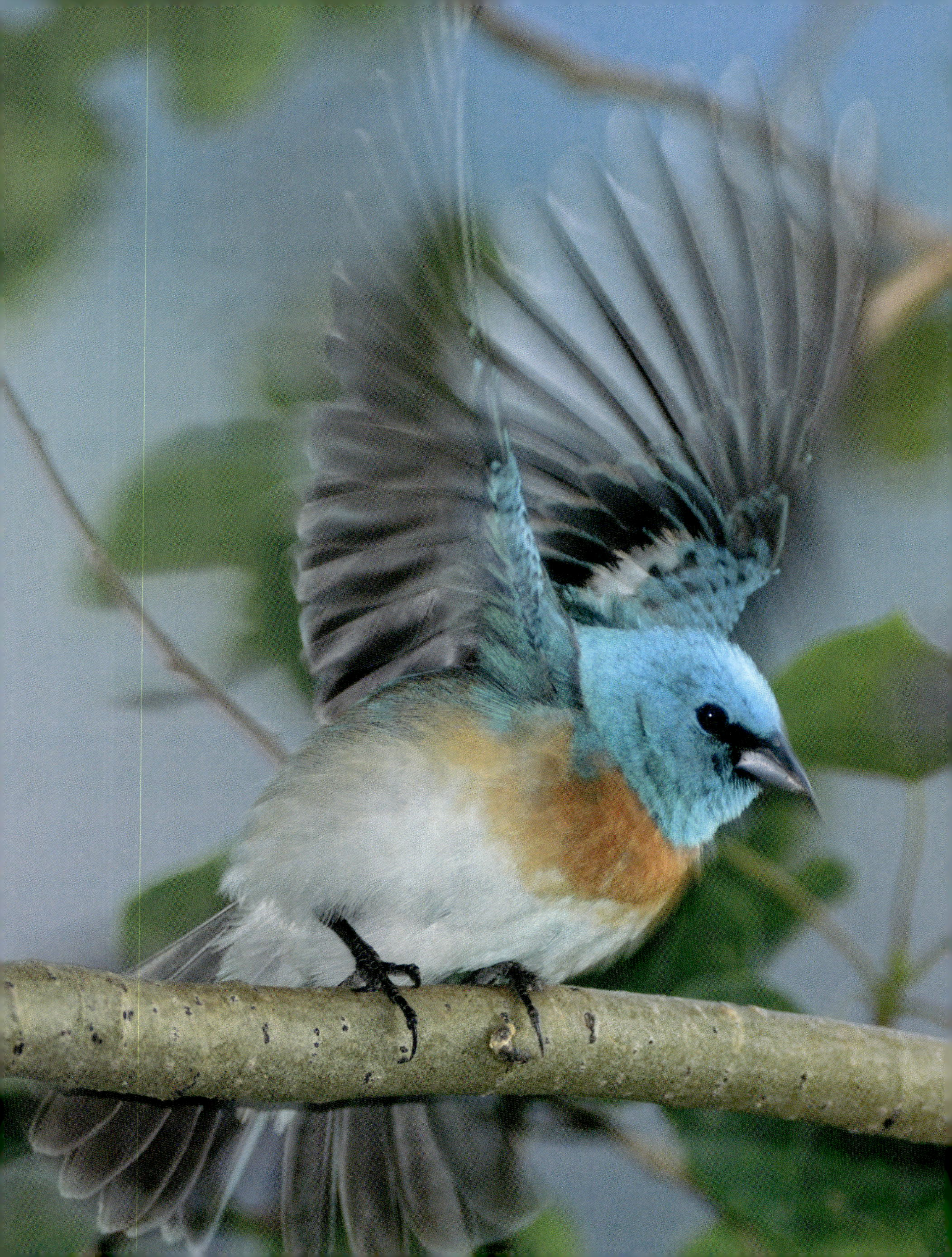

CHAPTER 10

Special Techniques and Situations

A chapter on special techniques and situations in wildlife photography could easily expand into an entire book. Photographers specializing in various aspects of wildlife photography have developed an outstanding array of creative techniques to capture the desired images. For example, a handful of experts have utilized multiple flash configurations triggered by light beams (like the one that keeps your garage door from closing if the beam is broken) to capture amazing images of owls and flying squirrels at night. Others have used cameras triggered by motion-sensing devices to document animal migrations where the timing of the creatures' travel through a particular location is nearly impossible to predict. However, those (and other) highly specialized techniques are beyond the scope of this book. We'll instead stick with the more common but

Lazuli bunting with flash. *Jack Ballard*

advanced situations encountered by wildlife photographers looking to increase the creativity of their images or shoot in challenging conditions.

FLASH PHOTOGRAPHY AND WILDLIFE

Flash photography is most often associated with taking pictures of people indoors, but a flash can be a valuable tool for the wildlife photographer as well. Portrait photographers working outdoors frequently use flash to lighten strong shadows on a model's face when composing portraits in a natural setting. Advertising photographers also use flash to accomplish things like reducing the dark shadow created on a model's face by the brim of a hat. Wildlife photographers can sometimes use flash for similar purposes, eliminating or reducing shadows, adding additional lighting to illuminate a dark subject, or enhancing the quality of light on a dreary, overcast day.

My most regular use of flash involves "fill flash." Used in this way, the flash does not become the dominant source of light but serves as a supplementary light source to illuminate dark areas of the photo. It may reduce shadows, but doesn't eliminate them completely. To function as "fill," the photographer needs the capability of adjusting the flash's output. This normally means reducing the flash's power via on-camera or on-flash controls (some systems may allow for both). The pop-up flashes on many DSLR camera bodies offer this control, as do the built-in flashes on some compact cameras. Using such controls to power the flash so it reduces its light by -1 stop is usually a good starting place for fill flash.

Right: Fill flash was used to create a point of light in the eye and brighten the shadows on this friendly white-crowned sparrow. *Jack Ballard*

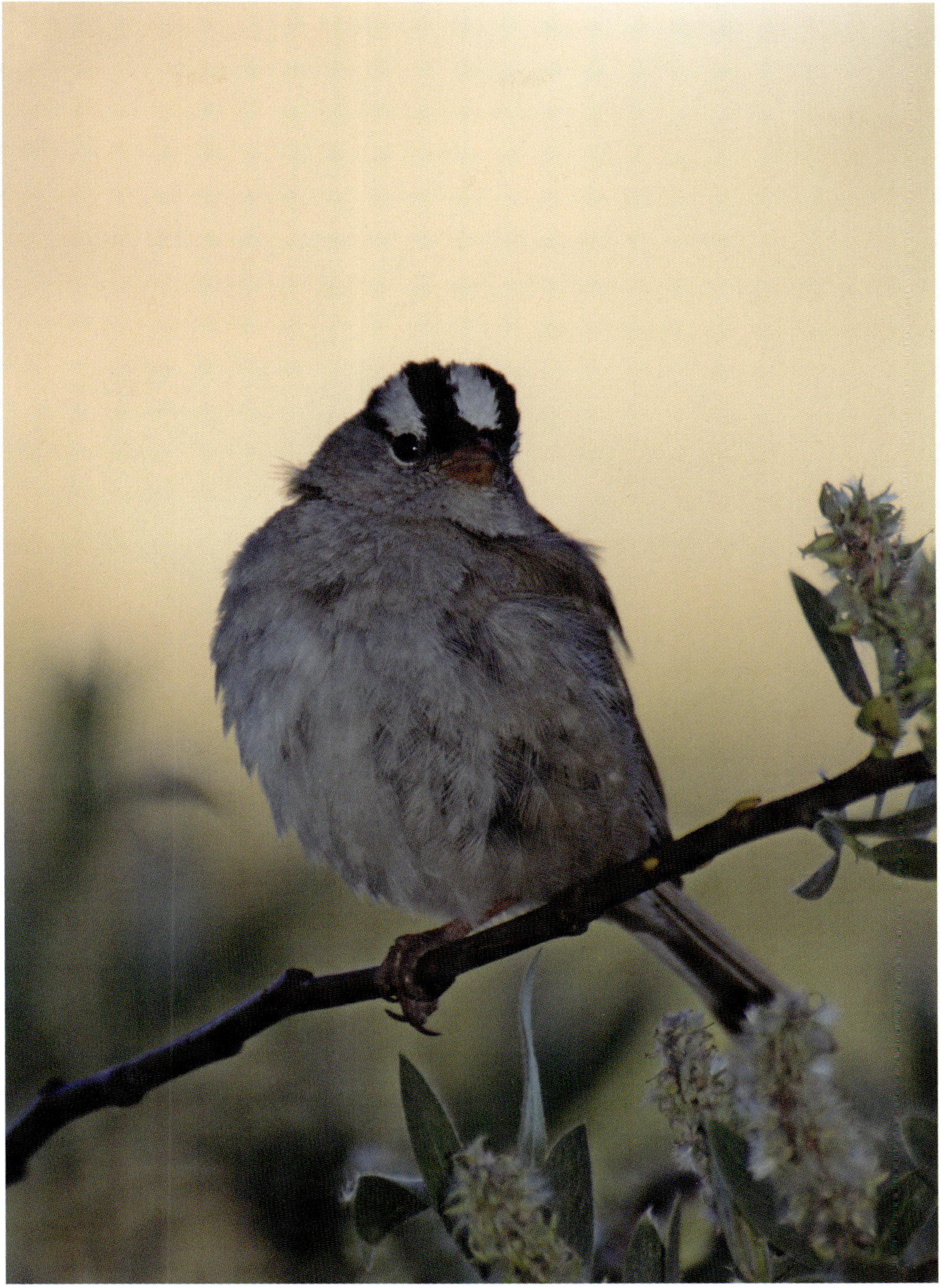

External flashes offer more power than those built into a camera. A powerful external flash may be able to illuminate a wildlife subject at 50 feet or more, completely lighting a subject at night or adding fill flash in the daylight hours. No matter what type of flash is used, some issues exist in flash photography with wildlife that aren't so much a concern when photographing people.

The first of these is the potential of the flash to startle the subject and cause it to flee. Oftentimes flash from the first frame will alarm an animal that is subsequently unbothered by the burst of light. However, some critters will not tolerate flash at all. When approaching a wildlife subject, fire your flash from a distance, first pointed at a right angle to the animal. If that doesn't bother

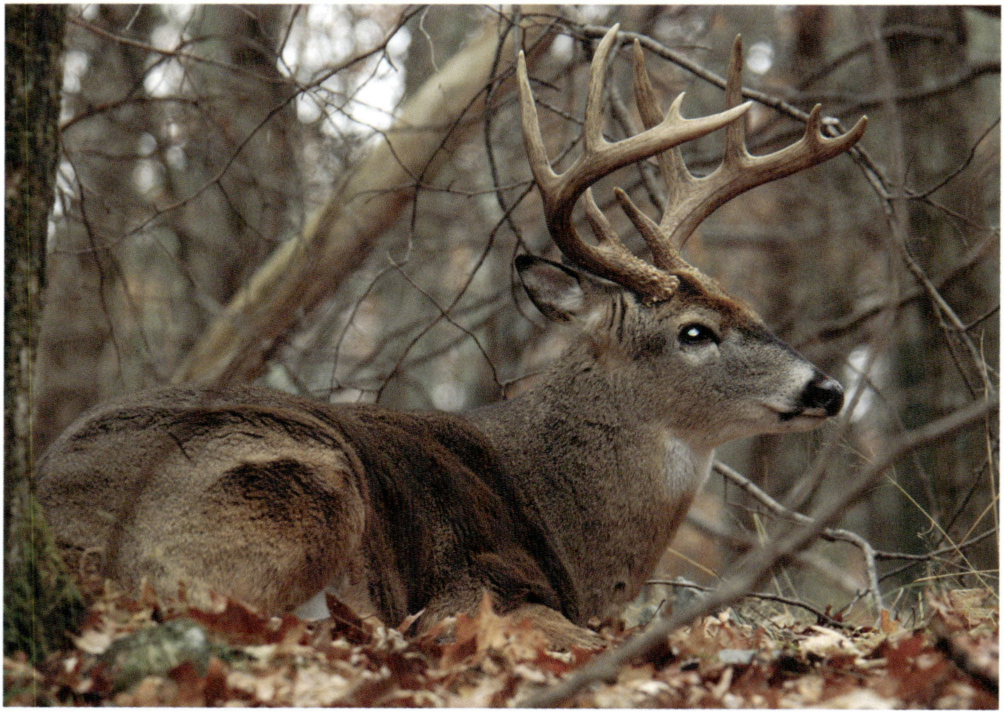

A powerful external flash was used to light this resting whitetail buck. The direct angle to its eye created the "glowing eyes" effect that is especially problematic when using flash on ungulates. *Jack Ballard*

the subject, fire the flash pointed directly at the creature. Many animals will accept flash when conditioned in this way, perhaps due to their experience with lightning or the shine from highly reflective surfaces in the natural world.

Another difficulty when using flash with some creatures is the equivalent of the "red eye" effect when a flash is triggered directly into the dilated eyes of a human. This is especially troublesome with species that have exceptional night vision, including canine and feline predators. Even more extreme is the "glowing eyes" look flash imparts to deer and other ungulates staring at a flash. This is caused by the very large pupils of the animals and a special layer of cells at the back of the eye known as the tapetum lucidum, which reflects light and enhances the animals' night vision. The annoying eye shine created with flash on these subjects can be lessened or eliminated several ways. One option is to take the picture when the creature isn't looking directly at the camera. Another is to locate the flash off-camera so it fires at an angle to the subject, using a cord or remote firing device. A final solution is to fire away and rely on your processing skills to correct the problem with photo-editing software.

ENHANCING MOTION

Recording an image of a cheetah, dust billowing from the furious pace of its pursuit of a gazelle, is a prize any wildlife photographer would love to obtain. Similar esteem is attached to a photograph of a swooping raptor intent on snagging a ground squirrel in its talons. Other readily photographed wildlife subjects in action include flying birds and running mammals. Exactly how the action is portrayed need not depend on the automatic settings of a camera, but can rather be highly controlled by the photographer.

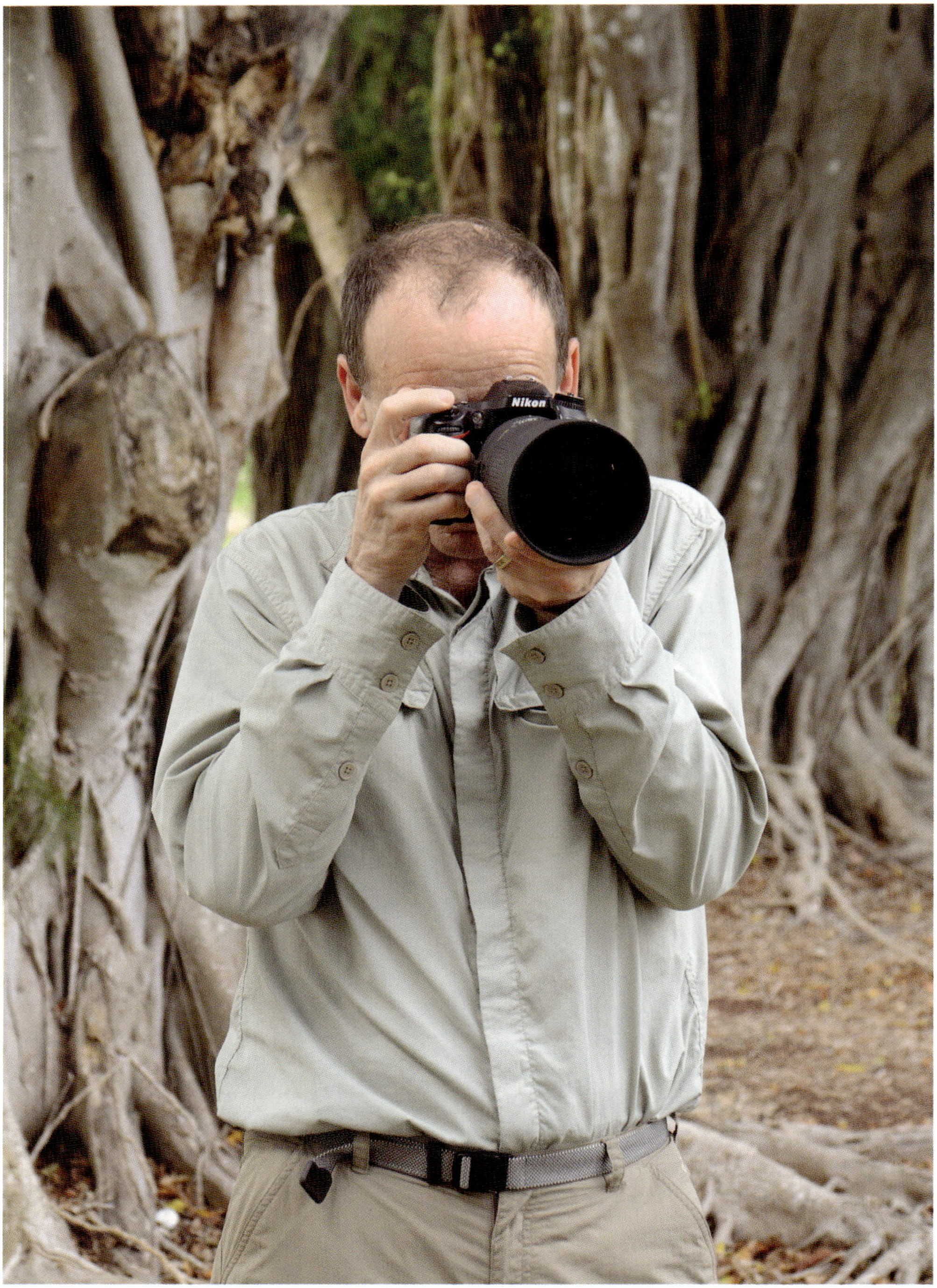
Nikon

Panning Techniques

"Panning" is the art of photographing while tracking a moving subject with the camera at various shutter speeds, creating an image where the background is blurred to imply motion while the subject remains in focus. Numerous variables influence the final effect of panning in a photograph. It is not a highly predictable technique, although with practice it's possible to have a fairly good idea of the appearance of the image ahead of time.

Effective panning starts with a solid camera handling technique. Photographers most often pan while standing. In this position, the elbows should be braced against the ribcage, the camera firmly grasped in the photographer's hands. The goal is to track the motion smoothly, with as little up-and-down movement or shaking as possible.

Camera settings and method are a matter of personal preference. Some photographers use a camera focus mode that tracks the subject. Others prefocus on a plane the subject is expected to pass through and trip the shutter at that point. One photographer may choose to shoot long bursts of frames, while another triggers just a few. A tripod is favored even when panning by some; others always rely on a handheld camera. Many of these decisions come with practice and are determined in part by the capabilities of one's equipment.

For beginners, it's helpful to think of the panning equation in terms of the subject's speed, the subject's distance from the camera, and the shutter speed. The closer the subject is to the camera, the faster the photographer will need to swing the lens to follow the motion, increasing the blur of the background. A fast-moving subject versus a slower one creates a similar effect. Calculated against these variables is the shutter speed of the camera. A standard rule in

Left: Elbows braced against the ribs and a fluid motion are integral to a good panning technique. *Lisa Ballard*

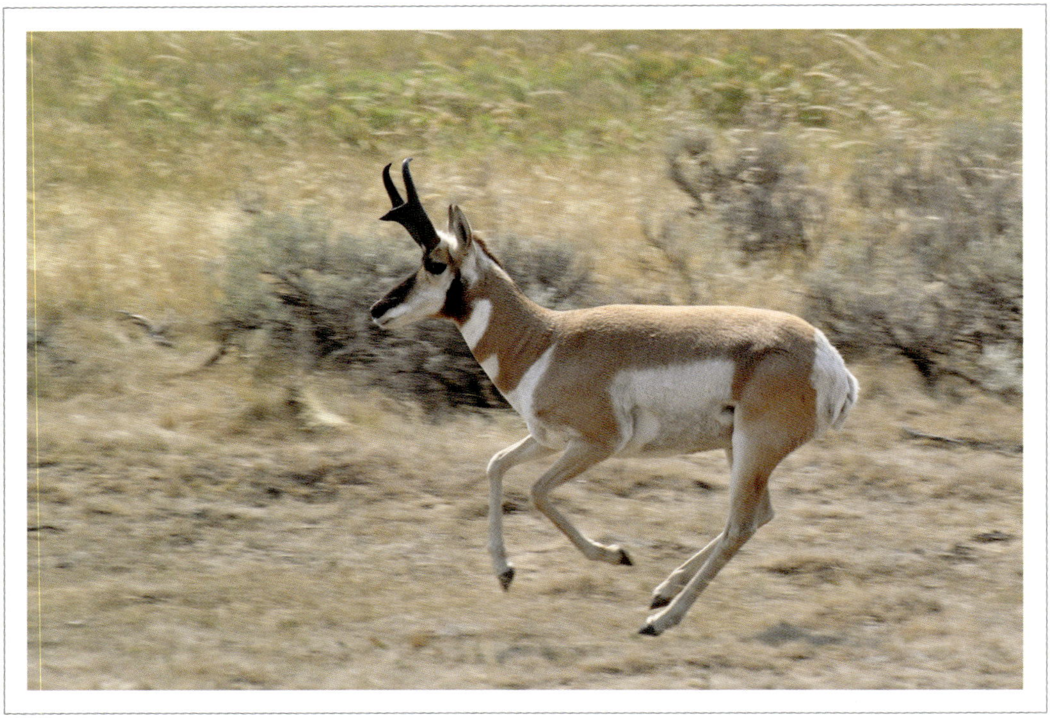

A smooth panning technique develops with practice and allows the photographer to suggest motion by blurring the background of the photo. This running pronghorn buck was photographed by panning in Yellowstone National Park at 1/320th of a second. *Jack Ballard*

relation to panned action photos is that at least one element in the frame needs to be in sharp focus. The faster the shutter speed, the higher the odds of stopping some action in focus. However, faster shutter speeds also reduce blurring in the background, which is largely the point of panning. A shutter speed of 1/60th of a second is often suggested as a place to begin when panning.

Shutter Speed

Shutter speed is operative in panning, but also important to action photography that doesn't require panning. For example, photographing a bird flying directly at the photographer may require minimal camera movement. However, shutter

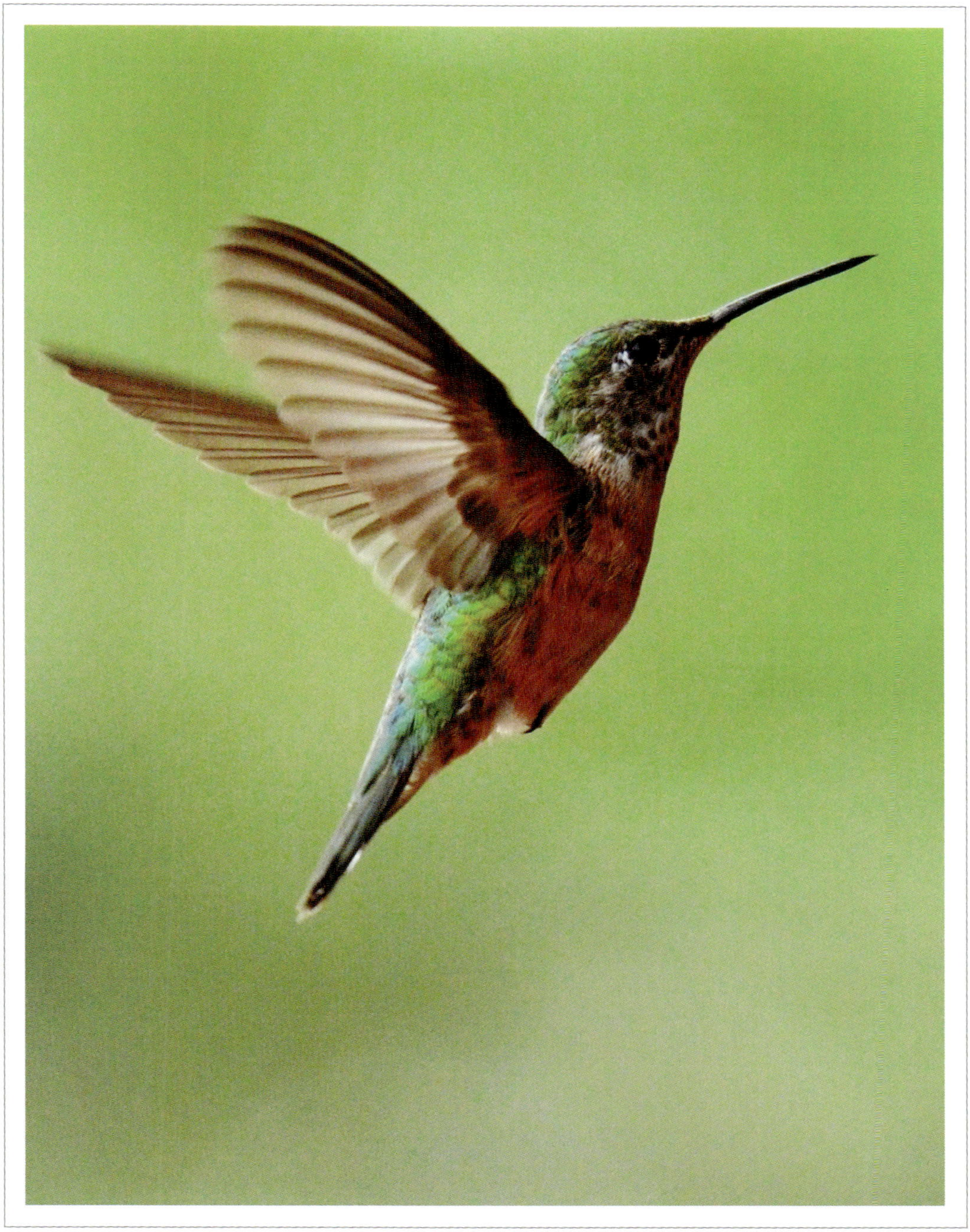

The wings of a hummingbird beat incredibly fast. A shutter speed of 1/1600th of a second still blurred the wingtips of this hovering hummer. *Lisa Ballard*

speed will be highly determinative of how much action might be implied by blurring of the wings. Many photographers favor shutter speeds high enough for "stop-action" results in which the subject and other pertinent elements in the composition are in perfect focus without blurring.

A slower shutter speed can stop action of subjects moving directly toward or away from the photographer more easily than those moving from side to side. The incredible advances in digital camera technology in the past decade have made stop-action wildlife photography much easier than it was previously. If completely freezing movement is the goal, there's no harm in shooting at 1/2000th of a second when only 1/250th is required. Reasonably good lighting conditions allow photographers with quality equipment to increase ISO settings for sharp images at very high shutter speeds. With the exception of the wingbeats of flying birds and some other motions, most wildlife action can be frozen at 1/1000th of a second or slower. Analytical photographers who photograph the same moving subjects over time (flying waterfowl, for example) often make notes regarding shutter speed in relation to action effects under various conditions to determine future settings.

PHOTOGRAPHY IN AND ON WATER

A host of birds and mammals are associated with water, not to mention amphibians and fish. I spend plenty of time in and on water photographing wildlife, sometimes wading, at other times perched on a motorboat or sitting in a canoe. Photography around water means being especially careful with your gear (doubly so in salt water), as the electronics in modern camera equipment are acutely allergic to moisture.

Wading into water is sometimes necessary to get within range of a particular subject. A handful of wildlife pros I know spend prolonged periods of time wading in shallow lakes and marshes stalking particular subjects. One uses a floating blind of sorts, which consists of camouflage fabric draped over an egg-shaped frame attached to an inflated inner tube from a large tire. He wades along very slowly in waist-deep water and is able to get within very close distance of many creatures.

While wading in calm water doesn't create much of a photography challenge, shooting in moving water poses some problems. Safety is an obvious concern. Attempting to photograph in a swiftly moving stream or walking on a treacherous river bottom can jeopardize the safety of both the photographer

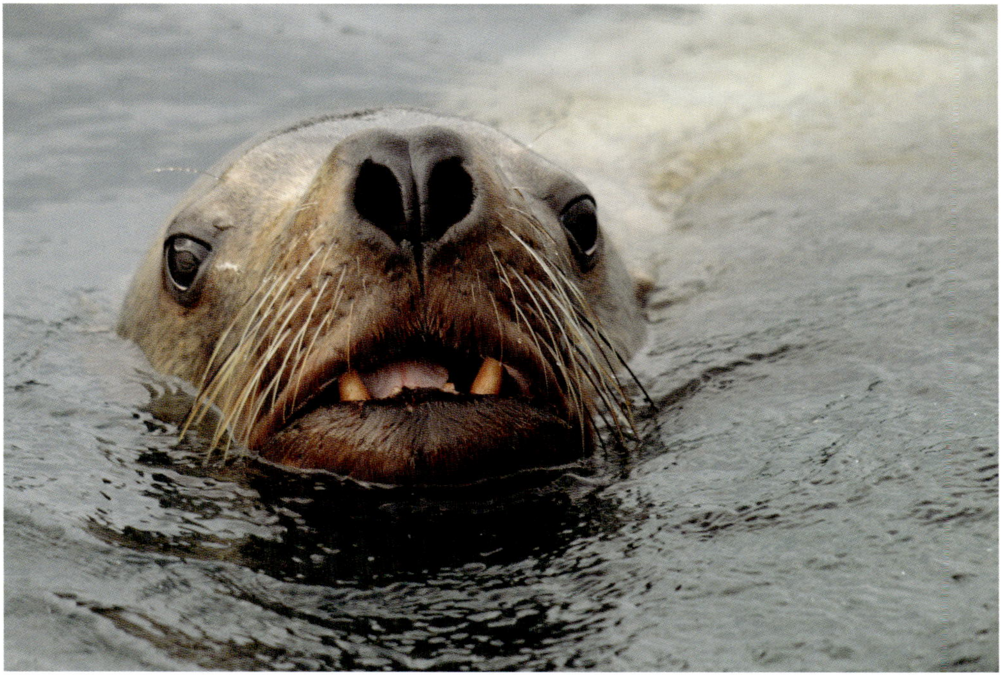

This sea lion was photographed from a small boat. A high shutter speed was used to counteract the movement of the craft on the waves. *Lisa Ballard*

and his expensive camera equipment. On the photographic side, the challenge has more to do with camera movement. Vibration transferred from moving water in a flowing stream or wave action in a lake or at seaside can cause the camera to shake, resulting in blurry images. This phenomenon affects tripod-mounted cameras as well as handheld. The best way to combat this sometimes subtle problem is to shoot at higher shutter speeds than would otherwise be necessary.

Shooting on the water from the platform of a craft can be very challenging. As a rule of thumb, the smaller the craft, the more prone it is to movement created by waves and currents. My wife and I frequently use an Old Town canoe for wildlife photography. We rarely shoot at the same time. Most often I paddle, keeping careful control over the craft's angle to the subject and speed. This allows Lisa to concentrate completely on the subject.

Whether shooting solo or with a partner, three problems are common to photographing wildlife from a craft. The first is camera shake. This can be countered by increasing shutter speed or using a lens with an image-stabilizing feature (make sure it's "on" before boarding). The second is maintaining a level horizon in the picture. Handle this by paying close attention to the shore or horizon line when composing. Create some margin for error by allowing room around the subject to tilt, and then crop the image when editing if necessary. Finally, shooting from a craft, especially a small one, often involves the likelihood of spray reaching the camera. Carry a drying cloth and protect the camera in spray-likely situations, such as motoring or paddling into waves.

UNDERWATER WILDLIFE PHOTOGRAPHY

Not too many years ago, underwater wildlife photography was the arena of wealthy hobbyists or pros who tended to specialize in imaging aquatic and marine creatures. Waterproof, underwater cameras were expensive. Special housings to protect normal cameras underwater were often awkward. For several hundred dollars, a snorkeler or lake-goer can now pick up a waterproof compact camera. Many of these have a variety of underwater shooting modes and produce surprisingly good images in competent hands. What's more, a waterproof compact is an excellent addition to the traveling photographer's arsenal when shooting in rain, snow, or other moisture-rich environments.

Whether using a waterproof compact or wielding a more sophisticated underwater camera, photographers new to this medium should be aware of a few basic issues. First is the ability to see the image in the viewfinder or on the camera's viewing screen before shooting. Looking through a viewfinder usually means having your head in the water, tough to accomplish without at least a mask and snorkel. Cameras with tilting screens allow image composition in shallow water. Otherwise the photographer may have to point the camera at the subject and guess at framing, a method that yields a low percentage of acceptable results.

Photographing beneath the surface of a crystalline lake or the clear waters of a reef create ideal conditions for underwater photography. However, most waters are not that clean. Sediment carried in a current or bottom debris dislodged by the photographer's feet often creates problems. These include

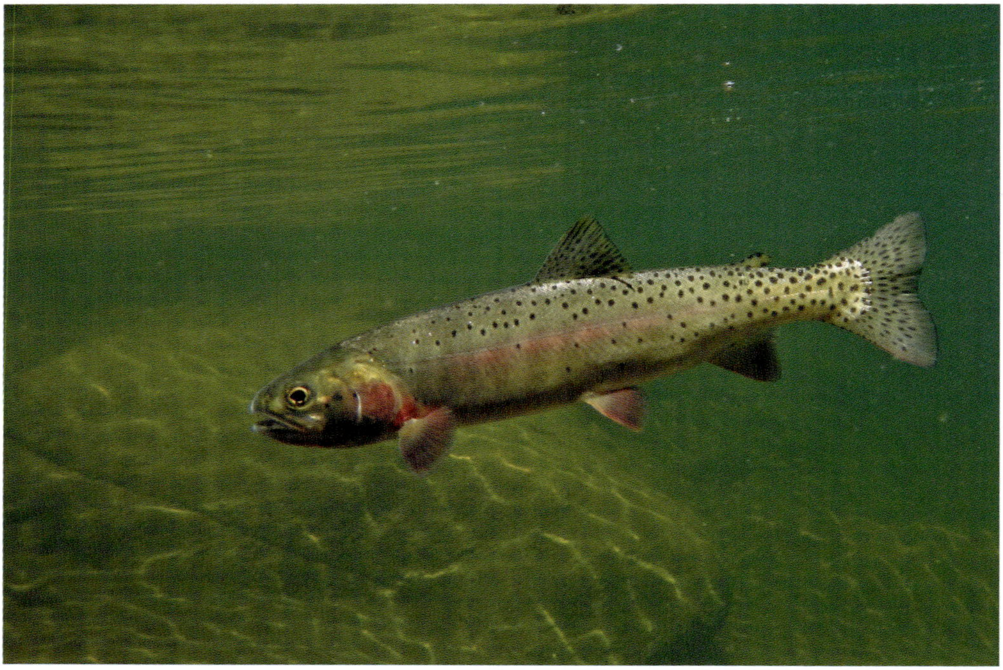

The gin-clear water of a high-mountain lake made this photo of a cutthroat trout possible from a distance of more than 10 feet. Clear water increases the lens-to-subject distance needed to obtain a clear underwater image. *Jack Ballard*

unsightly blobs in the photo, sometimes too numerous to be easily eliminated with editing software. They can also fool the camera's focusing system into thinking a suspended object in the water is the subject. Turbidity also reduces image quality; the farther away the subject, the more suspended particles affect the photograph. Additional range and magnification afforded by a zoom or telephoto lens aren't always helpful underwater. Along with magnifying the subject, they also increase the presence of any impurities in the water between the lens and the subject.

Another challenge concerns flash. Compact cameras often incorporate flash in their exposure equation. Flash works well in some underwater situations, but kills photos in others. The light from a flash will illuminate the presence of any suspended debris in the water. In moving streams that create tiny air bubbles or when bubbles are released from the bottom (often by the movement of the photographer's feet), the flash turns these into annoying bright blobs in the photo.

Finally, underwater photography frequently plays havoc with a compact camera's color rendition of the scene, often overemphasizing greens. This one, fortunately, is usually easy to correct with editing software and shouldn't cause undue concern when checking images in the field.

Underwater subjects can be difficult to approach within camera range, particularly when using a compact camera with limited reach. If you have a friend who fishes, there's an easy way to wiggle your toes in underwater wildlife imaging. The management of many fish species, both fresh and salt water, requires that fish of a certain size or species must be returned to the water. For example, Florida fishing regulations demand

ETHICS AND ETIQUETTE

UNDERWATER PHOTOGRAPHY

Underwater photography, even with basic equipment and everyday locations, requires some thought regarding its impact on creatures and their habitat. If you choose to photograph fish released by an angler, educate yourself regarding the best release techniques and incorporate them into your photos. Keeping fish out of the water deprives them of oxygen and increases physical stress, which can lead to mortality. Excessive handling can damage scales and the protective "slime" on the body of many fish.

Other aspects of underwater photography can also be a concern. Human contact with coral in marine environments can kill it. The possibility of transferring parasites, diseases, or invasive plants and organisms via clothing and footwear is of extreme concern in many places. Wading in areas where fish are spawning or other aquatic creatures have laid eggs can smother the eggs and reduce reproduction. Ethical wildlife photographers are astute biologists who educate themselves concerning the possible impacts of human activity in various environments and model the best practices to mitigate them.

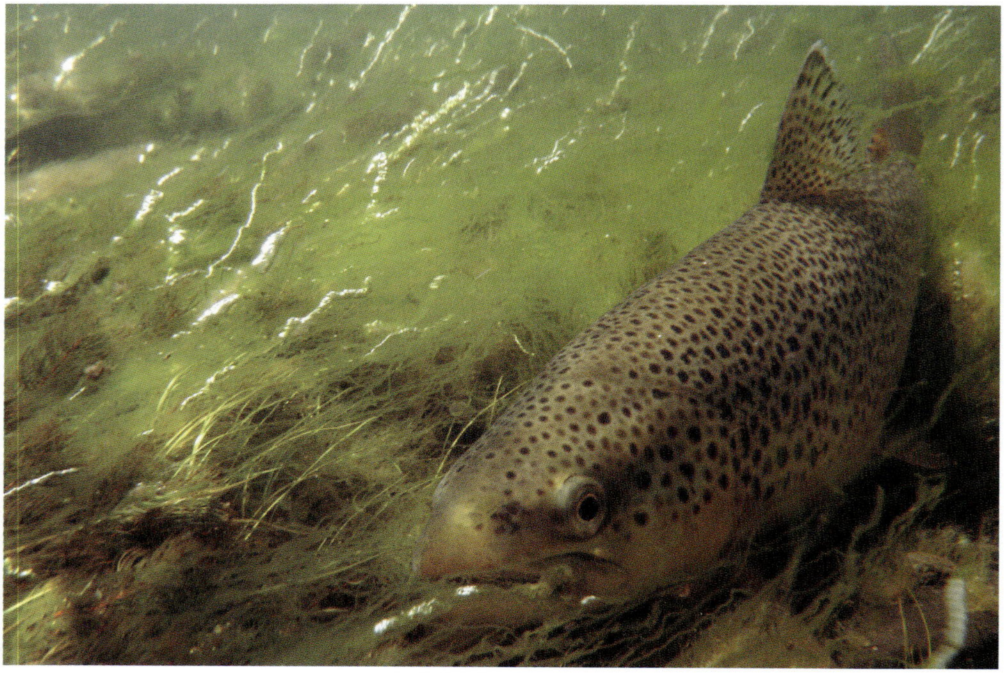

This brown trout was photographed in the Missouri River in Montana just after being released from an angler's hand. *Jack Ballard*

that redfish (red drum) under and over a certain size must be released. We often photograph fish just as they are freed from an angler's grasp. This allows a high level of predictability and has yielded some fantastic results.

DEALING WITH EXTREME ENVIRONMENTS

Wildlife photographers often dream of exotic locations: squinting through the viewfinder at lions on the Serengeti, nabbing images of penguins in Antarctica, or pursuing photos of a rare creature like the Bactrian camel in the Gobi Desert. But with the singular opportunities they afford, such extreme environments create hazards to both photographers and their gear. Keeping yourself safe from frostbite, dehydration, altitude sickness, and heatstroke are all potential issues when shooting in the toughest wildlife habitats on the planet. Protecting your gear is important, even when challenging environments can occur 10 miles from home, as they sometimes do near my abode in Red Lodge, Montana.

The four most common enemies of gear in extreme environments are heat, dust, cold, and moisture. Extreme dry heat can damage the protective seals on camera gear. Dust is pernicious in many places, reducing image quality when it clings to lenses, scratching glass and coatings, and invading the mechanisms of

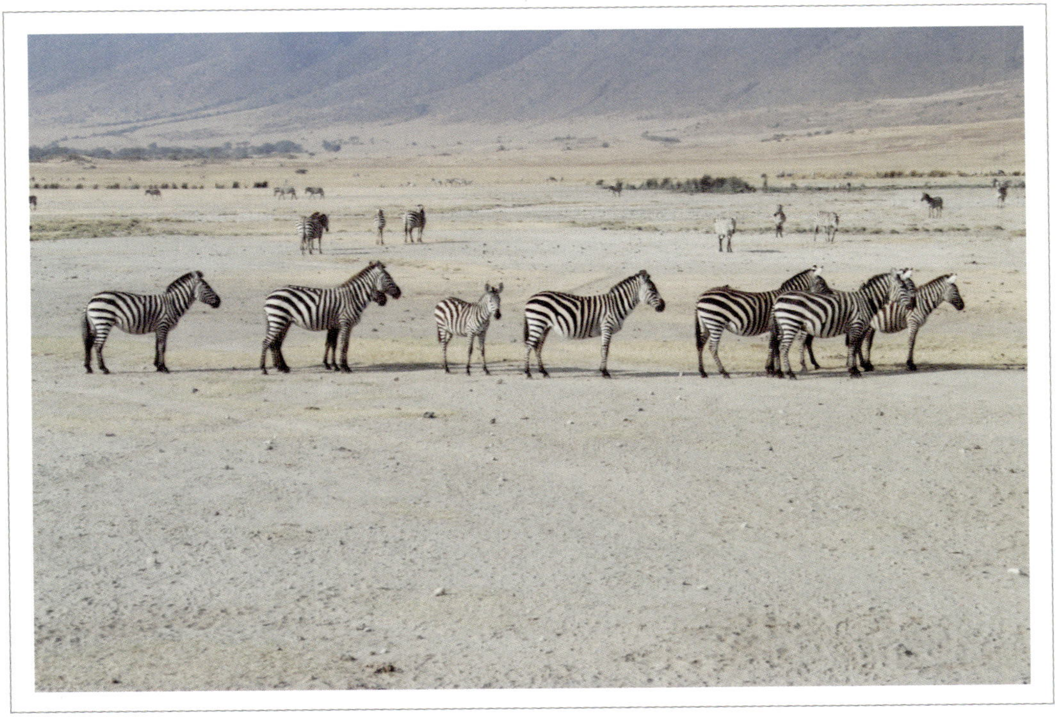

Dusty, arid environments create survival challenges for wildlife. They are also very hard on camera equipment.
Lisa Ballard

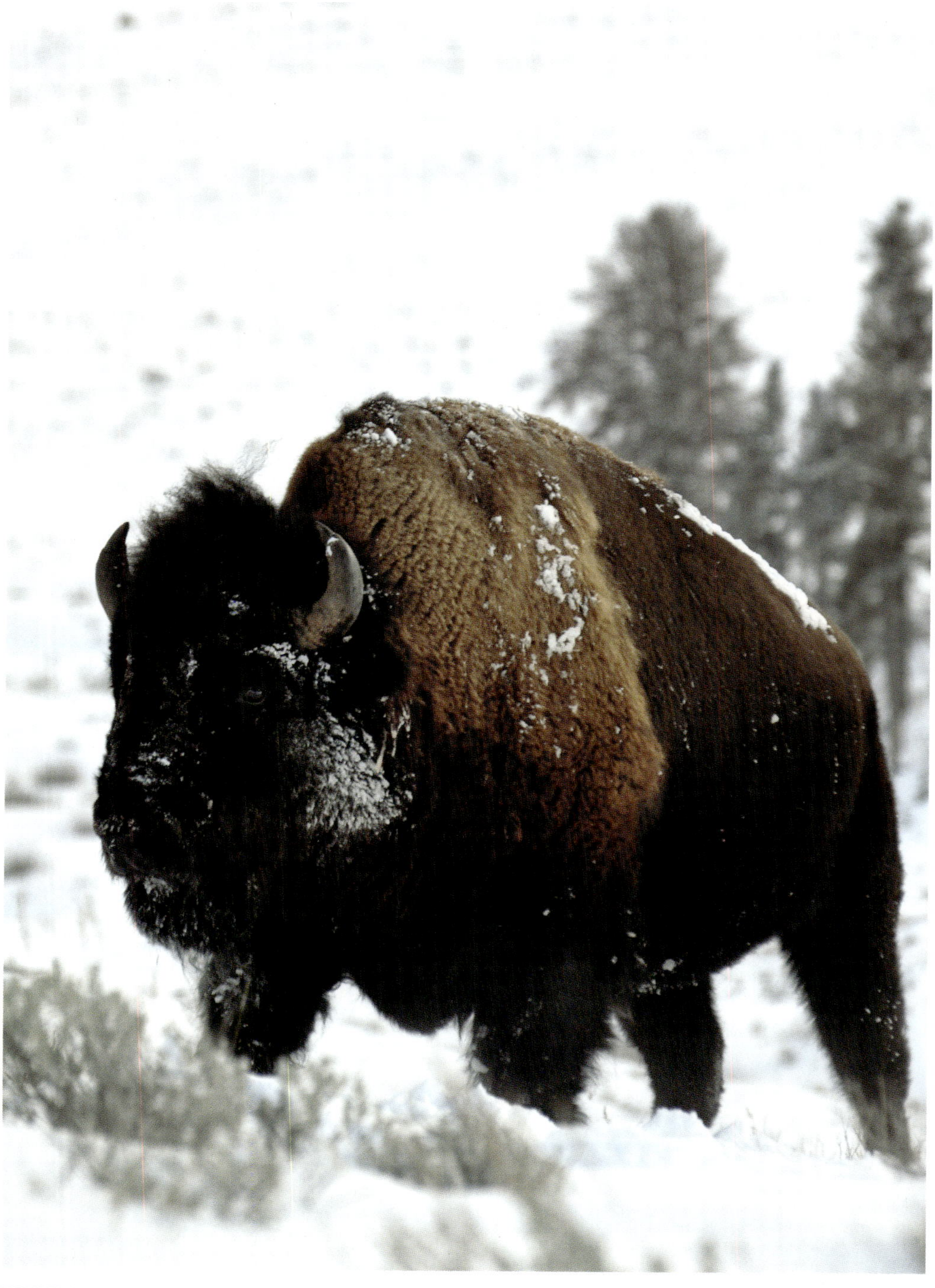

cameras and lenses, shortening their life. Heat and dust are often related, but not always.

Protecting gear in extreme heat means keeping it out of direct sunlight as much as possible, in the shade or a covered case. Cameras can take considerable heat when allowed to warm up slowly. Sudden temperature changes can cause condensation to form on and inside cameras and lenses, and is perhaps the primary cause of equipment failure in extremely hot or cold environments. Condensation can occur with heat, but is more common in the cold. A rule of thumb used by photographers in the winter states, "You can go from hot to cold, but not cold to hot." This refers to the fact that the external glass on cameras and lenses will fog almost immediately when brought from cold temperatures into someplace warm. Condensation forms on internal elements as well and in severe conditions can ruin equipment. The best option is to allow your kit to warm slowly. Removing the lens from the camera body, taking the cover from the lens, and opening the battery compartment will further allow moisture to dissipate from the equipment.

It should also be noted that severe cold drains camera bodies quickly. Battery efficiency is reduced in cold temperatures and focusing mechanisms require more power to move, creating a "double whammy" for battery life in the cold. Carry a spare battery and keep it warm. Single-use hand and feet warmers don't only protect people's hands and feet from frostbite, they can also be used to maintain battery temperature in a pocket or camera bag. Starting with a warm battery will extend its life in cold climates.

The thermometer read −20 degrees Fahrenheit when the author photographed this bull bison in Yellowstone National Park, Wyoming. Rapid, extreme changes in temperature subject camera bodies and lenses to stress and internal condensation. *Jack Ballard*

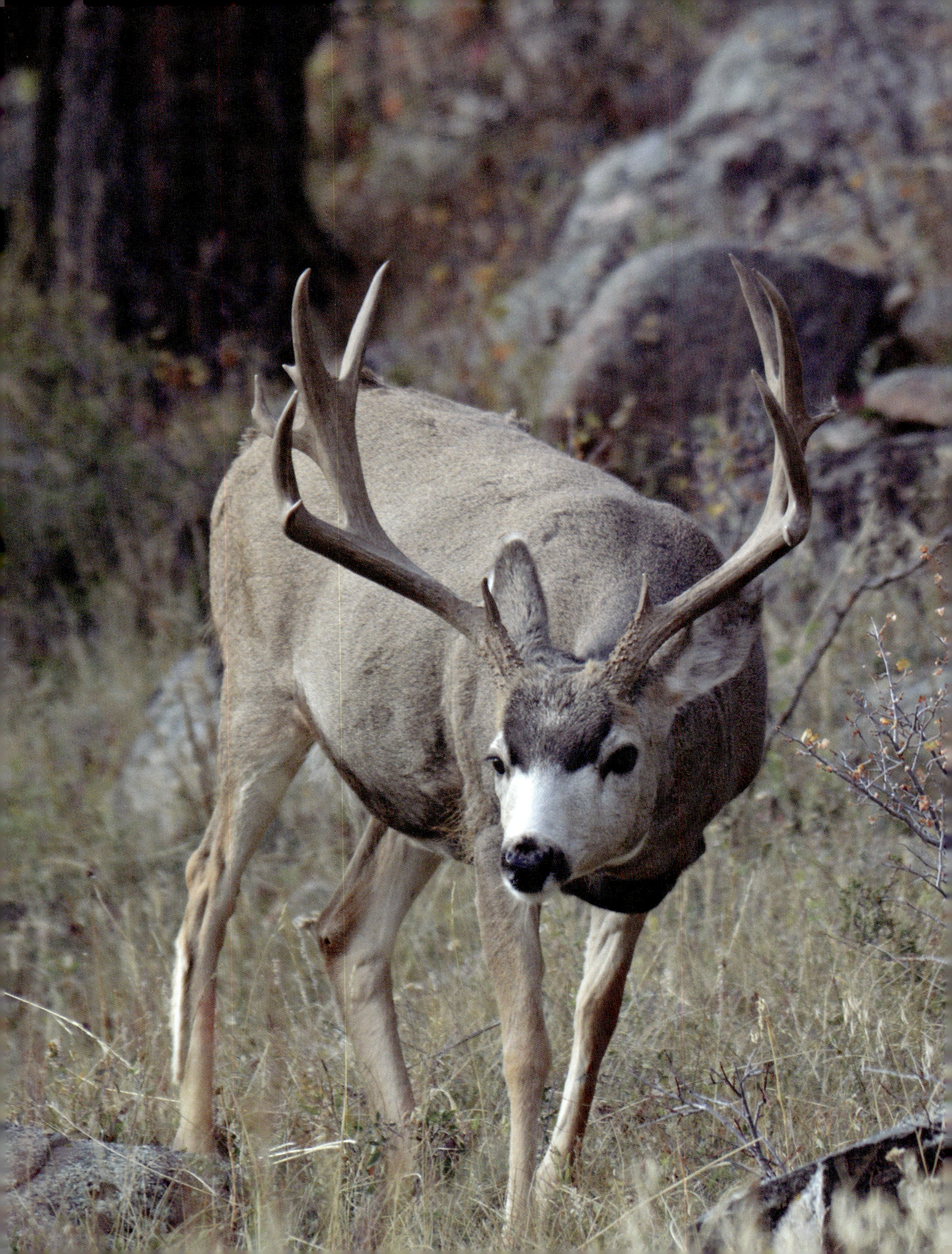

CHAPTER

11

Image Processing, Storage, and Sharing

My career has spanned the transition from transparency film to digital imagery as the standard medium for wildlife photography. Early digital cameras had some serious drawbacks (image quality, function, etc.), but their advantages quickly became obvious to professionals. Quite frankly, I miss the film days in some ways, one of which is in relation to editing and storing photos. The editing process with film was simple: If a photo wasn't perfect in every way (composition, sharpness, exposure), it went into the trash can. The price of film and its processing put a limit on how many frames I might shoot of a given subject. With an erasable memory card, there's no financial downside to recording hundreds of frames when shooting digital. Photos can be cropped and exposure tweaked. The temptation to retain flawed photos is very high,

Mule deer. *Jack Ballard*

creating more images to sort through when selecting photos for a magazine article or book project.

No matter how many wildlife photos you shoot, creating and maintaining a logical filing system, creating an archive, and making basic adjustments before printing and otherwise sharing images are all tasks confronting the photographer. When it comes to these jobs, the adage "the sooner, the better" certainly applies. It's a whole lot easier to develop a filing system when you have two hundred images versus two thousand. Here are the basics when it comes to dealing with your pictures when the fun of shooting is finished.

STORAGE AND BACKUP

Several options exist for the long-term storage of digital photos. The internal hard drive of a computer, an external hard drive, or "cloud" storage via the Internet are all options. Necessary storage amounts vary dramatically in relation to the capacity of your camera. The first digital camera I used for professional photography produced images of about 2 megabytes with its finest JPEG format. Four generations later, my current camera records similar JPEG files more than five times as large. Shooting in RAW format, the files are even larger. As my digital photo library has enlarged and file sizes have increased, so have my storage needs.

There is no "right" or "wrong" answer of how to store photos, as long as the system is satisfactory to the user. However, certain principles are used by professional photographers that apply to anyone who wants their images preserved safely. The first of these concerns backups. There's a saying in the business that asserts, "If it isn't in three places, it's not backed up." Although this idea seems like overkill to some people, the rationale behind it is sound. Files are kept and accessed from a primary storage source (probably a laptop or desktop computer). They are copied (backed up) onto another storage medium (probably an external hard drive) in case the computer's storage is irretrievably ruined. However, a fire or other catastrophic event might take out the building in which the computer and external hard drive are located. The third copy is kept off-site (on a remote hard drive or cloud storage). Thus the rational for three copies. Some professionals and many amateur photographers rely on a single backup, playing the long odds of a catastrophe simultaneously taking out the primary storage source and a backup.

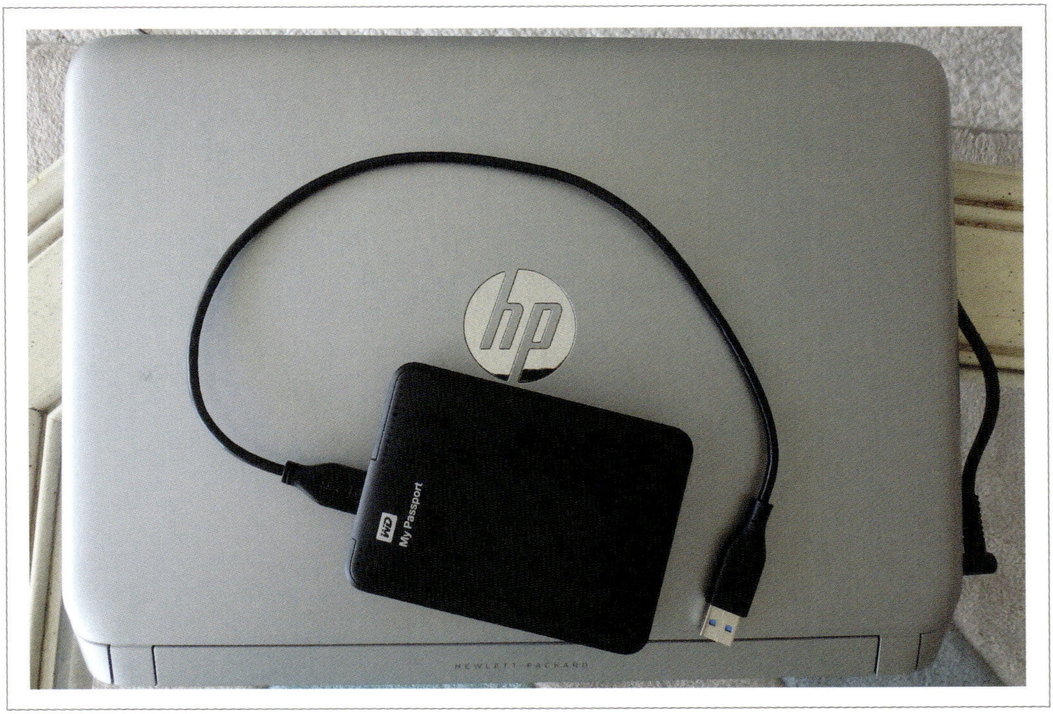

An external hard drive is a simple way to provide basic backup of a wildlife photo library. *Jack Ballard*

The "pain" for many photographers involves keeping the backups current. Many use software that automatically updates files from one location to another; however, a major error from the "mother" source (such as accidentally deleting a folder containing priceless images) can be transferred to the backup. Others accomplish the task manually. Either way, assurances should be made to make sure the archive system is up to date.

Both pro and hobbyist wildlife photographers are limited to storage systems in relation to budget. Should I buy or add to a system enough capacity to handle the next year's shooting, or spend more money on storage that should accommodate my needs for the next five years? I opt for the latter sentiment. Moving files from one storage system to another is usually fraught with annoyances. As with many other aspects of photography, you'll not likely regret purchasing too much storage, but you are guaranteed to rue too little.

FILING SYSTEMS

Time is money, or so the saying goes. For professionals, an image filing system that allows for rap d retrieval of stored photos allows the submission of more photos to potential buyers. An individual photo of a grizzly bear snagging spawning salmon from a river in Alaska is probably easy to find in a library of five hundred images. Could you access it within a minute in a library of fifty thousand?

The answer is "most certainly" if your filing system is logical and up to date. Once again, there's no correct or incorrect method, as long as it works. The keys are simplicity and consistency. Lisa and I share our wildlife photo library, but

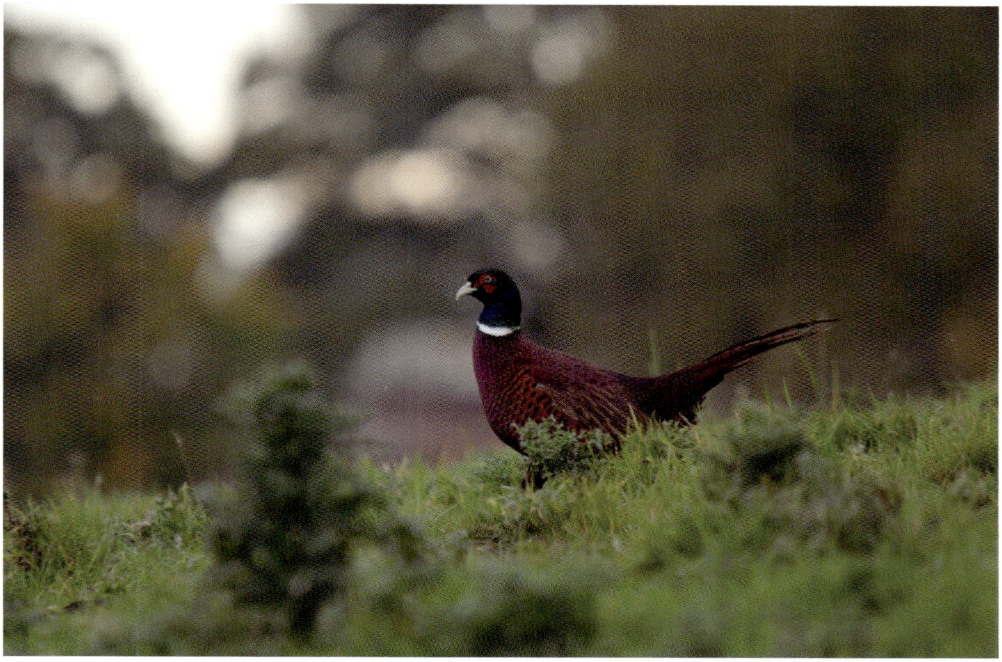

This photo of a ring-necked pheasant taken in the countryside in Devon, England, might be filed by location, species, or other parameters. The basic format of a filing system doesn't matter as long as it allows for quick and easy location and retrieval of images. *Lisa Ballard*

primarily due to the fact we merged our resources a number of years into our respective professional lives, we maintain separate filing systems. She organizes the photos into folders primarily by location. I prefer to file them according to species, in a manner similar to the organization of my slide library in the film days.

We overlap with regard to key words in the metadata of the images, and aim for strict consistency in this area. Although an image of a mule deer buck from Rocky Mountain National Park, Colorado, shot in October might reside in separate folders on our computers (mine in the "Mule Deer" folder, hers in the "Colorado" folder), we can both find it quickly by searching in relation to consistent keywords including: mule deer, buck, Colorado, autumn, and Rocky

Mountain National Park. After a shoot, we cull technically unacceptable photos and needless duplicates. Once ready for filing, the images are key-worded, which is integral to rapid retrieval in our filing systems.

PHOTO PROCESSING SOFTWARE

Serious photographers seem to fall into two distinct categories: those who love the manipulation of images with editing software and those who loathe it. I am adamantly in the latter category. My goal is to capture the image perfectly in the camera. But that doesn't always happen, and editing is inevitable. The photo editors of some publications who purchase my work do not want images manipulated at all, and I love them. Most, however, are much more prone to select photos that have been edited, at least in relation to basic processes.

The extent to which a skilled user can change the appearance of a photo via computer manipulation is nothing short of amazing. But the majority of the editing involves basic "fixes." Numerous programs and apps are available for photo editing. Some are free and work very well for standard photo adjustments. Others are exceedingly powerful but command a hefty up-front price tag or a substantial monthly subscription fee. Certain versions work well for some users, not so much for others. Between free software and free trials of paid versions, it's possible to try out several options before you settle on an editing platform. Although I use professional editing software, most of the tasks for which it's employed could be completed with a free version.

Right: Professional editing software was used to crop, brighten, and enhance the color on this photo of a badger. It also allowed the author to remove the barbwire in the foreground and eliminate the blade of grass jutting through the animal's eye via layers and a clone-stamping tool. For simpler fixes, free editing software will suffice. *Jack Ballard*

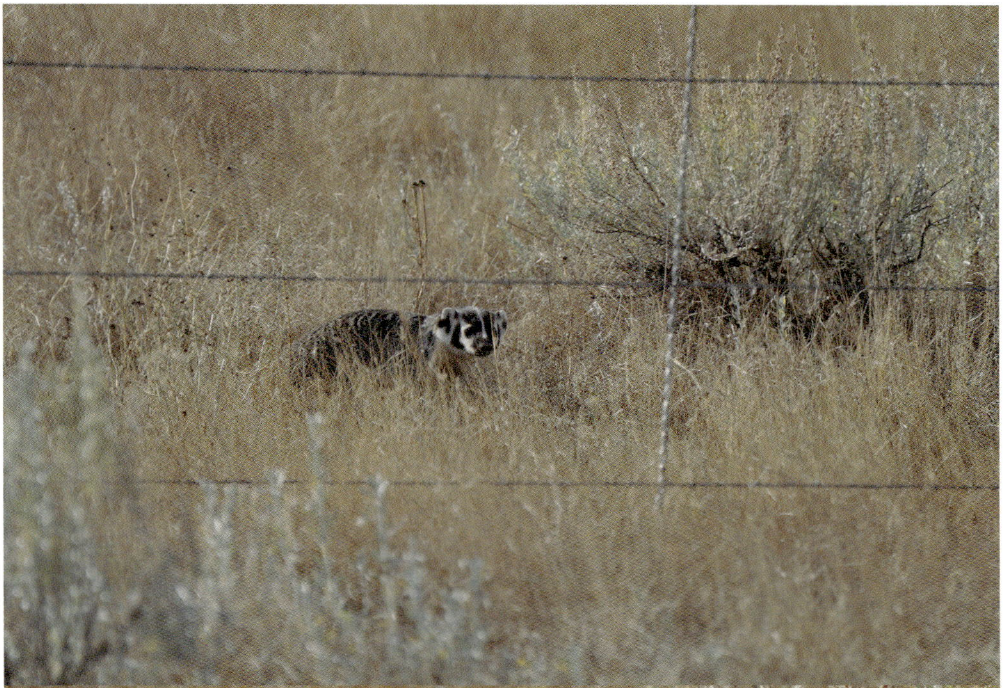
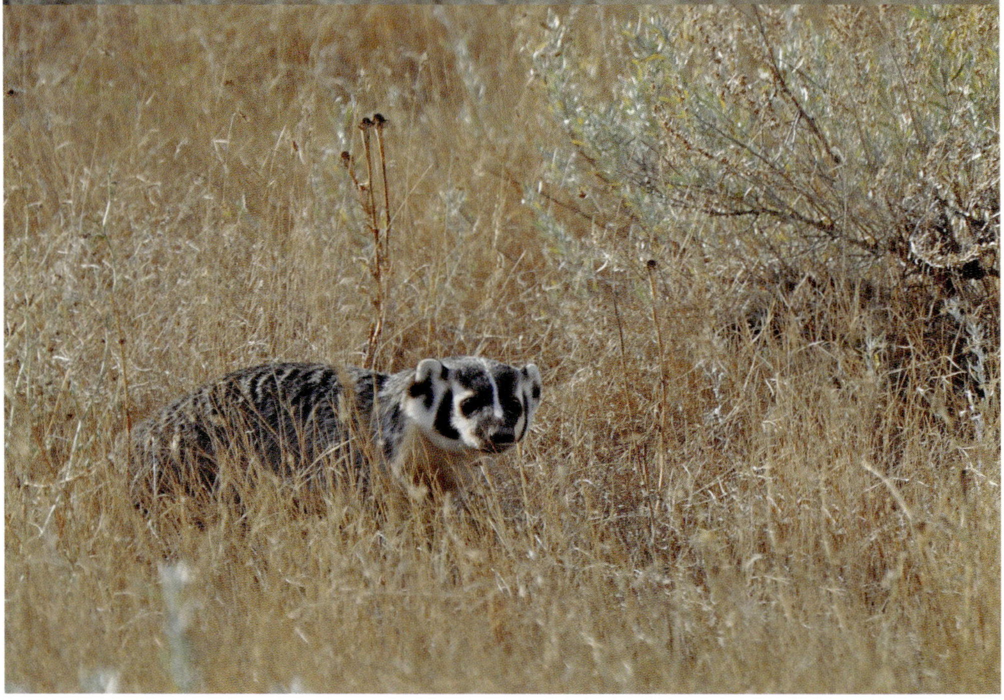

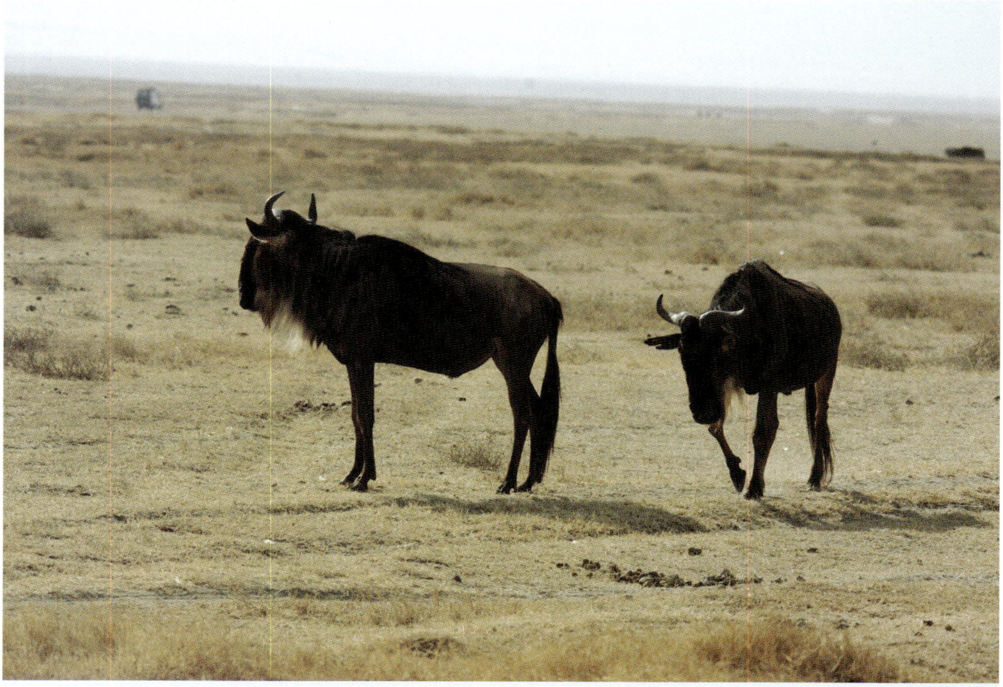
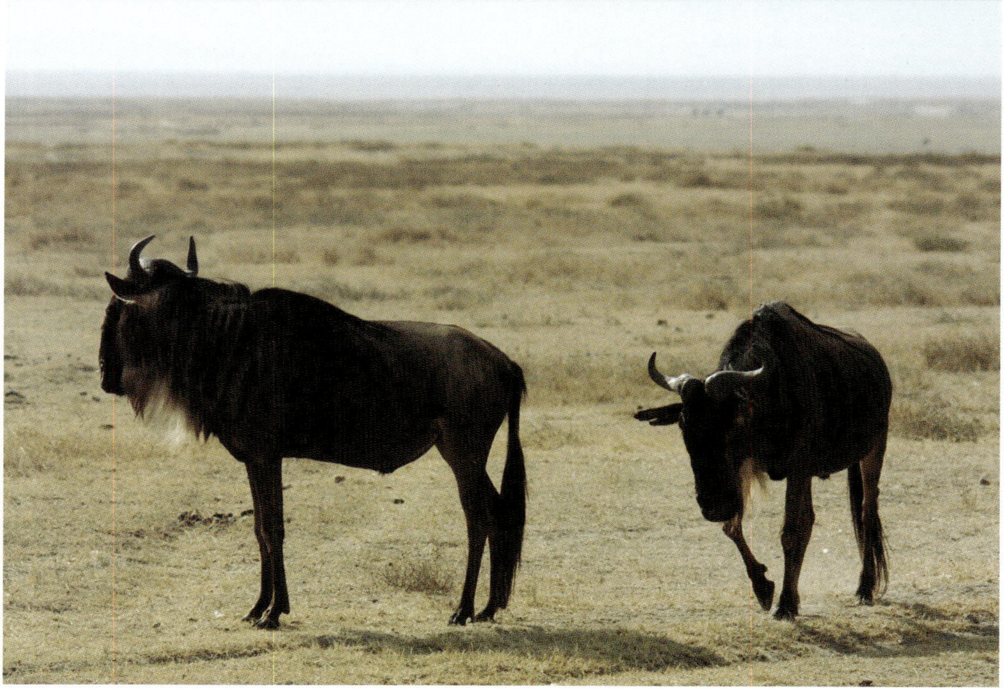

BASIC PHOTO PROCESSING TECHNIQUES

What are the minimum capabilities required for basic photo editing? This question might spur a heated debate in a roomful of photographers, but the most common editing tasks are relatively simple fixes of errors in composition and lighting. Here are the editing tasks you'll most likely use for wildlife photos. A useful editing platform should handle them with ease.

Cropping

Cropping is simply the ability to reduce the size of the photo, usually to enlarge the subject in the frame or eliminate extraneous elements from the photo. I usually crop at the same width and height ratio of the original photo, but editing software typically allows cropping at other dimensions. A standard crop for most professional purposes is rectangular, but some editing platforms allow cropping to other shapes.

Exposure Adjustment

Photos often come from the camera just a little too light or dark. Exposure adjustment allows the user to brighten or darken the image. Basic editing software normally does this in relation to the overall photo. More sophisticated applications can specify whether the adjustment applies to highlights, midtones, or shadows. The ability to lighten shadows independently is extremely useful.

This wildebeest photo was rotated to level the horizon and cropped to eliminate the dung in the foreground and the vehicles in the background. *Lisa Ballard*

Contrast adjustment also shows up under exposure controls in many software programs. Increasing the contrast of a photo can make the subject "pop" against the background. Simple software often treats this as an automatic adjustment, while more powerful versions offer precise control.

Leveling

When shooting quickly to capture action or photographing wildlife from watercraft, it's easy to tilt the subject in the frame. Leveling the image in relation to a shoreline, the horizon, or an animal's body are regular editing tasks. This necessitates rotating, and either cropping or cloning the background to expand photo size.

Color Correction

Color rendition is a problem for some cameras, often in relation to a particular color or certain scenes. Some cameras, for example, tend to overemphasize the greens in landscape images. Difficult lighting situations can also result in aberrant color. Even basic editing software has some color correction capabilities. With simple software this is often limited to "auto color correction," which may or may not render color as desired. More sophisticated editing platforms allow the user to tweak color in relation to specific hues and give much more control over the outcome. Free software is often limited in this area, but certain camera/software combinations work very well together with auto color correction. For the most precise results, it's essential to use a viewing screen that has been color-corrected for making such adjustments. Most software also allows color to be eliminated to produce a black-and-white image for artistic or other purposes.

Software allows color to be removed from a photo to create a black-and-white picture. This image of an osprey taking off from its nest has been sold as a black-and-white decorator's print. *Lisa Ballard*

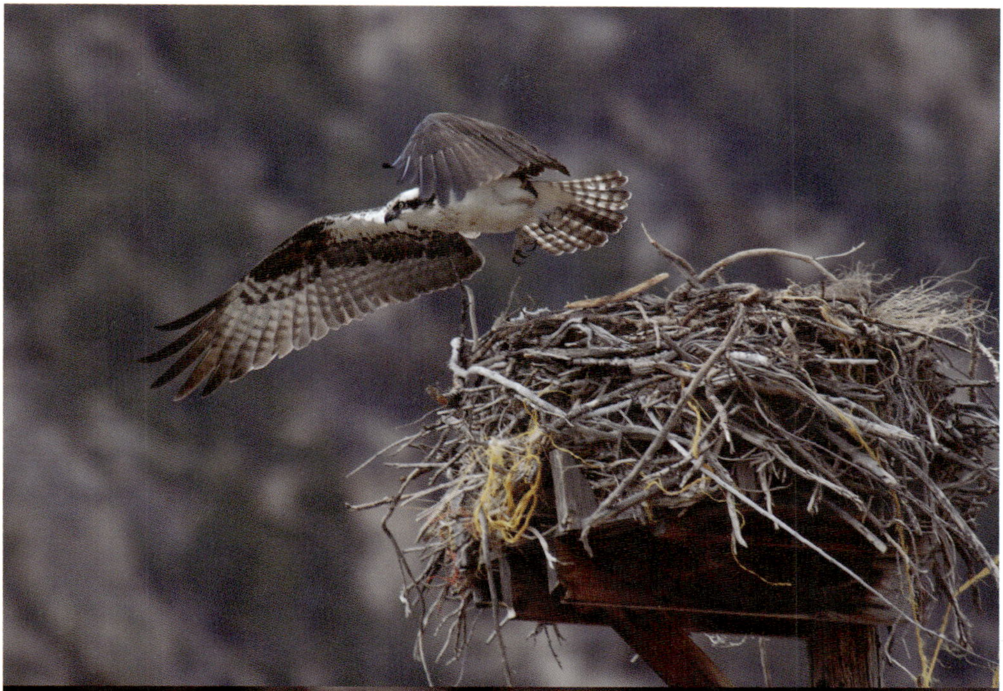
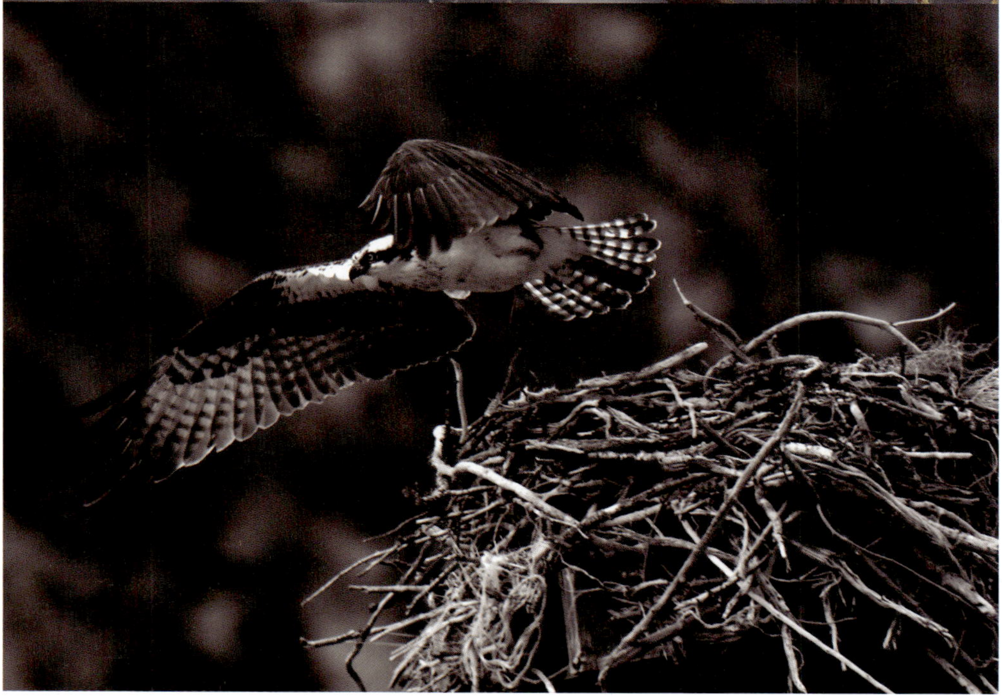

PHOTO SHARING

Some readers of this book remember the days of photo albums, scrapbooks, and binders crammed with printed photos. The primary means of sharing pictures in my childhood, most American families had numerous photo albums residing on the coffee table or gathering dust in an attic.

My household still uses versions of the photo album in the form of photobooks my wife often creates after a memorable trip. Like the albums of old, the latest version graces the living room coffee table, while others are neatly arranged in a bookcase. The source of these is a photo printing service we use via an online upload of the images that are found in the books.

From computer monitors to smartphone screens, most photo sharing nowadays has moved to electronics. A group of friends might cluster around a high-definition monitor in my office to view a slideshow of images from a recent assignment. Or a seatmate on an airplane, upon learning my occupation, might apprise me of a favorite photo on her cellphone. Amateur and professional photographers alike are confronted with an ever-changing and bewildering assortment of platforms for photo sharing. Which ones are the best? That depends upon your desired audience and the purposes for which you wish to share your images.

For most amateur photographers, social media sites such as Facebook are used to communicate with friends and acquaintances for other purposes and are a logical way to share wildlife photos. Other social platforms such as Pinterest and Instagram are more specifically oriented toward image display, along with a host of other sites that cater specifically to photographers.

Professional photographers often create their own website or use websites that allow the user to create a photo portfolio (often for a fee). These are usually intended to serve as a professional marketing tool and include options for displaying photos to their very best advantage. While it's easy to get caught up in the idea that one's images should be shared on numerous platforms, identifying a source or two that most efficiently links you to your intended audience keeps things simple and reduces the time needed for photo sharing. Like most wildlife enthusiasts, I prefer to spend more time in the presence of my subjects than manipulating and uploading photos to share.

Efficiently sharing photos online from a quality camera normally involves some resizing of the images. After a few modest tweaks, JPEG format files from

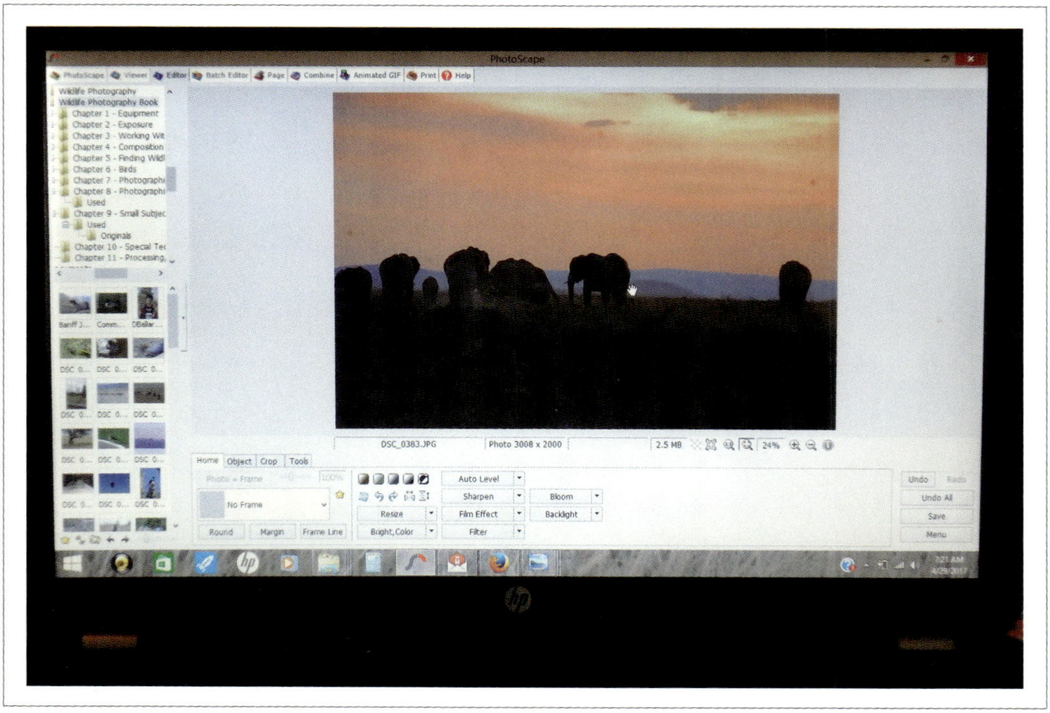

Images should be resized via editing software for easy uploads and to make it more difficult for others to "pirate" shared images for printing or other purposes. *Jack Ballard*

my current camera may exceed 20 megabytes in size. However, for the vast majority of applications, a 1-megabyte image is all that's needed to maximize its size and sharpness on the typical computer screen. Reducing image size for sharing speeds uploads. It also reduces the ability of a thief to swipe your favorite wildlife shot from a sharing site and use it as a glossy, full-page photo on the cover of his marketing brochure. Photos can be manually resized by reducing their overall dimensions or resolution in terms of dots per inch (dpi) or pixels per inch (ppi). Higher-definitions computer monitors are available, but most computer screens still display images at a resolution of 72 dpi. Photo-editing software that includes a "batch processing" feature can reduce the size of numerous images for uploading to sharing sites in a single operation.

TO SELL OR NOT TO SELL?

Similar to other artistic endeavors in which a very skilled individual might make a profession from a passionately pursued hobby (oil painting, woodwork, ceramics, etc.), obtaining income from wildlife photography is alluring. Even more titillating is the notion of becoming a pro. What could be more fun and rewarding than traveling the globe or specializing in the photography of a favorite wildlife subject to make a living? It is not easy. Many aspects of the job (clerical work, photo filing, marketing, dealing with the unreasonable demands of cheapskate clients) are just as mundane and stressful as in any other occupation. But oftentimes these are more important to success than skill with a camera.

Right: Wildlife images, such as this one of a less than common black-headed grosbeak have commercial value. How to realize it is one of the greatest challenges of professional wildlife photography.

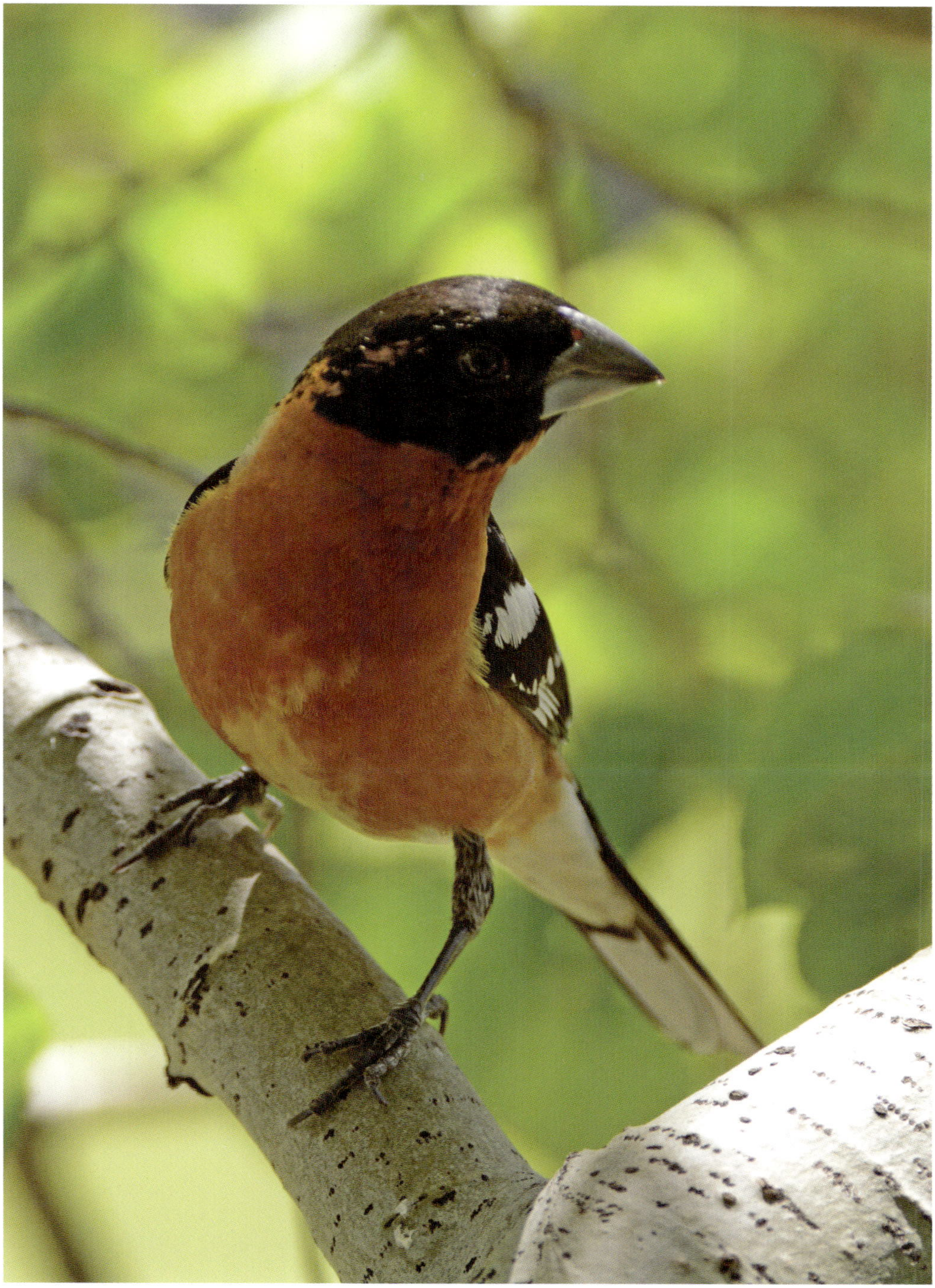

The reality of the profession is that many who appear to be "professionals" are not. There is a critical difference between being a "full-time" wildlife photographer and a "professional" wildlife photographer. The term "professional" suggests that all or a very significant portion of one's income is derived from the pursuit. Many of the full-time "pros" leading photo safaris, selling images to magazines and advertising agencies, or teaching nature photography seminars have another, more important source of income such as a trust fund, a pension, or, in the language of the ranching community in which I was raised, "a spouse with a good job at the county courthouse." In addition to the income I derive as a wildlife photographer, I make a living writing books and articles and undertaking other photo projects for commercial clients. The individuals who claim wildlife photography as their single source of income are very few.

That said, exceptional wildlife photography has value. Depending on its use, the rights to reproduce a single wildlife image may command a payment of $10 or $10,000. Regaining some of the investment in equipment and travel expense is an attractive option for skilled amateurs, some of whose work may be on par with the best professionals.

Wildlife photos might garner income as greeting cards, illustrations in print or online publications, advertising images, or prints used for interior decoration. If you choose to sell, allow me a simple suggestion: Demand the same compensation for your work as a professional. With the proliferation of online "stock" photography sites, it has become more difficult for professional wildlife photographers to make a living. "Why pay a real pro two hundred dollars for rights to use a photo of a grizzly bear when I can get it from a stock site for twenty bucks?" reason many photo buyers. Much of the stock photography online is sourced from amateurs happy to get an occasional ten or twelve dollars

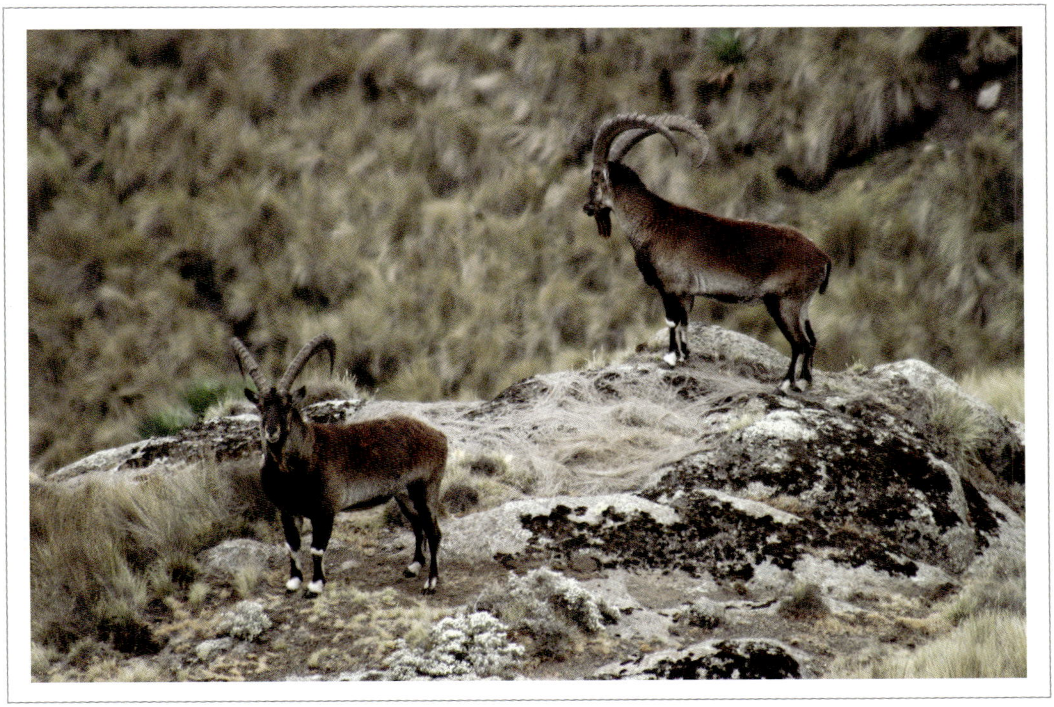

Wildlife images, like this one of endangered walia ibex in Ethiopia, may encourage citizens and politicians to conserve their habitat and ensure their survival. *Lisa Ballard*

from a photo sale, undercutting the professional. If your goal is a supplemental or full income from wildlife photography, your interests, and those of others in the profession, will be best served if you expect appropriate compensation for the use of your images.

Selling wildlife photos is really an aspect of sharing. Perhaps more satisfying than the income I receive from a wildlife picture used as a magazine illustration is the delight a child experiences when viewing it or the renewed appreciation of its species sparked in an individual who may be motivated to conserve its habitat. Here's to the belief that the photography of wild animals can play a role in their survival as well as create great delight in the lives of those who capture their images.

INDEX

Note: Page numbers in *italics* indicate photo captions.

Absaroka-Beartooth wilderness area, 103–4, 105
accessories, camera, 21–26
  flash, 23–24
  packs and bags, 25–26
  tripods, 21–23
African elephant, 45
alligators, photographing, 184
American alligators, 175, 179, 182
American avocets, 106
American goldfinch, 122, *123*
American martens, 104
American robins, 113, 123
  nesting, 131
American toad, 177
amphibians, 171–85
  changing appearance, 182–83
  dangerous, 184–85
  movement patterns of, 174–78
  seasonal activities of, 178–79, 182
  senses of, 174
  touching, 180
Andean condors, 111
animals. *See* wildlife; *specific animals*
apertures, 16–17, 36–37, 39
  changing, 41
  and depth of field, 82–83
  and exposure, 43
  settings for sharpness, 18
  and teleconverters, 20
  See also lenses; cameras

backlighting, 55–56, 58
  See also light, working with
backpacks, 25–26
badgers, 156, *232*, 233
bags, camera, 25–26
bald eagles, 54, 116, 117
  photographing in flight, 134, 136
bats, 145
bears, 165, 166, 168
  young of, 161
  See also black bears; grizzly bears
beavers
  approaching, 155
  ponds of, 106
bighorn sheep, *56*, 57, 158–59
Billings (MT), wildlife near, 106
binoculars, 26
  and smartphones, 27
birds, 113–41
  backyard, 121, 123–24
  in flight, 8, 134–40
  migrations of, 119, 121
  movement patterns of, 115–17
  nesting, 129–34
  seasonal activities of, 117–19
  using a blind, 124–28
  See also specific species of

bison
  behavior of, 145
  bull, 82, 143, 224, *225*
  danger of, 165, 166
black bears, 146, 147
  babies of, 159
  danger of, 165, 168
black-chinned hummingbird, 115
black crowned crane, *96*, 97
black-necked stilt, 106
blinds, using, 124–28, 131
  at beaver pond, 106
  for mammals, 168–69
blue grouse, 130, *131*
blue wildebeests, 108
bobcats, fur of, 161
broad-tailed hummingbird, 107
brown trout, 222
bugs. *See* insects, photographing
Bug's Life, A (film), 201
bull bison. *See* bison
bull elk. *See* elk
bullsnake, 84
bumblebees, lens for, 202, 204
burrowing mammals, behavior of, 145, 159
  See also mammals
butterflies, 205
  lens for photographing, 202
  monarch, *188*, 189, *202*, 203

California condor, 113
calliope hummingbird, 113
cameras, 1, 3–29
  accessories for, 21–26
  caring for, 28–29
  compact, 12, 13, 193–94
  exposure control of, 6, 31–47
  in extreme environments, 223–25
  and flash photography, 208–11
  image capture speed, 9–10
  image quality of, 5–6
  lenses for, 14–20
  mirrorless, 11
  and motion-sensing devices, 207
  settings for flight photography, 134, 136
  settings of and exposure, 43–48
  shutter speed and motion, 135–36, 137, 214–16
  using underwater, 219–22
  See also DSLR cameras; digital cameras
Canada, bird species in, 113
cars, photographing from, 124–25, 128
Cascade frogs, 175–76
cases, camera, 25
caterpillars, photographing, 205
cattle egret, 104
cedar waxwings, 118, 123
cellphone cameras, 14
  See also cameras
chameleons, 183
chickadees, 115, 116, 131
chipping sparrow, 122, *123*
chukar partridges, *136*, 137
close-up photography. *See* macro photography
collared lizard, 172
common garter snakes, 170, *171*, *172*, 173
  touching, 180
common goldeneyes, 8
common loon, 51
common raven, 47
common redpoll, 34, *35*
common snipe, 64
common yellowthroats, 120, *121*

compact cameras, 12, 13, 14
built-in flashes on, 208, 220–21
and macro photography, 193–94
composition, 69–89
depth of field, 82–83
errors in, 88–89
and focus, 78–81
and level horizons, 74–75
perspective in, 83–87
rule of thirds, 71–74
subject framing, 76–78
See also photographs
Cooper's hawk, 19, 123
coral, photographing, 221
cottontail rabbits, 144, *145*
in urban areas, 163
coyotes, 56, 100
approaching, 155
behavior of, 146–47
coat of, 161, 162, *163*
in urban areas, 163
crocodiles, approaching, 184
cropping, photos, 235
See also photographs
Custer State Park (SD), *99*
cutthroat trout, 220

dark-eyed juncos, 123
deer
bucks, 165, 168
coat of, 161
fawns of, 161
in urban areas, 163
whitetail deer, 60, *61*
digital cameras, 14, 227
exposure factors in, 35
image capture speed, 9–10
ISO, aperture and shutter speed, 38, 42, 216
metering modes in, 6
photo processing software, 232–33
sharpness of, 17
storage and filing systems in, 230–31
storage of photos, 227–29
See also cameras
downy woodpeckers, 123
dragonflies, *198*, 199, 202
drones, use of, 20
DSLR (digital single-lens reflex) cameras, 3–5, 11
exposure control of, 6, 43
focus capabilities of, 8–9
image capture speed of, 9–10
image quality of, 5–6
lens magnification in, 14–15
pop-up flash in, 23, 208
"spot meter" function of, 45–46
ducks
mallard hen, 75
photographing in flight, 139
dusky grouse, 104

eagles, photographing in flight, 135–36
See also bald eagles
eastern salamander, 185
eastern screech-owls, 123
elk, 102
behavior of, 145, 148
bull elk, 10, 52, 86, 159, 165, 166
coat of, 161
photographing, 70, 79, 152, 161
in urban areas, 163
equipment. *See* cameras
exposure, 31–47
adjustment of, 235–36

and aperture, 36–37
and camera settings, 43–44
for difficult subjects, 44–47
in DSLR cameras, 6
and ISO, 37–39
relationship of elements of, 39–42
and shutter speed, 35–36
and sidelighting, 55
and wildlife silhouettes, 63
See also cameras
external flashes, 210
external hard drive, 229

Facebook, photo sharing on, 238
feeders, placement of, 123
field, depth of, 82–83
firebug, 191
fish, photographing, 221
fixed lenses, image quality of, 15–16
See also lenses
flash photography, 207, 208–11
external flashes, 23–24, 210
See also cameras
flight photography, 134–40
See also birds
"f-number." *See* lenses
focus. *See* composition
foxes, 161
approaching, 155
babies of, 161
in urban areas, 163
f-ratio. *See* lenses
frogs, 183, 184
eyes of, 174
movement patterns of, 177–78
seasonal activities of, 178–79
touching, 180
front lighting, 51–53
See also lighting
gear. *See* cameras
geese, photographing in flight, 139
gelada baboon, 63
gemsbok, 169
Glacier National Park (MT), *100*, 101
golden-mantled ground squirrels, 68, *69*, 104
grasshoppers, lens for, 202
great blue heron, 87, 140
great egrets, *136*, 137
great gray owl, 121, *140*, 141
great tit, 111
green-winged teal, 135
grizzly bears, 102, 107, 143
behavior, 148
danger of, 165, 167, 168
photos of, 2, *3*, 90, *91*
young of, 159
ground squirrel, 143
guides, for photo tours, 109–10

hoary marmot, 59, 157
horizons, level, 74–75
house wrens, 123
humidity, and light, 67
hummingbird, 215
hyenas, 164, 167

iguanas, 182
impala, 89, 154
insect repellent, and equipment, 28
insects, photographing, 201–5
Instagram, photo sharing on, 238
International Crane Foundation, *96*, 97, 98
International Organization for Standardization. *See* ISO
ISO, 37–39, 40
and shutter speed, 3, 41
See also cameras

J. N. "Ding" Darling National Wildlife Refuge, 136
jackrabbits
coat of, 161
in urban area, 163–64

Komodo dragons, 184

latitude, and light, 67
least weasel, 143
lenses, 14–18
apertures in, 16–17, 36–37
for backyard birds, 123–24
caring for, 28–29
for DSLR cameras, 4
for flight photography, 134
focusing on reptiles and amphibians, 178
ISO of, 37–39
lens flare, 58
macro lenses, 190–93, 200
magnification of, 14–16, 188–90
for mammals at a distance, 151, 152
and mirrorless cameras, 11
and sharpness, 17–18
for shooting from blinds, 124, 128
and teleconverters, 19–21
telephoto, 194–96, 202
for wilderness photography, 104
zoom, 12, 21
leveling, images, 236
See also photographs
light, working with, 49–67
backlight, 55–56, 58
daily changes in, 64–67
front light, 51–53
midday light, 67
overcast (flat light), 58–59, 61
sidelight, 53–55
silhouettes, 61–63
little blue heron, 58
lizards
color changes in, 183
movement patterns of, 175, 177, 178
lorikeets, 24

macro photography, 187–205
and backgrounds, 196–98
cameras for, 193–94
and compact cameras, 12
depth of field in, 199–201
high-magnification lenses, 188–90
of insects, 201–5
macro lenses, 190–93
telephoto lenses, 194–96
mallard drake, 118
mammals, 143–69
behavior of, 145–58
coat of, 161–63
dangerous, 164–68
newborn, 160
photographing from blind, 168–69
seasonal activities of, 158–59, 161
in urban areas, 163–64
See also specific mammals
mice, in urban areas, 163
midday light, 67
See also light, working with
mirrorless cameras, 11, 14
See also cameras
moles, 163
moose
danger of, 165–66, 168
seasonal activities of, 158–59
moths, photographing, 205
motion, enhancing, 211–16

panning techniques, 213–14
shutter speed for, 214–16
mountain bluebirds, 132, 133
mountain goats, *76*, 77, 104
coats of, 161
mountain lions, 145
behavior of, 148
danger of, 164, 168
in urban areas, 163
mule deer, 99, 226, *227*

national parks, wildlife in, 99–103
nest boxes, placement of, 123
Ngorongoro Conservation Area (Tanzania), *108*
night photography. *See* flash photography
northern flickers, 123
northern scorpion, 192, 201
nuthatches, 131

osprey, 139, *236*, 237
nesting, 134
photographing in flight, 135–36
overcast (flat light), 58–59, 61
See also light, working with
owls
baiting in winter, 138
great horned owl, 50
short-eared owl, *92*, 93

painted turtle, 197
panning, 134, 213–14
body position for, 212, *213*
perspective. *See* composition
photographs
color correction in, 236–37
composition of, 69–89
and exposure, 31–47
filing systems for, 230–31
processing software for, 232–33
processing techniques, 235–37
selling, 240–43
sharing, 238–40
storage of, 228–29
working with light, 49–67
See also cameras
photo tours, 107–10
etiquette on, 110
guides for, 109
pikas, *79*, 104
Pinterest, photo sharing on, 238
polar bears, 164
predators
danger of, 164–68
mating season of, 159
See also specific animals
private property, photographing on, 106, *107*
pronghorn antelopes, 15, 106, 214
pronghorn sheep, 158–59

rabbits, 159
raccoons, in urban areas, 163, 164
raptors
baiting, 138
and blinds, 128
red-breasted nuthatches, 123
red crossbills, 115
red fox, *100*, 101
reflectors, 26
reptiles, 171–85
changing appearance, 182–83
dangerous, 184–85
movement patterns of, 174–78
seasonal activities of, 178, 179, 182
senses of, 174
touching, 180, 181

"rim lighting"
See also backlighting
"rim lighting", 55–56
ring-necked pheasant, 53, 231
river otters, 96
Rocky Mountain National Park (CO), 102, 148
rough-legged hawks, 112, 113
migration of, 119, 121
ruffed grouse, 38

safaris, 107–10
salamanders, 179
dangerous, 184, 185
salt spray, and equipment, 28, *29*
sea lions, 217
Shenandoah National Park (VA), 102
shutter speed, 39
and DSLR cameras, 43
for flight photography, 136
See also cameras
sidelighting, 53–55
See also light, working with
silhouettes, 61–63
skunks
babies of, 161
in urban areas, 163
SLR cameras, 3–4
See also DSLR cameras
smartphones, cameras in, 26–28
snakes
common garter snake, 170, *171*, *172*
dangerous, 184, 185
movement patterns of, 175
senses of, 174
touching, 180
snapping turtles, 179
snowshoe hares, 104
approaching, 155–56
coat of, 161
snowy owls, 119
sparrows, photographing, 134
spring peeper, 200
squirrels
approaching, 155
in urban areas, 163, 164
state parks, wildlife in, 99–103
subject, framing of. *See* composition

tablets, cameras in, 26, 27
Tarangire National Park, 154
teleconverters, 19–21, 196
telephoto lenses, 15, 16, 17, 37
for macro photography, 194–96
See also lenses
travel, and local wildlife, 111
See also photo tours
tripods, 21–23
and sharpness, 18
tundra swan, 30, *31*
turkey vultures, 134

underwater photography, 219–22
and compact cameras, 12
ungulates. *See* mammals
United States
bird species in, 113
national parks in, 107

wading birds, 118
walia ibex, 111, 243
warblers, 134
warthogs, 169
water, photographing in and on, 216–22
waterbuck, 169

waterfowl, photographing, 139
water sources, placement of, 123
weasels
fur of, 161
least weasel, 143
western painted turtles, *80*, 81
western yellow-bellied racer, 176
whales, 145
white-crowned sparrow, 104, 105, *208*, 209
white pelican, 114
whitetail deer, 48, *49*, 94, 102, 146, *152*, 153
approaching, 155
buck, 168, 210
fawn of, 160, 161
white-tailed jackrabbit, 148–49, 163–64
whooping crane, *6*, 7
wildebeest, 234, *235*
wilderness areas, 103–4, 105
wildflower photography, light for, 59
wildlife, 91–111
birds, 113–41
enhancing motion of, 211–16
and exposure values, 33
in extreme environments, 222–25
and flash photography, 208–11
lenses for photography, 14–18, 19–21
light patterns for photographing, 49–67
local, 106, *107*, 111
mammals, 143–69
migrations of, 207
and photo composition, 69–89
photo tours and safaris, 107–10
silhouettes of, 62–63
in state and national parks, 99–103
underwater, 218–22
urban and backyard, 92–94
in and on water, 216–18
in wildlife refuges and wilderness areas, 103–5
in zoos and other facilities, 95–98
See also specific wildlife
wildlife, small. *See* macro photography
wildlife refuges, 103–4
wild turkey, 126
wolves, 107
coat of, 161

yellow-headed blackbirds, 119
Yellowstone National Park (WY), 100, 102, 146, 152
grizzly bears in, 102
yellow warblers, 123

zebras, 142, *143*, 223
zoom lenses, 12
for flight shots, *135*
gyroscopic device in, 21
magnification and quality of, 15–16, 190
See also lenses
zoos, photographing at, 95–96, 98

ABOUT THE AUTHOR

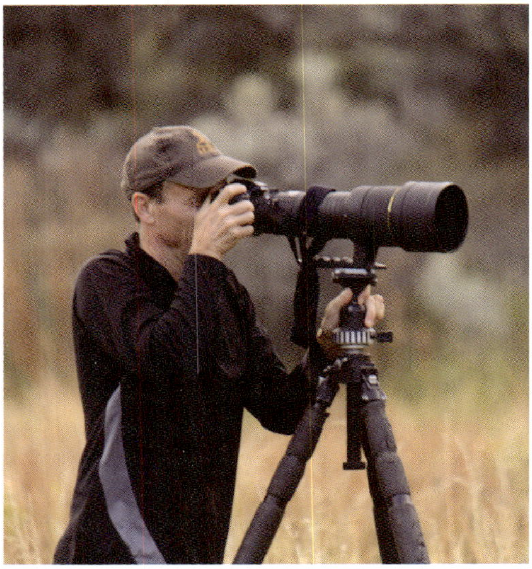

Jack Ballard's photos have appeared in over one hundred regional and national magazines in the past two decades, along with posters, billboards, and other media. He works as an assignment photographer for educational institutions, conservation groups, and other entities. His photos have been published in numerous books (Smithsonian Press, Heinemann Library, Rowman & Littlefield, etc.) and calendars. Jack has received multiple awards for his writing and photography from the Outdoor Writers Association of America and other professional organizations. He is the author of a dozen books and hundreds of magazine articles. Jack lives in Red Lodge, Montana, with his wife, Lisa, and English setter, Percy. See more of his work at www.jackballard.com.